Campus Ministry Memoirs
The Way It Was
1964-2014

Celebrating the 50th Anniversary
of the National Campus Ministry Association

Recollections and Reflections
by the "Sages" of Ministry in Higher Education

Edited by Betsy Alden

Contents

Preface

An image of golden autumn leaves illumines the path we have journeyed together as campus ministers over the past fifty years. These 54 memoirs, written by colleagues and friends on the Golden Anniversary of The National Campus Ministry Association (NCMA), evoke a spirit that continues to infuse our profession. Although most of us are now retired and in the autumn of our years, often a time of reflecting and recollecting, we hope this volume is as much about reviving as reminiscing! We offer it as a resource and gift to our successors, and as a grateful response to the churches that paid us to do work that we loved. Even as one era of campus ministry recedes, new paths are being creatively forged as seasons change.

Over the years, we came to call the elders among us Sages ("those who are wise through reflection and experience"), realizing that they still had much to impart to new generations of campus ministers. At our annual NCMA conference in 1997, George Gunn, Jim Pruyne, Tom Philipp, and others suggested that we begin to collect our stories. Last year, as we approached the 50th anniversary of NCMA, the time seemed ripe to create a Wordpress Blog of the Sages' Pages, to which we urged our friends to contribute. Our authors, from 33 states, on 100 campuses, and representing over 1,500 years of campus ministry, have written their individual retrospectives and reflections-- ranging in length from three paragraphs to fifteen pages; now we extend this collection into a book we can share widely with others.

For the majority of writers, campus ministry was our life-context—whether we served on one campus or on seven! As professionals, in the best sense of the word, we represented our denominational and ecumenical sponsors, and we interpreted to our churches the issues and values on our campuses. We worked collaboratively with campus faculty, administrators, and program staff to integrate ethical and spiritual concerns into the total fabric of institutional life on both public and private campuses.

In many ways, this was a "golden" era of ministry in higher education. We were encouraged to create new paths for doing ministry on campuses and with our communities, to bear witness to the church's concerns for compassion, justice and peace. We had frequent opportunities to encounter provocative leaders and speakers at collegial gatherings and stimulating conferences.

Many of our living mentors/sages are represented in these pages, and we are mindful of many other saints who are no longer with us. As editor of this collection, I have chosen to let the authors speak in their own words; none has been edited for content, so they reflect the diversity of personalities, interests, and perspectives of each individual. We have arranged these in order of the chronology of service—from 1950 to 2013—to present the evolution of campus ministry itself.

Soliciting, collecting, and editing these memoirs has truly been a labor of love for me. In a way, this collection brings me full circle from the beginning of my work as National Communications Coordinator for United Ministries in Education (UME) from1984-89, interpreting our work to seven denominations and about 1500 campus ministries. It is amazing to me now that most of the activities described in these memoirs occurred with no technology but a typewriter and mimeograph/copy machine. Until the 1990's we had not even heard of telephone conference calls, much less faxes, email, Skype, or Fed Ex. We relied on print media, stamped mail, occasional (costly) phone calls on land lines (no mobiles), and traveling across the country to in-person meetings to communicate with each other!

I am grateful for the collaboration of everyone who contributed and responded to my multiple emails for this collection. Special thanks to NCMA for allocating funds to begin this project; to Meghan Florian for her technical skills in copy-editing and layout; to Helen Neinast for finding the perfect image to illustrate this book; to Geoff Dunkak, for his graphic design expertise on the cover; to Robert Thomason for his insightful commentary (through more than thirty drafts) and for getting this book into your hands, and as always, to my partner-in-everything, Mark Rutledge, for good cheer and backrubs along the way.

The inscription for this book can be no other than the one I use in my email signature—a poem by Mary Oliver:

> *Pay attention.*
> *Be astonished.*
> *Tell about it.*

—*Betsy Alden*
November 2014

An Introduction to the Sages' Pages
By George Gunn

George was a Founding Member of NCMA and is the Sage who proposed this collection of Memoirs one year ago on the NCMA website. Here is his initial invitation to tell our stories for our 50th Anniversary.

The year was 1964 – 50 years ago!

Some might call it the midpoint of the Golden Years of Ministry in Higher Education. Others, including those who have made initial contributions to the on-line volume of Our Stories and Our History, would call it only the end of the beginning!

Fifty years is not long in the annals of Higher Education in America. Fifty years earlier – 1914 – was just before World War One, prior to the birth year of any of us who are now identified as "Sages" in the membership of the National Campus Ministry Association. We are another "greatest generation" that led the historic expansion of higher education opportunities, from the G. I. Bill after World War Two to the community college movement and service-learning and civic engagement in the late decades of the Twentieth Century.

We also are the generation that led the civil rights movement in the 1960s, who mentored the rise of a social conscience in the nation, who nurtured campus-centered movements toward peace and justice, toward equality and inclusiveness, and toward a culture with a more universal compassion toward all people. We have sought to make "mission" the hallmark of campus ministry, and service its heart.

At this crossroads we offer a living history, to use our stories to bear witness to the providence of God in our journey of faith and to demonstrate the integrity and credibility of the Church we love and serve.

We hope this living history will include the unique testimony of individual campus ministers from many parts of the country, both denominational and ecumenical. Each ministry was founded and each continues to be grounded in the faith that we are led by the Holy Spirit into the realm of higher education, and that it is a love of truth to which we are called in each generation.

Not only in each individual campus ministry, but also in the initiatives taken by specific denominational and ecumenical "support" services for ministry in higher education, we have a story to tell! In this context you are invited to go on line and add your stories, with a brief personal update, including the positions and campuses you served.

Press Release --Dateline: St. Louis MO / October 27, 1964

National Campus Ministry Association
Launched in St. Louis
(originally published in denominational newsletters)

Higher Education Ministry leaders from major Protestant denominations gathered in late October at the historic Mark Twain Hotel in St. Louis, Missouri, to give a face and a name to an ecumenical organization of professionals engaged in ministries in higher education.

Building on a history of denominationally based fellowships of those who serve in college and university faith communities, the development of a national body, by ordained campus clergy and lay student workers, is seen as a significant movement in the evolution of campus based ministries.

Student organizations of four denominations merged in 1960 to form the United Campus Christian Fellowship (UCCF). These four were the United Presbyterian Church, the United Church of Christ, the Christian Church – Disciples of Christ, and the Evangelical United Brethren Church. These four denominations also had leadership roles in the creation of the United Ministries in Higher Education (UMHE) in 1964.

This movement represents the reality of a growing ecumenical spirit in many campus settings and the need to forge cooperative and united ministries with a wiser and more faithful witness in the use of professional leadership and in the utilization of campus facilities. UMHE has affirmed the wisdom of continuing the employment of regional and national staff by the several denominations, but their deployment in the service of the greater good, in the strengthening of the whole of the Churches' ministries in higher education.

With the formation of the United Campus Christian Fellowship (UCCF) in 1960 and the United Ministries in Higher Education (UMHE) in 1964, both the student movement components and the national professional staffs were out front as visible and viable partners in the realm of higher education. Concurrent with these new alliances comes now **an ecumenical association of professionals engaged in ministries in higher education.**

As early as the summer of 1963, there was a consensus found for moving toward "a single association." An increasing number of denominations were joining the movement and supporting annual gatherings of ordained clergy and lay student workers. At the same time, as these "fellowships" began to be more inclusive and inter-denominational, there began to be a greater mix of students, faculty, and campus ministry professionals on individual campuses and in regional gatherings.

Delegates here represent the ministries of the United Church of Christ, the Christian Church - Disciples of Christ, the Evangelical United Brethren, and the United Presbyterian Church, U.S.A. Joining them in this historic venture are Campus Ministry Associations of the American Baptist Church, the

4

National Lutheran Church, and the Presbyterian Church, U.S. (Southern). Also present and participating are individual ministers in higher education, representing the Methodist and the Episcopal Churches.

The name chosen by the assembled representatives is the National Campus Ministry Association. An Executive Committee made up of representatives was named and Dick Yeo, a long time Campus Minister of the United Church of Christ, serving the campuses of the Washington DC area, was named the first President.

We share a common calling as ministers in higher education, and we share a common faith, focused on our common journey and a commitment to the deepening of faith and knowledge wherever we serve.

Press Release prepared in October, 1964 by George Gunn, campus minister, University of Arkansas, representing the Presbyterian Church (U.S.) on the Executive Committee.

A Life/Career in and with Campus Ministry
By George Gunn

Picture This: Sitting on the Bus by Rosa Parks

The year was 1950. The month was April, a month filled with decisions, chiefly who and when to marry and where to begin my ministry. The place was Five Points in downtown Atlanta. I walked there from Terminal Station, where I had deposited my suitcase. My destination was suburban Decatur. I had a late afternoon appointment to meet Paul Garber, a Bible professor at Agnes Scott College. I would return to Louisville that night on the train.

My mind was on the events of the previous two days in Athens. I had come by train from Louisville to interview for the Minister to Students position at the University of Georgia. All had gone well and I left Athens with the position offered and my acceptance all but assured. I would graduate at Louisville Seminary in late May and come by early June to begin my ministry in higher education in Georgia. The stop in Decatur was to visit with a member of the Synod Student Work Committee who could not be in Athens the previous day.

My bus sat at the curb in front of F. W. Woolworth. It was surrounded by diesel fumes and hurrying passengers, homeward bound. I boarded the bus, its destination, clearly, "Decatur." I paid my 15 cent fare and looked for a seat. Only one space appeared to be vacant. It was in the first double seat past the parallel bench seats nearest the front. I sat and waited for the bus, now full, to depart.

We sat. One of the men seated in front of me leaned toward me. "The driver is talking to you," he said forcefully. I looked up to the front of the bus. The driver was turned in his seat, facing me now. He stared directly at me and spoke each word slowly and for all to hear, "Hey, buddy, you are sitting by a nigger!" "Buddy?" His tone did not sound very friendly in the context.

I did not move. Finally, after a very long pause, I rose to my feet. I turned to my embarrassed seatmate. "I'm sorry," I said. I looked down into the brown face and tired eyes of my new found buddy and prospective fellow Georgian. "Thank you." she said, in a whisper. I was caught by surprise, even though I had ridden busses and boarded trains in every southern state and city in which I had lived. I knew about arbitrary color lines and segregation. I knew too that to refuse to move would create a crisis in which there would be only one victim, this quiet woman. Her calm and confident demeanor reminded me of my mother.

One of the white men on the bench seat moved over to make room for me. It was 1950, too early for non-violence and peaceful protests and freedom rides. Perhaps, by that very corner, past Five Points and Woolworth's, and down Auburn Avenue, a 19 year old Martin Luther King, Jr., had walked two years earlier, on his way home from an afternoon class at Morehouse College. I believe I passed him there, as I boarded the bus, but I couldn't call his name.

We rode in silence, rumbling down busy Auburn Avenue, passing "Daddy" King's Ebenezer Baptist Church. I studied the faces of the white men seated directly across from me, trying to fathom their fears. I was a color-blinded Saul, stumbling down his Damascus road, on the brink of receiving a new name and a new calling. I was a persevering Jacob, wrestling with a heavenly messenger before dawn, and like Paul, being given, by God's grace, a new name and a new mission.

This day, two voices were raised, the white man's who called my attention to the bus driver, and that of the driver who delivered a loud judgment and ultimatum on behalf of the State of Georgia: "Hey, buddy, you're sitting by a nigger!" Only two voices responded, both whispers: "I'm sorry" and "Thank you." The voice of hatred thundered. The voice of peace whispered. Would the day come, I wondered, when I would hear the voices of justice thunder in these streets and the see hatred and fear reduced to a whisper?

On the bus to Decatur, I was on my way to receiving a new name and, perhaps, the blessing I sought was to be found both in my wounded spirit and in the confirmation of my calling, to be an agent of reconciliation and a proclaimer of God's peace and justice.

I believe now, looking back, that the bus to Decatur was taking me toward who I was called to be and to the place I was meant to be.

On to Athens: The Classic City

In early June of 1950 I drove my new 1950 Plymouth from Louisville to Athens, Georgia. I had graduated from Louisville Seminary in May, finalized the purchase of my new car ($1,825), and had driven to Cincinnati to meet Sally. She was en route from Lynchburg, Virginia, to her home in Salem, Oregon, at the end of her junior year at Randolph-Macon Women's College.

I was putting Sally on the train in Cincinnati and then returning to Louisville to load my earthly possessions and to move them to Athens, where I would begin my first job as Presbyterian Minister to Students at the University of Georgia. I would also be finding an apartment to rent and to return to after my drive to Oregon in August and our return as "Mr. and Mrs."

I have related my early encounter with the customs of the deep south in my bus ride from downtown Atlanta to Decatur two months earlier. In the fall of 1950 I was to be confronted anew with the politics of segregation and the reality of racial injustice. I went to the Clark County Court House, across Hancock Street from First Presbyterian Church and my office. My purpose was to register to vote. As I waited my turn, I witnessed the exam being given to a colored citizen twice my age. "African-American" was a term destined to come into usage some twenty years hence, after the passage of the Civil Rights Act by the U.S. Congress

An oral exam included details of the U.S. Constitution and of American history, facts which could not reasonably be known. It was quickly apparent to me that the State of Georgia had no intention of registering this fellow citizen to vote. The sham of the exam was clear when he was denied and no exam was mentioned when I presented myself as the next in line. I did have to pay a Poll Tax.

My four year tenure in Athens and on the campus of the University provided ample and frequent occasions to reflect upon the injustices present in the deeply divided culture of a segregated society. In both the university realm and in my relationships within the religious institutions there, I was confronted daily with challenges to my growing sense of the immorality of racial segregation and the complicity of "good people" in its perpetuation.

"The Varsity" was, and still is, a time honored and student frequented hamburger joint, then on the corner across from the main campus of the University of Georgia. This corner is a short three blocks from First Presbyterian Church and the office of the Minister to Students. Early on I walked over for my first taste of a Varsity burger. I entered and stood at the counter, getting a "what are you doing here?" look from the counterman. Only then did I recognize that I stood between two young black customers. There was no sign to distinguish it, but this was the counter at which any consumer of color stood to order and receive his "take out" from "The Varsity" The color of our money was the same, but the color of the sit down customers was not the same as those who had to find another venue in which to do lunch.

All this came to my mind when Atlanta journalist Harry Golden wrote a piece for the Atlanta Constitution. He proposed that integration of Georgia restaurants and other eating establishments be accomplished by removing all tables and chairs! His "stand up" integration plan was judged facetious, but as "sit in" protests and demonstrations in college and university communities like Athens were soon to be initiated, the role of activist students came to personify the moral integrity present in the civil rights movement, a movement which would flower in the 1960s.

Athens calls itself "The Classic City." First Church stands on Hancock Street next to the downtown Post Office, and only three short blocks from the front campus of the University. It is an imposing classic, columned building, built in 1820, using slave labor. One of its most visible features are the gated pews, with their little doors that define the half pew sections - no through traffic! Many of the pre-bellum members had paid for their family pews and placed a name plate on or near its door.

One week day as I walked through the sanctuary, I observed Mr. Hugh Gordon attaching a silver plate to his pew, with the single word "Gordon" on it. I learned later that he was the grandson of General John B. Gordon, CSA. My wife Sally took a place off a side aisle and received a warm welcome from its occupant, who welcomed her at the conclusion of the service, "to our family pew." She turned out to be a Russell, kinswoman to U.S. Senator Richard Russell. Weeks later Sally took her place in the same pew and encountered an equally hospitable member who also welcomed her to "our family pew," only

8

this member was a Talmadge, part of old Gene and son Herman's clan, former and then current Georgia governors.

This reminded me of the story of a G.I. during World War II who took a seat in an equally sequestered spot in a large house of worship in Washington DC. A ruffled seat warmer next to him passed him a scribbled note, "I paid a thousand dollars for this pew!" The serviceman turned it over and wrote a reply: "You paid too damn much!"

Campus Ministry: Student Work Revisited

The campus of the University of Georgia in 1950 was typical of most "flagship" campuses in the U.S. The G.I. Bill, in the first years following the end of World War II, had resulted in the rapid expansion of every college and university. Major denominations moved to strengthen their higher education mission presence in both public and private institutions. "Student Work" took on a revival, and this oldest "special ministry" of the Presbyterian Church in the United States began to flower with new forms and faces across the South.

The campus at Athens was no exception. The Women of the Church of the Synod of Georgia made a statewide appeal to secure funds to support the ministry to students at Athens. The Synod named a Student Work Committee and the allocation of designated funds and the naming of personnel to lead this effort was initiated. Congregations in the college and university communities took a fresh look at how they might provide "a home away from home" to resident students. Each saw the need to go beyond welcoming students to corporate worship and recognized the opportunity present to engage them in study and service.

It was this Synod Student Work Committee with whom I had met in Athens on that fateful day in April. The Committee members represented ministers and lay leaders of campus related congregations, both men and women, and faculty members of public and private colleges and universities. The Committee Chairs, during my tenure, were Senior Pastors of congregations in these communities: Dr. Kerr Taylor at First Church, Milledgeville; Dr. Dickson Phillips, First Church, Thomasville; and Dr. Wade Huie, Vineville P.C., Macon.

Students from the various campuses composed a statewide "Westminster Fellowship," and they gathered throughout the year in both conference and retreat settings for worship, Bible study, and inspiration. The presidents of each state organization also attended a higher education conference at Montreat in June each year. Art MacDonald, one of our undergraduate students, destined for an illustrious career in higher education and the arts, was president of the Georgia Westminster Fellowship!

This P.E.A.S. Conference (Presbyterian Education Association of the South) was the occasion in the 1950s when the students took an action in response to Montreat's exclusion of one of their number, an African-American student, denied the privilege of swimming in Lake Susan. They moved their conference out of Montreat and over to the campus of Warren Wilson College! "It didn't take courage," one student observed, "just common sense." Another asked, "Why is there a problem? In the cold water of Lake Susan everyone turns blue!"

Another incident along the racial justice journey came when the ritual of Sunday Night suppers at First Church was interrupted after I invited Lawrence Bottoms, a well known black Presbyterian pastor, to speak and, of course, to engage in conversation with students around the dinner table. When I learned that I was judged to be out of order and that I needed to withdraw the invitation, I countered that I could not do that, and if hospitality at the Church was not available, Sally and I would entertain him in our apartment and come to the Church for time with the students. When that was also vetoed, I realized the stakes were getting higher by the hour and that I needed to fashion some compromise.

My fellow campus minister and director of the Wesley Foundation saved the day by giving me the name of a local A.M.E. pastor who graciously issued a supper invitation to his church for our visitor and the dialog with Presbyterian students took place after the dinner hour without incident. Years later, after Lawrence Bottoms' election to be Moderator of the Presbyterian Church, U.S. General Assembly, Sally and I recalled that incident in our shared history and voiced our abiding deep regret to the new Moderator, evoking from him only the most kind and gracious words of understanding.

In the early 1950s, the University of Georgia was the site of major denominational expansion of campus ministry. Along Lumpkin Street, from the downtown churches out to its intersection with Milledge Avenue, and back to Prince Avenue, properties were being purchased for religious centers. For generations antebellum homes along these tree lined avenues had been transformed into both fraternity and sorority houses. Now mixed with them were substantial residences owned and adapted for the ministry to students.

Presbyterians initiated conversation and speculation about joining the movement, but it was not until 1956 that property on south Lumpkin was secured, at 1250 Lumpkin Avenue. Call it an "edifice complex," if you will, but the faith communities took on the generation of growth and vitality, reflected in the development of these centers of nurture and social witness in the decades following.

For me, a call to serve a college town congregation in Arkansas came at an opportune time in 1954, and we moved as a family of four to Arkadelphia, Arkansas, arriving the same week as the Supreme Court ruled in the Brown vs. the Board of Education case and we entered a new setting for ministry in higher education.

The Sixties

From 1954 to 1960 I served as Pastor of the First Presbyterian Church in Arkadelphia, Arkansas, home of Henderson State College (now University) and Ouachita Baptist College (also now a University). This opportunity to work with Faculty and Students and a multi-generational congregation deepened my appreciation of the wholeness of the pastoral task, and the disciplines of preaching and teaching. At the same time I became involved in the leadership of both Presbytery and Synod higher education agencies and became Chair of the Board of the Ministry at the University of Arkansas at Fayetteville. I also gained experience in fund raising and in the planning and construction of a new building in a new location in Arkadelphia.

In 1960, I found myself making the drive from Arkadelphia to Fayetteville. I had made the 200 mile trip alone at least twice a year for the past fe years. This time Sally was at my side. It was February 1960 and the Joint Committee (Board), which I chaired, was scheduled to meet with the Local Board to consider calling me to be the next University Pastor and head of Staff at Westminster House, the Presbyterian Center at the University of Arkansas.

I had known well the last two Campus Ministers, Bill Gibson and Ben Smith and also the Senior Ministers at both Fayetteville churches. One was Bill Knox at First United Presbyterian and previously at Central Presbyterian Church (U.S.A) before its merger with First Presbyterian (P.C.U.S.) to form a Union congregation as "First United." Now seemed the right time to return to Ministry in Higher Education and to give this campus ministry my full attention.

Ralph Madison, a student at Austin Seminary, had come on board at the Center as a Student Intern the previous Fall and anticipated serving out the academic year. The Westminster Fellowship and its student officers were in place to provide continuity and leadership into the year ahead. A new campus ministry manse on Rockwood Trail had been purchased and was ready to be occupied.

Since the mid-forties the campus ministry had been under a Joint Committee and a local board represented the two congregations. Students were active in both congregations and continued attending a Sunday morning class for Bible study

In the early fifties Van Howell and his wife Mary purchased a one-story brick residence at 902 W. Maple Street, at the heart of the Campus and opposite the Student Union. This building became the first Westminster House. After some remodeling to create two offices, a chapel, and dining and meeting areas, title was given to the Presbyterian Student Center and its trustees. The Howells received a small lifetime income from the Center and continued a lifetime of interest and support of this ministry. With the consolidation of the two congregation's student ministries at the campus, a single Sunday morning Class at the Center was offered.

Time and Space Facilitated

In 1960 I had inherited a Ministry with a rich history and a future ready to be claimed and defined. Both the Synods of Arkansas and Oklahoma were in the midst of capital campaigns to strengthen the mission and outreach of both Churches. Both had included Student Work or Campus Ministry, based on the advocacy of the Westminster Foundation in the Synod of Oklahoma-Arkansas (P.C.U.S.A.) and of the Synod of Arkansas-Oklahoma (P.C.U.S.)!

It appeared that another building project was in prospect for me. The years 1961 and 1962 had seen the successful conclusion of the capital gifts effort by the two Synods and the securing of the needed property. We knew from early on that any significant increase in the space needed for an expanded ministry, and for parking at the Maple Street site, would require the purchase of adjoining property.

The decision was made first, that we should have an architect from the University faculty as a sign of our recognition of our being a part of the University community. Our choice was Keith McPheeters, a disciple of Fay Jones, an architect who had made a name for himself in the region. Keith himself had recently designed a home in nearby Bentonville for Sam Walton, Walmart's founder and CEO. Keith began with an exhaustive examination with us of our goals and expectations, i.e. what is the ministry we want to facilitate by and in our building? Keith's visionary skills and the A.I.A. Honors he received led him in due time to the School of Architecture at Auburn University, where he eventually was named Dean. We made a wise choice.

As the detailed planning was concluded and the architect's plans approved, a contract was made for construction of the new Campus Center. The contractor we hoped would be the low bidder, came in with a bid of $200,000, less than $200 under the next one! In the meantime the student group was active and attendance good for the traditional Sunday night suppers. For the year of construction, these suppers moved to the manse out on Rockwood Trail, on the eastside of Fayetteville, with Sally as the hostess and chef.

We also had occasional student retreats at Devil's Den State Park or Eureka Springs. One especially memorable retreat was at War Eagle Farm near Beaver Lake, when then-rare whooping cranes were sighted on the pond.

As the Disciples considered the cost and feasibility of a new Center on their property, just a block from our new building, the wisdom of a merged ministry became a reality. Another factor was our shared commitment to see Child Care at or near the campus as a priority in our future ministry to and for the University. A graduate student, arrested for neglect by leaving her baby in her car while she made a class, dramatized the need. Presbyterians and Disciples led in the undertaking, with strong support from the University. All this led to the Incorporation of a Board and the designing of The Infant Center, built on the site of the old Disciple Center.

12

When Arla Elston, the Disciple Campus Minister, left us to become a Regional Executive in Oregon we sought another Disciple to fill her shoes and to share the leadership of the United Campus Ministry. This is when Peter Ray, a recent graduate of Texas Christian University's School of Religion, drove in aboard his VW Bus. Its colorful graffiti gave class to our parking lot!

The Deep End Sighted

It started out with the building, rising from the rubble of the old. It was not beyond our imagination, but due to the imagination of dreamers and doers with a vision for a generation that was now eager to create a setting for dialogue, a showcase for indigenous talent, an open mike for voices at the grassroots, and a center for hearing from the margins. Providing a place for socializing convenient to the campus residential population and within walking distance was also a goal.

A Coffee House Ministry was a high priority for the bunch of Dreamers who gathered to "bluc sky" the future. Most were already involved in some way with "The Center." More specifically, we were involved with each other in the congregations and community to which we had been drawn. The lowest level of the four level building design was dedicated to this venture. It had an entrance from the street, marked by a custom made sign with the name "The DEEP END" divided by an arrow pointing down below. Its furnishings, lighting, sound system, the menu, and the decor, together, created a welcoming and intimate setting for both student and faculty participation.

The core innovators included Marilee and Bob Frans, Mary and Dick Pulley, Carolyn and Tom Jefferson, Sarah and Wade Burnside, and Sally and George Gunn, of course. These, with a loyal student contingency, became identified as "The Deep-Endables." From the start both students and faculty members of Fayetteville congregations volunteered to serve tables and do kitchen duty.

"The DEEP END" took shape during the summer of 1965 and evolved as the fall term unfolded. Student support and participation was immediate and enthusiastic. The development of the Menu is remembered with nostalgia, in particular the trial run one night with the preparation and serving of the first Reuben sandwich, the jamoca coffee, the choice of teas and cheeses, and a mixed fruit punch, concocted by Christy Oliver and Sally Gunn and christened, "CoupdePong!" Open 8 to 12 PM each Wednesday, Friday and Saturday nights, the work crew of three arrived by 7 to set up the kitchen, light candles, put on the tablecloths, cut down the lights and cut on the music and the mike.

Friday night ordinarily featured a musician or live performance. The best attended nights were those that featured a University faculty member in an hour of "Prof Off the Pedestal," and Wednesdays often featured reruns of old movie clips and classic short subjects. The University sponsored "Symposium," a lecture series brought name speakers to the campus, and it became almost routine for the open forum and reception following to be at The Deep End or our Forum Room.

A small red journal kept in the kitchen recorded the date, the weather, the attendance, and the featured artist or speaker. Among these are found the names of U.S. Senators Fulbright, Thurmond, Hatfield, Brooke, and men like Ralph Abernathy and women like The Peace Pilgrim.

The Forum Room was a place for dialogue and provided seating for 60-70 people in a comfortable and spacious meeting room. Here were scheduled occasional lecture series and special services. A new Presbyterian congregation used this space for Sunday worship for several years. It was not the only setting for worship. The fourth level of the Center included three offices, a library, and a Chapel: The Servants Chapel.

This space was furnished with two square custom made tables and four movable benches, easily rearranged to seat 10 to 12 for meditation, for worship, or Bible study. Two stained glass windows, one representing the Old Testament Suffering Servant as "a root out of the dry ground," and the second the New Testament "Towel and Basin," symbols of the Servant Lord's washing his disciples' feet. Over the door one could read, as one exited to go out into the world, the words "Servants Entrance."

The Center over time became both the meeting place or supporter of a variety of campus related organizations. When two graduate student women proposed a Women's Center and needed an office in which to meet and do counseling and provide resources, one of the two rooms adjoining The Deep End was provided. Both Peter Ray and I also began to do Draft counseling and to see women in our offices who were referred to us from the Dean of Women's office. We had joined a network of Campus Ministers in states where abortion was illegal who had contacts in cities and states where a so called "Problem Pregnancy" could be legally and safely terminated. Ultimately, we were able to identify local medical personnel to address this need.

Working for PEACE and JUSTICE

A weekly "Peace Vigil" was held on the corner across Maple Street and opposite the Student Union. Because the Vietnam War had made "peace" a timely topic and a divisive issue, we provided a forum in the Coffee House format for advocates of all persuasions to be heard. When Martin Luther King's Poor Peoples March in Washington was organized in the summer of 1968, students and their mentors, including our teenaged sons Wilson and Herb, joined the thousands who made that journey. The next year a Peace March on the Mall in Washington drew an estimated hundred thousand who marched past the White House to shout the name of a fellow American who had died in Nixon's war. The night before, in the National Cathedral, one of four speakers was an Arkansas student, the wife of a seminary student who had given up his deferment to serve in the military.

B.A.D. (Black Americans for Democracy) was a student organization that took a leadership role in advocating for the growing numbers of African American students on campus. At a point in the early sixties, a sit-in in the University President's office sought assurance that black students would be admitted to the resident halls and have equal access to all the facilities of the University. Jim Loudermilk, the Wesley Foundation Director, led this failed effort and took the heat from the Administration and from his own Bishop, who moved him to a less visible post.

About the same time the "Game of the Century" was to be played in Razorback Stadium, a title game between Arkansas and Texas, two undefeated football teams, ranked No. 1 and No. 2 in the national polls. President Nixon would attend and would award a mythical trophy to the winner. Anticipating trouble, the Secret Service blanketed the campus and stadium area. There was a impromptu pep rally each night all week. With full press coverage, it appeared to the B.A.D. leadership to be the perfect time to make a statement to protest the continuing racist policies of the University. I heard talk of a plan to disrupt the game itself with a barrage of broken glass and bottles thrown from the stands.

Then, on Friday night, there was a drive-by shooting, wounding one black student. I was at home when I received a phone call about nine o'clock. "Eric asked me to call you. Can you come to a meeting going on right now down on Dickson Street?" " Eric" was a name I recognized. Months earlier I had joined a group of students and faculty, both whites and blacks, who had gathered on Maple Street in front of the Student Union. A single student had climbed a sycamore tree in front of the Union, near the spot where the weekly Peace Vigil formed. He proclaimed that he would not come down until "peace" was declared in Vietnam. Now, in the second day of his protest, a bunch of frat boys announced that they would throw the bum out of his tree if he was not down by 9 PM.

Eric was among the black students who showed up to help protect the tree and its occupant, and to defend his rights. Also joining the defensive team were the few black faculty and a significant number of other faculty and students. We formed a human circle around the tree, and locked arms, facing outward. As we faced down the rowdy mob, my right arm linked with Eric's and my left arm with that of Jim, a husky English prof, who I knew had been a lineman on his college football team. As the assailants failed to prevail, one at a time they drifted away, leaving only a drunken few to give up jumping to reach low limbs.

The issues of race and of peace have a way of melding, as Dr. King often reminded us, each advocate needing the other for balance and wisdom. "Want PEACE?" the bumper sticker asks, "Work for JUSTICE."

I honestly cannot remember what I might have said to the black students who crowded into Eric's apartment, that night, but I felt privileged to have been invited and trusted to be a part of the movement toward consensus and

15

toward a non-violent resolution to a crisis that called for patience and for perseverance in the 1960's, the golden years of campus ministry advancement!

A.D., A Journal of Opinion

At its inception it was *A.D. 1964*, and the year changed as the years passed, 1965 . . . 1966 . . . 1967 . . . While this publication became an extension of the United Campus Ministry, it was in fact an ecumenical venture to generate communication in print around campus related issues. *A.D.* could be translated in its traditional "Year of our Lord," or as "Arkansas Dialogue." I designed the first issue and provided its name, but soon enlisted a Catholic journalism student to carry it on. It was close to an underground newspaper, circulated by placing free copies in the Student Union and in religious centers that welcomed dialogue and diversity.

A.D. was a place for the exchange of views and commentary - a journal of opinion. The publisher was actually Margaret Engles, our United Ministry's stalwart secretary, receptionist, surrogate mother-confessor, and advisor. Her busy mimeograph, and its ubiquitous brown ink, left its mark on everything in sight!

An interesting sequel in publishing history occurred in the 1970s. The Presbyterian Church (U.S.A.) came out with a new look and name for its official subscription magazine. Its name was *A.D. 1974*. I wrote the Editor and congratulated him on "continuing the fine journalistic tradition we initiated in Arkansas in 1964." His reply was cordial but guarded, as he assured me that they had done research to find that no copyright was to be found for the name!

George Gunn, and his wife, Sally, have retired to the Givens Highland Farms Retirement Community in Black Mountain, NC. After 20 years of life in Banner Elk, NC, where George "flunked" retirement by serving a small mission-minded church in Newland, NC for 18 years, he is now writing his memoirs, using photography as a metaphor. The title of his memoirs is "Time Exposures - Shot by Gunn." He exhibits his art and photography at the church and at Highland Farms.

Empowering Students Through a Center-Based Ministry:
The University of Texas at Austin in the 50's-70's
By Bob Breihan

At age 18 my career aspirations were simple: be an electrical engineer. I had no idea what a campus minister was, but was fortunate to arrive at the University of Texas where one of the best, Paul K. Deats, filled that role. I quickly realized the strength of such a presence in student and campus life – Paul was simply there: smart, confident, personable and not afraid to speak his mind. He made a lasting impression on me in a very short time. Later, after two more years in the Navy as an engineering officer, and a year to collect necessary credits to graduate, I would come to my "Jesus Moment:" shall I work with machines and electricity or with people? After thinking, praying and talking to almost anyone standing still (or even walking slowly), I chose seminary (over law) and so the journey began

In my senior year at Perkins Theological Seminary in 1952, I was asked by a Methodist Conference leader to lead a program of youth work and leadership education. He was eager to have me start and sent me to a conference in Michigan the next day! A short 18 months later, the Wesley Foundation at the University of Texas asked me to follow Paul Deats, who was dismissed for being too "pink." (Remember this is the early '50s.) Again, I agreed, with no further instruction for my new task than: "Just don't do what Deats did" (which was to attract all manner of criticism for his espousal of pacifism and liberal views in general). They added, "Since you were in the Navy we know we can trust you" -- I decided not to mention my own relatively recent conversation to pacifism and forged ahead.

As a newbie, I worked under this mantra: "Ask all the questions you can think of for one year – people will be glad to talk." Just seek to understand the context – and keep a log privately. I reasoned that if you ask the same questions in the second year, folks will begin to question you and wonder. "Be interested but not persuaded by what you hear. Say 'I hear you' and 'we'll see' as often as you can."

The Wesley Foundation at that time had no set program, no structure -- except a student council -- so I spent a lot of time with those students, with Methodist faculty and administrators at the University, probing their thoughts and opinions.

We had the traditional format of the time: several Sunday school classes on Sunday morning, taught by university faculty, church members, and state officials – all were well attended. Sunday night was the main event – dinner, followed by singing, then a speaker for 45 minutes, but always finishing up in time for evening service at the church!

One of my enduring concerns was to help students get connected with the issues of their time and their context in Austin. During the week, groups of students volunteered in city social service programs, many in East Austin, the

17

traditionally African-American side of town. Staff from these agencies often gave presentations that helped students see both the potential and the challenge involved in such work. Then there were state and national Methodist Student conferences – I worked to get students there so they could realize the broad scope of student activities at that time.

Also, I made it a practice to talk with students about their studies and their professors – who pushed them to grow, by challenging their beliefs. In this way, I encouraged a bridge of conversation between the university setting and the students' faith connection. One such example was a botany professor who regularly questioned their beliefs in God. Conversations with him and others in the sciences led to some special programs where high school kids were brought to the campus from all over the country. The purpose was to keep the dialogue going, opening the students to a new way to look at science.

My own values and my willingness to cross over into different areas of inquiry and action in this way repeatedly brought new commitments. For instance, my pacifism led me to Friends meetings and to the program work of the American Friends Service Committee. In addition to helping set up workshops in Austin, I became involved in strategic planning for a six-state region which included establishing the first integrated child care facility west of the Mississippi.

Another fruitful exploration came through my contact with Dean Page Keaton of the UT law school. An SMU law professor and a professor of ethics at Perkins School of Theology (both in Dallas) had been teaching a joint course focused on abortions. When I told this to Keaton, he readily took to the idea and for several years we ran a weekly seminary between the Presbyterian and Episcopal Seminaries in Austin and the students and faculty from the law school.

In the midst of these endeavors, in 1959, 25-30 campus ministers across Texas came together to press the Texas Methodist Student Movement to appoint me as interim (then permanent) director, replacing a strong nominee from the more conservative, church-centered part of that commission. This involved extensive travel within the state, attending to 25-27 campuses, meeting with school presidents or deans and sometimes mediating between a campus minister and an administration when the minister took a position on a controversial social issue.

It was heady work, often satisfying, but took me away from family more than I would have liked, so I was ready when the Wesley Foundation board requested me to drop this broader assignment and return to lead the local program in Austin. A Bible chair position was staffed for academic student courses and a creative colleague, Rev. Eddie Shaw, developed "The Guild of Lay Theologians," in which about 100 participants each dedicated two hours a week to private study of a paper on a theological issue, then spent one hour of participation in a 12-member Guild group led by a local clergyperson. Those involved went through a 4-year program in this way and "graduated" with a certificate signed by the United Methodist bishop at the time.

About this time, I was elected president of a newly forming Citizens Commission on Human Relations. With others, I worked to integrate restaurants downtown and around the university campus. While students participated in sit-ins, I would go to the various managers and try to get their cooperation, but instead many downtown stores chose to close their lunch counters rather than integrate. One manager did agree initially to welcome black students and their families; soon others were eager to come as well, so the Nighthawk Restaurant soon welcomed any and all black citizens. A list of those places that agreed to serve the students was then compiled and circulated in the black community.

The Citizens Commission pressed in other areas as well, demonstrating at a newly opened skating rink and making steady efforts to integrate Austin movie theaters also. Students were very active in all these efforts but success was very slow. A meeting with a well-known civic leader and the managers of the downtown theaters resulted in one small victory: allowing blacks to use the balcony of the Varsity Theater on the edge of the campus.

The location of the Methodist Student Center across the street from a large state university campus presented numerous possibilities, and some problems. The center was open until 10pm every night, often for outside groups to use the building. We reasoned that students needed to have a safe space where they could freely discuss social issues important to them. The Center became associated with open-minded approaches to all faiths as well; when an Islamic student association could find no other place to meet, we welcomed them once a week for quite some time.

A further expression of this kind of commitment was ICHTHUS Coffee House, open every Friday and Saturday night from 7-midnight, which served coffee, tea and bakery goods, and displayed the work of local artists. Students were recruited to oversee the Coffee House and were also informally coached to listen to students who came in and also to explain in purpose of the Coffee House in nontraditional language.

Each week, a speaker was invited to make brief remarks throughout the evening and engage in dialogue with anyone who wished. We also had singers (including Pete Seeger and Janice Joplin!), poets and occasionally a staged drama in a nearby auditorium. Another innovative use of the Center space itself was for major theatrical productions. At one time a group of African-American students had a small 'company-in-residence,' in cooperation with the coffee house.

The times they were "a-changin'" in the late 60's, and the emphasis on dialogue and speaking one's mind led to my participation in the Southwest Regional Draft Counselors. This group developed as the military draft had increasing presence in the life of program students. They cooperated to publish the regulations for local selective service boards, and we also made sure to

19

have someone on stage whenever military personnel made a presentation at local high schools. I had many occasions to sit with young men as they struggled with the question of becoming a conscientious object to the deepening war in Vietnam.

Another issue arose from a different direction when the director of student health services approached me regarding the vexing frequency of 'problem pregnancies' among University students. Together we formed the Coalition for Sexual Understanding, to educate teachers, counselors, and social workers across the state who were involved with adolescents and young adults. Guidelines were developed through this process for sex education and counseling in whatever context they might occur. Additionally, I joined the Clergy Consultation for Problem Pregnancies, a nationwide network which began to address the need for safe and legal abortions to be available for those who desired.

The students associated with the Wesley Center were themselves initiators of programs as well, including a work camp each year over Easter weekend (this was prior to the advent of longer spring breaks). Fifty to 75 students went in car loads to help with specific projects, such as building a summer camp for the Centro Sociale, a program of the Methodist Board of Missions. They were completely in charge, a source of great pride to them and center staff as well.

Community-building and providing hospitable space for students, who were often overwhelmed by a large university, was always a priority. Through my community involvement, I and several others established a volunteer-staffed all-night Hotline to Help for the larger city. It was a natural extension to tend to students in a program called The Listening Ear, which took place at the Center.

We enlisted volunteers from one of the strongest churches, and each was asked to be at the center one evening a month, from 10pm to 6am, simply to listen, without judgment, offer coffee – and discourage those who came from trying to sleep overnight there! This program was very successful, with a consistent flow of folks sitting and talking through most of the night. Many years later, these same volunteers speak of all they learned by serving in this way and how grateful they were for the opportunity.

I look back on my experiences in campus ministry with wonder – that there were so many diverse opportunities for programming and services. Basically, the times were right for empowering students to think and act for themselves. The University and surrounding businesses were very responsive to student interests and needs. The Church itself was still a potent influence in communities across the nation, and as a result there was a great interest in tending to student needs when they left home for college.

But by the early 1960s, this cohesive set of interests began to come apart. Over the following years, careful listening and attention to ways that campus ministry could play a creative role, kept our programs going until the mid to late 1970s.

By the 1980s, the Church's overall influence had steadily waned, large centers such as the Wesley Foundation were a thing of the past (ours was taken down in 1981), and much smaller, often fragmented, campus ministry coalitions were left to respond to students' spiritual needs. I give thanks for those who have continued in this calling -- shedding old ideas and structures and seeking to imagine new forms and styles of ministry that provide a solid, God-based presence for students today. May their efforts be blessed!

Bob Breihan was active in student and campus ministry from 1951-81, after which he served as Associate Pastor at University UMC in Austin till 1986. He was NCMA President from 1983-85. From 1986-2001, he was the Founder/Director of the New Life Institute, a center for Counseling and Spiritual Growth, then the senior therapist there till 2012. He and his wife Sarah Bentley are happily retired on a hillside in Austin, enjoying the flora and fauna, and spending time with family.

NCMA: An Obvious Thing To Do!
By David Burnight

I was happy to be an APUP delegate to the 1964 gathering in St. Louis which created NCMA. It was an obvious thing to do. We were all pleased that the wheels of denominational structure could move in such a reasonable way. We welcomed each other!

Looking back, it strikes me that connections with WSCF (World Student Christian Federation), APUPs(Association of Presbyterian University Pastors), NCMA, and all the gathered campus brothers and sisters thereof, have added to my education as much as any course or seminar. What a great bunch of people I have been privileged to know! Experimental forms of spirituality, ways of doing intercultural education and exposing justice issues, contact with movements like Taize -- all these have been gifts to me.

Extracurricular gifts were often surprises. One was in 1954. Just three years out of seminary, I was happy to be preparing for a visit to our Cal Aggie Christian Association at UCDavis, from a young man in Guatemala who was to tour the U.S. under the sponsorship of WSCF, talking about Christian faith and international sharing. Abruptly, he called it off! Our U.S. had sponsored a coup which overthrew the democratically elected president of Guatemala. It quickly came out that John Foster Dulles, Secretary of State, and his brother Allen Dulles, CIA Director, had large holdings in United Fruit Company. President Arbenz wanted to nationalize United Fruit, or at least arrange for Guatemalans to get a bigger share of the banana business. He was labeled a "Communist." Our young Christians protested America's arrogance. This all startled me, because one seminary professor had held up J.F.Dulles, a Presbyterian elder, as a shining example of Christian involvement in political life! My naive view of the way our nation and churches work was seriously modified!

Actually, a similar confrontation for me occurred in 1952, but it took a while for it to sink in. At the Presbyterian General Assembly, a missionary from Iran came into a meeting of the Missions Committee. He reported that the American/English upsetting of Premier Mossadegh was very disturbing, and likely to have dire consequences. Churches, in general, paid little attention. . ..
The rest is, of course, history!

In 1964 my associate John Pamperin and I chartered a bus to take 30 students, faculty, local clergy and townspeople from Davis, CA to meet MLK Jr. on his march into Montgomery, as he had invited. We were not surprised at the sullen reception given by the white people there. But we were inspired by the gentle sturdy faith of the black church folks who hosted us. Singing hymns together that night brought tears to everyone's eyes! After King's speech, next day, we started back, reading the local newspapers on the bus. The coverage of the event was so skewed and misleading that it was really a lie. The big side story was that a black man and white woman had been found fornicating on the fringes of the march! If the press could so misrepresent what we had just experienced, what might this mean back home about our own newspaper's coverage of the Viet Nam war? Another eye-opener! (The faith experiences were good sympathetic material for talks to churches in conservative parts of California.)

APUP and NCMA gatherings were always awareness openers and learning experiences. When the Nicaraguan revolution was going on, the first clear whispers of it came to me from fellow UP's at our national conference. So in 1981, Jim White and I took some students from SDSU and Long Beach State to Nicaragua, for a 10 day visit. Though missionaries and other aware Americans were holding weekly protests outside the American Embassy in Managua, the American press ignored them, and repeated the Kissinger line about the "brave Contras." The interviews and photos which we took back became provocative material for student discussions and for sermons in local churches.

These are a plus to all the personal gifts of growing faith and love which I had from students and faculty. We were trying to be a community which understood and practiced spiritual Universals, and welcomed everybody's Truth. Now this seems to be happening in many quarters! There is hope!

My campus ministry assignments were at the University of California at Davis, 1951-1966 and San Diego State University, 1966-1994. These 20 years of retirement have been lively, but they are difficult to describe. For a while I hung in with the Presbytery, chairing the Peacemaking Committee and then the Social Concerns committee. The committee folks were fine, but the stupid hassles over homosexual policies became such a block to anything else that I stopped having any part of it. Ginny is a Vatican II Catholic, and I have participated with her in a lot of activities of her parish (even though I can't say the Nicene Creed with them!) Bible study with liberal Catholics can be fun. We went to Turkey with Pacifica Foundation, and since then have been in a Muslim-Christian dialogue group, including Ramadan meals together.

David Burnight and wife Ginny are living in the little village of Crest, in the hills high above El Cajon, California. David keeps track of about 150 former students, with an annual Intersection House alumni newsletter. He is the "Welcome Wagon" person on the board of the Community Association. They enjoy walking, the waves at La Jolla, gym workouts, the San Diego Symphony, and singing with a Crest guitar jam.

Life in Campus Ministry
By Robert and Shirley Cooper

Probably not too many seminary graduates have spent their entire careers as campus ministers, but for Bob and me it seemed a natural thing to do. We both were active in a student group while in college in the 50's – in fact, we met at a national Methodist Student Conference in Urbana, Illinois. We both have vivid memories of the first worship's opening hymn: 3500 voices from all over the world joining in singing "For All the Saints." After we married, we followed in the footsteps of role models we admired as students, Maye Bell at the SMU Methodist Student Movement and Cecil and Faye Matthews at the Texas Tech Wesley Foundation.

The Texas Methodist Student Movement had recently been organized when Bob finished at Perkins in 1952.He was happy to be appointed to serve with Ferris and Marion Baker at the Wesley Foundation for schools in Denton, now called North Texas University and Texas Woman's University. The '50s offered opportunities for state and national student conferences to enrich Methodist students' spiritual, intellectual, and social awareness. They also fostered a deep trust and commitment among campus ministers. Local retreats, worship services, cell groups (called prayer groups and other names in the anti-communist years to come), service projects and recreation were offered. We lived in the second floor of the Methodist Center at TSCW, now TWU. The early morning prayer group saw us off to the hospital to have our first child.

Counseling was always needed, since students were mostly young in those days, and suffered the stresses of growing up, succeeding in school, choosing a career and often a mate, as well as meeting challenges to their faith. Older students often had settled some of these issues, but had other stresses instead.

After our four years spent in Denton Bob was assigned to what is now Texas A&M, Canyon. That became a one-year assignment when Bob refused to sign a "loyalty oath" required of all teachers during the worst of the McCarthy persecutions. Our friends Bob Monk and Bob Breihan found a way to finance a position for Bob Cooper as part-time program director for the state and regional meetings and part-time associate director at Texas A&M in College Station. After a year Bob Monk left for graduate work at Princeton U. and Bob Cooper was Wesley Foundation director for three more years.

Then we were off to Drew University in New Jersey for a Masters Degree in Theology. (In those days, three years at seminary entitled students to a Bachelor of Divinity Degree only, and some universities required those who taught Bible courses to have a Masters degree. Yes, Texas allowed campus ministers to offer courses for college credit back then.) As was our custom, we moved towing a U-Haul trailer and car packed with boxes and a baby bed mattress on top. We had two little boys and another on the way. My feet were on a box and our turtle was in his bowl on my lap.

Finishing his degree, Bob was appointed to Texas A&I in Kingsville as minister for Presbyterians, Disciples, Episcopalians and United Methodists, and to S.M.U. for 27 years, where Bob was first director as part of the Wesley – Presbyterian – Christian Fellowship. This morphed into the United Campus Ministries which included Roman Catholics, Campus Y, and others. Later, Bob's job title was changed to Associate Chaplain, an office which included many of his former duties along with some new ones. These included a shared responsibility for the Sunday chapel service and coordinating a campus ministry organization of all religious groups on campus. This group planned all-campus service projects and encouraged cooperation between ministries.

The styles of clothing, music, political and economic philosophy, and even theological viewpoint changed cyclically through the years, but students, staff and faculty all were still people with the same basic needs.

Our three sons cut their teeth on the campus upheavals of the '60s and '70s, but also had the unforgettable experience of hearing in Sunday Chapel great preachers like Claude Evans, Schubert Ogden, John Deschner, William Sloane Coffin, etc. and great music led by Lloyd Pfautsch, Carleton Young, and Robert Anderson. And our children enjoyed the extra attention the students gave them. We remember 8-month old Glenn sitting on the ping- pong table while a friendly game was played over his head. Graduate psychology students, who were required to test children, found the boys to be willing subjects.

Before SMU, Bob worried that he had to spend too much time on maintaining Wesley Foundation buildings and grounds, and so was pleased and relieved that SMU would give us space in the Student Center that someone else cared for. Imagine our surprise when the next campus minister thought that being at a separate building was a primary need!

As times change, ministers and ministries change, but Wesley's challenge to unite "knowledge and vital piety" remains.

Since retirement Bob Cooper has been active at Casa Emanu-El UMC, Dallas Area Interfaith, Lake Highlands-White Rock Democrats, and plays tennis twice a week. Shirley taught three and four year olds in day school and was younger children's secretary at Highland Park UMC. She became secretary for the Dallas Hotel-Motel Association and then for the North Texas Conference. They have recently moved into CC Young retirement residence in Dallas. Bob says, "We hope to get ahead of the need."

Working For Racial Justice in the 1960's
By Harry Smith

During the efforts to achieve equal rights for African-Americans across the South during the Civil Rights struggle, CORE The Congress on Racial Equality) decided to focus its efforts on several communities, including Chapel Hill, North Carolina, the location of the University of North Carolina.

Campus ministers at UNC participated in a variety of ways to support what the students and CORE workers were doing to achieve equal treatment in local eating establishments, theatres, and motels. Strategies included staging sit-ins in restaurants and undergoing arrest to emphasize the need for a Public Accommodation Law.

I recall one evening when the students were focusing their efforts on Brady's Restaurant. After the mixed group of students had been refused service, the police were called to arrest them for trespassing. Facing arrest, the students "went limp" and were lying about the floor of the restaurant. Mrs. Brady, who was not known for her liberal views, decided to dramatize her contempt for the students' effort by straddling one of the students and urinating on his face.

Later the students were discussing what charges, if any, they might bring against Mrs. Brady for this gross and demeaning act. Someone suggested "Assault with a Deadly Weapon" while another recommended "Breaking and Entering."

I was deeply impressed by the students' ability to respond to the hostility their actions provoked and to use humor to cope with the tensions which they were experiencing.

At one point, following a series of arrests for civil disobedience, one of the students, who held one of the University's most prestigious scholarships as a Morehead Scholar, was ordered to appear before the Honor Council to face possible expulsion for his violations of the law.

The Honor Council had the responsibility of determining whether John's civil disobedience leading to his arrest constituted "conduct unbecoming a Carolina gentleman."

It was a very important moment in the University's history when the Honor Council voted that under the prevailing circumstances such conduct was, indeed, not "unbecoming" but completely justified and that all charges against John should be dismissed.

Subsequently, knowing that his actions might mean the loss of his Morehead Scholarship, John went to Selma and was later incarcerated in the State Penitentiary in Raleigh. I recall taking a copy of Bonhoeffer's *Letters from Prison* for him to read in prison, much to the puzzlement and consternation of the prison officials.

Upon learning that the City of Chapel Hill was planning to open a new municipal cemetery out on the Durham Highway, the campus ministers led the effort to insure that it would not be segregated. Drawing up a petition, we sought the signatures of the various ministers in area churches.

Unfortunately, we encountered some opposition and a refusal to sign by the Lutheran minister who said he "believed in the separation of church and state," by the Baptist minister who had the local mortician in his congregation and did not wish to get involved in his business, and the Methodist minister who said he no longer signed petitions after an unfortunate experience in a previous charge.

Undaunted, we took the petition with as many names of religious leaders as we could muster to the City Council meeting. We were informed that the sale of cemetery lots was a business matter and that most people were very concerned about insuring that their property would not be devalued by unacceptable neighbors. We pointed out that most burials took place without knowledge of who was buried in adjacent lots, but to no avail. Furthermore, we were informed there would probably not be enough demand for burial in an unsegregated cemetery to justify integrating it.

After much discussion, the Council offered a compromise. They would designate an integrated area of the new cemetery if we could get someone to consent to be buried in the unsegregated section.

Fortunately, we learned that a retired economics professor from the University of Chicago had been diagnosed as having terminal cancer and would be glad to pioneer our effort to insure that the new cemetery would be integrated. As luck would have, Mary's cancer went into remission and she did not die until much later. By then, the City Council had agreed that the cemetery should indeed by integrated, making further action unnecessary.

Needless to say, this episode provoked a number of dubious comments, about our "unsuccessful undertaking," the "grave issues we had raised," and the "controversial ministerial plot" that we had perpetrated.

Fortunately, changes in the racial atmosphere and the eventual passage of the federal Public Accommodations Law and the Civil Rights Act, moved us far beyond the discrimination of events in 1963 and 1964 in Chapel Hill.

(Written in 1998 in response to an NCMA request for anecdotes.)

Harry Smith served as Presbyterian campus minister at the University of North Carolina from the early 1950's till the late 60's, when he went to Yale to teach. He became President of Austin College in Sherman, TX from 1978-1994 and retired to Santa Fe, NM, where he died in 2002.

Recollections at Age 88
By J. Emmett Herndon

Let me introduce myself. From 1955-90, I spent 35 years in campus ministry at Stetson University and Emory University. While at Emory, I also worked with faculty groups at Agnes Scott College, Georgia State University and Oglethorpe University. And inherited the ministry at Georgia Tech.. So, here goes.

I remember
- being nominated to be the NCMA president but losing the election to a friend at Duke;
- being a dorm chaplain in a large women's dormitory with office hours 9-12 P.M. on Sunday nights;
- having 60 nursing students attend a series on Pain, Suffering and Death, an idea I stole from Harry Smith at UNC;
- developing special ministries with medical students;
- moderating 8 faculty-staff discussion groups monthly;
- coordinating the programs of the Biomedical Ethics Group for 18 years;
- getting 25 phone calls on a Sunday night from women with unwanted and unplanned pregnancies;
- being a plaintiff in our case against Georgia's restrictive abortion laws;
- taking 80 students from Emory and the Atlanta University complex to an ecumenical conference in Athens, Ohio;
- our stopping at a barbeque place in Ohio for dinner and having Father Scott and me persuade those good old boys that they should serve us in their dining room;
- training students and providing draft counseling for students and faculty and winning every case;
- being charged with heresy by a nearby Presbyterian Church and it almost went to trial;
- a committee that I chaired to plan the college conference at Montreat deciding to move to Banner Elk because of certain racial restrictions on conferees;
- hate mail I received on occasions and spook telephone calls;
- choosing to stay in campus ministry after being considered to be a dean in student affairs at two universities.

Emmett Herndon, now 88 years old, lives at Lenbrook Retirement Center in the Buckhead section of north Atlanta. He leads the Great Decisions discussion group and, as always, reads extensively on a wide array of topics.

What I Have Learned After 40 Years of Ministry on the Same University Campus

By James Pruyne

The Beginnings

In the fall of 1955, my wife, Gwen, and I returned to what is now Illinois State University, after a three-month honeymoon in Europe. It included three weeks of study at the World Council of Churches' Ecumenical Institute on the shores of Lake Geneva in Switzerland. I had spent the previous year in a seminary fieldwork position at the First Presbyterian Church in Normal, Illinois, where Illinois State U is located.

The first thing we did after returning to "Normal," was to rent a large house adjacent to the university campus which would provide us with a small apartment, space for a student gathering place, and space for five students to rent rooms for the coming school year. This was necessary to have enough income to rent the house. We registered our housing accommodations with the University and waited for students to show up. The first one to do so was a young African American student named Donald McHenry. I showed him the rooms available and let him choose whichever room appealed to him. Thus began our experience and love of campus ministry.

Donald McHenry lived with us for his last two years at ISU. Our relationship with Don, as with so many students, became a life-long friendship. Later, he became the United States Ambassador to the United Nations in the Carter Administration. During the George W. Bush Administration, he returned to campus, bringing Madeline Albright with him. (We have a cherished photograph of the two of us with the two of them.) Together, they carried on an excellent discussion of current American foreign policy. Before the presentation, we sat with him during lunch and, for the first time, I asked him if, when he first knocked on our door, "Was he testing us?" His reply was, "You will never know." He returned several times over the years, sometimes at our request and sometimes at the request of the University. In the beginning, I was the go-between for Don and the University administration. First, would he leave his papers to ISU? Answer: "Yes." Then, would he serve on the ISU Foundation Board? Again, his answer was "Yes." At one point, he set up an account for us in the ISU Foundation to which he contributed some of the funds he received for serving on various boards of directors. It was a match system. He contributed and the companies matched his gifts. I took students to Washington, DC, a good many times for a spring break study seminar. Whenever we were there, Don found the time to meet with our students, often at Georgetown University where he was on the faculty.

During the time he was a student and living with us, he and friends organized the campus chapter of the NAACP. One night, when I was out at a meeting, he went to Gwen and said: "I am going out to the Green Lantern Restaurant (one of our better restaurants at the time) to see if they will serve me. If I am arrested will you and Jim come get me?" Gwen replied, "Of course!" and off he went. He did not get arrested. They let him in, but refused to serve him. Thus began several weeks of challenging all the restaurants in the community. In the end, the students succeeded, but it was not without having to threaten a lawsuit. Don is an amazing man. The Jacksonville newspaper referred to him as "the quintessential diplomat." This was the beginning of our ministry's involvement in the civil rights movement and the many issues surrounding it. Other actions we have been involved in over the years include:

Housing

When we arrived at ISU, there was only one residence hall on campus. It was Fell Hall for women. African American female students were permitted to live in it on one wing of one floor if they had an African American roommate. There were no dorms for men. Therefore, most students had to live in rooms rented from what were called Householders. The only area where African American students could find rooms to rent was the area in southwest Bloomington where most of the African American community lived. There were no public buses available after six o'clock in the evening. Hence, they often had to walk, sometimes a distance of two or three miles.

- Our students developed a "covenant of open occupancy" and went two-by-two to all 295 householders in Normal to ask them to sign the covenant. Only five did so. We were one; the Methodist pastor was one; and three others.

- We opened the "first integrated coop house for men," as it is reported in *The Grandest of Enterprises*, the history of ISU's first one hundred years.

Other actions and spring break trips

Our students worked with the student chapter of NAACP to desegregate the barber shops in town. They were prepared to challenge the theaters, but when the theater owners heard about it, they opened their doors before action was taken. In this, the student leader from the NAACP was Reggie Weaver, later president of the National Education Association for several years.

In 1957, a group went to Mary Holmes Junior College in West Point, Mississippi-- a residential school operated by the Presbyterian Church for African American students. So incensed were our students at what they saw that they voluntarily did the necessary research and wrote a paper outlining the realities of the "separate but equal" defense of segregation. They shared the report with our local churches. It was reported to me that this was the first group from the North to come into Mississippi in support of the Negroes since reconstruction. I cannot confirm this, but the source seemed reliable.

In the spring of 1963, 18 students spent their spring break in Savannah, Georgia, doing voter registration in the African American community. This venture was arranged for us by Larry Jones, campus minister colleague from Fisk University, and Andrew Young. I was told a couple of years ago by one of our students who has spent his life addressing these issues that our trip was the test case that led to "Mississippi Summer," the summer that the south was flooded with students--Black and White, Christian and Jewish-- registering voters particularly in Mississippi and Alabama.

New Campus Ministry Facility

In 1969, we opened a new ecumenical campus ministry center which included ministries supported by The United Church of Christ, the Christian Church (Disciples of Christ), The Church of the Brethren, The Mennonite Church, The Presbyterian Church, The American Baptist Church, The Evangelical Lutheran Church, The Episcopal Church and the Christian Scientists. This center over the years has also been used by Jewish Hillel, the Muslim, Hindu and Buddhist Communities at various times and in various ways. The building, known as The Campus Religious Center, was constructed out of black brick, as our expression of the "black is beautiful" affirmation at the time. The building immediately became the "home" of the Interdenominational Youth Choir, a gospel group that was the largest African American group on campus.

Just shortly after the building was opened, I received a call one afternoon from Lonnie Pruitt, now an Episcopal priest, who was the President of the Black Student Union. I knew him well. He had been a part of one of our study seminars at the U.N. Lonnie said, "Jim, we want to hold a press conference this afternoon, can we use the Center?" I checked with my Lutheran and Baptist colleagues and then told Lonnie, "The building is available to you." In that press conference, these students stated their demands to the University. They included:
- more students of color on campus
- more faculty of color
- courses in black studies
- the naming of a University building for Malcolm X

During the following week, other press conferences were held; the faculty members of color met; the faculty and students met together. They negotiated with the administration on an almost continuing basis - and all in our black Campus Religious Center. The University administration agreed to almost all of the requests in one way or another. They did promise to name a building after an African American, but they refused to name it Malcolm X. After all negotiations were complete and changes approved by both groups, we received "thank you's" from both students and the administration. *The Importance of Place cannot be overstated!*

Special Efforts with High School and College Students

Working with the Chicago Urban League, we arranged for a dozen students of color to spend ten days on the campus of ISU for academic enrichment. The University's residence halls were not open in the summer, so we arranged for these students to spend time in small communities and farms near the University.

A grant from the Presbyterian Church allowed us to work with a dozen African American Chicago high school students, providing mentoring and tutoring for them during the school year and bringing them to campus for two weeks of academic enrichment every summer.

We received an Illinois Board of Higher Education Higher Education Cooperation Act (HECA) grant permitting us to create mentoring programs for male African American students on four college/university campuses: ISU, Northern Illinois University, Eastern Illinois University and Elmhurst College. Then we received a second HECA grant to support the Student Volunteer Center we created. We staffed it with student interns who received three hours of academic credit for operating the Center and doing some workshops on race relations. Nine departments provided me with interns: art, music, theater, English, Communications, Political Science, Sociology, Educational Administration and Special Education. There were as many as twelve interns each semester. The music majors organized a choir from their friends. We shared them with the smaller churches surrounding Normal. One brought together not only a choir and soloists, but also a small orchestra. They did a portion of the Messiah in several small congregations. He later worked with the Robert Shaw Chorale.

Theater students presented a different children's play each semester to the same small communities. The art student did all of our graphic arts, posters, brochures, etc. I talked with each group explaining my Christian understanding of the importance of community service, using the Parable of the Good Samaritan to do so. I was surprised to discover how many of them had never heard of this parable nor any other one. I also introduced them to the community's human service groups with whom we would be working. One time, we did a study to see how we were doing. Students were the second largest source of volunteers in the agencies, exceeded only by senior citizens, and that was not by much. Students staffed after-school mentoring/tutoring programs in two Normal elementary schools and one Bloomington school. They did an amazing job! They also worked with the hospitals, neighborhood houses, etc. The University Student Affairs Office provided me with two graduate assistants each year. Two master's degree candidates did their practicum with me. One doctoral student did his in-service requirement with us, including among many other things, leading one of our spring break trips. At the high point, we were sending out six different groups each spring to various service/learning projects all across the country. Many of the interns were either African American or Latino/a. After graduating, one of the students wrote me to say that he had received a graduate assistantship only because of his intern experience with us.

The Development of Peer Ministers

With a grant from the Presbyterians in the early 1970s, each school year, we recruited a dozen students and trained them to be what we called "associate campus ministers." Later, "peer ministers" became the accepted term. One of our Board members, Betty Rademacher, a staff person in Student Affairs, had prepared a workbook for training residential assistants and other students in some "peer" student led activities, and she and I trained these peer ministers. The students did a superb job with this effort at outreach. They were also involved in leadership roles with various campus ministry programs, for which they were given a $1,000 scholarship each semester.

Efforts with Faculty, Staff and Administrators

In the 1950s, the Presbyterians did not use the term "campus minister." We were called, "University Pastors." This is still the best name for who we are and what we do. We are "University Pastors!" The large, ever increasingly secular public universities are our "parish." We were not called primarily to be pastors to a collected group of Christian students, but to be a pastor to all those who live and work in a university -- a very diverse and ever changing institution of learning. From the beginning, we were educated to love and, sometimes, to criticize out of that love this monstrous collection of communities bound together by the love of teaching and learning. We must be concerned for students, but we must be equally concerned for faculty, staff, administrators, etc. From the beginning, our ministry sought to embody this concern. Here are some of the ways we went about it over the years:

We began with a small faculty group gathered to read and discuss books dealing with theology and the Christian life. This was not enough. We soon discovered that there were no scholars from outside-the-campus coming to speak to our faculty and staff as well as students. So - - - --

We created what we called "The DeYoung Lectures." We gathered together a small, but disparate group of faculty representing a variety of disciplines. This Committee, each year, invited an outside scholar to address the issues in higher education from the perspective of their own discipline. Each gave three lectures on campus. After the first year, the University asked if they could publish the lectures in their quarterly journal, and we, of course, agreed. Scholars who gave these lectures included Harold Schilling, a physicist from Penn State; Robin Fleming, President of the University of Michigan, Nevitt Sanford, perhaps the most outstanding scholar on higher education, itself, from Berkley; as artist from the University of Illinois; Tom Green, a favorite of campus ministers at the time, who taught philosophy of education at Michigan State; a philosopher of science from Wayne State; a physicist from Carleton College; and David Berlo, a professor of communication, from Michigan State. One faculty member said to me that she was grateful to us for these lectures because it meant that we had not forgotten that those who spend their time teaching others, also needed to be taught on a continuing basis.

When the University began to bring in speakers on their own, we moved on to new things.

We moved on to "Faculty Forum." With a new faculty committee, we would pick a theme for a semester, divide it into sub-topics and knowledgeable individuals, most from off-campus, but sometimes from on-campus would be asked to address them. Each series would consist of six to eight weekly addresses over a luncheon in the student union. Well over a hundred faculty and staff would attend these presentations every week. We had six or eight presentations on a common theme in the fall and another theme and presentations in the spring semester. One semester the theme was "The Liberal Arts." One faculty member told me that this series changed his whole approach to teaching.

"Humanizing Higher Education" was the next theme. The format changed to a once a month dinners dealing with this topic. Speakers came mainly from higher education: legislative leaders, Board of Regents and State Board of Higher Education. (A great opportunity for me to get acquainted with these people.) Others came from the various disciplines, primarily from within the liberal arts and education communities. Attendance numbered seventy or so. Participants came largely from central administration, colleges of liberal arts, education and fine arts - not many from business. Again, an interdisciplinary faculty committee made the decisions and ran the programs. Staff did the administrative work.

When the new Campus Religious Center was completed, much of our effort in this area took place in this building, which was adjacent to the University. At the high point, we had three groups meeting on different days of the week. The American Baptist colleague, Walter Fishbaugh, met weekly with a group of faculty who shared their research across disciplinary lines. He called the group, Eureka! Our Lutheran staff member, Gerald Kissell, met with a group called "The Guild of Soup and Salad Theologians." He was the best academic theologian among the staff. There were fifteen or so faculty and a couple of local pastors who read and discussed solid works such as Hans Kung's book on "Resurrection." I led a group that was composed of faculty, some students and townspeople. Topics ranged all over the map geographically, politically, economically, scientifically, religiously, artistically, and the like. These lectures were called The Fell Lectures, names for Jesse Fell, who founded the University. His two sisters, Alice and Fanny, provided in their wills funds to be used to bring lectures to campus for the "whole community." Annually, we received grants from the Fell Fund to support these lectures. Our center became known among faculty, administrators and students as the "place that was open to free and balanced discussion," with advocacy on many issues thrown into the mix.

We also used faculty in a variety of other ways:
• When the American Embassy was invaded by the Iranians and our embassy staff became hostages, we organized an all-day Saturday event on

Islam and the Middle East for high school teachers in the county to prepare them to deal with this issue with their students.

• In the early days, we did a workshop for public school teachers on teaching religion in the schools. When Mr. Justice Jackson wrote the findings on the role of prayer in the public schools, he went out of his way to say that though the schools could not pray, they ought to be studying religion. We were aided by curricula already prepared by three states: Florida, Montana and Pennsylvania.

• At one point, we were able to offer a group of local churches, a six-week Sunday School teacher preparation experience. Although we offered to pay the faculty for this--or at least pay their transportation--in every instance, they declined. One faculty member said to me, "This is the first time the church has ever asked me to use my expertise in support of the life and work of the church." Prior to that point, all she had ever been asked to do was to bring a dish to a potluck.

The Regular Aspects of the Campus Ministry

In the preceding comments, I have talked about the program. While all of those things were going on, we also often worked with a student fellowship of some type. We listened to students and mentored them. We counseled with them. We took them home when a crisis in their family required it. We married them. We fed them. My wife put together a small wedding reception on very short notice. In other words we were there for the students whenever and wherever we were needed. We did draft and conscientious objector counseling during the Viet Nam war. We did problem pregnancy counseling when needed. We helped students who wanted to tell their parents that they were gay or lesbian by listening, supporting them and sometimes going with them to talk with their parents. We were a safe place for them. We did this long before the church developed the terms "open and affirming" or "more light." We helped residence halls and those who lived there to find some healing when a fellow student died by whatever means. We took students on retreats. We prayed with them, studied with them and played with them, loved them, challenged them and were with them as they searched for their own spiritual identity.

We also listened to faculty and staff of the university. We did, in the university context, all those things that a pastor in a local church was called to do. The difference is that we were able to do all these things and many others with the members of our parish in the place where they worked. Five days a week we were there for them in the university. On weekends, if we were not doing something with students, we could often be found worshipping with them. We substituted for pastors on vacation and for those who were ill. We also became interim pastors when a nearby church was vacant.

What I Have Learned as a University Pastor

1. I have learned that campus ministry is a great ministry, important for the university and for those who live and work in and for it as students, faculty, administrators, campus police, secretaries, student affairs staff, alumni, et al. It is important for the church. Above all, this pastor is thankful that our churches had the wisdom to give birth to campus ministry. It has been a total joy for me. Let us hope that we will find ways for it to continue. The work is not done!

2. Place is important! Where would the black students have gone without our ministry and building? How could we have become the place where everyone felt safe and all issues were addressed fairly...?

3. Being "in but not of" the university is often an advantage in ministry. We can go anywhere, talk with anyone, do anything without having to get the permission of the University hierarchy. I mentioned earlier the workshop we did for public school teachers on teaching religion. The funds for this came from us, from the university and from a grant from the Danforth Foundation. I was sitting in my office with one of the faculty members who had helped plan the event and would be one of the leaders. The daily mail came and in it was a letter from the Danforth Foundation agreeing to our request, IF the university would put a little more money in it. I dialed the University President and explained the situation to him. He immediately approved a larger amount. When I hung up, the faculty member was amazed.

In the 1980s, I heard a number of faculty complaining that the University did not have a Faculty Club. I said, "Why don't you organize one yourselves? I will help you." Four female faculty agreed to work with me, BUT they could not begin until some administrator approved what we were doing. So, we did and they did. There is now The University Club with space provided in the Student Union and free membership for faculty and staff. Even though I am not faculty or staff, I served as president of the club for one year. The point is not what we did. The point is that a university is very hierarchical. A faculty member is hesitant to approach the top of the hierarchy without first getting the permission of those who stand between the faculty member and the President or the Provost. Being in, but not of, means that you have an access to all levels of the university that are not available to those who are both "in and of" the University. It helps us and the university as well that University Pastors can have this relationship. Occasionally, it makes it possible for the Pastor to become an ombudsman for a student or faculty person. It permits one to become an advocate for a person or an idea or program. Warning: use this relationship carefully and well.

4. Campus ministry is neither a ministry of presence, nor a ministry with program. It is both. They each support the other. Presence enabled me to know personally over 350 faculty and administrators. It made it possible for me to bring together a group of faculty to suggest they might want to consider developing a program in Latin American Studies and another group to suggest

a Middle Eastern Studies program. It made it possible for me to serve on a variety of University Committees. The first one came early when I was asked to work with faculty in psychology who wanted to develop the protocols and rules that would make it possible for them to use students in their research while offering counseling to them at the same time. There was no student counseling center at the time. It made it possible for the Provost to call me and to tell me that the University's curriculum committee would be spending the next semester studying carefully its general education program. They needed student input and wondered if I would gather together a group of twelve or so students and spend the semester working with them on this question. At the end of the semester, the committee held a retreat and the students presented the papers. It also led to the creation of many of the programs described above and then made it possible for me to know even more of the university community.

5. Local church pastors are often taught that they should not stay in a local church for more than six or eight years. For the University Pastor, a long tenure is advisable. It takes time to gain the trust of the University. Faithfulness to the calling and time does make a difference.

Lastly, What of the Future?

It doesn't look good for our mainline denominations. Our membership continues to decline radically, causing us to lose churches, as well as members. In the 1980s, I did some research and found:

- At that time, the birthrate in our churches was at least one whole child less than the population at large (< than one child per family).

- The average age of our denomination was 58 and climbing. The median age of the population at large was 32.

Since I began in ministry in Illinois in 1954, each of the three major denominations I served (United Church, Disciples and Presbyterian) has lost more than 100,000 members in Illinois, alone. At one point, all or most of our funding came from the central offices of our denominations. Today, at best, our denominations cannot support even one ministry, let alone the fourteen or so ministries we once had. In Illinois, for example, campus ministries receive no support from the Presbyterian Synod or the Disciples Region. The UCC Conference support is important, but token at best.

And yet, I think our mainline ministries are more needed than ever before. Why?

The importance of the separation of church and state is vital to our life as a nation, but it is under strong attack from the right wing of both the political and religious communities. Right wing Protestantism and Catholicism has never been supportive. Both would be happier if the church--their church--had some control over the universities. Our ministries are the only religious bodies in support of the separation of church and state and thus in support of our public higher education.

Religion has always been close to higher learning. It founded the earliest of what we today call universities. The first one was founded in Bologna, Italy in the 15th Century; The University of Paris came next. The type of contact we have provided and need to continue to provide is summed up in the words of a little book entitled *Excellence*, written by John Gardner in the 1970s. He says:

There are a lot of people who love higher education, but are not critical of it; and there are a lot of people who are critical of it, but do not love it. What the University needs is people who love it and are critical of it." We have been these people! Both the church and the university – and I dare say the nation – need us to continue to do so.

Higher education is under attack in this nation. In many ways it is in disarray. We need to be a part of the conversation that works these issues through. Some of the issues include:

1. How are we going to pay for it?

2. What is the proper role for technology? Can a degree be earned entirely over the internet, and if so, what is lost and what is gained?

3. Are our universities and colleges to educate our young men and women, or are we to be satisfied with only training them for work that is available?

4. What is the role of community in learning, and what is community anyway? Does it require people being bodily present to one another in particular place, or is seeing and hearing them over the internet sufficient?

5. The "for profit" institutions get the lions' share of federal and state support for student aid. Do they, indeed, provide Bachelors and Masters Degrees and often doctorates that have the integrity that we believe the same degrees provided by the residential colleges and universities do?

6. Our founding fathers (and I daresay, mothers) thought that when they created Harvard and William and Mary, they were doing so in order to have "an educated clergy and an educated citizenry." Are our colleges and universities doing this now?" Should this indeed be part of the purpose of any accredited institution of higher education?

These are but a very few of the questions that have been raised or need to be raised. Each radically affects the other. Where are they being addressed now? How are they being addressed? Should our progressive Christian community be a part of these conversations or even the convener of groups to address them?

In Illinois, our dormant state commission has decided that what our universities need right now is an inter-faith center on each campu– that our progressive Christian ministry needs to occur in an interfaith context. What does that mean and how could we move in this direction?

I am sure the readers of this list are aware of them and many more. I remind you of them because I believe that although we may be declining in number, there may still be questions we should consider, ministries we must try to address.

If we move in any direction, indeed, if we are to continue to exist, we will have to fund ourselves. Is that even possible?

We cannot count on the structures of our mainline churches for any significant support. In many cases there is, or will be, no support at all. My own conviction is that we may need to separate ourselves structurally from dioceses, synods, presbyteries, conferences, regions and the like. In its place we might seek to build a group of Christian, Jewish, Hindu, Muslim, Buddhist, secular humanist individuals who would become the supporters of these interfaith ministries. We could become a ministry of religious individuals rather than a ministry tied legally to structures. The Parliament of World Religions works like this. The Student YMCAs that still exist on some of our campuses function in this manner. And I do believe that NCMA itself needs to become an interfaith association.

Jim Pruyne spent 40 years as University Pastor at the University of Illinois in Normal, IL, often in partnership with his wife Gwen. He has been active in NCMA since its beginning. They still live in Normal and continue to be advocates for higher education ministries.

Evolving Trends in Campus Ministry on 8 Campuses Over 52 Years
By Mark Rutledge

Introduction

As one of the NCMA "Sages" who is contributing to this Retrospective on the trajectory of campus ministry, I have attempted to distill my 52 years as a still-active, paid (now very part time) campus minister into some brief episodes for each of my eight campus ministry settings. I hope these reflections illustrate how changes in higher education, society, the church, and the world affect all our work. These interacting social contexts, interwoven with some individual personalities of my mentors friends, students, and colleagues, offer fragments of my continuing vision for ministry. At the best, I hope it will be suggestive and instructive. At the least, I hope it will amuse. We know the tricks memory plays and how one thing leads improbably to another, in the formation of who we are ever becoming as persons and professionals in ministry in higher education.

1. *University of California at Berkeley: Stiles Hall (1956-57).* After three years at Oberlin College I transferred for my senior undergraduate year to UC Berkeley, where I was involved in Stiles Hall, the Campus YMCA, known for its advocacy of civil rights, free speech, and social justice. After graduating in 1956 I worked part time at Stiles with Pierre Delattre, a Presbyterian minister later famous as the "Beatnik Priest" of a coffee house in San Francisco's North Beach. Our project was to develop a Religious Awareness Week with the University. The "Religious Emphasis Week" was a significant model being developed on many campuses across the country at that time in order to make churches' resources and presence more widely known among students.

Setting: At that time Berkeley was a sleepy little college town with book stores, pizza restaurants, and small businesses along Telegraph Avenue. Many of the students were WWII vets on the GI Bill, who took their studies seriously. But even then, in the midst of this conventional atmosphere, there were signs of liberal ethos. I would walk along the streets with Pierre, who was constantly looking for any magazines that might have just published one of his stories he had submitted. These stories were humorous, creative fantasies with characters whose loving-kindness flowed from universal religious grace. Once when he was perusing the stacks, he burst out: "Here's one!" It was a girlie magazine featuring the usual fare of nudes interspersed with short "literary" stories. When I was a bit surprised to see his gentle, spiritual fiction in "this kind" of magazine, he said, "Well, right now these are the only places that will publish my stories." Pierre has gone on to publish many articles and books, one of which, "Tales of a Dali Lama," has become a cult classic.

2. *Pacific School of Religion (1957-1961).* I entered seminary as an agnostic, on a personal religious quest, without any idea of becoming a minister. My experience with professors there showed me it was possible to have a deep faith and a sharp critical mind without sacrificing either. I had no intention of becoming a parish minister and no idea what form my ministry might take, although my experience with Pierre showed that there were many creative possibilities and a variety of non-parish settings that might provide salaries. On weekends I hung out in San Francisco, often going to the Church for the Fellowship of All Peoples where Howard Thurman was minister of a fully racially-integrated church. At some point during my first year, I had a kind of mini-conversion while studying the Old Testament prophets, whose first-hand overwhelming God-experience of what my teacher called a "divine-human encounter" flowed into a passion for social justice. In other courses, such as church history and pastoral psychology, I learned that such profound epiphanies occur for many people across times and cultures and are a universal part of human experience no matter how they are described. I was no longer an agnostic. I decided to complete seminary and see what came of it.

During my 2nd year I took a course with Clarence Shedd, national student YMCA leader who had just retired from Yale, whose book "The Church Follows Its Students" was our text. He was succeeded by Charles McCoy who offered courses in ministry in higher education, and who later was involved in the major Underwood Report for campus ministry, and I realized this was a field that was meant for me. {Note: the Underwood Report saw the mission of campus ministry to be the development of centers of "prophetic inquiry"—a vision which was implemented only sketchily across the country and was never sufficiently supported by the churches). I did an internship in campus ministry with John Hadsell at Westminster House, which further encouraged me in the directions of a traditional campus ministry, and also one that was oriented toward the total university.

Setting: The context for my internship was to work with a college age/young adult group based in a local church. I enjoyed the people with whom I developed relationships. For some reason the group never grew to the large size the lead pastor had envisioned, and he started calling John to complain. John carefully explained the dynamics of such groups in the context of small congregations near large universities, defended my work, and eventually became exasperated with what he called this "neurotic" minister. Thus I was able to see some of the dynamics and tensions of town-gown, church-university, and campus-based versus congregation-based ministries which have been persistent in many campus ministries.

3. San Jose State (1961-1967). I graduated from PSR in 1961, a year that saw the field of campus ministry expanding. We were to have a famous graduation speaker (name not revealed at the time) and when the ceremony began, Georgia Harkness, our theology professor, took the stage to say that unfortunately our anticipated speaker, Martin Luther King, could not be present because he was in jail in Mississippi for advocating civil rights. Her charge to our graduating class was "Go and do thou likewise."

I was shortly ordained as a minister in the United Church of Christ and accepted a call from United Campus Christian Ministry, an ecumenical campus ministry at San Jose State University, as an associate campus minister on a two person staff. I was there six years and was part of many changes. At first we organized Bible studies, worship, service and fellowship opportunities with students. Then an ecumenical consortium, Lutheran, Episcopal, along with UCCM (Presbyterian, UCC, Disciples of Christ), were able to raise funds to construct a modern chapel next door to the old house which served as our center. Shortly after the Chapel was dedicated funds became available to build a new ecumenical campus ministry center where the old house had been. These were expansive years for campus ministry when mainline churches could still fund it. We had weekly Sunday morning worship services in the chapel and continued to engage in traditional "student work." On my own time, apart from campus ministry, I remember my first experience on a protest picket line sponsored by CORE, a black civil rights organization demanding better jobs and pay for the bank's minority employees. This was also the era when ministries were starting coffee houses on campus to encourage dialogue and attract a wider clientele, as well as supporting civil rights activities and movements questioning the war in Viet Nam. Our coffee house, Jonah's Wail, became a popular center and rallying point for some of these initiatives. But budgets began diminishing and our staff of two was reduced to one, and my associate position was ended.

Setting: San Jose State was an urban university, with some residence halls and many commuting students who were relatively conventional. In 1961 many responded to our Bible studies, theology-oriented programs, and worship services, but as the decade commenced, and the Viet Nam War pervaded more and more of our lives, civil rights took front and center along with the emerging rock music scene and our ministry changed. Two examples: 1) we received an invitation from Cesar Chavez, who was organizing the farm workers in Delano, to bring a group down to help picket in the grape fields and assist in painting one of their offices. A number of students in our ministries responded and were transformed by what they saw, especially meeting the founders of the United Farm Workers, which included Dolores Huerta. 2) Every Saturday night we sponsored an "open mike" forum at the coffee house, where students and faculty took the podium to offer thoughts, rants, poems, and personal views on topics of the day. One of our student speakers used what is today called the "F-Bomb" in the context of making the point that the real obscenity of the day was violence and war. This event made the student newspaper, and created a firestorm of objection from some of our supporting churches. We wrote responses to the churches, along with editorials in the campus newspaper, defending not only free speech but the context in which real obscenity can be defined. We survived what we later called our great

"F...Flap," but it was a lesson for me to be prepared for blow-back if certain boundaries are crossed--a perpetual theme for campus ministry which repeated itself in many other settings-to-come.

4. Iowa State University, Ames (1967-71). Being jobless (another recurrent theme), I circulated my dossier through our national campus ministry personnel offices (yes, those were the days when the churches provided such a service!), and accepted a call to join an ecumenical campus ministry of four: the head of staff worked with faculty and administration; a more conservative staffer worked with traditional students; a young staffer worked with non-traditional students; and I was to work with the activist students. One of the groups that interviewed me for the position, and had a vote, was the campus chapter of Students for a Democratic Society (SDS). With the full support of the staff and our ecumenical board, I helped organize and/or support anti-war actions including the March on Washington in the fall of 1967. I helped form the Ames Draft Counseling Center and worked with many students considering their options, ranging from military service to conscientious objection. Frisbie House, the center which was my office and which was the oldest building in the country dedicated specifically for campus ministry, was referred to by some as a "staging ground for peaceful revolution." The University administration gave some credit to our campus ministry for avoiding the violence that consumed many campuses at this time. I earned my FBI file for accepting the draft cards of three students in a public ceremony (a parabolic action), and representing the church standing by those students who protested the war. We also supported the students who chose military service, as well as conscientious objectors.

But funding cuts were beginning to affect campus ministries in more and more settings around the country, and we were told by our supporting denominations to reduce our staff by one. In light of shrinking finances for our ministry, it was natural for me to soon be that one selected to move on, cutting staff from 4 to 3.

I anticipated this and began circulating my dossier again, this time not only for campus ministry positions, but because I had just earned my master's degree in counseling from ISU, for jobs in college counseling centers. I was delighted to receive an offer to join the counseling staff at the University of Victoria in British Columbia. I told our Board of my decision, set a time for my resignation, and set a date for a moving van to take me to Canada. Two weeks before I was to depart, I got a late night call from the Director of the Counseling Center who told me the startling news that the President of the University of Victoria had personally intervened, in what she called an "unprecedented action," and cancelled my appointment. His stated reason: he didn't want any "troublemakers" on his campus. Letters of recommendation from my board had obviously emphasized my activist work!

Setting: Iowa State University of Science and Technology was a largely residential campus and it earned the title of "Moo U" in a magazine feature the year I took up residence.

The town of Ames was remarkably cosmopolitan in spite of its being surrounded by prairie and corn fields, its television station WOI being a model of contemporary public broadcasting. I experienced all the controversy that my activist position elicited, while garnering support from the University, our Board, and the judicatories of our five supporting denomination, yet this was not enough to forestall the inevitable financial realities.

My wife and I divorced in 1969-70, which did not cause as great a stir as I had anticipated, partly because we modeled a process which earned the respect of many. We co-wrote a religious ceremony for the dissolution of a marriage which was celebrated by a local UCC minister; we sent out divorce announcements which looked like marriage announcements, saying that we were announcing an "Amicable Divorce," and requesting our friends and families not to take sides but to stay in touch with both of us. (Iowa had just passed a "no fault" divorce law, and the judge who granted the divorce said he was doing so only because the law compelled him to.) We hosted a divorce party where we cut the couple on top of the cake in two. We developed other rituals involving friends and families and we lived together for several months following the court decree. Our process was reported in a detailed article in the Christian Century, and our ceremony was later included in a book of contemporary worship services of the United Methodist Church, *Rituals for a New Day*.

5. *Monterey Peninsula College (1971-73)*. Being jobless (again), I traded on my shiny new master's degree in counseling from ISU and was hired by Monterey Peninsula College as a drug abuse education and treatment counselor at a salary twice that of my previous jobs. I was back in California. MPC was a community college which offered two year degrees guaranteeing transfer to a California university and others in many technical and professional fields leading to direct employment. My job was funded by a short term grant from the California Criminal Justice Division to respond to increasing drug and alcohol problems. The second year I was at the college, I worked as a counselor with physically handicapped students. Fort Ord was nearby, where many returning Viet Nam veterans began their civilian lives, one day in the field in 'Nam and the next in sunny California, so the college initiated a major program to help veterans begin to make the difficult transition from war to college life. Drugs were an issue with many students. Even though I was not an "expert" in drug abuse counseling, I was learning that a helpful ministry could consist of developing relationships and helping people find a different kind of "connection" where they could discover positive life and work alternatives to drugs.

44

Setting: The California Community College system was a model for state of the art education at the two-year college level. Having spent my life thus far in university settings, I was impressed with the community colleges' commitments to serving the local community of which it was a part, as well as to preparing students equally for vocational employment and/or transfer to four year universities. And it was exciting to work with "older students," --returning housewives, unemployed men who had been in successful careers, people seeking second careers, and others who had never been to college before. I taught courses in psychology and orientation to college life. Newly divorced, I rented a small house two blocks from Monterey Bay, bought a motorcycle; spent weekends cruising the Big Sur coast, and reveled in the freedom of the days. I was granted ministerial standing as a chaplain laboring "beyond the local parish" by the Northern California Conference of the United Church of Christ. I was "learning-by-doing" within a whole new form of ministry in higher education, which would occupy me for several years after I left MPC.

I attended our 1972 Annual Conference where the big decision was whether or not to approve the ordination of Bill Johnson, the first openly gay ministerial candidate to seek such a call to full time ministry--first not only in our denomination but, to my knowledge, in any mainline Christian denomination at that time. His photograph was on the cover of Time Magazine under the heading, "Better Than Lying." There was a lengthy debate on the Conference floor, where Bill answered such questions as: "What ethical criteria will you follow in deciding how to exercise your sexuality?" His reply was: "Why, the very same ones you do in exercising yours—and we all know what those are, don't we?" Another question I remember was, "If we ordain you, do you plan to practice your sexuality?" He replied, "Well, I didn't know that celibacy was a requirement for ordination in the United Church of Christ." After this kind of Q&A for a while the question was called for a vote which was overwhelmingly positive in favor of ordination. I left that meeting exuberant that the issue of "gays in the ministry" was now fortunately behind us. How naïve I was.

In the spring of 1973 the grant which funded my position expired and once again I found myself looking for work. At the same time I married a woman I had met after my divorce as a colleague at Iowa State. where she was director of the campus YWCA. And once again I availed myself of the national campus ministry personnel and job hunting network, through which I received a call to United Campus Ministry in DeKalb, Illinois. Back to the Midwest.

6. *Northern Illinois University (1973-1980).* NIU was a "suitcase" school, a large commuter university which catered to students from Chicago and the Northern tier of Illinois. Students did not respond to traditional appeals to "join our Christian group." I recognized this environment as mirroring, at a university level, a similar kind of social context and dynamic as the community college I had just come from. Several members of our ecumenical board were faculty or administrators at the local community college, and they told me that there were six community colleges within the NIU "service area." At the same time a national campus ministry consortium of seven denominations came together as "United Ministries in Education" (UME) to develop and support networks of ministries around the country. One of the process models they promoted was described as "Live Wires," created by campus minister J Springer and Earl Lowell in Pennsylvania and New York, where an itinerating organizer enabled local colleges and councils of churches to unite to jointly serve the people and communities in which they resided. This was a vision to which I resonated. With the support of our board my job description evolved to include exploring how ministries might be mutually developed using the resources of both local churches and community colleges.

While developing this model, I also enrolled in a doctoral program in counseling psychology at NIU, with secondary emphases on career counseling and community college administration. With my board's support, I was able to merge my doctoral thesis with our campus ministry to focus on the effects of counseling on college women with unintended pregnancies who choose abortion. I conducted my research at the student health service, seeing 78 students over the course of a year who agreed to participate in the study. I counseled the women pre-abortion, referred those who chose abortion to a nearby clinic, conducted controlled measurements pre-and post test on several psychological variables, and included follow up post-abortion counseling. A major finding of the study was that the women decreased in anxiety, increased in internal locus of control, and increased in positive self concept. Many said that their experience in decision-making helped them feel stronger. No one regretted making the decision they did. Many expressed natural feelings of sadness while acknowledging it was the "best" decision they could have made under the circumstances. No one made their decision lightly.

Setting: These were challenging new forms of ministry for me and pushed my natural introverted personality to the limits. After receiving my doctorate I took the national exam and was licensed as a clinical psychologist, so I decided to see a few paying clients on the side and make a little extra money, (Our salaries being what they are!) I think my experience doing abortion referral must have spread to others because I will never forget one day when an older woman came to my office asking for an abortion referral for her daughter, and asked if I would see her, which I did. I recognized the mother as one of the leaders of the pro-life, anti-abortion advocacy groups who was frequently quoted in the newspaper as opposing all abortions. When I mentioned this to her (non-judgmentally of course) she said, "Well when it comes to your own daughter…"

Most of my work at NIU was focused on developing campus ministry with community colleges, but though my experience on staff at Monterey Peninsula College provided background for the "college" half of that, I had no models for how to begin to relate that to the church's ministries. In 1974 I started with the help of my board members who were faculty at the nearby CC, and arranged a meeting with a couple of local pastors and the director of community services at the college to explore possibilities. We discussed our mutual interests in becoming allies, including a religious "presence" on campus (undefined), using church facilities and/or other resources to augment college offerings, and potential courses in common. There was definitely interest from all parties, and I was clearly on a quest in new and uncharted territory.

Right at this time (providentially?), I got wind of a major conference to be held in 1975 at Cedar Falls, Iowa on emerging models for the church's ministry with community colleges, sponsored by United Ministries in Education (UME). I knew on national staff from previous relationships (Bill Hallman, Earl Lowell, Clyde Robinson, and Bob Mayo) who were forming a new task force on this novel approach to campus ministry, so I immediately registered. The centerpiece of the conference was to engage in a simulation game, "Juco," developed by Wayne Bryan, campus minister at Drake University. The game was designed to acquaint the "players" with both the community colleges and the churches' stake in creating ministry with them. It was here that I learned more about the *Live Wires* model from J Springer's ministry in Pennsylvania. I was inspired to make that model the basis for my new job, and I returned to DeKalb to propose that I become the "organizer" of ministries with six community colleges scattered around the northern tier of Illinois in partnerships with local councils of churches and ministerial associations in those communities.

After doing this for a couple of years, with mixed results, I was invited to become adjunct staff to that same national UME Task Force on Community College Ministry. This was an exciting adventure, and one of my assigned projects was to convene a number of practitioners in this emerging field and write an article describing their theories and best practices, which was published as a UME monograph with the title "The Community Colleges: An Opportunity for the Church to Develop New Staffing Patterns for Campus Ministry." In 1980 it became a chapter in the book, *The Challenge of the Community College to the Church*, edited by Bill Hallman. Of course a major cause for creating different staffing patterns was the increasing concern of providing funding for full time campus ministers placed on university campuses. Our models were one attempt to address these problems creatively.

7. The University of New Mexico (1980-1996). After receiving my doctorate I decided to make a move that was entirely of my own choosing (for the first time in my career!), so I again made use of the national campus ministry personnel service and received an invitation to interview for a position at the University of New Mexico. This was a newly organized ecumenical ministry which included four denominations: Presbyterian (USA), United Methodist, United Church of Christ, and Disciples of Christ. I was offered and accepted the position as the first (and only) director of United Campus Ministries--a reality mirroring conditions affecting trends in campus ministry nationally.

UNM was an urban, regional, commuter university catering to both traditional undergraduates and older returning students—the average age of students was about 27. Very early, I realized that trying to start up a "traditional" model of campus ministry based on attracting and maintaining a "student group" offering Bible study, worship, service, and fellowship would not be feasible. So I sought to develop a ministry to and with the wider university community, partnering with both academic and student activities sectors of the campus itself, rather than to "hustle on the sidelines" creating our own little Christian enclave. This decision affected the following 16 years, and included many successes, some failures, and ongoing negotiations with our four supporting denominational governing and funding bodies. The Disciples, UCC, and Presbyterians mostly supported my preferred model, while the United Methodists, in the main, did not. That I was able to sustain it for 16 years is still a wonder to me, and included many ups and downs and continuing political and ecclesiastical maneuvering.

Setting: Overall I had a grand time. The ministry operated out of a center, an older house, right across the street from UNM. I experimented with new and creative ways to develop a variety of ministry initiatives to and with the university. I published a bi-semester newspaper, "The UCM Prophet," which eventually had a circulation of around 2,000, nationally as well as locally to churches, students, faculty and administrators. I either started our solo programs, worked with other community organizations, or partnered with campus units on programs such as: The Last Lecture Series; Theology for Lunch; a Peace Studies academic minor through the philosophy department. We were also involved in various social justice efforts such as the Sanctuary Movement related to central American wars of oppression; sponsored campus-wide speakers; supported and implemented a grant to showcase the art work of a Holocaust survivor; and solicited and published articles written by students, faculty and town leaders in our newspaper. I served on the Medical Ethics Committee of UNM Hospital. I taught courses in the UNM Honors Program, the Human Services Department, the Family Studies Department, and Psychology of Religion. We offered workshops and support groups on vocational planning, nuclear disarmament, gay and lesbian issues, and almost any current topic. We offered free lunches every week at our center, which was served by people from local churches, and which attracted a mix of students and homeless people. We sponsored a student to lead mission trips to Guatemala. We started a peer ministry program staffed by two or three students who lived in small apartments in our center. I offered non-credit classes on the findings of the Jesus Seminar, the latest incarnation of the scholarly "Quest for the Historical Jesus." --These all in the first 8 years or so of my "tenure." Needless to say, there was controversy over some of these things, which we weathered due to major support from a lot of people and many church agencies.

A shift in priorities began in 1987 and evolved to become the signature program of UCM, involving most of my time and energy. This was the year I married Betsy Alden, who had developed a nationally recognized ministry model of Service-Learning with seven community colleges in Dallas. Soon after our marriage she persuaded me to try out this approach at UNM. At first I was reluctant because I saw how much time and energy it would take to mount a new service-learning initiative at the same time I was involved in so many other programs. Service- Learning entails recruiting faculty who will offer credit for students in their regular courses to do community service projects related to course content, and simultaneously require that they engage in structured, small-group reflection on their experiences. I agreed to try it out on a small scale and recruited three faculty members, six community human service agencies that agreed to train and place student volunteers, and I decided to be the reflection group facilitator myself. The response from every participant was positive and overwhelming! I immediately saw the power of this model to engage faculty, provide support for community-based partners, and facilitate student reflection on their lives, faith or spiritual understandings, and vocational aspirations. I also saw that if I expanded the program it would take over much of our entire campus ministry. And that this might be a good thing! Nine years later we had over 30 faculty members from many different academic sectors, over 70 community agencies, hundreds of students participating each semester, and many reflection group leaders-- other campus ministers and student peer facilitators. It was about 75% of what our campus ministry was doing. Before I left UNM in 1996, the Vice President for Student Affairs had offered me a position at UNM as Coordinator of Service-Learning, but another fortuitous occasion intervened.

*8. **Duke University (1996 to 1997).*** In 1995 Betsy and I negotiated a never-before-tried experiment, a one-year "campus ministry exchange" with the Director of the Wesley Foundation at Duke, during which he would take over my ministry at UNM and we would serve together as co-campus ministers of Wesley during the 1996-97 school year. We wondered if we would be modeling an initiative which might benefit other campus ministers.

This move was a culture shock for me as most of my experience had been with public, mostly commuter, urban colleges and universities, the main exception being Iowa State University. Duke is a major residential, private research University, with elite status and prestige, where we found (unlike any other campus where I worked) that students wanted to gather, often, as communities and groups of worship, service, study, fellowship, and mission trips—traditional programs sounding like my first full time campus ministry at San Jose State-- almost like coming full circle. But the Wesley Foundation was grounded in spiritual and theological formation of exceptional students. When something was scheduled, students showed up and expected us to take leadership, mentoring and pastoral roles. The year was a steep learning curve for me, as I tried to keep up, learn from, and contribute my gifts to and with a remarkable community of student leaders. This was also the first time I discovered how to use email because this was how everyone now communicated with students—everyone could share a change in plans instantly!

Duke (1997 to 2013). As the end of our "exchange" drew near in spring semester 1996, Betsy was offered a full time position, which she happily accepted, as the founding Director of Service-Learning through the Kenan Institute for Ethics, a free-standing institute at Duke. We returned to Albuquerque to sell our house, celebrate my "UCC retirement" at age 63, pack up and move to Durham, North Carolina, where we simultaneously built our new house and she started her new job in fall semester 1997.

Duke is home to a large and intricate complex of over 24 denominational, interdenominational, interfaith and para-church campus ministries which reflects the diversity of the world's religious traditions. In addition, Duke Chapel is one of the country's largest University Churches, with a full panoply of Christian leadership, worship, and community outreach, including as part of its larger worshipping campus community an active Sunday congregation of 600 members.

One of the denominational campus ministries is Westminster Fellowship, supported by the Presbyterian churches of the area. During our exchange we had become colleagues with the Presbyterian campus minister, and when I proposed to her that the ministry become ecumenical to include the United Church of Christ, and appoint me as a part-time (volunteer!) Staff Associate, she readily agreed, and I became the first UCC campus minister at Duke. All campus ministers receive a small, $65 monthly "stipend" through Duke Chapel's Religious Life Staff, so in 1997 I was able to be "paid" in my retirement!

In 1998 Betsy and I convened a team of twelve university people to attend a major conference at Wellesley College on developing interfaith initiatives on campuses, and I returned to help organize Duke's first official Interfaith Dialogue Project funded by the Chapel and the Kenan Institute for Ethics. So then I had two retirement "jobs." In 2006-07 I invited Eboo Patel, who founded the Interfaith Youth Core in Chicago, and is currently on President Obama's interfaith council, to come to Duke to help jump start the university's interest in funding and staffing a more university-wide and centralized approach to interfaith ministry. Sam Wells, then Dean of Duke Chapel, responded by creating an interfaith council of existing campus ministry staff from different religious traditions. Duke was among the first major private research universities to hire a full time Muslim Chaplain and support a Center for Muslim Life to parallel our already well funded Center for Jewish Life. At the same time the university dedicated a prayer and meeting space for the Buddhist and Hindu campus ministries. The Chapel hired a full time Associate Dean to (in the words of Dean Wells), "help make Duke as well known and respected for its interfaith work as it has been for its Christian ministries."

As an "Ally" of the campus Center for LGBT Life, I supported an initiative in 2006 by Duke Student Government asking the college's Board of Trustees to change a Duke Chapel policy prohibiting same-sex commitment ceremonies. A committee was formed by the college President, Nan Keohane, to make a recommendation, and I advocated publicly for this change on the grounds that my denomination encouraged its ministers to perform such ceremonies and that current policy discriminated against my ministry. The committee considered this along with many other just causes for changing the policy, which was reversed following its final report. I advocated for LGBT concerns in other ways and was named "Ally of the Year" at a Lavender Graduation ceremony honoring graduating gay students.

In 2011 I left my position with Westminster Fellowship and became the advisor to the student Interfaith Dialogue Project, which is now my only work on the Religious Life Staff. We sponsor a credit course each year on interfaith dialogue, taught by students, and initiate other programs as appropriate. One of my other interests at Duke has been the dialogue of science and religion, and I helped convene a group of faculty and students who met informally for lunch over several years and engaged in discussions led by those who came on a rotating basis. I wrote a paper, which I gave at my 50th reunion of Oberlin College on "Science, Religion and Evolution," which helped me crystallize some of my own thoughts on the subject.

As early as 1998 I had started teaching regular courses in progressive religious studies through Duke's Osher Life Long Learning Institute, introducing findings of the Jesus Seminar along with other liberal theologians and biblical scholars. My most recent course last semester was "A Conservative and A Liberal in Religious Dialogue," co-taught with an evangelical minister, in which we modeled a civil, friendly dialogue across different viewpoints which are often infected with hostility and negativity.

In 2009-2010 I was one of the initial "subjects" in a research project sponsored by Daniel Dennett, one of the superstars of the "New Atheist" movements, and his co-author/researcher Linda LaScola, in which I was featured under a pseudonym in his article which came out under the title "Preachers Who Do Not Believe"

This has led to many interesting spin-offs in what I have come to call my "adventures among the atheists." I have been interviewed for some documentary films, featured in newspaper articles, and appeared on religious radio broadcasting shows. Although I have never called myself an atheist, I do see myself as a Christian freethinker and a post-super-naturalist, which gives me some credentials to dialogue with folks who see themselves both as "non-believers" as well as "believers." This has sparked some controversy which spices up my life in my elder years as a "Sage" in NCMA.

Reflections on Campus Ministry

Who we are (our identity as persons, our values, how we live) is formed in large part by the people we hang out with. I've been lucky to be around campus ministers all my professional life.

For a summary reflection on all our ministries, I can't say it better than Bob Dylan: "The times they are [always and still] a-changin'."

NCMA~

Early in my first ministry at San Jose State I was mentored by several veteran campus ministers in Northern California who introduced me to NCMA. I have been a member ever since, with the possible exception of a year of two when I failed to pay my dues! This Association has been important in helping me better understand what it means to be a campus minister, and to find mutual support among colleagues in what can be a lonely profession.

For a while I led the NCMA Partnership Program, which pairs a veteran with a new campus minister to encourage supportive relationships and to provide ways to share resources. I assisted George and Sally Gunn, Betsy and others who have developed the annual GNOME Awards which recognizes selected campus ministers for (having) "Gained Notoriety for Outstanding Ministry in Education" (and was honored to receive this award myself in 1988). I have attended many of our annual conferences over the years and have been inspired by colleagues who keep our vision alive. I now represent the Sages on the Coordinating Committee of NCMA. Ministry in higher education is a vocation worthy of our best energy and continuing commitment. In this I am a believer.

I have pretty much described my life in Retirement already, but the other big news is that I will soon be a grandfather for the first time, at age 80! (Yes, I've always been a late bloomer!) Betsy's five grandchildren have broken me in, but this will be a new adventure for me. Along with the vocational pursuits above, I enjoy walking in Duke Forest daily, reading good fiction for our two book groups, meeting with my men's group in Durham, spending summer/fall in our mountain home, and travels with Betsy.

Reflections on 40 Years in Campus Ministry
By Verlyn I. Barker

I have this suspicion that to be termed a "sage" in NCMA circles has more to do with my age, 82, than any wisdom I may have from years in campus ministry but I can at least offer some reflections from my 40 years in the ministry of the United Church of Christ, three years as Associate University Pastor at the University of Nebraska in Lincoln and 35 years on the staff of the Division of Higher Education of the United Church Board for Homeland Ministries with responsibilities related to campus ministry and the student Christian movement.

First, a disclaimer. I have been retired for 18 years and my professional papers and documents have been placed in the Archives of the Divinity School of Yale University, thus I must rely on a few papers I have retained and what I can recall. My closest colleague and friend over the last years of my ministry was Clyde Robinson of the United Presbyterian Church. Before I retired in 1996, we, with Clyde's wife Louise, should have taken a long holiday at the beach and written an overview of our ministry, clarity and accuracy assured with the assistance of George Dickel and Dewars White Label. Failing that, let me share something of my years in campus ministry.

I tend to think of this ministry with the titles that defined it over the years, the formative years, Student Work which was denomination-based; the great development years, Campus Ministry which began the ecumenical periods; and the broadest years of engagement, Ministry in Higher Education. The terms describing the ministry are directly related to what defined the Church at the time, its vision of mission in relation to its presence in the public sphere and the marks of leadership over the course of 60 years. My reference is to the "established" or "mainline" Protestant denominations."

First, in the 1940's, "student work" as discussed in the classic by Yale Divinity School Professor Clarence Shedd in his book, *The Church Follows its Students*. The "student workers" were located in a student center across the street from the large state universities. Students came to the center for worship, Bible, theological study and discussion of the meaning of being Christian, usually gathering on Sunday evenings for a fellowship supper followed with speakers and discussion, often professors and local pastors. Since religion was not taught in the university, courses were taught in the student center. It was a time when young people from the churches began attending the public universities rather than local trade colleges and church related colleges if they sought post-high school education.

I am not sure when this annual event began but it became common for there to be an annual Religion in Life or Religious Emphasis week in the universities when campus ministries brought prominent religious leaders to the campus for a series of lectures and discussions, when campus ministers were scheduled into the dorms, fraternities and sororities for discussion.

In the latter part of this period, universities began to accept religion as an academic discipline rather than constructs of the faith of individuals and provided opportunities for lectures. For example, in 1957 at the University of Nebraska, H. Richard Niebuhr was the invited lecturer for its "Montgomery Lectures on Contemporary Culture." His lecturers were published in his Radical Monotheism and the Western Culture.

Second, in the 50s and 60s, campus ministry was first denominationally oriented and gradually became more ecumenical. This was the time of tremendous growth in church membership, new church starts, and strong financial support of national and state/ regional mission agencies, including those responsible for campus ministry. A time when national assemblies prominently participated in public affairs, when the denominational leaders were public figures in the country. I think of Eugene Carson Blake and Bishop James Pike.

Also this was the time of the rapid increase in the number of ministries with funding from some national offices of the denominations. For example, under the leadership of Harold Viehman, whom I herald as the creative leader in establishing this ministry, the Presbyterians provided the funding for the campus minister as ministries were formed, first on the large state universities and then on the state colleges/universities. It was a time with national staff responsible for campus ministry, the Presbyterians, USA, being the largest with staff regionally deployed. The United Church of Christ had a staff of five, three national and two regionally based. The staff of these two denominations along with those of the Christian Church, Disciples of Christ, and the Evangelical United Brethren Church formed the United Campus Christian Fellowship, then the United Ministries in Higher Education.

The "campus minister" worked out of the center, some in houses others in newly constructed facilities at the campus. There was more of a total campus orientation, going into the campus rather than from the campus to the center, broadening from undergraduates to graduate students, faculty, international students and university staff. The campus minister met with faculty groups, student counseling staff, was invited to visit dorms, fraternity and sororities, and provide leadership in campus events.

The campus ministry centers became the place for discussion of controversial social and political issues, sometimes to the displeasure and even opposition of the university and people in the churches. Most notably these occurred in the Viet Nam War period. Because denominations, nationally, took liberal and progressive policy decisions in their national assemblies, campus ministers had a reference to legitimatize their actions and support their own convictions.

With this came exposure trips in which students, with the campus minister's leadership, traveled to places where they were confronted directly and personally to problem issues in the society and pondered the meaning for Christians. I first took a group to Omaha seeking understanding of the condition of the American Indian living off the reservation --on the TV evening news I was called "a wolf in sheep's clothing;" then a group to Chicago to encounter the destitute, "slum" areas of the city; and finally a group to Americus, Georgia, to visit the Koinonia Farm and Clarence Jordan, a sanctuary under constant attack for its stand against segregation. How well I remember the Jordans taking the men across the road for their night's lodging. Lights from a car were seen as we approached the road. Mrs. Jordan asked, should we stay on this side of the road or cross, to which Mr. Jordan replied, "Stay on this side, for if there is only the driver in the car it will be more difficult for him to shoot at us." In our cabin were marks of gunshots. We got the message loud and clear.

During this period, the denominational student fellowships began to be formed on the local, state and national levels, gradually taking ecumenical forms and marked by national student conferences during the Christmas holidays, always being exposed to prominent theologians, biblical scholars and leaders of the time, like Martin Luther King, Jr. --powerful experiences for students as well as campus ministers and chaplains. And likewise, denominational campus ministry organizations were formed with regional and national conferences, e.g., Association of Presbyterian University Pastors, United Church of Christ Fellowship of Campus Ministers. Out of these, came the formation of the National Campus Ministry Association in which I was a participant 50 years ago.

And third, in the 60s and 70s, ministry in higher education, again found a broadened view of ministry to include all aspects of the life and work of higher education, local, state, national. I am reminded of the issues we faced in the context of higher education, issues for which we were criticized but issues which sooner or later the churches would have to address. From desegregation and the struggle for equal rights, to the acceptance of students from other nations and cultures, to racial and gender inequality, to teaching of religion within the public universities, to the issues of faith and science, to war and peace issues regarding the Vietnam War and the complicity of the university in the industrial military complex, to issues related to human sexuality, to the policies affecting campus life, issues related to the welfare of students and academic freedom. But always central to the work of the minister in higher education were the students as they encountered new thinking and experiences in their faith and personal development.

The strongest and most effective advocates and interpreters were the magnificent cadre of highly competent ministers in higher education who responded to the call to this ministry with a vision and passion. Their service as pastors and teachers is the real accounting for this ministry. Out of these ministries came pastors and teachers in the churches, denominational, national and world leaders; in the public sector.

My past in this ministry still emerges in unexpected ways. A former student at the University of Nebraska has moved to Denver and, with her husband, we have lunch every week. She refers to her experience on the trip to Americus, Georgia, as having transformed her life. A month ago I was in meeting with the new President of Iliff School of Theology, Thomas Wolfe. When he saw my name plate, he said "I know who you are! I used to get letters and resources from you when I was Chaplain at Syracuse University." Only this week I had a student from my days at the University of Nebraska whom I had had no contact for over 50 years get in touch with me. While I do not dwell on my past, with these contacts I am reminded of my years in campus ministry.

Some refer to this as "the heyday" of this ministry, with Church-wise, highly effective national denominational leadership, strong ecumenical commitments, and effective participation in the public structures of society. Nationally United Ministries in Higher Education at its apex had the participation of ten denominations. There were ten national denominational agencies engaged together in UMHE in addition to the original four - (Christian Church, Disciples of Christ, Evangelical United Brethren Church, United Church of Christ, Presbyterian Church, USA): Moravian Church, northern province; American Baptists; Episcopal Church, Reformed Church in America; Church of the Brethren; United Methodist Church when it merged with the United Brethren Church. The professional staff were "contributed" to work as staff of UMHE, the number coming to 35 when I served as President of UMHE. UMHE's budget was provided by the denominational agencies' budgets.

There were three sections of UMHE's work, UMHE's nationwide ministries; UMHE's national ministries and the national offices, most notably the Office of Communications, the latter being the only staff supported by UMHE itself. The depth of the commitment and financial support varied greatly, frequently causing "difficulties" upon which I will not comment further! That belongs in a more private setting.

I. National Offices

The Office of Communications was key in developing the ministry networks, connecting ministries with a national directory, information and resources, a cohesion for a national identity. One of those leading the Office was Leon Howell, afterwards to become editor of *Christianity and Crisis,* and Betsy Alden, known for her development of resources used throughout the network, including *Connexion* and *ResUME,* a regular update of the work of United Ministries in Education.

Early in the formation of UMHE there was the Office of Personnel which I staffed in St. Louis, along with being a regional secretary. This grew from the practice of UPUSA of being involved in the selection of campus ministers who would serve in local ministries that were funded out of the national offices. The office collected resumes from those seeking positions; local committees seeking personnel obtained these resumes from which they issued their calls.

Later an unsuccessful effort was made to help local committees in their funding needs with an Office of Development, but reduction in the financial support from the state and regional denominational committees did not allow for this.

II. Nationwide Ministries

Most of the national staff were deployed to serve as resources and consultants to state commissions and local boards, some in other positions over the years. I can't recall all of these staff but I remember David Rich (ABC/UPUSA) in PA; Earl Lowell (UPUSA), Richard Nutt (UMC) and William Tibbitt (Epis) in New York; Samuel Slie (UCC) and David Wallick (UPUSA) in the Northeast; Harry Manon (UCC) in Pennsylvania; LeRoy Loats (UPUSA), Dale Turner (ABC}, Glenn Hosman and Cecil Findley (UMC) in LaGrange; Emerson Abendroth (UPUSA) in Kansas City; Sam Kirk, UMC in Denver; Verlyn Barker (UCC) in St.Louis; William Keys (EPIS) in the Middle Atlantic; on the west coast, William Hallman (UPUSA), Daniel Statello and William Shinto ABC), Paul Kearns (UPUSA) and Richard Nelson Bolles (EPIS). Others in the national offices included Donald Shockley, United Methodist; Nathaniel Porter, Mark Harris and James McNamee, Episcopal; Richard Tappan, William Belli, American Baptist; ABC); Bernie Michel and Gary Harke, Moravian; Ralph McFadden and Donald Lowdermilk, Church of the Brethren; George Conn, UPUSA; John Butler, Arla Elston, Larry Steinmetz, Christian Church (Disciples of Christ). When gathered in staff meetings, there was a comprehensive reporting on what was happening across the country, a thrilling and energizing experience.

National Ministries:

These ministries embodied the belief that it was important for the church to be engaged in national arenas of higher education which were addressing important issues. The two which became prominent in their impact were programs in medical education under the leadership of Dr. Ronald McNeur, a contributed staff person from the United Presbyterian Church and the program in career development under the leadership of Richard Nelson Bolles, a contributed staff from the Protestant Episcopal Church.

The work in medical education began in the 60s with the concern of two professors in the University of California Medical School in San Francisco who were concerned about the impact of the development of medical technology on the practice, teaching and research in medicine. The focus, the person as patient, in dealing with questions of the use of life-support systems, dying and death, abortion, euthanasia, ethics of organ transplant, genetic engineering. This program was a prime example of what it meant to being ministry in higher education, lifting up the national settings in which to be engaged.

With this came the formation of **The Society for Health and Human Values** which was a separate entity but a program of UMHE which provided the staff and received its primary funding for many years from the National Endowment for the Humanities. With seminars and workshops in the national meetings and conferences of medical educators, e.g., The Association of American Medical Schools emerged the Medical Humanities in the curriculum and staff in all of the 162 medical schools in the country. The program produced a major resource in a four volume series, Health and Human Values: A Guide to Making Your Own Decisions published by Yale University Press in 1983. In an effort to record the work of the Society, I wrote a monograph, Health and Human Values: A Ministry of Theological Inquiry and Moral Discourse, published in 1987. The Society's purposes are now found within The American Society for Bioethics and Humanities.

The work in career development emerged in the late 60s when the denominations began the period of membership decline and major reduction in funding for national agencies. Hard hit were campus ministries and the job losses by highly trained and effective ministers in higher education. There were no positions in this ministry to which they could go. One day when talking about the problem and pondering what UMHE could do, Richard Bolles said, " I want to be the nations expert in career change." With funding for his research came the first edition of What Color is Your Parachute? in 1970, revised annually ever year afterward, the latest being in 2014. I don't know exactly the number of copies sold over the years but the last I saw it was reaching toward 15 million. Life/work Planning is the process development, based on the belief that a person's skills and talents can be used in many areas in the work world. E.g., a minister has skills that are not bound only to the church's ministry. The book was translated into seven languages. Richard Bolles is and has been the speaker in professional conferences in this county and abroad and is often referred to as the guru in this field.

The Career Development Program was funded by the Lily Endowment. It included two week workshops for campus ministers, career counselors in college and universities and a host of others engaged in the field. As with our work in medical education, I often ponder the impact Richard Bolles has had on thousands and thousands of lives, including my own.

The Public Education Program grew out of the issues facing public education, e.g., funding, safeguarding the schools from the attacks of special interest groups like the fundamentalists. Our interest was challenging the growing presuppositions that education is to domesticate; rather, education is for the whole person, preparing students for life, how to learn rather than just being receptive of information. But the more action part of the program emerged around the issue creationism. An important resource for this program was Professor Douglas Sloan, Professor of the History and Philosophy of Education, Teachers College, Columbia University, earlier a leader in the Student Christian movement. His two books, *Faith-Knowledge: Mainline*

Protestantism and American Higher Education and *Insight-Imagination: The Emancipation of Thought and the Modern World* were two of most important books I have read about education. UMHE had two staff who began working in this area, Shirley Heckman, Church of the Brethren, and Barney Kathan, United Church of Christ. Their work with Margaret Shafer, in the National Council of Churches Office for Public Education, provided resources and tools for the church's advocacy for ethical public education policies.

In 1981 the General Assembly of the State of Arkansas, passed Act 590 "to require balanced treatment of creation-science and evolution-science in public schools ..." -the beginning of a nationwide hot discussion and debate on "creationism" fostered by the fundamentalists. In January, 1982, Judge Overton, a judge in the US District Court for Eastern Arkansas handed down a decision giving a clear, specific definition of science as a basis for ruling that creation science is religion simply, not science. While the ruling applied only to the Eastern District in Arkansas, it had national and nationwide consequences which affected every Public School Board in the country.

The public education program was incorporated with UMHE and the organization's name was changed to United Ministries in Education, public education being one of the program areas. Hal Viehman, retired, became the staff person for this program. He and other denominational leaders participated in the Council for Religion in Public Education which held that it was important to engage in the debate and discussion in order to increase understanding which included advocating respect for sound education and integrity of religious belief and clarifying the meaning of the freedom of religion amendment as it applied to public institutions like the public school.

Among resources developed for local churches was my *Creationism, the Church, and the Public School* and a monograph series on *The Church and the Public School*, the latter focusing on the importance of the public school in our nation.

The Community College Program was an example of how UMHE responded to the phenomenal growth and diversity in higher education, from the "flagship" state universities, to professional schools, to teacher colleges, to community colleges. The work focused on sustaining and strengthening the colleges' response to the needs of their communities and developing ways in which colleges and congregations might work together with their mutual resources. Much of the work of the national staff team was within the national conferences of The American Association of Community Colleges. The UMHE team included William Hallman and Clyde Robinson, UPUSA; Robert Mayo, an African American Episcopal priest on the staff of the UCC; Earl Lowell in New York; J Springer in Pennsylvania; Mark Rutledge in New Mexico; and Betsy Alden in Dallas. Resources developed by this team included *Live-Wires: Developing Campus/Church Connections for the 21st Century* by Earl Lowell and J Springer, as well as a series of monographs.

The Peace Education Program with the leadership of Shirley Heckman, from the Church of the Brethren, worked closely with Betty Reardon, Director of the Institute for Peace Studies at Teachers College, Columbia University.

III. Other National Interests

Latin American Interests, led by William Rogers, a minister in higher education in New York, focused on finding ways in which the church and university, with Anglo and Latino communities, could deal with the implications of the use of US power and oppressed people in Latin America.

UMHE provided funding for the **Women's Caucus** focused on issues in the emerging women's movement, i.e., the role of women in higher education and the church. We also helped to fund the **Ministry to Blacks in Higher Education,** organization with leadership from Frank Horton and Richard Hicks of the United Methodist Church and Robert Mayo from the United Church of Christ. This program focused on ways in which predominantly white campuses could respond constructively to the presence of an increasing number of African American students on their campuses.

When the AIDS epidemic developed, UME, in association with the American College Health Association, sponsored AIDS training events for campus ministers. The other national program that emerged in UMHE but quickly became independent as it was embraced by national denominational agencies was science and technology.

Science and Technology emerged first out of campus ministers' interests in the new conversations around the relation of science and faith, leaving behind the "two realm" theory with conversations between theologians and scientists in the U.S. and England. A second component was interest in the impact of new scientific knowledge and technology on the society. I don't know the developments in all of the denominations, but the United Church and the United Presbyterians formed specific groups to address the questions. The two met and worked closely together.

In the UPUSA, The Working Group on Faith, Science and Technology was led by James Miller, a campus minister at Michigan Technological University, and Kenneth McCall, Executive Presbyter in Mackinac Presbytery in Michigan. They edited the *Church and Contemporary Cosmology*, published by Carnegie Mellon Press. In the United Church of Christ, I formed and staffed The Science and Technology Working Group with the leadership of Ronald Cole-Turner, campus minister at Michigan Technological University and now a professor at Pittsburgh Theological Seminary, and Brent Waters, Chaplain at Redlands University, now a professor at Garrett Evangelical Seminary in Evanston.

Together the two groups sponsored a symposium and published the papers on *Rediscovering Alexandria: Science, Technology & and Churches* in 1990 in the annual meeting of the American Association for the Advancement of Science. The UCC group was responsible for developing policies on related issues for the General Synod, e.g., mapping the human genome, genetic engineering, stem cell research, dying and death (focused on the use for life support systems). Study resources developed for the churches included *New Genesis: Theology and the Genetic Revolution* by Ronald Cole-Turner and with Brent Waters, *Pastoral Genetics: Theology and Care at the Beginning of Life.* Brent also authored *Dying and Death: A Recourse for Christian Reflection and Ministry in An Age of Science* and *Technology: Genetics and Pastoral Theology.* Brent Waters and I also edited "Science, Technology and the Christian Faith: An Account of Some Pilgrims in Search of Progress."

There were similar initiatives in the Evangelical Lutheran Church in America and the Protestant Episcopal Church. The leader in the ELCA was the late John Mangum. John and I happened to live in the same apartment complex on the upper West side in New York City and became good friends. Out of our discussion came the conviction that it was time to form an ecumenical body, and we co-founded the **Ecumenical Roundtable for Science, Technology and the Church,** which sponsored annual conferences led by prominent theologians and scientists, attended by a large range of persons including campus ministers, pastors, theologians and ethicists.

In 1987, the ELCA with the World Lutheran Federation sponsored a global consultation in Larnaca, Cyprus, with the theme "The New Scientific Technological World: What Difference does it make to the Churches?" There were 45 participants from seventeen nations. A week of worship, lectures, and discussions, were all reported in *The New Faith Science Debate: Probing Cosmology, Technology and Theology* edited by John Mangum. I had the privilege of working with John in planning and participating in the consultation, a memorable experience marked by the presence and participation of some brilliant young people, including a 19 year old, called the "whiz" from Argentina, who reminded us of the importance of these discussions for his generation.

IV. The Student Christian Movement

To omit the development of the student Christian movement over this time seriously overlooks an important part of ministry in higher education.

Internationally, the vision and energy for an ecumenical student Christian movement originated in Europe in 1895 by the North American evangelist and global ecumenist, John R. Mott, with the formation of the World Student Christian Federation, a federation of the student Christian movements in nations around the world, organized into six regions: Africa, Asia-Pacific, Europe, Latin America and Caribbean, Middle East and North America, the number of movements changing over the years. When I was President of the WSCF Trustees, US, in the 80s, there were 105 member movements.

Briefly, students who participated in the SCMs were encouraged to study their Christian faith with the same depth and passion they brought to their studies. SCMs are known for their openness to searchers as well as believers and for a strong commitment of racial and social justice. Every four years, WSCF holds a General Assembly with delegates from each of the six regions, one of the richest experiences one can have. I participated in the General Assembly in Colombo, Sri Lanka, in the 70s.

This was during the Cold War with Russia. Somehow the WSCF leadership was able to bring a student from Russia to the Assembly under an assumed name. Vividly I remember one lunch in which I entered the room from the west, he from the east and we greeting one another and sat for lunch. At the end, we rose and embraced as the Assembly sang, "In Christ there is no East or West" --one of the most emotional experiences I have ever had.

Out of the 2004 General Assembly came this guiding vision:

Our mission is to empower students in critical thinking and constructive transformation of our world by being a space for prayer and celebration, theological reflection, study and analysis of social and cultural processes and solidarity and action across boundaries of culture, gender and ethnicity. Through the work of the Holy Spirit, the WSCF is called to be a prophetic witness to church and society. This vision is nurtured by a radical hope of God's reign in history.

WSCF sponsors an annual World Day of Prayer for Students with a common liturgy, the offerings from which are used for the Federation's Ecumenical Assistance Program which is given to SCMs in countries facing disasters and political oppression. The hymn sung at every gathering is one written by Walter C. Smith in 1867:

Immortal, Invisible, God only wise,
In light inaccessible hid from our eyes,
Most blessed, most glorious, the Ancient of Days, almighty, victorious,
Your great name we praise.

Nationally, the SCMs had several organizational formations over the years, their archives being a part of the archives of the Divinity School of Yale University. The first expression was the Student Volunteer Movement, SVM, formed in 1886, as a collegiate expression of the concerns of students for foreign mission. The Interseminary Movement, ISM, began in 1889 as a fellowship of theological students with concern for mission, unity and the renewal of the church.

The major resource for the student Christian movements that followed was the magazine for the Methodist Student Movement which was formed in 1941, ***motive magazine***. B.J. Stiles was the amazingly creative editor. More than a resource for the Methodist Student Movement, it became a major resource for the entire University Christian Movement. One found this magazine in every campus ministry center in the country. Noted and celebrated for its avant garde editorial and artistic vision, in 1966 *Time* magazine said it stood out among church publications "like a miniskirt at a church social." *(Motive* was the runner-up to *illas,* the Magazine of the Year in 1965.) Ultimately its strong stands on civil rights, Vietnam, and emerging gender issues became more than the United Methodist Church officials could take. They withdrew funding and it ceased publication in 1972. An entire generation of religious activists was shaped by its vision.

In 1944, The United Student Christian Council, USCG, became the national body of a number of national denominational intercollegiate movements of denominations and the Student YMCA and YWCA. Since the WSCF's membership was restricted to one ecumenical body from a nation, it was the member US movement in the WSCF federation.

In the 1940s when more students were attending college, denominations developed an extension of their youth ministries-- for the Congregational Christian Churches, a student adjunct to Pilgrim Fellowship. Before the actual formation of the United Church of Christ in 1957, students from the Congregational and the Evangelical and Reformed Churches formed the United Student Fellowship, USF.

In 1955, USF sent a formal invitation to all member groups of the USCG to discuss the possibility of forming a united SCM in the United States, These discussions held at Stephens College in 1960 resulted in the formation of the United Campus Christian Fellowship, UCCF, "believing that we are called to unite our campus Christian movements to carry out this mission in our campus life." Joining with the USF of the United Church of Christ were the student movements of the United Presbyterian Church, the Christian Church (Disciples of Christ), and the Evangelical United Brethren Church. From the UCCF "Articles of Union":

> The mission of the Church is to express God's love in the world....A campus Christian movement exists to help students carry out the mission of the Church in campus life....The purpose of campus Christian programs is not to raise up more faithful Presbyterians or Congregationalists. Christians in the university are to pursue their studies as a Christian calling, knowing also that through their participation in the life of the university they may more fully convey their faith in Jesus Christ to others.

Then came the zinger:

> Our campus Christian movements are church-related movements, and the fact of our disunity as denominations cannot be ignored. But as we face our responsibilities on campus, is God calling us to heal our divisions? It is above all in the attempt to carry our mission into the world that the Church is driven toward unity (as, e.g. in India)...Can we not expect that God may

use our experience of life together as a step toward greater unity of His Church.

From this came the challenge, why should the Boards that support our ministry be separate? Hence came the formation of United Ministries in Higher Education by the denominations which had formed the United Campus Christian Fellowship.

The UCCF continued its efforts to form a more united SCM in the US. In 1965 UCCF and the Methodist Student Movement discovered mutual interests in a more united mission but could not agree on a common strategy. MSM was more oriented on social issues; UCCF on higher education. The discussion did result in The National Student Christian Federation as a wider ecumenical forum for SCMs in the United States. Later, the University Christian Movement became the Council of Ecumenical Christian Ministry (CESCM) which included the United Church of Christ, The Protestant Episcopal Church, the Evangelical Lutheran Church in America, the Presbyterian Church, USA, and the United Methodist Church.

Whatever the ecumenical forum, the denominations had their student expression from which they participated in the ecumenical expressions. In the 1980s the United Church of Christ and The Christian Church (Disciples of Christ), as denominations, formed a partnership which gave rise to the Student Ecumenical Partnership (STEP). It was formed to unite and develop a national network of students and those committed to ministry with students in order to support their faith journey; to foster the churches' commitment of ministry with and for students and advocate for their needs and concerns; to encourage student participation in state, regional, national and international events.

In conclusion, I wait for others to share their thoughts and experiences in the contemporary expression of the churches' ministry in higher education. When I retired there was much discussion of congregation-based campus ministry. Whatever the form, I write to emphasize the rich tradition of which it is a part, recognizing that the condition and situation of the church and its leadership is determinative. Our present obsession with "growing the church" will surely give way to a healthier ministry and mission. I agree with what John Buchanan wrote in a recent issue of *The Christian Century*: "I have a proposal: let's call a moratorium on counting members. Let's consider that we are called to witness God's love in Jesus Christ and to do everything we can to be Christ's body in the world, to do what we believe he would do and is doing through us." I wonder if Pope Francis may be the one ushering in the Reformation we have been waiting for.

And, finally, a bit of wisdom. When I announced my retirement in 1996, two special colleagues and friends responded with cogent pieces of advice. Richard Bolles replied: "So now what are you going to do with your life?" And from Jack Harrison, who embodied the meaning of being a minister in higher education: "Just don't look for your footprints in the sand." In other words, the gift of life goes on. Claim it I have, but always with sincere gratitude for the challenging and fulfilling ministry I had in campus ministry and the student Christian movement.

Resources:

1. *The Campus Ministry*, edited by George L Earnshaw, published by Judson Press in 1964. Chapters on the formation and development of denominational student movements, including one I wrote on The United Campus Christian Fellowship.
2. *The United Ministries in Higher Education: A Historical and Critical Appraisal,* by Darrell W. Yeaney, Ph.D. dissertation at Boston University, 1975.
3. *The Church, the University, and Social Policy* by Kenneth Underwood, published by Wesleyan University Press in 1969 for The Danforth Study of Campus Ministries.
4. *The Journal of Ecumenical Studies,* Vol. 32, No 4, Fall, 1995. The issue is titled, "Perspectives on Ecumenical Christian Presence in U.S. Universities and Colleges, 1960-1995," edited by L Newton Thurber. This includes chapters on the Lutheran Campus Ministry, Methodist Student Movement, United Campus Christian Fellowship, NCMA (written by Charles Doak), and Student Movements of the YMCA and YWCA, as well as a historical bibliography of the WSCF Centennial compiled by Newt Thurber, Franklin Woo and myself.
5. *Seeking and Serving the Truth: The First Hundred Years of the World Student Christian Federation* by Philip Potter and Thomas Weiser, World Council of Churches, 1997.

Verlyn Barker retired in 1996 and moved to Denver, Colorado, where the major focus of his time has been on genealogy for his family, three branches of which came to America in the 1600s and one from Germany in the mid-19th Century. After 35 years with a daily schedule, meetings, airports, airplanes, and hotels, he is now happy to be "at home" in his condo with a panoramic view of the mountains and auto trips into the southwest. The freedom one has in retirement is an earned gift.

Campus Ministry in the 60's and 70's:
Context and Observations
By Howard L. Daughenbaugh

This paper was originally prepared for presentation in 2009 to the College Alumni Club at Illinois Wesleyan University in Bloomington, Illinois.

Between July 1958 and July 1973, I was a United Methodist campus minister at **Tulane University in New Orleans** for eleven years and the University of Illinois, Urbana/Champaign for four years, so I want to offer some comments on the dynamics of this important era in our history, along with observations about what we might have learned that can be useful today.

I begin by referring to an article, "My Hometown," by Martin Marty, which was published in *The Christian Century.* "With George Santayana I believe that one needs a *locus standi*, a place to stand to view the world. Santayana had two: the Spain of his childhood and the Harvard of his later years. My places are Nebraska and Chicago." For me those two places are actually three. They are Lake Charles, Louisiana; New Orleans, Louisiana; and central Illinois.

My wife Judy and I grew up in Lake Charles. In the days of our youth, it was the place where we had a marvelous educational and social experience. The educational experience was unique because it was a city-operated system provided by a community of some 50,000 people in the Deep South, and it was excellent because close to 50 per cent of our class attended college, with the majority completing at least an undergraduate degree.

The social experience in this community of our youth was developed by the high school we attended, the resources of the city, and the creativity of our parents. It was healthy, taught responsibility, and encouraged a high level of enjoyment. From it we learned how to relate constructively to one another, how to develop leadership skills, and how to be responsible citizens.

If you think I'm painting an entirely too idyllic picture of this place of our youth, you are probably correct. It did have its seamier side. Racially it was a thoroughly segregated community. Religiously it was dominated by white, mainline Protestants which left little room for folks from other religious persuasions. However, there were several independent Christian congregations, a rather large contingent of Roman Catholics, and a Jewish congregation in the community. Economically it became dominated by the petrochemical industry, so its environmental record left something to be desired.

Nevertheless, it remains as a "place to stand to view the world." We often measure what we see in this world today, both the realities that need to be changed and those that need to be preserved, by what we experienced in that place of our youth.

My second "place to stand to view the world" is New Orleans, Louisiana. I would risk the observation that New Orleans is to Louisiana and the world what San Francisco is to California and the world and what New York City is to New York and the world. These cities cannot be confined nor defined by the states in which they are located. In large measure New Orleans is defined by Latin American culture in the same manner as San Francisco is defined by Asian culture and New York City by European culture. These are, indeed, American cities, but they are also international cities.

In June, 1958 my wife and I and our one year old son moved from Perkins School of Theology and Southern Methodist University in Dallas, Texas to Tulane University in New Orleans. I had entered seminary in 1955 not knowing whether or not ordained ministry was the vocation God intended for me. I graduated in 1958 with some certainty about ordained ministry, but I was unclear as to what expression of it I should pursue.

One day during my senior year I was walking by a large bulletin board in the seminary's administration building and saw an announcement about a chaplaincy opening at a church related college. Intrigued I continued my journey straight down the hall into the seminary dean's office. As luck would have it, he had some time to give to a confused senior.

Merrimon Cuninggim was this gentleman scholar's name. Some of you may recognize him as having served as the Executive Director of the Danforth Foundation following his tenure as Dean of Perkins School of Theology.

Perhaps my interest in college chaplaincy had been sparked by my participation in Dr. Cuninggim's class, *The Christian Faith and Higher Education*. In any case, the results of our conversation heightened my interest, and he encouraged me to follow it.

Not many weeks later the annual Ministers' Week was held at S.M.U. At this event each year district superintendents from many conferences around the country would come to campus to interview students. That year I met with two superintendents—one from Montana and the other from my home district in Louisiana. Why I chose the one from Montana I have no idea.

The Montana superintendent discussed with me a new church start in Billings and the campus ministry position at The University of Montana. When I met with my superintendent from Louisiana I was startled when he told me he had been authorized by the bishop to discuss with me a new church start in a suburb of New Orleans and the campus ministry opening at Tulane University.

Upon discussing these conversations with my wife, Judy, Montana was quickly removed from consideration, and we decided campus ministry at Tulane sounded very interesting and challenging. In June, 1958 the bishop appointed me to the Tulane University Wesley Foundation.

You might recall that in 1958 the Civil Rights movement was gaining a head of steam. Our society was beginning to move from quiet social conformity into a time when the centrifugal forces began to overwhelm the centripetal forces. All of the component parts of our ordered society came under intense scrutiny. It began with the Brown versus Board of Education decision which produced Little Rock. It continued with the launching of Sputnik, and it shifted into high gear with the Montgomery Bus Boycott.

Jack Kerouac, Bob Dylan, and Martin Luther King, Jr. inspired us by word, song, and sermon to face the injustices of a conforming society where a hierarchy of accepted values was suddenly and substantially challenged. As we recited "On the Road" with Kerouac, sang "The Times They Are a Changin'" with Dylan, and read King's "A Letter from a Birmingham Jail;" it began to dawn on us that we were witnessing some significant alterations to the fabric of our society. According to these prophets in our midst, it was no longer acceptable for the economic franchised to control the economic disenfranchised, for women to be subservient to men, for blacks to be obedient to whites.

Though these disruptions of the established norms occurred throughout our society, there was a sense in which they were focused on the higher education community. It was in that community where the opportunity to question and challenge existed as an essential ingredient to its enterprise. It was also understood that the formation which occurred in a person's life during her/his higher education years would have a direct bearing and substantial influence on their adult life and the society of tomorrow.

The academic community was seen as the place of greatest flexibility, freedom, and focus on the future. It was thought that the seeds of a society characterized by greater justice would have their best chance of taking root in our colleges and universities. Yet no one seemed to be able to forecast the turmoil that this vision for higher education would create within the academy.

In such an atmosphere *in loco parentis* was no longer applicable. Students began to understand themselves as contributors to, not just receivers of, the educational enterprise. They wanted greater influence in the curriculum and greater governing authority on the campus. They thought house mothers were anachronisms and dorm hours incredulous. It wasn't long before the economic and civil rights revolutions were joined by the sexual and educational revolutions.

The educational enterprise began to question itself. Would the university continue to follow the traditional academic model or would it, in the vision of Clark Kerr, President of the University of California system, and Thomas Jefferson before him as he planned his beloved University of Virginia, become a collection of residential colleges fostering a sense of academic community between students and faculty? Would it be a research community, a teaching community, or both? Would it concentrate on specialized departmental education providing skills to be employed in careers or would it provide an education experience designed to create a purposeful and meaningful life or would it seek to offer both? To be sure these questions were really not new to higher education. However, they contained urgency about them in the 1960s and the early 1970s.

So the rather quiet decade of the fifties came to a close. Of course, the fifties had not been all that quiet. There had been warning signs of what was to come. If we had possessed the necessary eyes to see, and naturally some did, the Brown versus Board of Education decision would have alerted us to the Civil Rights Movement, Sputnik would have revealed to us the possibility of a technological revolution, and President Eisenhower's farewell warning of the growing military/industrial complex would have signaled the economic challenges ahead of us.

Although no one was quite ready for what was to come, very few of us saw the new decade as a foreboding time. We did not dread its arrival. Even with the growing racial turmoil in our society, changing student and faculty expectations in our colleges and universities, a Cold War that was especially hot at the time, and the discussions surrounding the role and purpose of higher education, the sixties dawned with a great sense of hope and with the eager expectation of exploring new horizons in space and elsewhere.

As the decade opened, there arose on the scene a young Roman Catholic politician who eventually became the symbol for the hope and promise of the decade. At the same time there was a book published by a young Harvard Divinity School theologian by the name of Harvey Cox. The title of his book was *The Secular City*. In it he proclaimed that there were no longer any unsolvable problems-- only unsolved problems. Today we see such observations as naïve. Then it was the expression of a "can do" generation.

On our national scene that young President from Massachusetts reflected the optimism and commitment of a generation. John Fitzgerald Kennedy described that generation as "tempered by war, disciplined by a hard and bitter peace,..and unwilling to witness or permit the slow undoing of...human rights."

On the international stage, a Scandinavian visionary served as General Secretary of the United Nations. Dag Hammarskjold talked movingly about cooperation, not conflict, between the nations of the world.

On the religious front a short, rotund Pope, elected almost as an afterthought, gave voice to an ecumenical spirit. This spirit, according to John XXIII, assured us of respect, even reconciliation, between the various expressions of the Christian faith as well as openness towards Jews, Muslims, and people of other religious persuasions. He reformed, nay, he revolutionized the church.

Indeed the decade began with abounding hope, falling boundaries, and limitless possibilities. At least it seemed that way at first.

In the midst of this idealistic climate campus ministry realized its task could no longer be nor did it want to be defined as a youth ministry of recreation and fellowship for young adults. If it was to be true to its faith, campus ministry had to offer opportunities for students to wrestle with the economical, social, and educational issues emerging at breakneck speed in the society. It had to engage the university in conversation about the purpose and style of education necessary in the changing society. It had to provide religious education for students struggling to relate their faith to a society where the ethical issues associated with the exercise of power and the pursuit of justice were paramount. It was a heady, energizing time to be alive.

There was this feeling in the early years of the decade that we were engaged in a truly important enterprise where significant affirming differences could be made in the lives of people, the university, and the church. The very title by which we were known changed. For example, I was no longer known as the student minister on campus or as the Wesley Foundation Director or as the United Methodist Chaplain. I was now the Wesley Foundation Campus Minister or the United Methodist Campus Minister.

This change was significant in private, non-sectarian and public higher education, because it declared that we were no longer compartmentalized in a segment of the university community. In some cases, probably most, our linkage to the university remained through the dean of students or the vice-president of student affairs. In some cases, we were given direct access to the provost or the president. In virtually all cases we became integral participants in most phases of the university's life. Our relationships with the faculty and the administration were as important as those with the students.

The change was equally significant in the life of the church. Until the 1960's most campus clergy were not clergy at all; they were lay persons licensed as directors of Christian education. Before the decade was half over the directors of Christian education were replaced by fully ordained clergy many with advanced degrees or post-graduate study under their belts.

What was not fully anticipated in both the university and the church was the profound alteration this made in our roles in each of these communities. We now engaged in serious conversations about the educational, theological, and ethical questions surfacing in face of the many issues arising in the society. We were seen as members of the university community as a whole. In the church we were identified as an authentic specialized ministry with a clear mission. With our emphasis on questions of ethics we bridged different academic disciplines. With one foot in the society, another foot in the church, our bodies immersed in the university, and our minds and spirits committed to all three we were able to communicate with all each of these communities in a manner quite unlike other vocations.

Some of the results of these changes were not comfortable for us nor for those with whom we worked and conversed. In the university the questions we raised about the educational process were not always appreciated. The activities in which we engaged, primarily those related to civil rights and later the Viet Nam War, brought discomfort to the status quo in both the university and the church. In the church we were thought to have developed a prophetic edge to the detriment of what was thought to be primarily a pastoral vocation.

Still, the advantages of this change in our role within the university and the church far outweighed the disadvantages. We were discovering realities of fundamental importance to our lives in our society, the university, and the church. It was a time of renewal and re-creation. There was energy, purposefulness, and hope about who we were and what we were doing.

Late in 1963 all this began to change. The decade had hardly begun. There was the assassination of the president on the streets of Dallas, Texas. The United Nations' General Secretary was killed in an airplane crash in Africa. The life of the Pope in Rome ended just as the reforms of Vatican II were beginning to take root. In 1965 Viet Nam began to explode onto the world stage. Early in 1968 that young African-American leader who spoke to us about a dream and taught us about non-violence in face of monumental oppression was cut down. A few months later another young Kennedy, an even more energetic and articulate presidential candidate, had his life snuffed out just as he was beginning to restore our hope and awaken our conscience to the plight of the poor in our midst and the possibilities for peace in the Far East.

It was said by one, "We will never laugh again." The reply by another was, "Oh, we will laugh again. But, will we ever hope again?" A decade that began with hope, commitment to the ideals of our nation, and a concentration on the needs of our less fortunate neighbors ended in despair, anger, and self-centeredness.

Nevertheless, New Orleans and Tulane University became my second "place to stand to view the world." It was a view filled with eagerness, anticipation, triumph, and hope tempered by tragedy, despair, and doubt. My life changed. My vocation changed. My faith changed. I believe all three matured as a result of standing and viewing the world from New Orleans and Tulane University.

However, the time had come to move on, and move on we did—big time. We left behind Lake Charles, New Orleans, and Tulane for the unknown possibilities of living in the prairie land of central Illinois.

All of my great grandparents and grandparents were from Illinois, so coming to **Urbana and the University of Illinois** was something of a homecoming for me. One of my great grandfathers had been a Methodist pastor in southern Illinois. Another great grandfather served in Grant's Army that secured Vicksburg, Mississippi and Mobile Bay, Alabama. Among all the Civil War veterans buried in a cemetery in a small southwestern Louisiana community his tombstone is the only one which bears the marking, "Grand Army of the Republic."

Not many weeks into my responsibilities as the executive director of an ecumenical campus ministry related to the University, we attended worship at Wesley United Methodist Church in Urbana. That morning the Associate Pastor of the congregation and the Associate Campus Minister for the Wesley Foundation introduced us to a Nobel Prize winner. I knew, then, we had moved into a different world.

I had this strange sensation of truly being in over my head. Besides "I am honored to meet you" what else do you say to a Nobel Prize winner? Words like "Wow" and "uh, uh, uh" came to mind, but I didn't think they were appropriate. I began to realize that we had moved to my third "place to stand to view the world."

While in New Orleans and at Tulane, the Civil Rights Movement and the changing environment in higher education and the church defined our view of the world. In Urbana/Champaign and at the University of Illinois, the Viet Nam War and its impact on life in the university and the church defined our view of the world.

The issues of war and peace, not to mention the birth of a broadened environmental movement, formed the context in which the university exercised its responsibility in the educational enterprise, and the church gave witness to its faith at work in the society. The Civil Rights Movement and poverty were still key players on the stage, but they were now matched by concerns for the environment and the trauma of Viet Nam.

It was here that the disarray we had begun to experience in our last years in Louisiana gained momentum. Students who once had thought there were no boundaries to their futures now began to feel betrayed by a stagnant economy, by a government which had been so promising and now was a part of the problem, and by what they thought was an endless, aimless war. University faculty experienced division in their ranks over the role social, political, and peace issues ought to play in the academy. Tensions arose between faculty and administrators, because one was perceived as too closely allied with the status quo and the other as desiring an academy too far removed from reality. Campus ministers found themselves separated from the denominations that supported them, and those who didn't experience such separation were, quite often, criticized by their colleagues.

All of this is grossly oversimplified; but I do believe it is fair to say that vision was lost and survival became the motivator in the church, campus ministry, and the academy. As a result, distrust and disillusionment with social and political institutions, including the university and the church, grew at warp speed.

Robert Bellah and his colleagues in their classic study *Habits of the Heart* documented the collapse of community responsibility in favor of individual rights. Entitlement became the operative goal. A decade which began with such promise ended in the throes of trauma. Preservation became more important than transformation.

As I conclude, I would like to offer a few observations from these "places where I've stood to view the world." I claim no particular uniqueness about them. Others far more articulate than I have spoken about them. Still, these gleanings from the sixties and seventies may have some relevance to us today.

First, we can remember that our best choices are seldom either/or. More often they are both/and choices. As a matter of fact, it is the tension existing with the both/and that most often produces creative results. As Robert Bellah would have us remember, we live as individuals in community. Once we

72

emphasize the one to the detriment of the other we start down the slippery slope of narcissism, on the one hand, and dominating control, even totalitarianism, on the other.

Beginning about 1965 we forgot what we had learned in the first half of the decade, namely that we shared responsibility for the well-being of our communities, nation, and world. Our enemies did not evaporate, but we had learned how, for the most part, to contain them, even isolate them. This was done by addressing the legitimate concerns and grievances of most people with whom we shared life.

Following the assassinations and confronted with the ever expanding war in Viet Nam despair rather than hope became dominant among us. We turned inward and began to lose our focus on the shared responsibilities we had in our communities, nation, and world. As we stared into our mirrors seeing only our personal pain, we lost sight of our neighbors. The word entitlement was substituted for responsibility.

Becoming focused primarily on what is good for *me* instead of upon what is good for *us* led to a concentration upon the accumulation of power rather than the pursuit of justice, though it is clear that justice cannot be attained in a given situation without the power to achieve it. Much depends, however, upon our focus. Is it on the power we want to accumulate or is it on the justice we need to pursue?

My second observation from the places where I have stood to view the world is one that I do not like to hear myself say, and it is probably entirely too cynical. Nevertheless, I have come to the uncomfortable conclusion that there may be something about us that can tolerate only so much hope. A cursory look at history seems to reveal that we, as societies, have not treated the conveyors of hope very kindly.

Fortunately, however, there have been those persons who have taken the challenge to repeatedly reintroduce the creative potential of hope into our lives. It is very encouraging to note that those who have been the most creative in their expression of hope gain our attention. So it would seem that even as we are unable to live with them we know we cannot live without them.

As a result, this observation from the "place(s) where I have stood to view the world" leads me to conclude that we may now be entering another era where a focus on our neighbors, particularly our neighbors in need, is receiving greater attention. Perhaps, we may be realizing that we need to turn from an era of entitlement to a time of responsibility. We may have begun to see that the exercise of self-centered power is, in the final analysis, self-defeating. It may also be that we are beginning, once again to ask the questions of justice for those among us who need it the most.

Of course, realizing justice and living hope will not be a journey without threats to its successful completion. The reactionary forces of fear and insecurity will emerge and gain their moments in the sun seeking to restore old systems of power and control. However, one can find hope in the midst of these reactionary moments by remembering there would be no backlash if there was no awakening.

Some have said we live in the midst of the Fourth Great Awakening in our country's history. No awakening has been without a struggle with the forces which would deny its vision. Still, the vision of a new future has been cast. It calls for stewardship rather than exploitation of God's creation. It summons us to a human community that embraces unity instead disunity, justice instead of domination, the honoring of different faith expressions instead of control by one over the other, and the living of hope instead of despair.

Sounds a bit like the 1960's and 1970's when I submit this vision of a new future—this new awakening actually began for our time. Yet, it is as ancient as the prophetic vision found in Isaiah, Amos, Micah, and elsewhere in the biblical story. And, on that note of hope I'll conclude.

Howard Daughenbaugh is living with his wife, Judy, at Luther Oaks Retirement Center in Bloomington, Illinois. He occupies himself with caregiving and enjoying his children, grandchildren, and newly born great granddaughter. He is also engaged in teaching a variety of seminars on theological and ethical concerns, preaching, promoting protection for the endangered red rock wilderness areas of our country; and seeking greater awareness of the need for a Christian response to violence in our society.

Ultimate Concerns: Prints and Drawings
By Thomas Niccols

Where did it begin? Perhaps with building a puppet stage when I was a kid. Or when I studied stained glass windows during boring sermons. Or because an aunt took me to the St. Louis Art Museum before I knew the difference between Raphael and Rembrandt, but was sure the nude sculpture in the front hall was neat.

Not long after I became Director of Westminster Foundation at *Ohio University* (1958-70), my dear colleague George Kennedy at the Wesley Foundation held a "University of Life" series which featured profs giving lectures on "Religion and (you name it)" topics. Dr. Stanley Grean, a philosopher, held forth with Tillich's Dynamics of Faith, while another class led by an active Episcopal layman, Dr. Fred Leach of the Art Department, talked about religion and art.

From that emerged a national competitive exhibition of religious art co-sponsored by our campus ministries. Leach and his colleagues in art were of inestimable help to us, complete neophytes in such a venture. We placed ads with a quote from Paul Tillich in national art magazines to invite artists to submit work for our show to be juried by printmaker Professor Mauricio Lansansky of the State University of Iowa. His national reputation got our project off to a very successful start.

Our first modest show, some 25 or 30 selected works, was hung in the University gallery, and we reveled in the opening reception which brought a good crowd, including the president and his wife. Lasansky recommended a few works as purchase prizes, and thus we started a nice collection of contemporary art which grew each year.

Often invisible in universities like fleas on elephants, campus ministries are usually ignored, but we got good press, and, even better, we had many opportunities for conversations, gallery talks, and panel discussions. The show brought enthusiasm among the faculty, students and even some folk in the churches.

The Tillichian title "Ultimate Concerns," of course, attracted debates and puzzlement. How was one to take the beautiful color woodcut called "Let's Make Love?" I recall Leach standing in front of the title when the president's wife was looking at the art works. Good thing Jesse Helms wasn't around.

Other works drew on the long tradition of history painting based on Biblical stories and images. I scrimped enough from our tight family budget to buy a fine intaglio by Frank Sampson called "Ezekiel's Vision," the first original art I had ever purchased. Incidentally, after 38 years on my wall, it inspired me to create my own three dimensional version, a large assemblage, to carry in the 1998 Parade the Circle sponsored by the Cleveland Museum of Art.

George and I soon learned that the growing annual show took long hours, for we had to un-pack submitted works, and then using the same packages, return all prints except the purchased prize works to the artists. Our lean budget was largely funded by artists' entry fees, and some artists who assumed our "foundations" were richly endowed, protested these fees. We side-stepped the issue with the dodge that since most artists did not object to this widespread practice, we would ignore the prophetic protests. Today I hope I'd be more ethically responsive.

After a number of years we did use other funds to circulate our collection of contemporary art among churches and schools. But we were unable to pay our student volunteers who helped us with the grunt work of un-packing and re-packing the art. Sad to say, the church is typically quick to preach justice for workers in the secular world, but often very miserly about treating its own workers fairly. Eventually our "Ultimate Concerns" expanded beyond our capacities so that we asked O.U. to take over the show.

What did I learn? Well, I became much more aware of my own interest in art, which led me to seek a Danforth Campus Ministry Fellowship for doctoral studies in comparative arts. Thus the exhibition set the stage for my later ministry at Hiram College where I taught courses in religion and culture during my twenty-one years as chaplain and professor.

I think the project also demonstrated conclusively that we minister best when we seek ways to involve people inside and outside the church at the points of their deepest commitments and concerns. Though now retired, I still assist annually with the endowed Hiram College Lectures in Religion which brings national scholars to our campus. Again and again I find that the lectures which touch the interests of other disciplines besides religious studies attract the most diverse and numerous faculty members, students, and area clergy.

Whether the church will ever again, as in the past, become a major patron of the visual arts remains problematic. But the enthusiasm of contemporary artists who would respond was surely proven by our project. I am convinced that even the most financially strapped congregation or campus ministry can find ways to affirm and release that marvelous creativity which helps us see with eyes not dulled by the banal and trite images assaulting our modern world.

(Written in 1996 for a potential collection of NCMA anecdotes.)

Getting the End of the Story
By Chad Boliek

Here's a little story from campus ministry days in the 60's at the *University of Idaho*:

One early spring afternoon Roger found me having coffee at the Burning Stake, the popular coffee house of the Campus Christian Center. "Chad, I just don't know what I'm going to do!"

"Yeah? Well, welcome to the sixties, Roger. What's up?"

"You know I'm about to graduate in a couple of months, and I've no idea what to do next."

"You mean about Vietnam?"

"Yeah, that mostly, I guess."

So we talked about that, mostly. Turned out Roger wasn't a conscientious objector. But he decidedly was wishing he could avoid a military career, or at least put it off for a while. More conversation. Roger was an English Lit major with some fuzzy career goals. He also was an idealist. He wanted to *help* people, not eliminate them.

A "light bulb!" Somewhere on my notoriously messy desk I'd seen some brochure or something about the new Peace Corps program. "What about *that*?" I asked. "It might mean a deferment, and a chance to do some reflection and maybe some good at the same time."

Before we were done, he'd made the decision and even filled out the application and put it in the mail. Later, I heard that he had been accepted and was indeed going to be a Peace Corpsman. Then you start wondering.

Normally that would end the story. A frustrating thing about working with students is that you get to know them for a year or two or so, and then they're gone. Feedback is a problem. Did your ministry have any effect for good, or did you blow it?

Years later. Ten to be exact. By then I'd hung up my Campus Ministry togs for a staff position at Ghost Ranch, the Presbyterian conference center in New Mexico. When who should stick his head in my office asking, "Remember me?" but old Roger himself!

Roger had done his Peace Corps service in Korea after having trained for the job at Ghost Ranch of all places. He was back with his friends for a ten year reunion. In the interim he'd gone back to school for his Ph.D . and was on the faculty of a prestigious university.

"But tell me," I could hardly wait to ask, "How was the Peace Corps, really?"

"It was absolutely the worst two years of my life!"

"Oooops!"

But he was smiling. Turns out, despite the foul-ups and stresses, the experience was rewarding in the long run and a true turning point for his life. He was grateful. And squared away!

One for the good guys!

(Written in 1998 for a potential collection of NCMA anecdotes.)

Chad Boliek served as Presbyterian Campus Minister in an ecumenical team ministry at the University of Idaho from 1960 to 1971. He then continued in ministry as the Business Manager of the Presbyterian Ghost Ranch Conference Center in New Mexico. He now lives in retirement near Las Vegas, New Mexico. He says of those exciting yet turbulent years of campus involvement during the 60's: "They were times of extraordinary crisis for many students and faculty - and campus ministers, too. Good for the church that saw the need and provided a presence!" He stays in FaceBook touch with a surprising number of students from those days who are still saying "no" to injustice and political idiocy, and "yes" to freedom, peace, and responsible action.

Chad now lives in retirement near Las Vegas, New Mexico. He volunteers as a teacher of 4th and 5th grade science; sings in the Presbyterian Church choir; and actively advocates for responsible stewardship of earth's resources.

Crises of Conscience
By Don E. Gibson

Introduction

I became a co-pastor with Don Scruggs, Director of Westminster Foundation, at the **University of Oklahoma in Norman** in November, 1961. I was called to work with Don in merging the denominational ministries of Christian Churches (Disciples of Christ) and the United Presbyterian Church, U.S.A. The merger (United Campus Christian Fellowship- UCCF) represented a wide-spread movement that resulted in creating ecumenical campus ministry centers across the nation. I became motivated to write about the formation of united ministries on the OU campus when I learned that 2014 is the fiftieth anniversary of the formation of the National Campus Ministry Association (NCMA). My tenure in campus ministry stretched from 1961 to 1983. Don Scruggs and I worked together for approximately ten years. After receiving his doctorate degree in Political Science from OU, he took a teaching position at Stephens College in Columbia, Missouri where he currently lives. Thus, we were what might be called "charter members" of NCMA. Indeed, I was privileged to serve as a Regional Representative to the national organization, which usually held a couple of meetings a year in Chicago.

Thad Holcomb followed me as campus minister at OU in 1983. He had previously served as campus minister at the University of Tulsa and later at the University of Kansas.

The Dramatic Change in Perspective

It is my intent to make objective observations and commentary regarding the advent of ecumenical campus ministry at the University of Oklahoma in Norman. But such objectivity is exceedingly difficult. The twenty two years I was engaged in this ministry stretched from my age of 27 to 50. It was a time in my life when I personally solidified my theological convictions; attempted to live out those convictions within the context of deep conflicts within our nation; was learning to be a husband and parent; and experienced friendships and vital collegiality among other campus ministers that included Presbyterian, Lutheran, United Methodist, Episcopal, Jewish, and Catholic colleagues. UCCF also included the United Church of Christ, although there were only 3-4 UCC congregations in Oklahoma.

Though we were not legally bound to one another, I would like to recognize the following persons with whom I had strong, vital personal and professional relationships: Jim Shields, Cathy Carlson, Clay Ballard and John Crooch--United Methodist (Wesley Foundation); Father Bill Ross, Father Charles Sweat and Father Joe Ross, Catholic priests; David Klumpp, pastor of University Lutheran Church; Norman Alexander and Father Don Owens, St. John's Episcopal; Rabbi Victor Epstein, Hillel Foundation. I also wish to acknowledge the special friendship and support from Mrs. Audrey Maehl, who was instrumental in the formation and leadership of the Oklahoma Commission for United Ministries in Higher Education. We also received valuable support and leadership from laity who were on the faculty and administration of the University and members of First Christian, First Presbyterian and Memorial Presbyterian congregations in Norman. This included two Presidents of the University, Dr. George Cross and Dr. Paul Sharp.

Three crucial changes took place within my first three years as campus minister at OU. First, the work changed *from denominational to ecumenical.* As denominational ministries both the Disciples Student Fellowship (DSF) campus minister and United Presbyterian Westminster Foundation campus minister worked as staff members of the local congregations, with representation from denominational judicatories. As ecumenical campus ministers, Don Scruggs and I worked under the guidelines and authority of a Local Board composed of representatives of local congregations and denominational judicatories. Most Board members were faculty, administration or students at the University.

Second, the orientation changed from *"student work" to ministry within higher education.* This change in orientation had immense impact upon staff and Board member's perception of our agenda...how we spent our time and available resources. The student work orientation focused primarily on contacting, inviting undergraduates to attend local churches, programming "fellowship" events and discussion groups for undergraduates and providing "pastoral care" to students as they adjusted to becoming young adults. I will describe the orientation for "ministry in higher education," as part of the third crucial change that took place on college campuses in the Sixties.

Third, the context of *life on the campus turned from casual to confrontational,* representing the controversial and conflicting voices that divided our nation. At this moment, 2014, I'm now 80, and easily forget that persons under fifty years of age today lack 'first- hand knowledge' about the specific issues and the intensity of feelings and rhetoric triggered by issues about abortion, war in Vietnam, civil rights movement, war on poverty, women's rights, gay/lesbian rights, freedom of speech, drugs, the "Hippie" movement and religious cults.

From my perspective, Don Scruggs and I had complete agreement with Board members of United Campus Christian Fellowship (UCCF) that the core purpose of our ecumenical ministry required that the agenda for our work was primarily defined as appropriate engagement and response to controversial issues spawned by the Sixties and Seventies. A foundational conviction for ministries in higher education is that Church and University share a vision and mission related to defining and implementation of views and values that serve "the common good." For instance, the so-called radical student group known as Students for a Democratic Society (SDS) held their weekly meeting in the UCCF Center. That did not mean we agreed or gave blessing to everything

SDS leadership said or did, but we were present and interactive with the leadership of SDS…and we were severely criticized for such involvement.

My approach in describing twenty-two years as ecumenical campus minister at OU is to co-mingle theory and practices, theology and deeds during those years. As grandiose as it may sound, I believe the theological foundation for this ministry, not only at OU, but across the nation, emerged from interpretation and wrestling with the implications of the following quotations:

"Let us make humans in our image, in our likeness, and let them rule over the fish of the sea and the birds of the air, over the livestock, over all the earth, and over the creatures that move along the ground." Genesis 1:26

Imperative: The human species is given rights and responsibility for partnership with God in the stewardship of creation. Both Church and University have missional assignments related to this imperative.

"The Lord said, 'I have seen the misery of my people in Egypt. I have heard them crying out because of their slave drivers and I am concerned about their suffering. ---So, go, I'm sending you to bring the Israelites out of Egypt.'" Exodus 3: 7,10

Imperative: The Judeo-Christian tradition requires that we listen to "The Human Cry!" and respond with compassion to any and all expressions of human suffering. Also, see Matthew 25: 31-45 – *"I tell you the truth, whatever you did for one of the least of these brothers and sisters of mine, you did for me."* The Church's agenda should be determined by sensitivity to and appropriate responses to "the human cry" within our world.

In highlighting the drastic change in perspective from "student work" to the ministry in higher education at the University of Oklahoma we adopted H. Richard Niebuhr's comments as our organizing principle:

Finally, the social responsibility of the Church needs to be described as that of the pioneer. It is the sensitive and responsive part in every society and mankind as a whole. In ethics it (church) is the first to repent for the sins of a society, and it repents on behalf of all. When it became apparent that slavery is transgression of the divine commandment, then the Church repents of it, turns its back upon it, abolishes it within itself. (H. Richard Niebuhr)

This perspective, *the church as social pioneer*, is in sharp contrast to what I describe as "The Fiasco" of post World War II religion in the United States. Here are two questions which help capsule the history of Protestant Christianity in the U.S. following World War II: Who was the most popular and highly respected religious leader in America after 1945 until 1965? What was the essence of his message and mission strategy? His name was Billy Graham. His message was personal salvation exclusively through Jesus and his strategy was mass revivals. I call this era "The Church-ianity Era." The Church as social pioneer is in sharp contrast to the focus on personal salvation and building mega-institutions based on personalities.

The Great War ended in 1945! We were jumping for joy and singing, "When the boys come marching home…Hurrah! Hurrah!" Another song hit

Broadway where Momma asked her husband, "Reuben, I've been thinking, said his wifey dear - Now that all is peaceful and calm, the boys will soon be back on the farm." Reuben starting winking and rubbed his chin. He pulled his chair up close to mother and he asked her with a grin -- "How you gonna keep 'em down on the farm after they've seen Paree? They'll never want to see a rake or plow and who the deuce can parleyvous a cow?" Reuben was correct. The boys came marching home, got married along with those already married and headed for college to learn a new career where the jobs were mostly in the city. Post World War II was the beginning of what we called "urbanization – moving from the farm to the city! They were having babies and going to church!

The chemistry of the urbanization, mass revivals and the church growth movement were at their peak from 1945 to 1965. We couldn't build new churches and expand the old ones fast enough to accommodate the birth rate and urbanization influx to our cities. After 1965 the trends of the previous 20 years slowly turned downward.

I call this era "The Church-ianity Era" because there was a gradual switch in emphasis from "Come, follow Jesus!" to "Come, join the church!" That may not sound like a serious change. But I believe it was a disastrous change. I became convinced that the Church-ianity era was what Soren Kierkegaard called "a crime against Christianity." We had lost focus. Kierkegaard's radical evaluation of the church led him to the conclusion that:

The Christianity of the New Testament simple does not exist. There is nothing to reform; what has to be done is to throw light upon a criminal offense against Christianity, prolonged through the centuries, perpetrated by millions whereby they have cunningly, under the guise of perfecting Christianity, sought little by little to cheat God out of Christianity, and have succeeded in making Christianity exactly the opposite of what it is in the New Testament. (*Attack Upon Christendom*, Beacon Press, p. 32-33)

To summarize the enormous dramatic change in orientation from "student work" to ministry in higher education, the church-ianity movement of post WW II began to run out of gas with younger generations. The balloon burst. By the middle Sixties, the growth pattern started a downward trend. It was the advent of a new breed...a new breed of student on the college campus and a new breed of ministers called campus ministers. I remember that the first book we used in discussion groups in the early Sixties was entitled, "The Noise of Solemn Assemblies" by sociologist, Peter Berger. It was critical of institutional Christianity that held worship at 11 a.m. on Sunday – the most segregated hour of the week!

The Crisis of Conscience

"What is a rebel? A man who says no, but whose refusal does not imply a renunciation. He is also a man who says yes, from the moment of his first gesture of rebellion." Albert Camus, *The Rebel*

How can we explain what brought about the rebellion and protests on college campuses in "The Sixties?" It seems to me that the roots of the issues of the Sixties were evident in the birth of our nation. Historically, unresolved conflicts, lingering hatred, fears, anger and guilt mixed together in the cauldron of our political, economic, religious and educational institutions again came to the boiling point.

Living in greatest nation in the world seems to require that *we repress and try hard to ignore the atrocities in our history* -- atrocities against Native Americans and African slaves. Repressing these atrocities requires that we practice self-deceit. George Orwell observed that "during times of universal deceit, telling the truth becomes a revolutionary act!" Forces had been at work within our society that triggered what might be called "an existential crisis" in our national psyche….a moment in which we were rudely forced to examine who we are and ask questions about where we're headed; as if we were engaged in a mid-life crisis. It was a look in the rear-view mirror and what we saw was a very confusing mixture of progress and failure. We had failed miserably, especially in keeping the promise of the Constitution that promised life, liberty and justice for all. We have proudly held up the vision expressed by the statue of Liberty:

> *Give me your tired, your poor;*
> *your huddled masses yearning to breath free..*
> *The wretched refuse of your teeming shore;*
> *Send these, the homeless, temptest tos't to me .*
> *I lift my lamp beside the golden door.*

Yet, we were continually reminded of those atrocities in our past, not yet resolved. Slave ships from Africa! Brutality! Klu Klux Klan! A Civil War that ended slavery, but the racism became institutionalized in segregation. Then in the Fifties, youth were leading sit-ins at lunch counters in Oklahoma City, a bus strike in Montgomery, Freedom riders found murdered, Bull Conner with his dogs and police knocking people down with fire hoses, five children killed in Birmingham church bombing.

Then came "that war!" Vietnam! Let's remember the warning issued by the former General and former President, Dwight Eisenhower (a Republican!), whose farewell speech in 1961 warned us of the danger of the military-industrial complex following World War II:

This conjunction of an immense military establishment and a large arms industry is new in the American experience. The total influence –

economic, political, even spiritual – is felt in every city, every State house, every office of the Federal government. Our toil, resources and livelihood are all involved; so is the very structure of our society...the free university, historically the fountainhead of free ideas and scientific discovery, has experienced a revolution in the conduct of research. Partly because of the huge costs involved, a government contract becomes virtually a substitute for intellectual curiosity. The prospect of domination of the nation's scholars by Federal employment, project allocations, and the power of money is ever present and is gravely to be regarded. (*Public Paper of the Presidents,* Dwight E. Eisenhower, 1960, p.1035-1040)

Eisenhower's warning anticipated the seduction and gullibility of the American public. We would do well to remember what happens to a nation filled with wine that makes us drunk with belief in what has been called our "Manifest Destiny." In 1900 Senator Albert Beveridge of Indiana, who later won a Pulitzer Prize, presented the reasons why the United States was justified, even obligated, to invade the Philippines and beyond:

God has not been preparing the English speaking and Teutonic peoples for a thousand years for nothing but vain and idle self-contemplation and self admiration. No! He has made us the master organizers of the world to establish system where chaos reigns. He has given us the spirit of progress to overwhelm the forces of reaction throughout the earth. He has made us adept in government that we may administer government among savage and senile peoples. Were it not for such a force as this the world would relapse into barbarism and night...This is the divine mission of America, and it holds for us all the profit, all the glory, all the happiness possible to man. We are trustees of the world's progress, guardians of its righteous people. The judgment of the Master is upon us: 'Ye have been faithful over a few things; I will make you ruler over many things. (*Endgame,* vol. 1; Derrick Jensen, Seven Stories Press, 2006, p. 221)

Two US ships were fired upon in the Gulf of Tonkin in August, 1964. Congress, in the spirit of our Manifest Destiny, gave authority to the President to send in the troops. To build sufficient military forces to fight this war required drafting young men. As the draft escalated so did the opposition to the draft. Opponents to the war began the chant –"Hell no! We won't go!"

With parades of people chanting "Hell no! We won't go!" and others singing "Ain't Nobody Goin' to Turn Me 'Round" and "I Shall Not Be Moved!" the "Establishment" replied, "America: Love it or Leave it." The nation was seriously divided! Which meant the churches were divided! Which meant the university campus became a battle ground. We were caught in the crisis of conscience!

- Covenant Study Groups. We held study/discussion groups that met weekly for 4-6 weeks, including biblical and theological studies.
- Mission trips to southwest Oklahoma. We worked with Hispanic migrant workers picking cotton four-five weekends each fall in a cooperative program with local churches in southwest Oklahoma; this included considerable involvement with Catholic representatives.
- Civil Rights Movement. One of my most memorable experiences was the role four campus ministers had in response to "The 19 Demands" presented to the University President, Herbert Hollomon by the Black Student Union on March 9, 1969 at the height of the Civil Rights Movement. Holloman's public posture was, "I will not respond to anyone's "demands!" But secretly he did respond.

Credit Don Scruggs as the one who suggested that we, four campus ministers, offer President Hollomon and Sterlin Adams, a graduate student and leader of the Black Student Union, our "good office." We had developed friendly relationships with both the Administration and leaders of the Black Student Movement. They accepted our invitation to meet in secret meetings in the UCCF Center, and we negotiated a few guidelines to be mutually respected in their discussions. We agreed to intervene only if the conversation became hostile.

Many of the participants in those discussions are deceased. I tell the story because it is an illustration of campus ministry that transcends "student work," and focuses on what's best for the university and best for our world. It is a real source of inner satisfaction to focus on what I consider to be a significant example and contribution made by United Ministries in Higher Education. In his book, *Race and the University* (University of Oklahoma Press, 2010), Dr. George Henderson, goes through each of the 19 Demands and documents positive responses made by the University to the Black Demands. Dr. Henderson was the third full time African American professor at OU, and the first Black family to own property in Norman.

- Project '68. It was commonplace for some students to engage in mission projects in the summer months. With encouragement from Scruggs, I made a proposal to our Board that I raise the funds and recruit students for Project '68, a summer service project in the inner city of Oklahoma City. I found an old deserted three story "mansion" and made a deal with the owner to rent it for three months. The house was surrounded by Black neighbors who welcomed us. I recruited 11 students to live with our family, when our three children were ages 8, 6 and 2. The day our participants moved into 'the Mansion' was the day Robert Kennedy was killed in California. Students were engaged in working in neighborhood recreation programs, voter registration, and assisting in churches' vacation bible schools. I was able to recruit only one Black student so we were highly visible as the only Whites in the neighborhood. Friendships among the students and with our neighbors had enduring meaning.

• The Eschaton Coffee House, which met at the United Methodist Wesley Foundation, was a focal point gathering place on weekends. Jim Shields and his associates, Cathy Carson and Clay Ballard, gave creative leadership that held lively conversations in an informal environment.

• Draft Counseling. Staying in school with passing grades was one way of avoiding being drafted and sent to Vietnam. Also, receiving standing as a Conscientious Objector (CO) required engagement in community service, but prevented being drafted. I went through extensive training to learn all the classifications and procedures related to the Draft. It was quite common to have requests for draft consultations from at least two young men each day for two or three years.

• Students for a Democratic Society held their weekly meetings in the UCCF Center. I mentioned this earlier, but want to comment on the significance of having SDS meetings in our Center. I well remember Mokey Webb, a lay leader in First Christian Church, who attended meetings of SDS. First he came to observe what really happened in their meetings, which was intriguing to say the least. He continued attending and I highly respect the voice that he became for our ministry. Mokey told critics of SDS meeting in our Center, "They have a right to think and express their views. We, as church, have a responsibility to defend their rights!"

Approximately eight years after SDS met in UCCF Center, an article appeared in the *Norman Transcript* (daily newspaper) interviewing a young man running as a candidate for the Norman City Council. He confessed that he had been active in SDS...*as a paid informant of the FBI*. I readily recognized his picture and name as a leader in SDS who was the most vocal person in wanting to escalate protests to the point of violence!

• The Gay Student Alliance. Within the first month of William (Bill) Banowsky's arrival as President of the University, he issued a ruling that the Gay Student Alliance would not be recognized as an official student organization. This prompted four campus ministers to submit a letter to the editor of *Norman Transcript* stating that we were disturbed and strongly disagreed with Banowsky's decision. We stated our belief that students who were members of the Gay Student Alliance should have all the rights to organize as other students on campus had. I had three quick responses to this letter to the editor. One, President Banowsky called to invite me and others signing the letter for a visit in his office -- "tomorrow." Second, I received an anonymous letter in the mail threatening my life! Third, information about the letter made it all the way to the village that raised me, igniting my father and an elder in the church who laid hands on my head at my ordination to jointly sign a letter that said I had lost my right to be called a minister in the Christian church!

So, I made friends with five or six gay students who agreed to be on a panel I moderated. The panel received invitations from a few churches who invited them to tell their story.

• Values Clarification Seminars. On a less controversial subject, I became very interested in a book entitled, *Values Clarification* by Sidney Simon and Howard Kirchenbaum (Hart Publishing Co., 1972). It was written to help public school teachers engage students in clarification of their values, being careful not to impose the teachers' values on students. Each spring I offered a Friday evening and Saturday morning seminar on a couple of weekends. I put publicity about the seminar in the College of Education where friends on the faculty encouraged their students to attend. I was asked to facilitate the seminar as part of a continuing education program within the Oklahoma City Public Schools.

My last story is one of my favorites. The UCCF center had a parking lot for about 18 cars. Monitoring the parking lot to prevent "poachers" from parking was a nightmare task. When a "violator" parked, we put a notice on the windshield: "This is your one and only warning. Next time, we will have police impound your car." One coed with a new black Buick continued to park, so I parked my car directly behind hers. There was no way for her to leave until I moved my car. The Center door opened and a voice yelled, "Whoever is parked behind me needs to move their car!

I replied, "Come in! Please be seated! Now watch while I call the police to have your car towed!" She said, "You touch that car and I'll call my Daddy!" I said, "Give me your Daddy's phone number and I'll call him!" She calmed down, and I moved my car.

About three years later, during a break in the values clarification seminar, a participant came to me and said, "You won't remember me, but when I was a freshman I parked in your parking lot..." I interrupted her and said, "And you drove a new black Buick!" She laughed! "You do remember! I want to apologize to you. I can't believe how arrogant and rude I was!" I offered my hand to receive her apology and she opened her arms requesting a hug! We had clarified our values!

Don Gibson is living in Oklahoma City. After retiring in 1998 and receiving certification with the national Interim Ministry Network, he spent 13 years as Interim Minister with Disciples of Christ congregations in Oklahoma. Now retired again, he says, "I'm busy with house repairs, writing, and in cursing the Republicans/Baptists who control Oklahoma."

My Life Work 1961-2003
By Delton Pickering

From my first appointment in ministry as an associate pastor at a church in Metarie, Louisiana, throughout my career in higher education and ministry, on through to my retirement from pastoring a church on the southern fringe of California's San Fernando Valley, faith and social justice have been inextricably linked.

1960-1961: Associate Pastor, Munholland Memorial United Methodist Church (UMC), Metarie, LA

1960 was the year that public schools in New Orleans were integrated. They picked on elementary school to start the process, and the only white person who chose to keep his child in the "integrated" school was my friend Andy Foreman, Pastor a UMC in the French Quarter on Rampart Street. He and his wife got a great deal of attention, along with death threats, etc. So several of us took turns driving him and his daughter to and from school and putting the family up in our homes. Each day we would have to run the gamut of rock-tossing, spitting white parents, often with infants in their arms, lining the street near the entrance to the school. It eventually died down, but my involvement got me the reputation of a "communist" and other unmentionables. Even the secretary at my church referred to me a a "card-carrying member of the Communist Party." However, most of the UMC hierarchy was on Andy's side, so I was still considered an "up and coming" young minister.

1961-1971: Director of the Wesley Foundation (UMC Campus Ministry) at Louisiana State University (LSU), Baton Rouge, LA

Toward the end of my year at Munholland Memorial UMC in Metarie, my bishop asked me if I would consider going to LSU as Campus Minister. In the back of my mind in those days it was only a matter of time before I went back to graduate school for a doctorate, with the aim of teaching religion on the college level; so a year of two on a college campus didn't seem so bad. But I got roped in in at least two ways: (1) I genuinely liked the work, and (2) I inherited a building program for a new UMC Student Center (Wesley Foundation). The ministry was then located in a simple, frame Army surplus building just behind fraternity row, and the expectation was that I would raise funds and design and erect a new building. This I accomplished in about five years, and I stayed on to enjoy five more. However, social justice issues were calling, especially on a big campus like LSU in Baton Rouge (the largest in the state).

First there was the free speech movement (remember Berkeley and Columbia?) The Louisiana legislature passed a law forbidding any Communist or Marxist speaker on a public college campus, under threat of the withdrawal of state funds. A group of students banded together on the grounds of academic freedom, and they asked me to be their advisor. We invited the First Secretary of the Soviet delegation to the United Nations to come and speak at LSU. He accepted, and it made the local press big time.

At first, LSU officials agreed that this ambassador could speak in the LSU Union; but under political pressure, they changed their minds and cancelled the speech. We decided to hold the event off campus, and it got a great deal of attention — and the university got a black eye for reneging on its agreement. We kept pressuring the university with other "offensive" speakers and, eventually, they caved in, and the issue was settled in the way you would expect an institution devoted to academic freedom to settle it. Needless to say, my reputation with conservatives was "in the toilet."

Then came the Vietnam War era.... Somehow I got roped into being the regional treasurer for the Vietnam Moratorium Committee, and our Wesley Foundation students offered the committee meeting space in our new building. I was not alone among the college chaplains in that involvement: Roman Catholic, Episcopal, Lutheran, and Presbyterian chaplains were also involved. We had a very successful Vietnam Moratorium Day on campus with thousands in attendance and nationally known speakers. But best of all, we had no violence, no burning buildings, and no arrests. Many said that was because of the close involvement of the campus ministers.

In the spring of 1971 I was selected to be the Louisiana Delegate to a *Citizens Conference on Ending the Way in Indochina.* There was one delegate from each state. We had a three day briefing at the United Nations and then flew to Paris for meetings with all of the parties to the Paris Peace Talks. The delegate from Colorado was the folk singer Judy Collins. We sat together on the plane. Interestingly enough, we observed that our every move in Paris was being filmed openly, and two years later every one of us was audited by the IRS. Upon returning to Baton Rouge, I accepted a lot of speaking engagements calling for the end of the war. Again, the conservatives were outraged.

At that time, I was also getting involved in civil liberties issues, having joined the Baton Rouge Chapter of the American Civil Liberties Union (ACLU). A very influential Methodist layman (Vice President of the Ethyl Corporation) wrote to my bishop, complaining of my activities. He suggested that if I really wanted to have an "influence for good" on the campus, I should protest the films that were being shown at the Varsity Theater, near the gates of the campus. The theater had late night showings of Russ Meyer-type films (*very soft* porn). What this distinguished gentleman didn't know was that every film shown at the Varsity had first received the imprimatur of three of us chaplains. The owner of the Varsity invited the three of us, along with an English professor, to preview every movie before he booked it, so that we could pass judgment on whether or not the movie had any "redeeming social value" (the then-current Supreme Court of the United States' standard as to whether or not material was pornographic). Fortunately, I don't think this activity made into the bishop's file!

I was involved in numerous other activities during my tenure at LSU, but the most disturbing to UMC officials was my allowing a Black student group, which had been accused of trying to assassinate the Mayor of Baton Rouge, to meet in the Wesley Foundation building. I personally knew most of the students involved and knew that the charges were bogus; but since the Mayor was a member of a local UMC, my involvement (even just the use of a room for meeting) was anathema to the bishop. He called me in for a consultation and gave me a year to find another position. That's how I wound up leaving LSU and Louisiana, my home state, in June 1971. By the way, the charges against the Black students were dismissed after being shown to be the result of perjured statements by racist Deputy Sheriffs of Baton Rouge Parish.

I was blessed with a very cooperative governing board of the Wesley Foundation at LSU. They genuinely believed that a campus minister's work would be enhanced by experiences abroad. So they allowed me to take three summers off for that purpose:

1964: I directed a student project in a rural community of the State of Puebla, Mexico. I was accompanied by 15 students, both undergraduate and graduate. We lived in extremely primitive conditions. For example, our quarters had to be fumigated weekly for tarantulas, and our alarm clock each morning was a burro that stuck his head through an open window and *brayed* over us. We had no running water, of course, and upon arrival had to build our only toilet. Our shower was improvised with a barrel on the roof that we filled each morning after dropping buckets into a mountain trench for water. We heated the water by burning corn husks. All in all, however, it was an enlightening experience. We grew close to the folks in the small village, and at the end of the summer we had to endure 15 mole (a dark gravy) banquets in the last week or so.

1968: I was supposed to go to South Africa at the invitation of that country's University Christian Movement, along with a group of other campus ministers. We had an orientation at the UN in New York City; but in those days of apartheid, the South African government refused to give us visas. So, after waiting a couple of weeks past our original departure date, we gave up. The week-long UN orientation, however, raised my consciousness considerably about what was going on in South Africa. Interestingly, the South Africa University Christian Movement became a banned organization that summer; so we would have been kicked out of the country, anyway.

Since I already had the summer off, I decided to do what I had always wanted to do and take a grand tour of Europe. It was *grand*, if you count using my *Eurailpass* to sleep on trains during overnight trips to avoid hotel or hostel expenses that I couldn't afford. I visited almost all of the Western European countries that way, including my favorite city, West Berlin. I happened to be in

West Germany when the Russians invaded Czechoslovakia. Many Czech students fled to West Germany. Most of them spoke English, not German, so I volunteered to help resettle them. That's how I spent my last couple of weeks in Europe.

1969: I was asked to direct a student study tour to Japan, Korea, and India. One of the highlights of that trip was a two hour audience with Prime Minister Indira Ghandi in India. She was very gracious to our group and extended our visit by an hour and half beyond our scheduled time. We were in Seoul, Korea, when the United States landed a man on the moon. I vividly remember watching the landing on a huge screen in a public square with thousands of others.

1971-1976: Director of the Wesley Foundation at Memphis State University (MSU), Memphis, TN

Of all the places I've lived and served, Memphis was probably the least satisfactory and most disappointing. For one thing, I went there under the false pretenses of the campus ministry leadership. Memphis State (now the University of Memphis) was a large, urban university of some 30,000 students, 90 percent of whom were commuters. At that time in my life, I was interested in pioneering what I called "urban campus ministry," by which I meant tapping the resources of both the church and the university in behalf of human needs in the urban community. So the situation at MSU promised to be a good fit. When I was invited to two interviews with the governing board of the MSU Wesley Foundation, I made my interest very clear. The board, in turn, seemed excited about my ideas and offered me the job, even though a local UMC pastor had also been interviewed and was thought by some to be a "shoo-in" for the position.

Not long after I arrived, the man on the board most responsible for advocating for my hiring left to become president of another college. He was succeeded on the board by a somewhat conservative law professor who did not buy into my vision of campus ministry. Furthermore, I found out later that the UMC Conference Committee that evaluated the campus ministry program was upset that an "outsider" had been hired instead of the local pastor. Well, you can see where this was going... I had several strikes against me from the early days of my tenure at MSU. Despite all of that, I was able to accomplish some innovative and useful programs while in Memphis, such as:

The development of a Women's Center — I applied to the national UMC for funding of a two year intern and was assigned a very bright, articulate and energetic young woman who had just graduated from the University of Virginia. In the meantime, a group of professional women in Memphis had been working on the concept of a women's center which would advocate for the needs of women throughout the city. However, they had no funds for staffing and no place for housing their center. Since my new intern was a strong feminist, with her approval, I offered to allow her to spend half of her time to staff the women's center. I also arranged for a centrally located UMC to donate space for offices and a meeting room. It all worked out very well. The center got off the ground, developed some good programs (including feminist art shows), and eventually had enough resources to hire its own staff.

Death and Dying in the Curriculum of the University — The Roman Catholic chaplain and I saw a need for a course on Death and Dying in the MSU curriculum. Elizabeth Kubler Ross's book, "On Death and Dying," was currently a bestseller, and the time seemed ripe. We approached MSU requesting that we be allowed to organize such a course, and the university agreed that we could do it in the continuing education division. We thought we'd have around 15-20 students, but the first night of class over 200 showed up! We had to move the class from a seminar room to an auditorium. We had invited a number of guest lecturers, including a local physician who had authored the American Medical Association's (AMA) definition of "brain death," a nurse practitioner who had spent her career in hospice care, lawyers, theologians, and social workers, among others. The course was a great success and so popular that the university picked it up for its regular, credited curriculum in the next academic year.

Veterans Advocacy Project — While I had been a vociferous opponent of the Vietnam War, I also developed a concern for the plight of Vietnam veterans. I conceived the idea of a *Veterans Advocacy Project* for Memphis. I hosted a luncheon in our Wesley Foundation building and invited all of the veterans affairs staffers from the various campuses in the metropolitan area, along with representatives from the Mayor's office, the U.S. Department of Veterans Affairs (VA), the Chamber of Commerce, etc. At the initial meeting, we discovered that those folks had never met together before and seldom communicated with each other. Yet, they all worked to serve military service veterans. The group decided to continue to meet and to cooperate on several projects. One project was the development of a discharge upgrade program. We trained volunteers to be counselors in assisting vets to have their other-than-honorable discharges upgraded to honorable, thereby making them eligible for medical and educational benefits from the U.S. government. The project was still going when I left Memphis.

American Civil Liberties Union (ACLU) — I was a member of the board of the local ACLU that held its monthly meetings in the Wesley Foundation building. Eventually, I was elected President. By tradition, since we had no staff, the ACLU telephone was located in the office of the President. I had the phone installed on my desk so that I — and I alone — would answer it. You cannot imagine the forlorn calls I received, most of which the ACLU could not respond to since the complaint did not involve any action by the government. Eventually, I was elected President of the Tennessee State ACLU, also. One of my first actions in that role was to get the state board to approve moving their office from Knoxville to Memphis, the state's largest city. We hired our first full time Executive Director (a young man who had been a parole officer and knew the legal system firsthand) and set up an office in a downtown high-rise near the court houses. We had a battery of volunteer lawyers across the state, so we were able to respond to genuine and egregious concerns in effective ways. Needless to say, my heavy involvement in an organization that favored abortion rights, opposed religious education in public schools, and opposed reciting "The Lord's Prayer" at government-sponsored events, did not stand me in the good graces of the church.

The *coup de grace* came when I attended a national ACLU board meeting in New York City where the ACLU became the first national organization to call for the Impeachment of President Richard M. Nixon. I returned to Memphis on a Saturday to fulfill a long-standing Sunday morning commitment to speak at the Memphis Unitarian Fellowship, which just happened to rent meeting space in the Wesley Foundation. I had planned to be very low key about the call for Nixon's Impeachment, knowing how the idea would play in conservative Memphis. But when I arrived for my engagement, the TV cameras were already in place. I had no choice but to explain to the public why the ACLU had taken its action. This, of course, resulted in many calls and letters to church officials asking why the UMC was calling for the Impeachment of a great President, and why, oh why, was a non-Christian group being allowed to meet in the Methodist Student Center at MSU? I saw the "handwriting on the wall," and at the next meeting of our board, I submitted my resignation — before I could be fired.

I had no job when I resigned, so I requested and received a sabbatical leave from the ministry of the UMC. About that time, the guy I had hired as ACLU Executive Director began suffering burn-out from his 12 hour long days on that job. So I secured positions for both him and his wife at a UMC facility for youth offenders in Kentucky and took over from him as Acting Executive Director of the Tennessee State ACLU. It was an interesting five months and provided me with a complete break from "church work."

One of the most exciting things I did was the development of a project on *Privacy in a Democratic Society* that was funded by a grant from the Tennessee Committee on the Humanities. It was a week long event held at a Presbyterian college campus, featuring a number of seminars and lectures by well-known persons in the field of privacy and related issues. While the project was underway, word got out that the Memphis Police Dept. had been spying on citizens for political — not criminal — reasons. It was revealed that the department had a whole room of files detailing their long-running spy program. We were afraid that the glare of publicity might lead them to dispose of the files, so we got a federal court order mandating that they be secured. Our chief lawyer rushed over to police headquarters with the court order, but it was too late. They had torched all of the files the previous night. The press was all over the story, and it resulted in a much bigger attendance at our event that we expected. Ultimately, it resulted in the termination of the police chief and the failure of the mayor to get re-elected.

1976-1988: Executive Director, Ecumenical Campus Ministry (ECM), Baltimore, MD

In the fall of 1976 I got an invitation to apply for a campus ministry position in Baltimore with Ecumenical Campus Ministry, Inc., an organization that sponsored campus ministries in Maryland and Washington, D.C. After interviews I was offered the position of Executive Director of ECM. I moved to Baltimore the day after Jimmy Carter's election as President in 1976. ECM was supported by the United Methodists, Presbyterians, Episcopalians, Roman Catholics, and United Church of Christ. It was an interesting period in that I spent most of time reporting to and seeking funding from those judicatories. After I'd been there a year, the United Methodists in the region (the Baltimore Conference) created a position that would give oversight to all of their campus ministries in Maryland, the District of Columbia, and a part of West Virginia. The UMC asked me to write the job description for the new position, so I wrote the best I could muster, having no interest in the job for myself. But the UMC bishop of the area decided that he wanted me to fill the job, and after a little arm-twisting, I accepted. In actuality, I subsumed the ECM position into the new one, so that I became supervisor of both the UCM and ECM campus ministries, a position I held until mid-1988.

Working in the Mid-Atlantic region of the country was much less stressful for me than I had experienced in the South. For one thing, church people in the area were much more liberal and progressive. The more active one was in working for social justice, the better. I continued my association with the ACLU, having become a member of the Maryland State ACLU Board of Directors, and later, a member of the National ACLU Development Council (many trips to NYC). I also became President of my professional association, the National Campus Ministry Association, and chair of the UMC National Campus Ministry Committee (many trips to Nashville). I served on the governing boards of two colleges, also (St. Mary's College and Seminary in Baltimore and Morristown College in Tennessee, an historically Black college). I chaired the Maryland Interfaith Legislative Committee (working to impact the State Assembly on behalf of human needs in the state). And I was asked to design and teach a course on ministry in higher education at UMC related Wesley Theological Seminary in Washington, D.C. All in all I kept pretty busy during those years in Baltimore.

After the AIDS epidemic hit the nation, I became very involved in ministry with persons living with AIDS. I was one of the founders of the AIDS Interfaith Network of Baltimore, the purpose of which was to enlighten church folks, in particular, and the public, in general, about the real nature of HIV/AIDS and to dispel superstitions, falsities, and other misconceptions prevalent at the time. I also co-founded the AIDS Interfaith Housing Project that provided housing with dictician and nursing support for persons with AIDS, especially those who were far along in the disease. Those efforts took a lot of my time, but my "bosses" were pleased that I was doing it. So there was practically no flack.

After about ten years, the UMC in the Mid-Atlantic Area decided to redesign their regional staff. As a result, the campus ministry position was eliminated, along with a number of others. My choices were to accept an appointment to a parish or to find another job. After so many years out of parish ministry, I wasn't anxious to be sent to a church I knew nothing about; so I started searching. Friends I had worked with in national campus ministry groups put my name in the hopper for a position supervising UMC campus ministries in the California-Pacific Conference that encompassed Southern California, Hawaii, Guam, and the Northern Marianas. I got the job.

1988-2003: Council on Ministries of the California-Pacific Conference, UMC, Pasadena, CA

I moved to the Los Angeles area in early August, 1988, to be on the staff of UMC regional conference. My focus was to be on campus ministry, but a number of other areas of ministry were added to my portfolio. That went smoothly for a number of months until December, when the bishop decided to move my boss to another position. That left the top staff position in the conference vacant, and I was urged to apply. I did, and I was offered the position of Director of the Conference Council on Ministries — a role I filled for the next six years. The Council included 16 in-house staff persons, plus about 25 out in the field. So, personnel management quickly became one of my time-consuming tasks. The other was travel. Since our region included Southern California, Hawaii, Guam, and the Northern Marianna Islands, my job called for me to attend meetings throughout the region (although, in truth, I only went to Hawaii every couple of months and to Guam and the Mariannas only once each). Also, my position put me on a number of regional and national committees that required travel across the country. It seemed like I was boarding a plane every other week or so — and sometimes, I was.

My social justice involvements had to be somewhat limited because of my hectic schedule. I was elected President of the Southern California Ecumenical Council and served on the Board of Directors of the California Council of Churches. Both groups focused on the needs of the poor and dispossessed and pressured governmental bodies to pass laws and regulations that would help, not harm, the poor, including immigrants. (California had and has a huge immigrant population.)

The Northridge earthquake occurred while I was in Galveston, Texas, attending the annual meeting of the Association of Conference Council Directors (my peers in the UMC), of which I was President at the time. Of course, I had to rush back, and I spent much of the rest of the year working on relief in the Los Angeles Metropolitan Area and coordinating UMC efforts.

As it turned out, there was a six year term for my Council Director position. So, at the end of it in 1995, not ready to retire and not wanting to pack up and move again (I loved living in Pasadena and still do), I allowed my name to be placed in consideration for a pastorate within commuting distance of my Pasadena home. After rejecting several appointments, I accepted the offer of Sherman Oaks UMC. Sherman Oaks was a smaller congregation in Sherman Oaks, CA, an upscale community, just over the hills from Beverly Hills, and on the southern fringe of the San Fernando Valley. I was a little anxious about the appointment, since I had never been a local church pastor and certainly wasn't used to writing weekly sermons; but I was well-received by the congregation, and after a while, the preparation of sermons became routine.

My sermons were generally well received, and some even elicited applause! The church badly needed attention to its organizational structure, its budgeting process, and its governance process. All of those needs played to my strengths. It took several years, but eventually we got everything reorganized into a more efficient operation. I stayed on past my 65th birthday (traditional retirement age in the UMC), but finally decided to retire at 67. My eight year tenure became the longest in the church's 55 year history. I had a wonderful send-off and continue to look back fondly upon my one and only pastorate.

Since retirement, I've continued to stay active in several organizations, most importantly as a member of the Board of Directors of Scarritt-Bennett Center in Nashville, Tennessee, for over ten years. The Center focuses on justice and anti-racism issues, as well as women's concerns.

My personal health has limited my involvement in the past two years, but I look back with satisfaction on the work I've done and with appreciation for the many gifted and dedicated people with whom I have associated.

I've generally enjoyed retirement since 2003. I travel as am able, finished reading all 100 of the Modern Library's "100 best novels in English of the 20th Century," and spend most of my time attending to health issues: every Tuesday, Thursday, and Saturday I'm on dialysis for 4 hours, and every Monday, Wednesday, and Friday I go to cardiac rehab at a nearby hospital. God is great and life is good!

What Fallout From the In-between?
By Wayne Bryan

Well. . . it began when my phone rang in the Fall of 1961 and my friend Pat said, "I thought you would like to know that the Pastoral Search Committee here in Nacogdoches has your name on their list... and I, for one, am encouraging them to choose you!"

"Oh, tell them to forget it." I replied. "I'm very happy where I am. Besides I've been here for less than three years. And the other thing is that I don't have any desire to live in East Texas."

Four months later I was installed as the Pastor of Westminster Presbyterian Church in Nacogdoches, Texas and Pat was the church secretary. We were quite a pair!

And. . . it ended in the late Fall of 1989 when Mimi and I packed our car and preceded the moving van on its trip from Austin, Texas eastward to Columbia, South Carolina. Or, I guess to be really truthful, it ended several months earlier when my supportive board members in United Campus Ministry of Austin counseled kindly with me to say that we were not going to have enough money to continue our enterprise and they would advise me to start looking for a new job.

A geographer and an historian surveying the "in-between" of that beginning and that ending would present extremely different reports.

The geographer would survey what appeared to be relevant street addresses and discover no evidence of campus ministry programs in Nacogdoches, Texas; Des Moines, Iowa; Gainesville, Florida; and Austin, Texas with my name attached. The easy conclusion would be that, if they ever existed, they are all gone. Vanished. Closed. And such is the truth!

The historian would search differently, probing the "files of impact, the venues of effect" in the lives of people now scattered around the world, and say something dramatic, like: "Oh, my!"

I can't do anything about the elements of the geographer's report. But I can speak some words about what the historian discovered. So let's talk about the pieces of the in-between.

1962-1966 Stephen F. Austin State University, Nacogdoches, Texas

When I arrived in Nacogdoches it was to be the pastor of Westminster Presbyterian Church. There was no history of ministry in relation to SFASU except an occasional faculty member or student who came to worship. But I did not allow this vacuum to continue. Within a very few weeks, I was "hanging out" at the student union and the faculty club. I had arrived in March and by the beginning of the Fall Semester of 1962 enough contacts had been made that I started a Sunday School Class for students. And shortly after that I had put posters out on campus for United Campus Christian Fellowship which was organized and meeting on Sunday evenings for dinner, study, and fellowship.

Quick fall-outs from this were students appearing for worship services and volunteering to be part of our music program. And, as one might expect, my office at the church (and the tables in the Student Union on campus) became the site of counseling and advising for students.

This relationship with students on campus (in classes for which I enrolled) and at the church was pretty well matched with similar experiences with faculty and staff. In the faculty club and in private homes where we were frequent guests, my pastoral relationships and personal friendships expanded.

For the last two years I was in Nacogdoches, the campus ministry also included *The Exit*, a coffee house which we organized for Friday nights using the fellowship hall at the church. This program drew lots of students and faculty who were not participants in UCCF or in the worship and congregational life of the church. Some of my best relationships with students were those I developed at *The Exit*.

And remember, I was still full-time pastor of the church, director of my Presbytery's camp and conference program, and writing Sunday School curriculum for our national church to be used all across the country.

All of this continued at a healthy pace until I took the next step of filing my vita with United Ministries in Higher Education. In the summer of 1966 there was that second phone call! This time the call was not from a friend but from the chairman of the board of United Campus Christian Ministry at Drake University. The move came in October!

1966-1975 Drake University, Des Moines, Iowa

The Iowa United Campus Christian Ministries Commission (later named the Iowa Commission for United Ministries in Higher Education) was the parent organization for ministries at the University of Iowa, Iowa State University, the University of Northern Iowa, and Drake University. It was the joint ministry of the Presbyterians, Christian Church (Disciples of Christ), United Church of Christ, American Baptists, and Church of the Brethren. That state commission employed the staff for the four universities and provided the funding as contributed by the five statewide denominational judicatories. There were a total of nine staff members when I began.

In my position at Drake, the diversity of the job and the breadth of personal interests were as broad as in my previous positions. A local board, as the representative of the state agency, oversaw and directed the ministry. The basic part of the job was teaching short term courses on issues related to the emphases of the local board, counseling students, directing worship, publishing a newspaper related to the religious and social issues of our concern, developing personal and professional relationships with faculty and staff, and managing all the structures of the board, the student association, finances, and communications.

Much of that sounds like a list which almost every campus minister would make about his/her job. What I think I will do is to point to some of the unique tasks, opportunities, and responsibilities of those nine years. I will try to keep this as short as possible:

• Serving as a liaison to the Office of the Vice-President for Student Affairs, nourishing the great working relationship between Student Affairs and campus ministry. Much later, in 2010, Dr. Donald Adams, our VP for Student Affairs, said to me in an email: *You were the one, along with Nick, Harold (*campus ministers*) who made my first year much better than it would have been without you!! You were an important colleague.* (After naming about ten students, all who were active in our ministry and student leaders on campus) he ended his note with: *"A great group of people, a wonderful time for all of us to be together at Drake in the late 60's and early 70's. Thanks so much for keeping in touch.*

• Organizing and leading semester long study groups (generally called "Covenant Communities") for students on a variety of topics which included contemporary theological issues, cultural issues, human sexuality, the nature of the human, creative educational designs, etc.

• Sharing management of the Coffee House (named "The Cellar") with the United Methodist campus minister with whom we also shared a building. This had a number of purposes – social gathering, venue for displaying musical and artistic talents, discussing social justice issues, outreach to recruit participants in other parts of the campus ministry program.

• Participating in unique counseling assignments including draft counseling and problem pregnancy counseling (this latter was in a national organization affiliated with Planned Parenthood).

• Producing arts weeks at the ministry center for three or four years. This featured student art from Drake and other Iowa colleges/universities as well as art produced by people in the community.

• Serving as a strong force for the university in the lives of its freshmen. This included creating and leading a simulation named "Freshman Year" and a slide show introducing the Office of Student Affairs, both of which opened the university's Freshman Orientation Summer Program for 4 years (and the simulation was published and used by more than 100 other universities); and creating and directing "Freshman? Freshman!", a semester-long orientation and support program in which about 50% of the freshman class participated and which had a dramatic impact on student retention.

• Serving as an adjunct faculty to college of education on creative teaching. I began an independent company called: "The Creative Educator" where I wrote and published a whole series of simulation games.

- Writing and publishing articles, reports, interpretation, etc. on campus ministry programs, structure, and governance for the national publications of United Ministry in Higher Education.
- Creating teams of students who interpreted student activism and campus unrest at presentations before church groups, civic clubs, etc. and developing the "40-Hour Weekend Program" introducing the public at large to college life and issues of the 60's and 70's. These developed many good community relationships for campus ministry.
- Acting as a resource on leadership and service to Pan-Hellenic and the Inter-Fraternity Council. Their generous response was electing me to Gamma Gamma (the Greek national honorary fraternity).
- Speaking in local churches and national conferences on the role, purpose, and content of campus ministry and serving (very often) as a visiting preacher in churches around the state.
- Attending Presbyterian General Assembly (the national governing body) meeting in Omaha where I chaired the Family Life committee.
- Continuing to write Sunday School curriculum for the national Presbyterian Office of Education for use in congregations around the country.
- Serving in the summer of 1969 as director of a 40-student summer staff at Ghost Ranch (a national Presbyterian conference center) in New Mexico.
- Hosting, in 1975, a national conference on community college ministry under the auspices of United Ministries in Higher Education. The major agenda was a 2-day long simulation which I had created.
- Accepting the position as State Executive for Iowa UMHE, overseeing a 2-year restructure of Iowa UMHE and its four Centers – Drake, Iowa State, University of Iowa, and University of Northern Iowa. This was a part time assignment while my regular ministry at Drake continued.

And . . . it was in this period of restructure (and reduction of the Iowa UMHE staff from 9 to 5) that I looked around and, although I was encouraged to stay on at Drake, accepted the call to become the campus minister at the Disciples-Presbyterian Center at the University of Florida.

1975-78 University of Florida and Santa Fe Community College, Gainesville, Florida

This was a different world!

The Disciples-Presbyterian Center was a cooperative ministry of the United Presbyterian Church U.S.A., the Presbyterian Church U.S., and the Christian Church (Disciples of Christ). It was housed in a building which it owned across the street from the College of Business and between the Methodist Student Center and the Episcopal Student Center.

As at Drake University, the basic part of the job was developing and maintaining a student association with weekly meetings, teaching short-term courses on issues related to the emphases of the local board, counseling students, directing worship, developing personal and professional relationships with faculty and staff, and managing all the structures of the board, the student association, finances, and communications.

Programmatically, I tried to find my way in some of the same areas that had been successful at Drake. First I tried to build on the basic student group who participated in study sessions and social events at the campus ministry center. This was always a small group, supported by the fact that four male students lived in the apartment at the center and provided much of the contact and leadership for the student group.

Because the Vice-President for Student Affairs, the Dean of Students, and four or five other student affairs staff people had been on the staff at Iowa State University just before coming here and knew Don Adams and the staff at Drake, building relationships with this group of professionals was very easy. Because of that relationship and my rather rapid rise in leadership with the campus ministers, I was soon meeting with the Dean of Students staff weekly as the representative of campus ministry. This gave me a visibility on campus and a wider awareness of life at the university.

One of the helpful structures that came from this relationship was a response network for emergencies and needs. We formed about 7 or 8 teams, each composed of a campus minister, a student life professional, a counselor, a campus police member, and a faculty leader. Those teams were available to be the "first responders" whenever there were emergencies on campus. They also were the ones to analyze situations and organize larger responses when needed.

As would be expected, I was also soon engaged in freshman orientation and its larger system of development. Although this never grew to the size we had developed at Drake, I was able to bring some of the same insights and dynamics from my earlier experience and my doctoral program research into the structure here.

One new and successful part of the ministry was campus ministry at Santa Fe Community College, which was located on the west side of Gainesville. The first steps were getting acquainted with the student services staff and faculty of the college. Since the college was outside the city, a large number of students rode the city bus to campus and the transfer point on that bus line was just in front of our campus ministry building and students sat on our porch while they waited for the next bus.

I took advantage of that bus stop by hanging around the porch and engaging in conversations with the students. Then I started having Breakfast at the Bus Stop on Thursday mornings. This meant providing coffee and donuts, conversation and information about the college, friendships and, eventually, counseling sessions that developed.

In my usual community-building style, I started introducing campus ministers and local pastors to the faculty and staff of the community college. This group became a strong resource for counseling, advocacy, and support for the students. Because students were all day students with few expressions of community and social life on campus, most of our work was done one-to-one with the students. Those conversations ranged from personal growth and plans for a profession to very strong religious and life questions.

Building on these experiences with the community college, I developed and lead a state-wide conference on ministry in community colleges utilizing a simulation I created to reflect the structure in Florida. The fallout from this was indeed felt across the state.

A unique program that I created at the university built on my concern for freshmen and their development. I got acquainted with many faculty members who taught the beginning courses in departments which would become majors for the students. Then I invited a faculty person, a professional in the field, and a dozen or so students who thought they would major in and become professionals in that field to come to my home for dinner and discussion. This was very successful and helpful. Students got to look at themselves, talk about their dreams and plans, and ask questions about their future academic life and eventual careers.

Note: While I was writing this piece of my report I discovered that the Alban Institute weekly newsletter for January 20, 2014 contained an article titled "The Congregation as Resource Center" which said:...*congregational leaders could play a mediating role in connecting members with others who share their interests or linking college students with professionals in their area of study*. Hmmm! Sounds familiar, doesn't it?

And, finally, I completed the Doctor of Ministry Degree which I had been working on at San Francisco Theological Seminary. This had included two years of weekly class work, one summer on the seminary campus, and a dissertation/project. My dissertation/project was on life, support, and adjustment of university freshmen with emphasis on the particular role that campus ministry played.

As I said, this was a different world. Following the great community and personal relations at Drake and in the Iowa UMHE, I was faced here with a troubled (and troubling) board and support system. Sadly I found myself following the experience of several predecessors and staying only for a brief period of less than three years.

1978-81 The Creative Educator, Columbia, South Carolina

I guess the best name for this period is *An Unexpected Interim*. Or maybe *Telling Others About Campus Ministry* (Are publicists still considered professionals is their field?)

I left Gainesville, Florida and joined my wife in Columbia, South Carolina just in time to start the fall semester of 1978 in the Department of Media Arts at the University of South Carolina. For some strange reason I thought I was taking some time out to be a student but in actuality I was only a month into the semester when I got drafted to also be an Interim Professor in the

102

department. Even with both jobs, I managed to complete a Master's in Media Arts degree within twelve months.

With this credential, I was able to open an office as The Creative Educator and expand on my experiences in media production, communications, and creative education. Not surprisingly, my major client was the national office of United Ministries in Higher education for whom I produced an extended series of simulation games, many slide-tape shows interpreting campus ministry at a number of sites across the U. S., and articles in their publications. This was a wonderful education for me as I got such a close-up view of a huge variety of programs in campus ministries around the country.

Now a confession: working for UMHE (and a few local clients) did not keep my table with enough food so I also worked as an interim minister in churches in the state and had a job as a Kelly Girl. In case you don't remember Kelly Girls, it was a company providing temporary office workers (mostly women). But I guess I did something right in that work because in my first year I was named "Employee of the Year" by the Columbia office of Kelly Services!

I guess all this montage of activity kept me adequately "in the loop" because in the spring of 1981 I was hired by the board of United Campus Ministry of Austin to be their head of staff and director of ministries.

1981-89 University of Texas and Austin Community College, Austin, Texas

United Campus Ministry of Austin was the local expression of Texas United Campus Christian Life Committee – the statewide agency formed by the Christian Church (Disciples of Christ), the United Church of Christ, the Presbyterian Church U.S., and the United Presbyterian Church U.S.A. Here in Austin much of our life and programming was also in tandem with the campus ministry program of the United Methodist Church.

As at my other venues, the basic part of the job was staff supervision, developing and teaching short-term courses on issues related to the emphases of the local board, counseling students, directing worship, developing personal and professional relationships with faculty and staff, and managing all the structures of the board, student-oriented programs and groups, finances, and communications.

Our office was in the Congregational Church of Austin (United Church of Christ). Since we did not have a campus ministry center in the usual sense, all of our programming was done on campus, in churches, and in other venues. Pat Russell, a UCC minister, was our associate with special attention to ministry with students and relations with local churches. Claudia Highbaugh, a Christian Church (Disciples of Christ) minister worked part time for UCMA with African-American students at the university and part time as the chaplain at Huston-Tillotson College (a traditional African-American college related to the United Methodists and two black denominations).

Along with programs related to traditional students, we put great emphasis upon work with student families, international students and students preparing for international experiences. Within a year or so, we developed the University of Texas Student Parent Association, a ministry directed toward the university's more than 5,000 student families.

The initial ministry was a child care center, a service not provided by the university and greatly appreciated by the student families. It was housed first in University Methodist Church and later in a facility owned by and rented to us by the university. The child care program had a full-time director, James Fisher, and seven staff members. This added to my schedule through administration and personal counseling.

New to the life of UCMA, we developed a program in conjunction with the office of the Dean of Students at Austin Community College. As had been the program in Florida, the structure at ACC was related to faculty, participation in classes, and personal counseling. All of the students lived in the city and just appeared for classes on campus, thus traditional campus ministry structures were not able to function here.

At UT, we created an international program through which the University of Texas became a sister university with Irkutsk State University in Siberia, USSR – a program which I directed. And we helped form the group in Austin who became the local expression of Christmas International House, a program of the national Presbyterian Church and which brought international students from colleges all over the U.S. to Austin for two weeks at Christmas.

I accepted an invitation from a member of the University's counseling center to join him in establishing a service project in Jamaica and to recruit and train students for the project. This was a two week experience in which the students lived and worked in a small village there. We sent about 15-20 students to this program each year.

Expanding on the international touches, I became the local director and national board member of USA-USSR Citizens' Dialogue, promoting peace by bringing groups of Americans and Soviets to each others' country. These were professional people from all walks of life and generally stayed two to three weeks on each visit to the other country.

Not wanting to let any grass grow under my feet, I still continued writing curriculum and magazine articles for the Presbyterian Church – including a regular monthly magazine column of games and puzzles related to the teaching curriculum for junior highs. And I continued producing media for United Ministries in Higher Education and other groups.

Finally in this list of unique features, I received a grant from Texas United Campus Christian Life Committee to monitor legislation on higher education underway in the Texas Legislature and report on this to the TUCCLC parent denominational bodies. And, again, I was a commissioner to the General Assembly of the Presbyterian Church (USA) where I chaired the committee on peacemaking.

Reflection on the In-Between

As I said at the beginning of this report, the campus ministry phase of my life ended when the funding for the work in Austin died in 1989. And, as I noted, that "death through the departure of dollars" came to all four of my venues. But I want to say a few words about what I can see in the reflection provided by the rearview mirror of years.

That mirror lets me identify a healthily-large number of ministers, church administrators, and counselors. It shows me people with productive educations who were dropout-bound when I first met them. These have become many, many educators in public schools, colleges and universities all the way across this country. I see professional and service-oriented citizens around the world who went back home after their education in the U.S. I cannot see but can easily imagine people in many countries whose lives are changed by the ministries of students who came back to them to serve. Business people, public officials, artists, musicians, peacemakers, social service providers, and so many more!

I cannot claim responsibility for who and what they are. I can only kneel in prayer to say "Thank you, Lord, for calling me to this ministry and allowing me to be part of all these lives!"

Wayne Bryan lives in Columbia, South Carolina where he followed his campus ministry career with ten years as the director of the SC Council of Churches and five years as the director of an international visitors program for the U. S. State Department. He and his wife, Mimi Parrott, spend much of their retirement time in service to their local Presbyterian church.

A Memoir
By Darrell W. Yeaney

This memoir, written at the request of those planning the 50th anniversary of NCMA in the summer of 2014, is divided into three sections for the convenience of those who have little time or inclination to read it all. The first section is a brief sketch of my career in "professional ministry" which includes my recent retirement years in which my work in and through the church has continued, though on a nonpaid basis. The second section is a listing of some of the major influences on my life that have helped to determine my choices both positive and negative. And finally, I include a collection of musings or beliefs about life that are random statements of values by which I attempt to guide my daily living. The reader is invited to choose any or all sections to be read in any order.

I. Brief Professional Sketch

I attended Westminster College in New Wilmington PA., graduating in 1953 and moved to Pittsburgh PA with my new wife, Sue Brown, where I enrolled at Pittsburgh Xenia Theological Seminary and graduated from Pittsburgh Theological Seminary (a merger of Pitt-Xenia and Western Theological Seminaries) in 1956. I then inexplicably accepted a call to be the pastor of a small, 180 member congregation of the United Presbyterian Church in North America, located in Manhattan, Kansas home of Kansas State University and the "Fighting Wildcats."

The U.P. Church in North America voted to merge with the Presbyterian Church USA in 1959 which led to the decision of the ruling Presbytery of Kansas City to dissolve my little U. P. congregation since there was a much larger "First Presbyterian Church" located only four blocks distant. At the same time, a new congregation was to be organized and a new church built just west of the University campus. I then agreed to be the organizing pastor of that new congregation. The new congregation was organized, the new church built and I served it - Trinity Presbyterian Church - for three more years.
During those 6 years in Manhattan, Sue and I brought our three children into the world. Linda Sue in November 1956, Timothy Dale in December 1958 and Jennifer Kay in November, 1960. Nice planning wouldn't you say?

In 1962 I accepted my first invitation to be a campus minister at the Emporia State Teachers' College, Kansas, as the organizing minister of an ecumenical United Campus Christian Ministry (UCCM). After seven exciting, challenging and rewarding years, during which the NCMA came into existence, I received a Danforth Foundation grant to enroll at Boston University in a PHD program in Social Ethics.

With three young children, we moved into a rented house in the Auburndale suburb of Boston in 1969. Sue took a job at a food brokerage while I luxuriated through three years of intense but stimulating study, writing, and consulting with the Consultation and Education Division of the Boston University Hospital's Mental Health Unit and its Human Relations Center.

With a dissertation well underway, I accepted a surprise call to be the campus minister (UCCM) at the University of California, Santa Cruz in 1972, where I worked amid the beauty and bounty of the UCSC campus and California coastline for 14 years. Our three children all graduated high school and entered various universities during this tenure and I finished my dissertation and received my Ph D from Boston University. Sue created and directed a community organization which she dubbed the "I-You Venture," that ultimately recruited upward of 4000 volunteers to work in nursing homes in Santa Cruz County.

In 1986 Sue and I moved to Iowa City where I began a 12-year tenure as Campus Minister with UCCM at the University of Iowa. While there I also taught professional ethics at the College of Dentistry, expanding the curriculum from one to five courses. Sue also worked at the University with Aging Studies and then with Iowa City Hospice as the Coordinator of Volunteers.

I formally retired in 1998 and we continued to live in Iowa City doing volunteer work until 2006 when we moved back to the Santa Cruz area to be near our youngest daughter, Jennifer, her husband Ti and two daughters, Emily and Katy. To the present, I have been active with the Peace and Justice Task Force of the Presbytery of San Jose, the Palestinian Israel Action Committee of the Resource Center for Non Violence and as Parish Associate with the Trinity Presbyterian Church of Santa Cruz. Our chosen locus of international attention and activity has been focused on the Middle East and in particular, the conflicted relationship between the Palestinian people and the nation of Israel. We have traveled there eleven times leading tours including a national student peacemaking tour in 1991 and creating the Congressional Accompaniment Project in 2006.Our final trip to the "Holy Land" was a Peacemaking tour with our entire family of three children & spouses, five grand children and five close friends over the winter holidays, 2013-14. We recommend it as a gift of peace and justice to the future.

II. Some Major Influences

While the major influences on my life have been primarily personal, they often occurred at crucial times in my personal evolution and are associated with peculiar circumstances that reinforced their impact. Below is a selected list, presented here in connection with the circumstances of my evolving self and career.

My parents were lower middle class protestants and raised their children as active members of a local Presbyterian church near Pittsburgh PA. My standard WASP upbringing was altered significantly at the "New Wilmington Missionary Conference" in the summer of 1948 when I was sixteen. The Rev. Wall, a evangelical Presbyterian pastor invited me to give my life to Jesus. I did and it altered by life trajectory. I entered Westminster College in the fall of

1949 as a "pre-ministerial" student for which the college had created a triple major in Bible, Philosophy and Psychology. I "grew up" at Westminster, quickly outgrowing my narrow "fundamentalist" naïve outlook on Christianity under the influence of older students like John Rock, Robert Garvey and John Geldmacher, all brilliant yet quiet mentors.

Of the many other important personal influences at Westminster I limit mention to Paul Weirman, a roommate whose stellar character and steady friendship has remained over the years, and Professor Wiley Prugh, who in a time of crisis at the college, taught me the importance of courage and integrity in personal and professional life.

It was at Westminster where I met, by serendipitous accident, a beautiful and bright upper-class student named Sue Brown and later persuaded her to become my wife and life partner. Meeting her extraordinary parents and gifted siblings sealed the deal. Professor Gordon Jackson, who performed our wedding, was perhaps the most influential seminary faculty member who taught us the ethical tradition of the Hebrew prophets that is traceable in the life of Jesus and nearly all of my other historical hero guides to the present day.

In my first pastorate in Manhattan KS, I was "taken in" by a group of **campus ministers at KSU** who served as my mentors throughout my campus ministry career. They include "Abby" Abendroth, who invited me to assist at the Westminster Foundation, Warren Rempel at Wesley, Dale Turner at the Roger Williams Center, who introduced me to Paul Tillich's_*Dynamics of Faith,* Bill McMillan at the Episcopal Center, and David McGown who followed Abby at the Westminster Center and whose unique laughter echoes still in my memory. Later, Cecil Findley, a fellow pastor, joined these campus ministry colleagues as mentors and lasting friends.

When I began my work as **campus minister at Emporia State Teachers College in 1962**, it was Glenn Hosman, at the Wesley Foundation, who welcomed me and in 1964 accompanied me along with Robert Goodman and Professor Elinore Hoag on our Civil Rights trip to Mississippi, who joined me for a short time in jail there and who later invited UCCM to office in the new Wesley building in Emporia.

Local Emporia Black pastors, who allowed me to help them first shut down and then integrate the only swimming pool in Emporia, taught me both courage and the importance of creating a public demonstration to break open social consciousness and focus accountability for pervasive racial discrimination. And it was the Chaplain at Mary Holmes College in Mississippi who invited us to join him in bringing a dozen students and my reluctant parents to teach a two week Vacation Bible School there that was a learning event surpassing all formal education.

While at Emporia, I took time in the summer to learn more about urban ministry, first at the Urban Ministry Program at McCormick Theological Seminary and later through participation in a two week "Urban Plunge" with the Urban Training Institute also in Chicago. These hands-on opportunities gave me insights into the realities of urban poverty, and industrial labor issues, insights that rarely occurred in seminary or academia.

Campus ministers, I discovered, had greater liberty to live and speak a prophetic message to the church and world than parish ministers did and that task became, for me, a conscious choice. In the midst of my campus ministry work at Emporia State, I achieved an MS degree in Social Science which enabled me to more closely identify with the academic community and taught me how to do academic writing.

It was also in Emporia that we first became home owners, which was and is a significant identity and social status experience in America. The whole process of dealing with local state and national government bureaucracies and financial institutions became more complicated and consumed a larger and larger part of my time and attention and consequently became a somewhat compromising distraction from commitments to social justice and economic equality. But it also introduced me to mundane concerns like dealing with termites, clogged sewage drains, roof & foundation leaks etc. I gained a deeper respect for skilled tradesmen and honest financial advisors as well as a keener sense of possible dishonesty and corruption in the business world and market place.

We left Emporia in 1969 for *three years at Boston University* on a Danforth Foundation grant. Working under Dean Walter Muelder, dissertation advisor Paul Deats and Human Relations Director Kenneth Benne pulled my mind and heart in directions I did not know they could be stretched. Ken Benne was the founder of the "T Group" therapy movement and I learned its usefulness and errors close up. We found deep and trusting friendship with these men and other graduate student friends such as Dean & Elsie Fruedenberger and Sunny Robinson. Dean was a pioneer in putting Social Ethics to work in global agriculture, helping to promote the "green revolution" in Africa and elsewhere in the world. Sunny put Human Relations to work in the civil rights struggles of that time and also in personal life. Her integrity of character has been a sustaining force in our life-long friendship.

The student movement was still strong and the campus ministry staff in the Boston-Cambridge Campus Ministry-- Larry Hill and Jack Cornfield -- offered helpful insights into both the wisdom and the folly of identifying, sometimes too closely, with that generational dynamic. I also got a different view of Campus Ministry by serving on the Boston-Cambridge Campus Ministry Board of Directors.

I chose as my dissertation topic *The History and Dynamics of the United Ministries in Higher Education*, which was the national ecumenical structure that gave professional support to a number of mainline Protestant campus ministers. The effort gave me a birds-eye and critical view of my own work and its setting in the 20th Century protestant church's effort to influence higher education and its denizens from a progressive Christian perspective and commitment.

My research on the dissertation brought me into close association with several denominational executives who managed the higher education work of their respective denominations. Hal Vieman and Vernon Barker were most helpful in this effort. But by far the most influential was Clyde Robinson, an executive at the Presbyterian office on Higher Education. Clyde, a true "southerner," carried in himself all of the best of southern cordiality and suave ability to maneuver through the church bureaucracy, always remaining loyal to his constituents – the campus ministers whom he served. Under Clyde's able guidance, I served on the national campus ministry advisory committee and for a term as President of the Presbyterian Campus Ministers' Association. It was a learning curve where I felt continually supported by Clyde's personal friendship and professional knowledge and ability.

We passed up the first invitation to interview for the campus ministry job at *UCSC Santa Cruz*, but when it came again a year later, we saw it clearly as a divine intervention, flew to Santa Cruz and accepted the call, beginning work there with the UCCM in the summer of 1972.

The first Northern California-Nevada regional Campus Ministers gathering occurred in Santa Cruz that Fall and it came as a rude awakening to learn that the position of campus minister at Santa Cruz was regarded as folly by most of the other staff who were forced to take budget cuts due to declining revenue. For the first time I found myself unwelcomed by colleagues and had to overcome resentment of a policy decision about which I had no foreknowledge and for which I had no responsibility. However, the misplaced personal resentment was soon acknowledged, and a long tenure of 14 positive and supportive years followed. Once again I discovered able and creative colleagues such as John Dodson, Pete Koopman, Marna McKenzie, Bill Ng, "Lefty" Schultz, and others who, like other campus ministers, were "progressive" in their theology, philosophy and social action long before such insights became more mainstream.

At UCSC my local Lutheran Campus Ministry colleague Herb Schmidt became a life-long friend and constant source of encouragement and amazement. Politically savvy, ecumenically committed, imaginative and collegial, Herb was able to be theologically progressive while maintaining support from the conservative Missouri Synod Lutheran Church -- quite a trick. We continue to work together in retirement on issues of social justice and progressive religion.

It was in Santa Cruz that I first met Mark Rutledge who was working at Monterey Community College and who asked me to assist him in designing an innovative wedding service. Mark's quirky sense of humor and indefatigable pursuit of meaning has made him a life- long buddy on the journey of life and the work of campus ministry.

Five other persons must be named as "persons of special influence" during this tenure in Santa Cruz. The first is Noel King, who was professor and head of Religious Studies at UCSC. Sometimes affectionately described as a cross between a Pakistani Holy Man and Santa Claus, Noel was beloved by his students and treated me as his religious advisor though the truth was quite the opposite. Herb and I worked as adjunct members of the University Counseling staff and, while all of them contributed to my self understanding and professional work, it was Ray Charland who stood out as a close friend and counseling mentor. Ray invited me to conduct his wedding to Marcia and both have remained as trusted life companions.

Then there was Scott Kennedy, founder and Director of the Resource Center for Non Violence. Scott arrived in Santa Cruz at about the same time as I did and his sudden and unexpected death a year ago has left a void in the civic leadership in Santa Cruz (he was twice elected Mayor) and of what a non-violent life might look like in the modern world. Scott had a profound influence on my life and my own commitment to a personal and social strategy of non-violence. Scott also became a tutor to me, unraveling the complexities of the Israel/Palestine conflict and highlighting the importance of that area of the world for my international peacemaking agenda.

Jim Douglass, founder of the Pacific Life Community, whose courageous commitment to living a prophetic life of non-violence, gave the 20th Century world a living example of what that might mean in every aspect of life. Jim's writings, especially *The Non-Violent Cross* and *Contemplation and Liberation*, gave me a practical theology of prophetic non-violence in a nuclear age and a sense of hopeful urgency to confront the conventional wisdom of the national security state. Finally, I must mention Paul Niebank, first Provost at Oaks College, UCSC, whose commitment to truth and wise collegiality let me know what a model of administrative leadership in higher education might look like.

In 1980, I spent two weeks at a conference sponsored by the Guild for Psychological Studies at Four Springs near Calistoga, CA. which was a life changing experience, The Guild had developed a course of study that examined the Gospel accounts from the perspective of the writing of C G Jung, & had published a parallel *Records of the Life of Jesus* assembled by Henry Burton Sharman. By means of a unique curriculum of group study, art and meditation I began to see deeper meanings in these canonical accounts than I had learned in seminary.

Also during this period of my life I spent a week with Matthew Fox and company at his school for religious progressives in Oakland, CA. Along with his physicist colleague Brian Swimm and others, Matthew led me into deeper insight and courage to abandon the sterile doctrines of orthodox Christianity for an open-ended search for meaning within a broadened spiritual understanding of Christianity and its teaching of *Original Blessing*. I still recommend Brian's book *The Universe is a Green Dragon* to beginners on this Way.

In 1985, I joined a group of 20 west coast people on my first of ten subsequent visits to the Middle East. This tour was led by the American Friends (Quaker) representatives living in Amman, Jordan. We traveled through Jordan, to Damascus, Syria and throughout Israel and the Palestine occupied Territories of the West Bank and Gaza. We met with numerous people from the U.S. Embassy, the Israeli Defense Ministry and PLO staff, to Human Rights workers, to Palestinian and Israeli academics, Israeli Settlers and Palestinian refugees. My entire perspective and understanding of the Israel/Palestine conflict changed as did my long held assumptions about Israel gained from Jewish-Christian Dialogue groups.

Not surprisingly, on my return home, I found myself speaking a distinct minority voice among standard brand Christians when the subject of Israel vis-a-vis Palestine arose. I was amazed, not so much at the ignorance of most Christians about this conflict, since I had shared that ignorance before my trip, but at the stubborn resistance and even vehement defense of Israel as the victim nation in spite of all the evidence to the contrary. It eventually became clear to me that this peculiarly "pro-Israel" American consciousness was due to the pervasive work of what has become known as the "Israel Lobby" in American religious, political and cultural life. After returning with Sue in 1989 on a trip with a group of campus ministers sponsored by PAX Christi, I have returned nine more times, including a trip in 1991 with 25 university students and later led four trips with the Congressional Accompaniment Project which we founded in 2006. In 2008 we joined in founding the *"Israel Palestine Ministry Network" of the Presbyterian Church (USA)* and have chosen this area as our principle focus of international peace and justice work.

It is important to add several names here as persons whose life and work in Middle East (Israel-Palestine) peace and justice work has had profound influence on my life and work.

Abba Chacour, recently retired Bishop of the Melkite Church in the Middle East, and founder of the Mar Elias Educational Institution in Ibillin, Israel, is well known for his book *Blood Brothers*. Chacour's work and contribution to Middle East peacemaking and especially Palestinian education and advancement can hardly be over estimated. I am grateful to be able to know him as a friend and mentor in my own efforts to be a Middle East peacemaker.

Alongside Chacour is Naim Ateek, founder of the Sabeel Christian Ecumenical Liberation Theology Center in Jerusalem. A former Canon at St George Cathedral, Naim has constructed a global program called "Sabeel" for educating people in the importance of making justice central to any peacemaking efforts in Israel/Palestine.

The affable friendship and work of Jewish Israeli Jeff Halper, founder and director of the Israeli Committee Against Home Demolitions (ICAHD) in Jerusalem, has been another central influence on my life and work in this area. Jeff's vision, brilliance, persistence and now global influence is quite remarkable and serves as an inspiration to me.

Pastor Metre Rahib at the "Christmas" Lutheran Church in Bethlehem has developed that parish into a dynamic service & education center and has become the second largest employer in Bethlehem. His courage and persistence under fire – literal Israeli military fire – is remarkable and a source of sustaining hope in the midst of the crushing Israeli occupation.

I must also mention Saed Abu Hijlah professor at the Islamic University in Nablus and former student at the University of Iowa where I first met him. A gifted poet and charismatic leader, Saed was wounded when an Israeli squad of soldiers shot and killed his mother on their doorstep in Nablus in 2003. His ability to rise above this senseless tragedy and continue to demonstrate a kind of transcendent human love and yet a persistent non-violent resistance to the forces that brought such grief into his life, continues to amaze and strengthen my resolve to speak truth to power in my own society of complicity in the unjust and inhumane policies behind this personal tragedy.

In 1986 I accepted an invitation to move to Iowa City, IA, and I became the *UCCM pastor at the University of Iowa.*

This was the most widely diverse campus ministry I had experienced, challenging my physical, mental, emotional and spiritual abilities to the limit. It was, fittingly, at the end of my campus ministry career, and led appropriately to my retirement – in the nick of time – in 1998.

The UCCM House in Iowa City hosted an "international Student Loan Closet," (a furniture and household goods loan service), a Guest Hostel for outpatients at the University Hospital across the street; and a pre-school for 25+ children at the house and yard next door. Managing all of this in addition to a student group ministry, teaching one-quarter time the Professional Ethics curriculum at the University Dental College, hosting an annual lecture series at the School of Religion, raising funds from local congregations and supporting judicatories and by parking cars during home football games (the UCCM House was located adjacent to the football stadium) proved a full-time challenge to my energy, time and ability.

A few highlights of this period of campus ministry include taking students on service-learning trips to places like Washington DC, the Chicago Parliament of World Religions and work camps in Chicago and in Juarez Mexico, plus annual canoe trips with Wesley to the Canadian Boundary Waters; training student "Peer Ministers;" meeting with a group of women students for open discussion each Wednesday morning and later officiating at all of their weddings; joining Tom Boyd in "Conversations with Tom & Darrell" dorm discussions; teaching professional ethics and watching graduate students separate themselves into those seeking integrity and those seeking wealth. All these were instructive and often exciting gifts of doing campus ministry in Iowa.

Another significant influence during these years was my participation in a two year training program in Spiritual Direction at a Roman Catholic Adult Education Center in Des Moines and later participation in a Spiritual Directors support group for a number of years with Dorothy Whiston as Director. This was an excellent balance to my deep and long standing commitment to active work for social justice and peacemaking.

III. Reflections of a Sage

I was 31 when I entered the profession of campus ministry with six years of local parish ministry experience and a college and seminary degree. I had been president of my college honorary fraternity, vice president of the Student Council and president of my Seminary class. Although I was an average student academically, I had established a sense of accomplishment and leadership in my own mind and, more importantly, had achieved a reasonably positive sense of self worth. However, I was still restless with the orthodox theological and institutional box within which I was raised and trained. It was the institution of campus ministry, and the larger church's support of it, that gave me the freedom to explore and grow on the frontiers of theology, philosophy, psychology, spirituality and social practice. And for that I am forever grateful.

Below are a collection of musings and quotes that express some of the ideas that have prompted, nourished and guided my evolution of consciousness over these last 50 years:

I am not impressed with the crowd pleasing success of the evangelical fundamentalists or the commercial success of the new atheists, both of whom, it seems to me, are tilting at windmills and having their own rewards. I have participated in those enterprises and have found them barren. Wisdom it seems to me, admits to mystery not certainty, and maturity exhibits humility, not arrogance.

Religious awakening, at its best, consists of a conscious break out of the cocoon of the socially conditioned ego-self, allowing both the deeper divine self to emerge and connect to the wider transcendent or cosmic Divine Self that unites a person to other sentient beings, to nature and to the Ultimate - God. This conscious awakening experience is common to all deep religions and is the means whereby human community is established above and beyond all culturally conditioned boundaries of tribe, class, race, nationality or religion.

"Only as we know for certain in our hearts that love never fails and never loses its own, can we attain that eternal relaxation that achieves the maximum through creative concern." -Nels F.S. Ferre

"Whoever seeks to gain his/her life (ego desires) will lose it. But whoever loses his/her life for my sake, will find it."-Jesus

"I see quite plainly that God has no favorites, but that he who reverences Him and lives a good life in any nation is welcomed by Him." The Apostle Paul, (Acts 10:34-35)

"No one is born a new being. He bears in his psyche the imprint of past generations. He is a combination of ancestral units from which a new being must be fused. yet he also bears within him an essential germ, a potential of a unique individual value. The discovery of this unique essence and its development is the quest of consciousness." -Frances G Wickes

"For Thou hast created us for thyself, and our heart cannot be quieted till it may find repose in thee." -Saint Augustine

"Die and Become.
Till thou hast learned this
Thou art but a dull guest
On this dark planet"
  -Johann Wolfgang Goethe

Darrell's Philosophical Musings--

The insight of Rene Girard, has helped me to see -- once again, and, as if for the first time -- the truth in the concept of "original sin" as basic to my self understanding. This notion of original sin, however, is not a static formula of spiritual genetics wherein we inherit guilt from our ancestors, which is the orthodox interpretation. Rather, it is an ancient insight into the dynamic choice-making of all human beings.

By learning through imitation, all humans learn to desire what others desire and in the competitive struggle that automatically ensues, we choose envy and jealousy over generosity and creativity; fear and hatred over curiosity and appreciation; and retaliation and violence over understanding, empathy and forgiveness.

We tend to ignore, forget or deliberately deny our own participation and complicity in the competitive, win/lose struggle of life and blame the "other" for weakness if he/she loses, or for wickedness if he/she wins.

We join in the group battles of families, tribes, religions, political parties, nations, races, etc. in their efforts to win over others. These group battles usually, if not always, allow the means of winning to corrupt any good goals the group may espouse.

The solution to this human propensity toward competitive violation of the human rights and well being of others lies, I believe, in an awakening to and recognition of our own complicity in choosing to imitate the competitive violence of our human society instead of accepting the invitation to a different way of responding to problems and life challenges - a way that includes cooperation, collaboration, and appreciation of differences - a way that is based on empathy, forgiveness and love.

This solution is the most fundamental challenge we face in life and it is the only path toward a truly human global society.

A few of the more prevalent and personally experienced social expressions of the "original sin" as described above are racism, sexism, communism, capitalism, nationalism, anti-Semitism, Zionism, Islamicism, Americanism and colonialism.

The way out of these social patterns of "original sin" is first. a recognition of our complicity; second. a full and cleansing acceptance of God's love and forgiveness; third. a firm and respectful resistance to all social injustice and scapegoating violence; and fourth, a daily personal commitment to the path of forgiveness, reconciliation, non-violence, respect for all life, universal human rights and ecological welfare.

This is a faith-act and will require spiritual as well as moral and intellectual disciplines and social and emotional (communal) support, which is why the church exists.

- Being out of favor is not equivalent with being wrong.
- Being unpopular is not the same as being stupid.
- Creative innovation will always meet the opposition of convention.
- All religions foster a contradictory double movement: one toward expansive inclusion and another toward restrictive exclusion. But a choice is always available.
- The human capacity for doing good is restricted by its propensity for doing evil.
- The disciples of Jesus, like other normal followers of a charismatic leader, fought each other for priority and status in their imagined future of an all-powerful kingdom. Jesus knew the corruption of the human spirit when power was sought over others – the powerful human instinct and drive to dominate and control. So he directly intervened and set a new and opposite standard: humility and service. They didn't get it until later when the power of his sacrificial love made it clear. Many religious leaders since have forgotten this lesson.
- Some ideas that are frequently confused, poorly defined and often conflated in the popular mind are religion, spirituality, the church and Christianity.
- Belief in God is in itself no guarantee of responsible moral or consistent ethical behavior among people or in a single individual. Rather, it is the kind of God – the moral and ethical character attributed to the God one believes in – that makes all the difference.
- Religion, in its offer of support for a hopeful worldview and belonging to a community of acceptance, is a useful contribution to human life, so long as that worldview is humane, inclusive and ecologically positive. If this world-view is also encouraging and inspirational in a way that enables persons to deal constructively and positively with pain, suffering and abuse, religion can be a very constructive contribution to human life. On the contrary, when a religious worldview is exclusively tribal, entitling one group over another, or promising exclusion from suffering and pain, or

attributing magical, superhuman abilities to one person or class of persons, it can be destructive to human flourishing and human community and ecological sustainability.

• There is no conflict between the human constructs of science and religion when their basic quests are properly defined and understood. Science is the human quest to understand how the universe exists and works and to manipulate its dynamics for good or ill. Religion is the human quest to understand why the universe exists and works as it does and to conform human behavior for good or ill to that understanding. Both science and religion are ennobling when they are pursued in the service of universal humane and ecological values. However, both enterprises are corrupted and corrupting when they are pursued for lesser ends.

I awoke from a dream in which I had become lost in a strange neighborhood of a strange city. I knew my name, but could not remember the name of the family or the address from which I had wandered. My attempts to retrace my steps only led me into more unknown and stranger neighborhoods.

The significant aspect of this dream is the feeling of lostness, or disorientation and of being a stranger, uncertain of how to get "home" or back to some familiar and certain world.

So the mind is able to imagine a situation of lostness that in itself engenders feelings of fear, even panic; feelings of growing vulnerability, almost like being caught on a spinning amusement park ride and unable to stop it or get off. You are not in control of your life. Death becomes a desired option to escape these feelings of lostness and powerlessness.

This dream of disorientation and lostness which is a projection of deep inner psychic feelings onto an imagined personal situation, tells us of the need for stability, and a sense of belonging to a real and known world or universe. Faith in such an ultimate reality is essential for rational, secure human living. Everyone must accept the reality of some experiential world to function as a human being. And, the larger or most comprehensive and inclusive that world is, the freer is the person to function with security in one's surroundings and in one's ability and capacity to cope, to thrive as a fully functioning and appropriate part of that world. Every human must have faith in his/her world as a real one and as part of an ultimate and eternal universe that gives meaning to one's own small existence. A person needs to feel and believe that his or her life counts for something that has lasting value.

So Jesus' metaphor about building your life on a rock and not sand, refers to this existential need for permanence and connection to ultimate reality, a reality usually called God.

A major problem in this human world is when humans accept a limited worldview that is circumscribed by racial, religious, ethnic, class, nationalistic or other identity boundaries that exclude others and privilege those who "belong." Friction and tension inevitably arise from these limited social identities, which too often lead to violence and devolution.

While earth's people are gradually becoming used to a more pluralistic community and language, the racial, ethnic, class and national boundaries still pose major blocks to the development of a truly humane world. We have a long way to go. Every effort to overcome these barriers through peaceful effort and to nurture a universal human consciousness is to be commended.

In retirement, I have continued my activity in peacemaking and social justice, helping to found the Palestine Action Committee in Iowa City and later the Palestine Israel Action Committee in Santa Cruz. Sue and I created the Congressional Accompaniment Project and organized and led four tours to Israel-Palestine. In 2011, Paul Seever, a Presbyterian layman, and I organized the Progressive Christian Forum in Santa Cruz which has conducted four annual public forums and numerous seminars for progressive Christian in the area. I continue to serve as its Convener.

I became a "Parish Associate" (unpaid helper) at the local Trinity Presbyterian Church where I work with the Worship and Education Committee and write a column called "The Non-Prophet Corner" for the church newsletter. While I suspect no one reads it, I find writing stimulates and organizes my thoughts. Sue and I work with the church's homeless shelter program which keeps us grounded in the underside of an otherwise affluent society. We also serve on the Presbytery's Peace and Justice Task Force that struggles to provide opportunities for pastors and lay leaders to move beyond "comforting the disturbed" and toward "disturbing the comfortable." These activities keep my mind and body engaged in dealing with the challenges of a 21st century world.

Reflections and Projections on Campus Ministry
By Richard Bowyer

For a number of years, even before my retirement in 2005, I have enjoyed a once a week breakfast with a handful of clergy. It is an ecumenical and diverse group in terms of age, gender and ethnicity. The nature of the gathering has morphed at times from a more devotionally based conversation to essentially a social and fellowship get-together. Some participants are quite regular in attendance while others are more occasional. Over time and as pastors come and go according to denominational processes or their levels of community involvement, medical situations, etc, a progression of folks have participated in the group.

Two of these clergy friends are now retired pastors whose entrances to ordained ministry were influenced in part by my role as their campus pastor. One of those two served a few years as a campus minister. Three of my successors at *The Wesley Foundation at Fairmont State University and Pierpont Community and Technical College* have been participants. My first successor was a regular until he left to attend graduate school and later return as a full time faculty member. The two subsequent successors, both female and one African-American have been occasional participants. One other, a Pakistani-American, came to the United States and eventually to West Virginia and the West Virginia Annual Conference of the United Methodist Church as a consequence of an elder brother who had taught at West Virginia Wesleyan and a younger brother brought to the US to attend Fairmont State as the first full time international student sponsored and funded by the Wesley Foundation while I was campus minister.

On a recent morning a conversation with one of my former students, now retired, led to my reflections on some basic guiding principles of campus ministry. The upshot of that led to the title I have placed on this essay. We were talking about the fact that much if not most of the leadership, clergy and lay, in our various churches and communions are at least verbally concerned about the disconnection between the current youth and young adult generation and organized religion and "the church." Our perception is that many, and perhaps most, of these same persons see campus ministry in terms of nurturing church connection and including "traditional" local church like programs and opportunities. They expect regular or at least scheduled, if occasional, worship experiences and some degree of an identifiable group or "membership" or affiliation. Quite often the measuring sticks of evaluations are geared to such factors: how many or how often?

My comment in the midst of this conversation was that from the earliest times my ministry, where this particular former student was involved, was guided by a style and approach that was still quite appropriate and relevant to the current "disconnected" and unaffiliated generation that increasingly identify themselves as "nones" in terms of religious affiliation.

The guiding principles for me have been basically those of presence and relationship. More than half a century ago, as an undergraduate student involved in an ecumenical campus organization and as a student pastor, I was asked to contribute an article to the campus newspaper. The theme or essence of that article was my understanding of Christianity as essentially a matter of relationship, with Christ and with one another.

Certainly groups and organizations, whatever their nature and purpose are matters of relationship. That needs no further comment. But one of the major problems of organizations is their tendency, if not their intent, to be exclusive and in-grown. Keeping the focus on campus ministry, I can still recall many years ago conversations with "my" Wesley Foundation "members." The students could only identify participants in the organization with the relatively small number of students in the campus community who came regularly to the programs and activities that they enjoyed. They were unaware of other students with whom I had ongoing and often very meaningful connections and relationships. Some of those were just clusters of students who happened to be drinking coffee or playing cards in the Student Center. In those early days, the various Greek organizations tended to have their own tables in the Center. I would often sit with them and engage in whatever was being shared. Often those conversations would not be acceptable in church or perhaps other "polite company." These persons, too, were "members" of our campus ministry. The group was broader and much more inclusive than the regulars at Bible Study or Sunday evening "vesper services." Some of them have gone on to become leaders in local congregations wherever they reside and with whatever communion they are affiliated. One or two even ended up in ordained ministry. I make no claim to influencing them nor those outcomes, certainly not as much as I might those with whom I was more actively engaged in campus ministry programs and activities. But I have had one or two comment to me many years later that my presence and influence was in some way meaningful to them.

I have always understood campus ministry to mean just that: *campus ministry*. I recall that about 1964 the Methodist Church (well before we became "United") officially changed its terminology from "Student Work" to "Campus Ministry." No longer was the Church engaged only in ministry with and to students, but to the whole of the campus community.

Here again relationships have become crucial. Many faculty, administrators and staff are active in their faith groups and local churches. Others have not had a church affiliation at all. And some have been turned off by incidents or situations that have soured them on the church. For them a pastor with an open mind and heart, a listening ear and attitude of caring has often been significant. The number of counseling situations, weddings and funerals or memorial services those connections have educed are noteworthy. But those faculty, staff, and administrative relationships have led to many referrals of students in need of assistance-- whether merely financial or

120

academic or actually spiritual or vocational. Relationships are crucial and at the very heart of effective Campus Ministry.

At the core of all of this is the matter of presence. It is simply important "to be there," wherever "there" happens to be. I can't begin to recall nor cite the numerous times across my 45 years of active campus ministry that I was stopped in a hall way or in the library or a faculty lounge or even the Student Center by an administrator and invited into her or his office. Many times it was to ask for assistance with a problem faced by a student. At times it was to share freely a problem, issue, incident or concern that they were too intimidated to share with colleagues let alone voice to their supervisor. They knew, or trusted and hoped that my relationships would open a door and perhaps the ear of a higher level of the administration where a concern might be addressed. There were a few times when that administrator was at the top of the power chain.

One of the more memorable experiences of the ministry of presence occurred at half time of a basketball game. Two students approached me. One, a student leader both officially as a student government officer and as a person of character, brought a fellow student to me. It was between semesters. The one in need of help had withdrawn the previous semester due to a family crisis. His financial aid for the next term was rejected because he had not made "due progress." He was given an opportunity to appeal but found difficulty in writing his appeal letter. I was asked to talk with the Financial Aid Director. I did that. Several days later, the Director called to me in the hallway and proceeded to tell me that based on my recommendation the young man's financial aid package was restored. That young man became a campus leader, graduated the next year and has become a counselor in a facility that works with troubled youth.

Presence and relationship are at the heart of effective campus ministry.

Such connections are certainly not limited to persons with Christian or church relationships or affiliations. Several have been with students and faculty of other faith traditions. Years ago our Wesley Foundation received a grant from the General Board of Higher Education and Ministry of the United Methodist Church to develop a video about Campus Ministry. It was entitled "A Ministry of Accessibility." Among those included in the video was the President of the college and a student who was Muslim. In fact that student's father was the Imam in his African home and his uncle a noted faculty member in Islamic Studies at a prestigious US university. The student, who actually became a member of our Board of Directors, stated on the video that even though he was of a different faith, he found his source of spiritual strength at the Wesley Foundation. That man is now a director of human resources for the International Monetary Fund.

On the occasion of the infamous 9-11 tragedy, I sent an e-mail to our two Iraqi Muslim faculty members offering them support and asking to be informed if either experienced any negative or hostile instances. One wrote back simply, "You are a good Christian." I had been at his bedside after very serious surgery a few years before and with his permission, as Islam allows, prayed for his recovery. Presence and relationship was well beyond the bounds and scope of traditional or certainly institutional Christianity.

My conversation at breakfast with a person whom I first knew as a student more than 50 years ago turned to the relevance of such a style of ministry to today's generation of "nones" and unaffiliated or disaffiliated. I recalled a conversation over lunch with a group of faculty many years ago. One at the table was more than non-religious. He would have self-described himself as "irreligious." Somehow the table talk turned to me and my role on campus. I don't recall anything of the nature of the conversation or what prompted it. But that man said to his peers, "Dick is God's man on campus." What an affirmation! What an application of incarnational ministry. And it was rooted in presence and relationship. That man was in the theatre department. My attendance at plays and engagement with students in the department, as well as with him and some other faculty who were somewhere outside the bounds of acceptable views and play selection at a then very conservative campus, made a difference.

I have long believed that campus ministry at its best is or should be a prototype for ministry and something of a laboratory exploration of what might be the future of the larger ministry of the church. These reflections lead me to the projection that the model of ministry needed today and in the future is simply one of presence and relationship that is certainly not confined to the facilities and activities of "the church."

In retirement we still live in Fairmont, WV where I serve on the Board of Directors of the Wesley Foundation and several other community agency boards. I have served as a chaplain on four cruise ships and my wife Faith and I spent two months in both 2006 and 2010 on the staff of the East Belfast Mission in Northern Ireland. I enjoy collecting baseball cards and attending baseball games around the country, attending plays, sports and other activities at Fairmont State.

Out on a Limb: 33½ years (1963-1996) in Campus Ministry
By Hugh Nevin

In retrospect it's easy to say where I've been as a campus minister: 16 years on Long Island (in two positions); 3 years (in as many positions) traveling New York State; and 14½ years in New York's Capital District (in two positions). Fleshing that out a bit and providing some flavor takes a little more doing. But to stay with the overview for a minute, the Long Island and Capital District positions were all new when I came to them; the State level positions were all interim. More, in the Capital District the positions were half-time; the other part of my time was as interim pastor in seven churches (plus an eighth in a three-year installed relationship). At the time the changes simply unfolded. In retrospect the question is there: was I being called to a career of staffing startups and transitions?

I. It was a conversation I had in 1962 with George Pera, Presbyterian University Pastor at New York University, that probably sealed my decision to become a campus minister. Though I didn't know it at the time of the conversation, George was a representative of an about-to-vanish breed, APUPs, the Association of Presbyterian University Pastors. With the founding of NCMA in 1964, APUPs went out of existence.

I was not at the initial gathering of NCMA in St. Louis in 1964; I was at Michigan State the following year. Beginning life as a campus minister by starting up an area ministry on the eastern two-thirds of the Long Island land mass kept my interests and attention focused locally in those first years. My family and I had arrived in Stony Brook in January, 1963. An initial objective was to cultivate the Board of The Campus Christian Federation of Suffolk County (later the *United Campus Ministries of Suffolk County*) and develop its activities, while at the same time creating a network of key persons on and near the four non-parochial campuses of the County. There was also an equally important project: bring Protestant student groups into existence on all four campuses. One had been in process of formation at Stony Brook when I arrived; the other three were added by the spring of 1965. The worship-study-service-fellowship model guided the development of these groups. The four campuses included: The State University of New York at Stony Brook (across the railroad tracks from our home in Stony Brook village), Suffolk County Community College in Selden (a 15-minute drive), Adelphi Suffolk (later renamed Dowling College) in Oakdale (a 30-minute drive) and Southampton College in Southampton (an hour's drive). By the late 1970s Southampton's student group had ceased activity and was restarted as part of a sub-area ministry including Southampton and the Riverhead expansion campus of the Community College; part time local staffing was engaged for this Peconic Ministry. Altogether the campuses were young or brand new and growing institutions; increasing enrollments, new faculty and staff, and building projects were the order of the day.

Regarding the pace and extent of ministry activity in the early years, a comment the Federation treasurer made to me is instructive: "You'll have to decide how much money you can use for program and how much you need to live on." Once we became a tax exempt organization, this pressure eased somewhat. Other examples of campus ministry activity/concern in the early years included the following: in several situations, local churches were active in developing student fellowships; the community college president let it be known that he (a leader in his local church) didn't want a campus minister living within ten miles of his campus. (A separate story: the Claritian priests conducting the Catholic campus ministries in the County waged the public and legal battle that opened the door for the establishment of religious ministries on campuses throughout the State University of New York system.) Students were active tutoring migrant children, and faculty and staff on campuses both advised groups and took the initiative to mount programs such as "The Place of Religion in the Academic Enterprise." The Stony Brook student group hosted the pastor of the Sweet Pilgrim Baptist Church of Hattiesburg, Mississippi, while the campus itself experienced a drug bust.

Three key events took place in the fall of 1965:

1. 37 faculty and staff from 9 Long Island campuses gathered in Riverhead (where the eastern forks of the Island begin) for a Consultation requested by the Nassau and Suffolk County campus ministry boards with lead funding from the Church in Higher Education Projects Committee in New York State. Colgate Rochester Divinity School theologian William Hamilton keynoted the event. Case study papers describing Hillel, Newman, Denominational Protestant, and United Protestant approaches formed the basis for discussion. The United Protestant paper was presented by Earl Lowell, Coordinator of the New York Commission for United Ministries in Higher Education in New York (UMHE). In addition to myself, two other local campus ministers were present, Paul Kaylor, Campus Pastor at Adelphi University, and Charles Kinzie, Campus Pastor at Hofstra and C. W. Post College.

2. Elsewhere that fall, campus ministers from six areas - Buffalo, Rochester, Canton-Potsdam, Troy, Nassau and Suffolk counties - gathered for a day-long consultation on the nature of area ministries.

3. A small university-community group at Stony Brook began a series of meetings on the topic of "Otherness" led by David Roomy, Associate Director of the Episcopal Council for Foreign Students and Other Visitors, Inc. The University was under a mandate to develop graduate programs at an unusually fast pace; it began recruiting graduate students from Taiwan (even a few from China through Hong Kong) and Japan. The University had no staff or program for their orientation to an American community and campus life. Out of the Roomy study group we developed an organization which we named Community Hospitality for International Students (CHIS). For a number of years it hosted sixty or more incoming international students each fall; they stayed with community families (identified initially through local churches) as

a vehicle for orientation before the semester began, many developing ongoing relationships. One evening, when host families were meeting in a campus dorm, the lights went out for a period of time: no one panicked. Hearing about it, the University President pronounced it a noteworthy example of improving town-gown relations that community residents would feel comfortable under such circumstances. The University finally added a foreign student advisor position and the program was then directed by that person. Eventually the Federation was no longer officially involved.

In the spring of 1967, on behalf of the state level UMHE Commission, a campus ministry review team spent three days in which they visited the four campuses, interviewed numerous persons on and off campus and held group meetings. To the extent a brief reference can capture the team's findings, it is this: "Although neither the Federation nor Hugh Nevin were known by everyone on each campus, their presence was felt on every campus...We would urge Hugh to continue to use his time in the area as he has."

The advent of CIIIS initiated a new stage in project work (a strategy that, by then, our Board had formally adopted): some projects could be developed and then spun off. The most long- lasting of such efforts was the next project undertaken, again in reaction to an emergent need. Psychology graduate students at Stony Brook who served as staff in the counseling center were rumored to be using their counseling information as the basis for academic papers. True or not, it precipitated a crisis of confidence on campus. Considering the situation, three of us - a tenured faculty member, biologist Jim Fowler (now deceased), local Methodist pastor John Paul Hankins, and I - set a goal. We imagined the establishment of a crisis intervention phone service, identified a facility for it (an unnamed local church), and agreed on a person who could staff the project once initiated. We then set about getting the ball rolling. Conceived in 1969, RESPONSE began operations in 1971 as a campus ministry program with a group of 50 to 80 trained student, faculty and community volunteers under the steady leadership of our chosen staffer, recently-graduated Stony Brook student Maureen Bybee. (In addition to significant phone usage, there was an unexpected byproduct: student volunteers bonded with older community volunteers.) After several years RESPONSE was able to receive funding from Suffolk County. Soon after that it was spun off as a separate agency. RESPONSE of Suffolk County is still active today.

Another project in the spinoff mode was the creation of a local agency, Community and Youth Services (CYS), with a variety of programs guided by a professional staff person and volunteer leaders and workers. A professor in the Stony Brook School of Social Welfare, a local church youth leader, and I provided leadership during the development stage. The key ingredient was the community needs assessment undertaken to fulfill a class assignment by students in the School of Social Welfare. Their final group paper was reworked as a proposal and a budget was added. County funding was forthcoming.

Two other areas of involvement deserve mention. Stony Brook's Administrative Officer, Karl Hartzell, spearheaded efforts over several years and eventually secured funding for a year-long study (1970-71) of the feasibility of establishing a major Center for Religion and Society at the University. For a variety of reasons, faculty opposition not the least of them, the effort faltered. In retrospect, a comment in a letter to me from the Director of the study as he departed (I was on vacation at the time) - helpful then in quelling opposition to our strategy by some stakeholders - seems more notable in retrospect as a suggestion of the common fate of our enterprises. Robert V. Smith (a Methodist, on leave from his position as Professor of Philosophy and Religion at Colgate University) wrote: "I'm sorry I did not accomplish more, but I did what I could. Since my present model for the Center is much like what you do, I hope you will continue to support it." The experience with the Center proposal did have one lasting impact: our ministry and others serving the campus developed a proposal for a modest interfaith center. Four years after Bob Smith's efforts, this initiative was successful in adding a permanent feature to Student Services - not least, as regards faculty support, because of the efforts of a member of the English Department, theologian Thomas Altizer.

Another example of church interest in creating new ministries in the growing Suffolk County area was a project of the Presbytery of Long Island. Its Nesconset Experimental Ministry led by the Rev. David Bos and his co-director, Father Peter Ryan of the local Catholic Diocese, developed programs in response to the needs of those living in the marketing area of a major shopping center under construction, Smith Haven Mall (three miles from the Stony Brook campus). Smith Haven Ministries (its incorporated name) was successful in securing significant space in the mall, opening with a full time staff of four. David and I discovered a variety of ways in which our ministries could cooperate together, often utilizing University personnel or students (programs with Schools in the Health Sciences Center were noteworthy). In addition to sharing office space for a period of time, while I was on sabbatical thanks to a Danforth Campus Ministry Grant, David served the Federation in a consulting role in my absence.

II. My second position on Long Island was created by developments at the state level in New York. Because it did not involve any physical change in living and basic work settings for me, it would be easy to imagine it was simply a transition to another stage. The change, however, involved a new call and the replacement of one working situation with a quite different one. The merging of the Nassau and Suffolk campus ministry boards was what happened locally to create one of eight area ministries covering New York State: the result, **Long Island United Campus Ministries (LIUCM)** was also UMHE on Long Island. Statewide, 28 separate local ministries became 8 area ministries, the unique history of each Area dictating the changes necessary - often from assignments to a single campus - to create area ministries in which staff were deployed in teams with both area and statewide portfolios. The New York State UMHE Commission process, completed in the spring of 1972, considered all local staff who wished to be involved and redeployed them, 18 in all, assigning Tom Philipp (previously at SUNY Oswego upstate) and me to the Island.

On Long Island, because I had already been working in a smaller area there that was now being enlarged -- from 4 campuses to potentially more than four times that number, I did not experience the change as dramatic; Tom did. One of the students active in the Christian Association at Stony Brook when I arrived over nine years earlier, Gerda Barber, wrote an article for a local paper describing the changes at a time when the new pattern was five years old, an article reprinted in the national UMHE publication, *Connexion*. In it Tom described the shock of going from being a well-known campus leader to a campus visitor known by only a few.

However, in the article Tom also described the development of a project initiated with his leadership. We had had a peace education - draft counseling project during the Vietnam War. When the War ended (troops began returning in 1973), a survey we conducted indicated that there were 16,000 Vietnam veterans on twelve of the campuses in our area, with many more in our communities. By creating a veterans peer counseling network, our ministry was able to provide a needed resource. Many veterans had problems relating to standard campus procedures; they could relate to their peers, who were able to provide both basic support and serve as guides or intermediaries in accessing campus resources.

Emblematic of what ministry meant during the UMHE on Long Island years was the statewide Lay Ministry Training Project, which I had a hand in initiating. In response to the World Council of Churches emphasis on the missionary structure of the congregation, a small group working under the title of the Metropolitan Associates of Philadelphia (MAP) -- represented most often, in our experience, by Richard R. Broholm -- had created the Lay Ministry for Organizational Change Strategy. A well-articulated training program introduced several of us as statewide staff to a process in which each of us with a non-staff partner from our Area was trained in the Strategy. Part of that training included each of these teams replicating the training with others in their own Areas. The Strategy was applicable for enabling ministry in whatever church and community or campus setting each participant chose to engage; I produced a local training workbook as a resource.

Long Island was the only Area to specifically identify its work as project-oriented. Staff in other Areas were quite effective in this and other ways in their own situations. One with special prominence was William Gibson, a member of the Southern Tier Area staff whose EcoJustice Task Force work was influential far beyond the bounds of New York State.

The issue we all confronted was the problem of replacing the familiar chaplaincy/campus ministry model with a way of presenting the area model of ministry in higher education that captured the imagination of both church leaders and people in the pews, or at least dissuaded its outright opponents. Truth to tell, most of us as staff would not have listed area ministry as a choice, though I can recall only one outright voice of opposition once the change was made. However, other incontrovertible facts soon became apparent: the reduction, between 1972 and 1979, of the statewide staff from 18 to 12; a pattern of declining income; and a projected 1980 deficit of $100,000 (roughly a third of our statewide budget).

The end came at a meeting of the UMHE in New York Executive Board on June 2, 1979 at which the following objectives were adopted:

1. Participation in the development of a new set of goals, strategies, structures and funding supports to carry on ministry in higher education in the state.

2. Cessation of the present program of staffing as of June 30, 1980.

3. Cessation of operations by the UMHE/NY Executive Board as of December 31, 1980.

I approached this development from a newly-acquired perspective. At the beginning of 1979, I had become the **Interim Executive Director of UMHE/NY**. In this role I now provided staff service to a high-level Futures Planning Committee that worked from July through November,1979 to implement the first objective. In addition, I worked with Jon Regier, Executive Director of the New York State Council of Churches, and the Council's Design Task Force as it developed a state level component for the emerging picture.

I also worked with the UMHE/NY Executive Board and Area personnel to prepare for the cessation of all area staff employment. Part of the effectiveness of these various operations was that they were guided by groups of people with single objectives: those looking ahead didn't have to look back; those winding things down didn't have to worry about what would happen next. As the one who staffed both kinds of activity, I did not enjoy the same luxury. At some point in the first half of 1980 I entered on a second interim position, becoming Higher Education Project Staff for the Council of Churches.

Once the Council's Design Task Force had determined that the Council should have a higher education position on its staff, a hiring process was instituted and Adam J. Kittrell, a Baptist pastor, was chosen to become the Council's Associate Director for Ministry in Higher Education. Adam brought good skills and church, campus and community experience to the position; what he lacked was familiarity with the New York State scene. As a result, in 1981 I stepped into a third interim position in as many years, Higher Education Consultant affiliated with IDEA, a New York State educational network under the direction of Christian Educator David Lewis. In this role I introduced Adam to the persons and institutions around the State with whom he would be working. At the same time I continued work across the State with localities that were seeking to redesign their approach to ministry in light of the events that had taken place.

The call for "an ecumenical ministry in higher education" saw the number of supporting denominations rise from the six in UMHE in New York (American Baptist, Christian Church, Reformed Church, United Church of Christ, United Methodist, United Presbyterian) to eight with the addition of Lutheran Synods and Episcopal Dioceses. Denominational funding, which had been provided to UMHE at the State level from which it was distributed to the Areas, was now returned to the direct support of local and regional ministries. The new scene was identified in a Directory of Cooperative Ministries in Higher Education in New York State issued by the New York State Council of Churches in 1982. It notes six models of ministry in use: parish-based ministry, institutional chaplaincy, shared or part-time ministry, denominational chaplaincy and appointment, cooperative or ecumenical ministry, and student-based organization. It lists 142 persons (by County) engaged in higher education ministry. Of these, 26 are identified as full time, 87 as part time, and 29 have no identification (most appear to me to be part time). For every one that was full time, approximately four were part time.

III. As my consulting role was beginning to run its course, a new position was announced at ***Union College in Schenectady***, made possible by the redistribution of funds that had taken place with the demise of UMHE/NY. As it happened my wife, Vaughn, and I had moved to Schenectady in the summer of 1980. She had been appointed to a faculty position in the Nursing Department at Russell Sage College in nearby Troy (she had previously occupied a similar position in the School of Nursing at the Health Sciences Center at Stony Brook). The move also made travel about the State easier for me. My office with the Council of Churches was at First Presbyterian Church, Albany, along with Elenora Ivory, the Council's Public Policy Director (ten years later I would serve First Pres as Interim Minister on the retirement of its long time pastor, Robert Lamar). I applied and was called to the position of Campus Protestant Minister at Union College, half time, in the winter of 1982. By the fall I had also become Interim Minister/Head of Staff at Albany's Westminster Presbyterian Church - where my colleague was Rick Spalding, now Chaplain at Williams College (site of my own undergraduate experience).

The 12½ years at Union had as background a continuing conversation within the local Board: how to make the ministry full time. We progressed in steps. For the first three and a half years I was on my own. The following year we added a part time ordained assistant. Then, for the next five years we had full time seminary interns (one staying a second year). Finally, for the last three years I served as Coordinator and two recent seminary graduates served full time as the Protestant chaplain. (Dr. Viki Brooks now serves full time, supported by both the College and the church community, in three roles: Campus Protestant Minister, Interfaith Chaplain, and Director of Religious Life. In between our times, Kathleen Buckley, now Chaplain at St. Lawrence University, was the Campus Protestant Minister.)

Union, founded in 1795, did not build its Memorial Chapel until the early 20th century. It was founded (thus the name) by three groups of early Schenectady residents and their churches: the Dutch of First Reformed, the English of St. George's Episcopal, and the Scots, Scotch-Irish and New Englanders of First Presbyterian. For years commencements were held in First Presbyterian's sanctuary. Not a few Presidents over the years have been members of the clergy. Most prominent was Eliphalet Nott, a Presbyterian who served as Union's President for sixty-two years in the 19th century. Indeed, during my first eight and a half years at Union the President was John S. Morris, a Presbyterian Minister and former Professor of Philosophy and Religion at Colgate University.

With the completion of Memorial Chapel, the College provided a position for a director of religious activities. By mid-century, this had become a member of the Classics Department who also served as Chaplain, Norman Johnson. With Norman's retirement in 1968, College funding for such a role ceased.

While the campus ministry board's oft-stated desire was to provide students the full time presence of a trusted counselor and leader in the faith, detailed above, it seemed to me that this intention needed to be supplemented by activities that were directed at repositioning what it means to be religious in relation to the College's history and the current educational enterprise. Over-simplified, this became a focus on values education, variously presented, and the use of orthogonal framing.

Worship, study, fellowship and service were still there for those who responded to them in their typical formats. For them, but especially for others, there were other opportunities. Here, in lieu of a description of the values education approach and orthogonal framing, are some suggestive recollections:

- Fresh from the completion of her seminary education, Protestant Chaplain Alison Boden (now Director of Religious Life and the Chapel at Princeton University) reciting the Gospel of Mark in a cabaret setting. Someone schooled in drama, as she was, taking the Good News out of the church and onto the student stage.
- President Morris, First Reformed pastor Dean Dykstra, my Catholic colleague Father Dennis Cox, and I, on an alumni weekend, concelebrating the eucharist using First Reformed's Lydius communion cup. The cup came from the period following the 1690 massacre of Schenectady citizens by French militia and native raiders, and had likely been touched by the lips of the fabled native American, Lawrence, a member of First Reformed who helped rescue captives led away after the massacre.
- Vermont artist Melinda White (now White-Bronson), in the College's theater-in-the-round, reflecting on her arresting sculpture, "We are the Angels: We are the Mortal People," with responses initiated by Rudy Nydegger, Associate Professor of Psychology and Management and a local

Hospice Board member. Using papier-mâché, leaves, wood, and burlap, the ten-foot high by seven-foot by five-foot sculpture depicts an angel leaning over a dying woman on her bed.

• Seminary Intern David Bodman (now Randall-Bodman) developing and presenting a first Interfaith event on campus titled "Reflections on Jewish-Christian Dialogue Today" and featuring guests Rabbi Leon Klenecki, Dr. Eugene Fisher, and Dr. Robert Everett. Opined Union's Associate Dean of Faculty Terry Weiner, in a next-day note to David, "The panel for the Interfaith Dinner was absolutely *first rate*! Bravo!"

• Seminary Intern Laurel Hayes (most recently campus minister at Webster University) initiating and moderating "Plateful of Questions," a student lunchtime discussion program that continued long after she had returned to seminary.

• Writer and preacher Frederick Buechner, resident for three days on campus, telling a class in the English Department how he writes to spark the imagination: long-hand, with colored pencils which he changes every few sentences.

• Seminary Intern Gloria Korsman developing and conducting an Interfaith worship service, "Living With AIDS."

• Malusi Mpumlwana, colleague of Steve Biko in the creation of the anti-apartheid Black Consciousness Movement in South Africa, sharing his experiences with students.

In nearby Albany, when UMHE in New York closed up shop, Lutheran and Episcopal ministries continued. Fourteen years later, the Albany-based Capital Area Council of Churches formed a campus ministry committee and advertised a new half time position. I applied and was accepted for the position; it was time for a fresh presence at Union (which Kathleen Buckley ably supplied) - and, as it turned out, a final new start for me.

My Protestant colleague at the University at Albany's Chapel House was Lutheran Chaplain Dennis Meyer, also part time (but in an installed local pastorate). It did not take long before we were agreed that Dennis should continue as the primary staff person for the gathered life of the Protestant community and I would take primary responsibility for the community's outreach activities. In practice we each did some of both; we also each shared responsibilities in relation to the rest of the Chapel House staff.

In sum, in two years, my contribution was to expand good working relationships with partners on campus and in the local church community. Two years later, in the fall of 1998, the Lutheran Board for Campus Ministry initiated conversations with its Council of Churches counterpart. A new Board with equal representation from each of the old Boards was in place by the following spring, the two half-time positions were merged, and a new full time Campus Minister, Sandy Damhof, was in place the next fall; this spring she will finish her 15th year.

There was one other project that I had begun while at Union that was completed while I was at the **University at Albany**: the nationally-attended Consultation, "Out on a Limb: Thinking About Faith and Ministry in the College and University Setting." This fall 1995 Consultation, generously funded by the Louisville Institute for the Study of Protestantism and American Culture, gathered some 120 persons over three days to talk together about the state of ministry in higher education, prompted by presentations from Episcopal Chaplain Sam Portaro, Professor of History and Education Douglas Sloan, Harvard Senior Research Fellow Sharon Daloz Parks, and Theologian Douglas John Hall, with responses by UCC Area Minister Donna Schaper and Auburn Seminary President Barbara Wheeler.

One denominational official later wrote that it was a "rare event." The letter writer was speaking of the caliber of the presentations and the design of what took place. It was, I believe, rare in another sense. Extended applause at the end of the gathering was prompted by an opportunity to thank me for my work as coordinator of the event. Yet, as the applause went on and on, it became clear that those present were also expressing, as Bob Lamar, moderator of the final session, said to me at the time, "something more." I would hazard the guess that what they were expressing was their heart-felt appreciation for their time together. Thoughtful conversation and fellowship, preceded and followed by artfully-crafted common worship/celebration (the contribution of Gail George, worship consultant, liturgist and dancer, now deceased) had evoked much of the best that nourishes the spirits of those who claim the title "campus minister," as well as those whose lives express the claim without the title.

There have been times over these years when my reaction to the prospects for this ministry has been anxiety, fear, and depression; a sober analysis of its statistical decline would say the same without the feelings. In addition, I could not even have considered the interim and, especially, the part- time positions in which I served had it not been for the steady employment of my wife. At the same time, I'm hard- pressed to imagine myself in a life's work that could equal it for energizing challenges, rewarding personal associations, and meaningful fulfillments, small and large.

Hugh Nevin, with his wife Vaughn, still lives in the Schenectady, NY house to which they moved on leaving Long Island in 1980. However, downsizing is now a serious project as a move to a nearby senior community is likely within a year. He sings regularly in the choir of First Pres, Albany, provides pastoral service occasionally, participates in a book club, enjoys the area's music and the arts and writing projects, mission activities and regular exercise at a nearby wellness center. Eight grandchildren (one married) ensure a continuing lively youth connection.

Creating Social Change
By Jim Ray

I am pleased to join other sages in remembering my 32 years in ministry in higher education [1963-1995] at the University of Illinois [Champaign-Urbana], the University of Pittsburgh, and Youngstown State University. I was appreciative in reading my friend Verlyn Barker's memoir for his historical look at how our unique ministry evolved over much of the 20th century.

Let me share some personal history, which in retrospect, helped to focus my concerns in ministry in our unique setting. I grew up in Columbus, OH in poverty conditions, which saw our family move 13 times just in Columbus, always into poorer housing. My dad got a degree in Business from the University of Pittsburgh in 1929, and was "a big man on campus". Given the "Great Depression" he had no full time job for over ten years until he got a position selling life insurance in 1941.

I graduated from a Junior- Senior High School which had only a half-dozen students of color then, while today it is 99% African-American, reflecting the "white flight" over the years since I left there. I entered Ohio State University in the fall of 1948, but my graduation was delayed by my being drafted into the Army during the Korean War. I ended up serving in the Prisoner of War Command on a tiny island off the southern coast of Korea, where our company of G.I.'s oversaw the guarding of 8000 North Korean prisoners, which was done by 1000 South Korean soldiers. Never had I been in such a diverse setting!

I was there for 16 months and speak of this because I encountered some ugly American stories, and actions, which affected my fairly simple perspectives on life and ultimately saw me going into the ministry. I was able to develop some personal relationships with four of the prisoners which produced some "AHA" moments.

Returning home, and being discharged from my two years of Army service, I completed my studies at Ohio State as a speech major and then went to McCormick Seminary where I graduated in 1960. I accepted a call to be the Assistant Minister at the First Presbyterian Church in Galesburg, Illinois where I learned about congregational ministry and enjoyed my ministry with the youth groups. After two and a half years I accepted a position on the campus ministry staff at the *Presbyterian McKinley Foundation and Congregation at the University of Illinois in January, 1963*.

I joined a staff of four campus ministers under the direction of Dr. James Hine, who was nationally known for his work on and off campus since he came there in the late 40's. Little did I know that the "student ministry" there was to evolve so quickly from what it was when Jim first arrived there years earlier. I saw pictures of students standing by the hundreds outside the McKinley Church waiting to get in for the second Sunday service. The sanctuary held over 600 persons and it was packed over most of those by gone days for both services. Jim Hine was a fine preacher and drew students in.

By the time I arrived, the times had changed dramatically on campus with students having access to more programs, having cars, and life becoming more complex for everyone. By this time there was only one service with perhaps 250-300 persons attending with the same good preaching and service that spoke to students and other university folk.

I had only been on staff at McKinley, doing "student work" for about a month when I got a phone call which was to revolutionize my life, as well as being a precursor to change on campus and the nation. A clergy friend was asking me to join him and other clergy to go to the March on Washington in August. My response was "What's that about?" I went and my life has never been the same since. There I not only heard speakers like Dr. M. L. King but Bob Dylan singing "The Times They Are A Changin'." That surely became the mantra for the Civil Rights struggle and the years leading up to the Vietnam War.

After only six months of doing bible study and programs and helping students understand their relationship with their faith and their church in a different university context, by the fall of 1963, as Verlyn Barker wrote, "Ministry in higher education had to come to grips with a whole host of issues, including racial and gender equality, war and peace, issues related to the welfare of students and academic freedom."

Those issues became a major focus of my ministry and I credit Jim Hine for allowing me and my staff colleague, Larry Hill, to be involved on campus, and off, in the Civil Rights struggle. Some members of the McKinley Foundation Board and the Session of the church disagreed with Jim but he stood his ground. Thus soon after the March on Washington I joined a large group of university faculty, students and staff in a protest demonstration in front of the home of the Chancellor of the University. We were there because the university was not hiring African-Americans and other persons of color in the numbers that should have been in place. I remember a time thirty years later at Youngstown State when I was chatting with an African-American staff person, and a friend of mine, who told me that out of over 1200 employees at YSU, from the President down to the lowest level employees, there were only about 50 persons of color working on campus in a city that was rapidly becoming a majority of black and Hispanic persons. In each situation, my concern, and action, was for me part of doing ministry in higher education, along with continuing traditional "student work" ministry.

At the U. of Illinois I started a weekly peace vigil in the center of campus. Several Roman Catholic sisters on the staff of the Newman Center joined in that prophetic presence with other students, faculty and staff.

Several years later these "sisters" and I joined forces to create a "Coffee House Ministry" in our foundation building. Those were the days!

134

I spent Holy Week of 1964, with another local pastor, when we responded to a call from the National Council of Churches for clergy to go south on picket lines in the South. He and I walked a picket line in front of the County Court House in Hattiesburg, Miss. We walked in a circle from 9-5 Monday- Friday. We lived in the black community with worship services in black churches several nights where I had never heard such preaching and singing. It was life changing of me. One day we were pulled off the line to go into the courtroom where a young black lawyer from Detroit, named John Conyers, defended and won the case against a young SNCC staff member. We integrated the courtroom for the first time in memory, and the judge was outraged and cleared the courtroom.

My friend and I were so nervous that we did not attempt to visit the local Presbyterian Church which was just a block away. All of this took place just weeks before the three young SNCC workers were found buried in an earthen dam several counties away.

Later that spring in the basement of the McKinley Church I joined other campus ministers and U. of Ill persons to do training in non-violence tactics with university students who were going to be involved in civil rights work in the Mississippi Summer Project-- doing tutoring, voter education and registration in local black communities in dangerous circumstances.

I spent six weeks in the summer of 1965 in southern Virginia, outside of Richmond, as I responded to a call for a campus minister to lead a group of college students to do voter registration and tutoring. We worked out of the local black Presbyterian Church in Amelia. The local Ku Klux Klan became more active in response to our presence. That program touched a lot of lives and gave hope to the black community. It also was a moving experience for the students, and I heard from several of them that fall about how much that had informed and changed them.

During that time my wife and our two young sons lived with a McCormick classmate and his wife in Richmond. He was serving as the first white pastor of a black congregation. I came in periodically to see my family as I lived with the students in the church in Amelia. That was certainly an experience for all of us.

I had three classmates from McCormick who went south back then to be white pastors of black congregations. I led a work project of U. of Ill students at one of those churches in Asheville, NC. As many of you who read this have experienced, one of our woman students on that project returned to campus and changed her major as a result of the work she did in Asheville. That challenged her perspectives and her faith caused her make this change.

During my time at McKinley Foundation the new anti-war organization, Students for a Democratic Society [SDS], held their first national conference in our Foundation building. Our staff took turns staying up until the wee hours as SDS held meetings long into the night to plan strategy for the next day to engage people in the community about their radical perspectives on the Viet

Nam War. Nothing at McCormick Seminary had prepared me for some of this, but my exposures in the Civil Rights struggle surely did. Thus I understood and agreed with much that SDS was dealing with on matters like the influence of racism and the power of the military-industrial complex on our universities and our nation. Much of that still pertains today as the power of the corporate world impacts our universities with funding that has strings attached.

In 1968 I received a Danforth Campus Ministry Grant which enabled me to return to McCormick to work on a degree that could help me move into an urban campus ministry position. I am grateful to another "Sage," Don Gibson, who wrote that by this time campus ministry had moved from "being casual to being at times confrontational." I had already experienced some of that during my time at McKinley. But the day after I moved up to the seminary was the day of the demonstration against the Democratic Party Convention which was meeting in Chicago. That was the day that police brutality erupted on the demonstrators in Grant Park who were tear gassed and many arrested. "Dump the Hump" was the mantra of the day. I went down to the park the next day, smelled the residue of the tear gas and participated in the concerns that were being voiced there about the Democratic policies being espoused at the Convention as the War in Viet Nam raged on.

At the end of my study year I accepted a position on the staff of *University and City Ministries [UACM] in Pittsburgh* to be in campus ministry at the University of Pittsburgh. UACM was a multidivisional ministry interfacing the Church with the university and the city. Located across the street from "Pitt" in a former Presbyterian church building, UACM was composed of: The Community of Reconciliation [COR], an intentional multi-racial congregation, Urban Ministry, Campus Ministry at three universities, the Hunger-Action Coalition, the Oakland Children's Center, with Mister Rogers as one of the initiators, and a full-time staff counselor helping young men deal with their questions about the draft during the Vietnam War

I had only been there two weeks when I joined many people in a street demonstration with the Black Construction Coalition which was confronting the refusal to hire black workers to help build the new U.S. Steel Headquarters Building downtown and the Three Rivers Stadium for the Pittsburgh Steelers. What both surprised and thrilled me in the demonstration was the participation of some of the members of the Community of Reconciliation. Except for some of the Civil Rights marches, I had never marched with the members from the congregation where I worshiped. That is as it should be for the people of faith who claim to follow Jesus should imitate his model that finally took him into the streets and to his death. Maybe that message has been too dramatically clear for church folk to handle.

COR was committed to a social justice ministry, and its members, white, black and others, were half from a black Presbyterian Church who wanted to be a part of a multi-racial witness to God's inclusive love, and many others

136

from other congregations, including Roman Catholic, whose concern for social justice were not being met by those churches. We had students from Pitt and Carnegie Mellon and some faculty. COR spawned an Inner City Youth Group which saw inner city young people going to suburban white congregations to meet with the young people there.

My work at Pitt was diverse, from traditional student work to being called one morning from the Student Affairs Office, the day after the Kent State demonstrations and the killing of three students there. That morning Pitt students were milling around the Cathedral of Learning, full of anger and frustration. Would I and other campus ministers come down to talk with them? Of course. I was able to meet the parents of the young woman Kent State student who was killed and was from Pittsburgh. I asked the father to come down later to talk with the Pitt students. That was helpful, both for the father and for the students who heard him, through his grief, counsel them not to demonstrate in an ugly manner.

My most challenging role in ministry, in, and to, higher education at the University of Pittsburgh was as the result of meeting a radical faculty member, who along with other activists in the Oakland area, which surrounded the university, had organized a neighborhood community group called "People's Oakland". Their goal was to confront the university about the ways in which it was not being a good "neighbor" to those who lived around Pitt. From my perspective it was a classic example of a university "doing their thing" to the detriment of the neighbors around it. People's Oakland received a sizable grant from the state with the intent to develop a master plan for the future of Oakland which would bring representatives from three universities, the several major hospitals, as well as persons from local block clubs and other community organizations, some of whom lived right across the street from Pitt. But the two bodies had never met to talk about what it meant to be neighbors. With the grant People's Oakland hired Urban Design Associates [UDA], an architectural and community planning concern.

I was asked to chair the monthly meetings of representatives of these various bodies, some quite large and others very small. But all had a voice around that table. I was excited because this effort was exactly what I had been looking for after my year of study at McCormick. There I read material from urban campus ministers who pointed out the great need for "neighborliness" to be an important factor between a university and the people who lived around it. For they were, and still are, in most places, strangers to each other, yet our biblical message is clear, that ministry is to be about the work of reducing the divide between the two parties.

The planning process, led by UDA, went on for several years with both confrontation and conciliation taking place. UDA held several large community gatherings where they asked homeowners, businesspersons, all types of "Oakland persons" what their concerns and hopes were for their sizable area. I marveled at their skill in listening, and engaging with, both individuals who owned or rented the places where they lived, and representatives from huge concerns like the universities and hospitals.

We hammered out a master plan, which some thirty years later I saw was still being carried out. As I reflect back now over the years, I know that my part in that important venture, which brought diverse people together, was doing ministry in higher education.

A few years later I made my last move in my career, which was to be the Protestant campus minister at *Youngstown State University* [YSU] in July, 1983. That ministry was called Cooperative Campus Ministry [CCM], as it had been formed years earlier by a cooperative action by the downtown churches in Youngstown. One of the highlights of my twelve years as Director of CCM was providing oversight for a Free Clinic which was held every Tuesday evening from 7-11 in the basement of First Christian Church, located on campus and also housed the CCM Office. The Clinic basically served as the health care center for the university students as YSU did not have such a facility. The Clinic was staffed by osteopathic physicians in the area. Over the years the population who came to the clinic changed as the fallout by the dramatic closure of the steel mills in 1977 in Youngstown meant many persons had no health care.

So they came to the Clinic. Over its twenty year history the Free Clinic served over 22,000 students and community persons. Finally YSU opened its own Health Care Center. Before that the President would on occasion slip me some money on the sly because he knew how important our service was for the students. The Clinic was another variation from traditional campus ministry and with its expertise we met the needs of many students and others.

I spent every Tuesday night for years at the Clinic talking with students about their situations, engaging with the doctors and ending the evening with a meal at a local restaurant at 11PM. A yearly highlight was a Christmas celebration which took place at St. John's Episcopal Church, just off campus. Following the work at the Clinic, on the Tuesday closest to Christmas Day, many of the Clinic staff would bring food and we would have our evening meal there in the Parish Hall. Then late in the evening we would go into the darkened sanctuary, sit in the choir pews and sing Christmas hymns played by the St. John's organist and the organ professor in the YSU Music School. That event always started the Christmas season for me, and I would recall the importance of the Clinic for so many diverse persons.

When I started my ministry at YSU I came with a keen interest in wanting to start an interracial dialogue group with students and any other interested YSU persons. I met an African-American woman who was a staff person in Student Affairs who wanted to join me and we formed the Racial Awareness Program [RAP], which met every Wednesday noon for a brown bag lunch. This quickly became one of the largest groups on campus and over the years evolved into The Coalition for Diversity. There were faculty, staff and students who took on every issue of diversity we could think of at a time when YSU evidenced little interest in this important issue.

When I arrived at YSU in 1983 the university was doing nothing to prepare students of color for what they would face in coming to live and learn in a primarily white campus. Beyond a few African-American faculty, there were no persons of color filling any leadership positions at the university. That fall some black faculty and staff who were on the CCM Board held a three hour "Introduction to campus" for incoming black students on the Saturday before classes began on the next Wednesday.

Over the years I believe that our emphasis on diversity had an effect on YSU and now it is a much more diverse university, though even now, nineteen years after my retirement, there is a long way to go.

Other parts of my ministry, which pick up my concern for the prophetic, include planting a Peace Pole in the center of campus, holding peace vigils and demonstrations over crucial issues of justice, and providing some support for key student groups that formed around these issues-- thus trying to inform the larger university population of the importance of engaging together on such critical matters.

With my Catholic campus ministry colleague we began a support group for older students returning to campus to start or finish a degree. The Non-Traditional Student Organization rapidly became an important base for those persons who came bearing additional burdens of family and jobs and wondered whether they could make it as students. They did so in grand style.

I will close by sharing the insight of John W. Traphagan, a professor of religious studies at the University of Texas at Austin. He wrote a recent article entitled "Does Higher Education Have a Customer Service Problem?" out of his concern that many universities around the country are moving to running on a business model where students are seen as customers and the university is thus "run with the idea of pleasing customers and providing a service to students". He believes "this changes the atmosphere from one where students are challenged to succeed and take advantage of all that they can as part of an intellectual community to one in which they view their education as a process of purchasing grades so they can get a job".

My experience in ministry in higher education formed by my life's experiences finds me agreeing with Traphagan when he concludes, "This degrades the mission of a public university, which is to promote the public good and improve society through research and education... .Thinking in terms of customer service deflects attention away from what we are--- a community of people interested in learning and creating knowledge that promotes the improvement of our society".

I have always believed that one of the primary roles of higher education is bringing about "social change." I was pleased to find Traphagan's thought agreeing with what for years directed my ministry in higher education.

I am grateful for the many campus ministry friends from whom I learned so much and with whom we did so much.

Jim still retains his passion for social justice and reconciliation, and is an advocate and activist at First Presbyterian Church of Youngstown, an old downtown church, working with faith-based organizations on ministry to the city and becoming a multi-racial congregation. He and his wife Sue together have six children and 14 grandchildren, scattered from Hawaii to Germany.

An Examined Life
By Don Shockley

It is sobering to realize that I may have lived my life in response to a Wesleyan cliché: "let us unite the pair so long disjoined: knowledge and vital piety." I guess it would be less unsettling if we updated the language to say that our task is to foster dialogue between learning and spirituality. Put that way, I am not reluctant to embrace the sentiment involved.

As a sophomore in a Birmingham, Alabama, high school in the fifties I got a wake-up call when my report card for the previous six weeks showed three F's and a D. Some of my friends teased me about the D. But my developmental situation was more complicated than these facts suggest. For example, it does not reasonably follow that I was at the time active in the Methodist Youth Fellowship and, in fact, one of its leaders in our local church's chapter; or that I was singing in the chancel choir at the time.

The Avondale Methodist Church (not United yet) was a good, solid congregation in the tradition of Wesleyan spirituality, i.e. it was not fundamentalist or even evangelical in the contemporary sense of those words. Suffice it to say that when I presented myself to our pastor at the close of the Easter service in my junior year in high school and told him that I came forward in response to his altar call, folks were surprised, myself not least of all. The pastor, who was elderly and ill and had not been with us very long, said something like, "Son, you are already a member here, aren't you?" I told him that I came down the steps from the choir to answer a call I heard in the closing hymn, "Take the Name of Jesus with You." I had a powerful sense that the text of the hymn was intended for me. It was a classic "call to preach."

That's how it all began for me. It was way too early; I was not ready for all the consequences that decision would bring, beginning immediately. As the report of what I had done went around the high school one of my classmates had an immediate response. "What a pity!" is what he said. There would be many moments when I thought his response was right on target. But, for the last half century the original calling has continued to echo in my mind and heart. And it has continued to be unsettling.

My immediate path was clear. I would improve my academic performance in high school enough to go to the Methodist college across town and after that I would go to seminary. What was not clear was that at the end of my first year in the college, I would be assigned as pastor of a small church about 35 miles from the campus. I was not consulted about this! A fellow student whose father was a district superintendent heard about it and told me it was a done deal. It is still hard to imagine this happening, but I was pastor of that church from the beginning of my sophomore year until I graduated from Birmingham-Southern College in 1959.

So, at the age of 19 I had the responsibility of preaching every Sunday morning and, in this case, every other Sunday night. And there began my lifelong task of trying to unite learning and spirituality. When you have Geology 101 and Western Civilization on week-days and preaching on Sunday you have to unite knowledge and piety as well as you can. I don't believe that, at that point in my life, I had even heard of campus ministry. I was not involved in the Methodist Student Movement on the campus because I had a church to look after. I had to study for my classes and prepare those sermons at the same time. And still have time for some social life. I was already in love with a wonderful young woman who had been my sweetheart in elementary school and to whom I have now been married more than 55 years. Needless to say I was involved in a complex life situation in which the foundation of my future was being sorted out. There would be nothing remarkable about that were it not for Robert Frost. In one of his great poems he said:

Yield who will to their separation
My object in living's to unite my avocation and my vocation
As my two eyes make one in sight.
Only where love and need are one
Is the deed ever really done
For heaven and the future's sake.

Frost was not only well represented in my American literature class; he came to our campus to read his poems and we all had the opportunity to meet him and get his autograph, which I still treasure. The point is that I was already hoping to find ways to reduce the distance between who I am and what I do and the great poet confirmed that such would be a worthy goal. In retrospect I know that, for me at least, campus ministry would offer the chance to do what I love and get paid for doing it. I was fortunate enough to have the opportunity to choose that path and that made all the difference for me. (Don't miss this further allusion to Frost's poetry.)

If you are still reading at this point, I hasten to tell you that I do not plan to go over the story of my life in the kind of detail this beginning implies. I had two more years in a rural pastorate followed by two years on the staff of an affluent suburban church in Birmingham. I already knew that the direction my life was taking had to change. I half-heartedly began to apply to graduate school in New Testament studies. Then someone told me that my alma mater was looking for a chaplain and, not really knowing all that would involve, I applied for the job and got it. I kept that position for eight years, then moved to the chaplaincy at the **University of Redlands** in southern California for seven years, followed by eleven years as chaplain of **Emory University** in Atlanta.

My final assignment was as a **general staff person for campus ministries related to the United Methodist Church**: Wesley Foundations, ecumenical ministries, college and university chaplains and more. It was a fortunate way to bring my active career to a close. In his research on the stages of human development Erik Erikson coined the wonderful term "generativity": creativity in behalf of the generations. How nice that after all the years in campus ministry I could devote myself to helping others find their way in the profession. From the beginning I had sought to understand and interpret our work to others. This involved a lot of writing and speaking long before it became a formal responsibility and although I have slowed down to a crawl now, I am still trying to help where I can.

I have never had a job that did not involve stress. Young people need to understand this when looking for their place in the world of ministry and work. The above may sound like once I entered the chaplaincy the rest was smooth sailing. That was by no means the case. I have frequently been on the other side of issues that some powerful people (e.g. college trustees, District Superintendents, et al.) were agitated about. I think I stood my ground without doing too many things that were stupid. In difficult times the caring and support of colleagues made a big difference. That is one of the reasons why professional groups such as the National Campus Ministry Association are so important. But they are also important because they are so much fun!

I retired fifteen years ago and, although I served on, and chaired, the board of directors of the Wesley/Canterbury campus ministry at Vanderbilt for a few of these years, I am aware of how out of touch I have become. The campuses have changed, the culture has changed, the situation of the churches has changed. Although I was extensively involved with all kinds of ministries on all kinds of campuses near the end of my career, I never attended as a student or served as a campus minister on any but private, church-related campuses. I wrote a book on campus ministry, *Campus Ministry: The Church Beyond Itself*, 1989, but it came out 25 years ago! (I can't resist saying, however, that the book was recently used in a class on campus ministry with the students saying it is still relevant.)

My final word is to express my gratitude for the opportunities I had to serve in, and love, campus ministry for so long. I am especially grateful for all the friendships that were born and nurtured among colleagues over the years, many of which were enabled by the National Campus Ministry Association, now celebrating its 50th year. Happy Anniversary NCMA!

Now here is the basic thing I want to say. I will have my 77th birthday this summer, and I have just admitted to feeling out of touch and over the hill. But that refers to the everyday, practical realities of ministry on the campuses. I am still very much engaged with the issues related to spirituality and learning that I mentioned in the opening lines of this little essay. I write a little, teach adult Sunday School classes a little, and engage in spirited conversations with friends all the time. A philosopher whose name does not spring to mind at the moment said that we have a moral obligation to be intelligent. How true! What we don't know—maybe refuse to know--hurts people. In whatever ways I can at this late date, I am still trying to find ways to help unite knowledge and vital piety!

Ministry to Blacks in Higher Education (MBHE)
By Jim Wilson

I became the campus minister at *Northeast Louisiana State University* in the fall of 1969. The university was located in Monroe, on the edge of the Mississippi River delta, and had integrated only a year or two before my arrival. Fewer than 500 of its 7500 students were black, and most were the first in their families to attend college. The only black employees of the university were in food service, custodial or maintenance work; there were none in faculty, administrative or secretarial positions.

The Wesley Foundation had integrated before the school, thanks to the prophetic insight of the former campus minister, Roy Nash. Our ministry included Sunday morning worship. We were the only worshipping community in walking distance from the dorms that welcomed people of all races and nationalities. The service was well attended.

Life in the delta was very harsh for people of color. Blacks greatly outnumbered whites, but most blacks were farmhands for rich planters, receiving low pay and often rude treatment. I noticed the black students usually did not look me in the eye when they shook my hand as they were leaving. I soon learned to hold on to their hand until they raised their heads.

A black student, Noah Riley, came to our chapel every day playing gospel music on our piano. We talked quite a lot about how to make a difference in the lives of black students and help them raise their self-esteem. Noah had a brainstorm and suggested we begin a gospel choir. Soon the Northeast Louisiana State University Interdenominational Ensemble was formed. We were its home and provided a practice facility. I was privileged to hear gospel music at its finest! The choir sang on campus, primarily giving the concerts at the Campus Ministry house. Before long, the Ensemble became a great choir!

In the early 80's, I received an invitation to come to the MBHE (Ministry to Blacks in Higher Education) gathering to be held in Jacksonville, Florida. I asked if they would like our Ensemble to sing. They said "Yes!" Our Campus Ministry and a local church had purchased an old school bus, and "old" is the operative word. We took off for Florida, but had lots of mechanical troubles. After patching the bus together about five times, we made it to Jacksonville with only fifteen minutes to spare. Harold Bell and Richard Hicks were waiting anxiously and rushed us into the conference. The students went in to sing without having an opportunity to change clothes. They held their heads high and brought the house down!

The students grew during their time together at the conference, because they were respected for their talents. It was a great experience, and these students basked in the warmth of the total acceptance.

On the way home, we stopped in Pensacola overnight. Just as we were pulling up at the church we had arranged as our hostel, the bus broke again. Sunday morning we fixed it and proceeded on toward Monroe, but it died again in Mobile. Several churches in Monroe brought vans and rescued the students. I got the bus fixed the next day and made it into Monroe that night.

Despite the problems, there were no complaints from this group of students. Honoring their gift for gospel music enabled them to survive in the university, which was in many ways a hostile environment. My understanding is that the Ensemble is still in existence, though it is now offered for class credit at the university.

I recently received this from a former student, now a pastor, and it describes one of the special fruits of campus ministry:

"I hope this finds you doing well. I haven't seen you in a number of years, so let me briefly bring you up to speed on my life. After spending 13 years in youth ministry, I stepped into the pulpit almost 14 years ago at the behest of my then regional minister. I served as pastor of Broadmoor Christian Church in Shreveport for 8 years while also working as a licensed professional counselor with the Youth Challenge Program. Just over 5 years ago, I made the move to Hot Springs, AR and have been serving as pastor of First Christian Church. I was ordained in the Disciples of Christ church 4 years ago on the alternative track to ordained ministry - but recognized my need to continue theological education. Two years ago, I enrolled in a program with Lexington Theological and am currently enrolled in my last two classes--Evangelism and Outreach, and Leadership in the Black Church Tradition.

"In my evangelism class, we were asked to define evangelism on a discussion board in 400 words or less. The following is what I wrote:

"According to page 337 of "Christianity for Dummies" the definition of evangelism is defined simply as "sharing with others the gospel of Jesus Christ." However, I believe the more important and more interesting question is not what is evangelism, but rather how do we evangelize effectively?

"I know from my own life experiences (as someone who wasn't raised in the church) that the most effective evangelistic effort toward me has simply been by example. I've been blessed with several great mentors in the faith in my life, but the one who comes to mind most often is my former campus minister – Jim Wilson. I grew up having the same stereotypical ideas about ministers as lots of other people. To me a minister was someone who had a lot in common with used car salesmen. Ministers were people with slicked back hair, cheap suits, people who yelled a lot, had great enthusiasm, and were always glad to see you – as long as money was potentially going to change hands. Ministers in my mind were judgmental people who exaggerated the last syllable of each sentence and tried to intimidate others with a "get right (with the Lord) or get left (behind)" attitude.

"Jim was nothing like what I had imagined. For two years, I served as the resident house manager at the campus ministry when I was in college, so I got to know Jim on a personal level. Jim was knowledgeable about scripture and

faith but challenged students to ask questions and to think beyond the text and the rituals. I got to know Jim as a minister and as a human being. He shared spiritual insights and thought provoking experiences as well as off-color jokes, and even a darker side of his personality. I saw him get angry, I saw him sad. I was nearby when his marriage dissolved and when he began a new relationship. Jim Wilson is far from perfect, but he was relatable, he was authentic, and he honored me by sharing (or at least not hiding) his personal struggles in the midst of his faith.

"I knew that I could never be a stuffed shirt pounding on a pulpit yelling about fire and brimstone. But after getting to know Jim, I realized that I didn't have to fulfill the stereotype in order to effectively "share with others the gospel of Jesus Christ."

"My daughter graduates from college in May, so she is now older than I was when I first met you. You are indeed one of the first people who come to mind when I think about my faith journey-- I just thought it was high time that I told you so. Take care and God Bless."

Jim Ray was campus minister 32 years, from 1963 until 1995. He served at Eastern Kentucky University and at Northeast Louisiana University, aka University of Louisiana at Monroe then pastored local churches until 2002 when he retired and moved to Tulsa, OK with his wife Ellen Blue, who became a professor at Phillips Theological Seminary. They currently live part time in Tulsa and part time in New Orleans and upon her retirement will move full time to New Orleans.

Ministry in Higher Education-A Journey
Robert L. Epps

In September of 1964, I moved my family (wife Richie, children Thomas and Elise) from Kansas City to St. Louis to be the Wesley Foundation Director for *Washington University*. The second week I was there, Mario Savio was pulled off a stage at the University of California-Berkeley, and the "60's" were underway in Berkeley and St. Louis.

I left Yale Divinity School in 1958 to go to Kansas City, Missouri, to teach at National College. National was in transition from being a training school for Methodist Deaconesses to a liberal arts college. That was a difficult transition. National failed to get accreditation or attract students. I taught one year, and two years later it closed and the property was given to St. Paul School of Theology.

From National, I went to be Associate at Central Methodist in Kansas City, and three years later went to a "soft money" job at the Psychiatric Receiving Center, also in Kansas City. At PRC, I edited one book and wrote another.

In each of these assignments, I had contact with students. At National, I sponsored the Methodist Student Movement, at Central we had a Sunday School class for students from the University across the street, and at PRC there were students for every medical and psychological field in training positions. Unknowingly, I was being prepared for my real Vocation-ministry in higher education.

Washington University in St. Louis is a high-quality institution with undergraduate and graduate students about equally divided. The "main line" Protestants campus ministries had no buildings, but I had office and program space in Grace Methodist Church. I early made contact with Jim Ewing, director of the United Campus Christian Fellowship, who became my friend and mentor. We each had a small student group and co-sponsored some study and on-campus worship events.

In the years 1964-65, St. Louis higher education was undergoing radical change. The Catholic schools (St. Louis University, Fontbonne and Webster Colleges) were opening up in response to the work of Vatican II. The St. Louis teacher training schools were combined into racially integrated Harris Teachers College. The University of Missouri established a St. Louis campus in the suburb of Normandy and a three campus Community College system was created. Eden, Kendrick, and St. Louis University were graduate theological schools. Across the Mississippi, the Illinois urban area had a unit of Southern Illinois University and a community college.

These developments made it necessary to "out-grow" the older traditional ministry base at Washington University and find ways, with no significant new resources, to serve the larger mission field.

The Episcopal Church was engaging in a "Pilot Diocese" program to use nine Dioceses to explore and study new ways to be in ministry in the changing culture of the closing years of the Twentieth Century. The Missouri Diocese was one of these pilots, and was the only one in the nation to include a higher education component. Richard (Dick) Tombaugh was the person employed to direct that aspect of the study.

Soon after Tombaugh's arrival, Ewing and I began weekly conversations with him around ways to understand and respond to the new higher education situation and its impact on the city, the church, and ministry in the various higher education settings.

Together, we did extensive interviews and more formal meetings with administrators, faculty, and students. Through these, we came to know a great deal about the developments in higher education and were well known as Christian clergy who honored and supported the mission of these institutions.

At the end of that year, I attended the first meeting of the National Campus Ministry Association at Michigan State University. Also, it became apparent that an organization, both more formal and accountable, was needed in St. Louis. The Experimental Campus Ministry was born with the consent of supporting boards and committees. Its use of "experimental" was a deliberate choice to indicate that it was a process, not a fixed institution.

During the following year, the civil rights events in Selma, Alabama, were underway. Without our knowledge or permission, the (misnamed!) *St. Louis Globe Democrat* announced in a story that the Experimental Campus Ministry was organizing buses to go to the closing of the march to Montgomery. The article gave the phone number of Grace Methodist Church as the contact. All hell broke loose.

The three telephone lines into the Church were busy night and day for three days. The congregation, an upper middle-class group, had vocal opposition to us and seemed to believe we had planned that. Relations with the Church were never warm after that.

The result, however, was eight buses that went to Montgomery gave us visibility with Church and higher education audiences, and served as a powerful entrée to the next six years. Jim Ewing left to be on the student services staff at Washington U. and Earl Mulley joined the team from Houston. Over the years we had seminary interns from Eden, St. Louis, and Perkins.

The ministry rented a store-front to be used as an office and base of operations. During the coming years we worked on issues and with groups that were not tied to one campus location. With faculty, we had on-going organized hospitality and conversation including an extensive set of week-end issue seminars. The University of Missouri-St. Louis was operating in a country club building, and there was no social or study space for students, so we coordinated the work of several congregations in the area to use Church space and provide refreshment and conversation.

Student worship communities were created and maintained, as well as study and conversation groups as needed or requested. Individual counseling is inevitable when staff is involved in faculty and student communities. Contact was maintained with denominational and ecumenical student organizations.

During this same period, the ministry maintained formal contact with the anti-war and anti-draft activities. This created serious difficulties in public relations and interpretation of the ministry. On the occasions where the concerned critics asked for explanations or conversation, there were fruitful insights on all sides.

There were problems, however. Some of the Church sponsors really only wanted the ministry in higher education to be done on the older Youth Group model. The concern for peace, civil rights, and the environment were not universally popular. Funding declined.

In 1973, I was invited to be Director of the Wesley Foundation at *Indiana University* working with co-Director, Hubert Davis. I accepted. In Bloomington over the next 19 years, there were close relations with the ministries of the American Baptist Churches, the Episcopal Church, the Evangelical Lutheran Church, the United Church of Christ, and the United Presbyterian Church. Compared to St. Louis, this ministry was more student-oriented and tended to the traditional.

Several activities were unique, however. Through the AELC, there was a weekly worship using contemporary, largely secular, music and committed to careful use of the Lectionary. In place of the "Sunday Supper" format, we developed "Agapes," a meal over several weeks limited to a dozen participants' and two staff. This always included Holy Communion at the dinner table. Each year, four groups of "deacons" were trained in the history and meaning of worship and served as worship leaders. A very careful program was developed with the Residence Life staff and student Resident Assistants. This program was taken up by the University, and the Psychological Counselors at the Health Center became involved. This project, and a parallel leadership education program, lasted for nearly a decade.

The relationships from these programs produced friendships that continue into the present. Most important were the relationships of those who worked together as staff at one time or another over the two decades: Susan Ban, Robert Boyer, Nevin Danner, Diana Hodges, John (Jack) King, Ann Larson, Joan Tupin, Robert (Bob) Turner, Roger Sasse, and William (Bill) Webster.

The campus ministry board decided to grant one-semester, full salary, sabbaticals after six years of work. I had two of these. In 1983, I spent several months in South Africa, visiting secular and religious student groups and looking at ways they were preparing for an end to apartheid. In 1989, I spent a semester at the Center for the Study of Islam and Muslim-Christian Relations in Birmingham, England. In each case, I traveled extensively and, on return, did speaking and writing, both in the Church and in higher education.

In addition to those trips abroad, I went to Israel/Palestine three times. The most significant trip was a traveling seminar sponsored by the Society for Biblical Studies, based in Boston University School of Theology, which explored the political and economic situation of the Palestinians and the remnant Christian community there.

In 1990, I was appointed to the pastoral staff of St. Luke's United Methodist Church in Indianapolis. St. Luke's is a mega-Church with a vast variety of activities. I did pastoral work, taught *Disciple* Bible Study, and oversaw local mission projects. In 1995, I was appointed to be the pastor of the Pittsboro (Indiana) United Methodist Church. This was an active congregation in an area moving swiftly from farm community to suburb. This was my only real "pastoral" assignment and I both enjoyed it and learned a lot. In 1997, I retired after 41 years in the ministry and moved back to Bloomington, Indiana.

The only breaks in my quiet retirement were a five month interim appointment as pastor of the Ellettsville United Methodist Church and service on the Board of the Area 10 Agency on Aging. The pastoral assignment was one in which I discovered I could help to heal a congregation that had experienced the removal of their pastor "under charges." That congregation still treats me like I am one of them. The Board membership and chairmanship put me in touch with a larger community and the finer points of state and Federal law and regulation.

I did a short assignment for the General Board of Mission of the United Methodist Church by sharing in the training of the mission team to Latvia and, later, going to Latvia to do "on-site" evaluation. Latvia has had a long history of Methodist involvement, interrupted by Russian and German military interventions, and is restoring its institutional life with new congregations and educational services.

In retirement, I was a part of organizing the Reconciling Ministry Community in the South Indiana Conference of the United Methodist Church. Reconciling Ministries is a nation-wide program seeking to welcome persons of all sexual orientations into the life of the Church.

My sabbatical in South Africa had been underwritten by **Campus Ministry Advancement, Inc.,** a foundation based in Ohio. On my return, I was elected to that Board and, when the founding officers retired, I became chairman. That has been both a time consuming and rewarding volunteer job. CMA, Inc. is in the process of closing.

As a family, we have traveled in England, Costa Rica, and did a two-week cruise through the Panama Canal. At the present time, we are in the process of moving to Bell Trace, a retirement community in Bloomington. Our new address is 800 N. Bell Trace Circle #305, Bloomington, IN 47408-4022.

In review, my journey has been eventful. I have had a patient and loyal wife, Richie, and two children, now adults. In large measure, the Church has set me to tasks that used my talents and responded to my interests. For that I am very thankful and grateful. My only regret is to see the "mainline" Protestant Churches in America retreating from creative ministries, especially the essential ministry of higher education. Surely this is not the end of the story since "the times are in the hands of God!"

Reflections on Ministry in Higher Education
By David C. Rich

It all began with a 3 by 5 card tacked to the Job Placement Bulletin Board at the Boston University School of Theology:

> *"Position as Protestant Chaplain, Maine Christian Association, University of Maine, Orono. ME. (for one year while the present Chaplain is on a one-year study leave.)"*

I was an American Baptist student finishing my senior year at Andover Newton Theological School in Massachusetts. I thought that it sounded intriguing and, at the least, would provide me with an opportunity to practice my interviewing skills. So I sent a resume. I received a phone call from the Chair of the Maine Christian Association (MCA) Board, inviting me to come to Orono for an interview, which included leading worship and preaching in the Little Theatre on campus, meeting the Board and meeting with students. And then, four days after Ginny, my wife, and I visited the campus, I received another phone call telling that they wanted me to come for one year. (It eventually was extended to two years when the study leave of the Chaplain was extended   for   a   second   year.)

I never dreamed that applying for that position in 1961 would lead to 24 years of ministry in higher education at the local, regional and national levels of the Church.

- Protestant Campus Minister, University of Maine. In the second year we developed an off-campus Coffee House. (1961-1963)

- Eastern Regional Director for Campus Christian Life, American Baptist Board of Educational Ministries. (1966-1967). In 1968, American Baptists joined UMHE and I became a part of national UMHE staff along with my American Baptist colleagues, Haydn Ambrose, Dale Turner, Bill Shinto, and Dick Tappan.

- Northeastern Regional Secretary, United Ministries in Higher Education, Valley Forge, PA. (1968 - 1975)

    In 1969 conversations were held between NCMA and UMHE national leadership about strengthening the working relationships between UMHE and NCMA. Out of these conversations came the recommendation that, as a part of my responsibilities with the UMHE National Staff, one quarter of my time I would serve as the Executive Secretary of NCMA. The UMHE office in Valley Forge, with Audrey Lightbody, would coordinate membership and communication services for NCMA. Someone described my position as a "go-between" and a

151

link between " labor and management." Perhaps. I also saw it as a way to increase communication and understanding between the two organizations with a common commitment to ministry in higher education.

My first trip was to fly to Boulder, CO to meet with Wally Toevs, President of NCMA from 1967- 69 and to begin the discussion of ways to strengthen the relationship. And then over several months I visited each of the 6 NCMA Regional representatives. We developed a plan that I like to think helped create increased communication and working relationships between NCMA and UMHE over the next few years.

- Executive Director for the PA Commission for United Ministries in Higher Education (1975 - 1990) It was a time of supporting on-going ecumenical ministries as well as developing additional models of ministries including ministries with African-American students on state university campuses in more rural PA communities, regional ministries with community colleges with J Springer as well as several models using persons to coordinate the ministry of congregations with state universities in their communities.

In 1990, I stepped down from my involvement with Pennsylvania UMHE Commission in higher education, changed my ordination affiliation from the American Baptist to the Presbyterian Church (U.S.A.) and concluded my last years of ministry serving as an interim Executive Presbyter of the Presbytery of Carlisle (1990-1991) and as the Director of the Retirement Planning program of the Board of Pensions of the PCUSA (1991-1999). I retired in 2000.

Some Reflections
I still carry a strong commitment to Ecumenism - always exploring what we can do together, and to Vocational discernment as lifelong process.
Last Spring (2014), I was in Maine and I talked with Tom Chittick, who was a student in the student group at the Maine Christian Association in 1961. Tom said to me: "You know, because of you, I went to seminary and became a Lutheran campus minister and I spent 30 years at three different campuses, and the last one was the Maine Christian Association at the University of Maine!"
A full circle! It has been a good ride. Thanks be to God.

Health and Human Values:
Reflections on a Ministry in Higher Education
By Thomas R. McCormick

In 1965, the career pathway that I had imagined for myself was interrupted by an unanticipated fork in the road. One branch was familiar territory, the other an unknown. After serving for five years in my first assignment post-seminary as pastor of a small, racially integrated congregation in the High Point community in West Seattle, I was ready to move on. On one hand, Rev. Loren Lair, Regional Minister in Iowa was inviting me to return to the region where we had become acquainted. (I had graduated from Drake Divinity School, Drake University, Des Moines, Iowa in 1960) He claimed that with five years of pastoral ministry under my belt, I was ready to step up and take a rapidly growing suburban congregation in eastern Iowa with a robust budget, a good salary and a new brick parsonage. He made it sound appealing. It appeared to be a far cry from our current situation, we had three small children and our family of five was struggling to make ends meet on the low-end salary typical for ministers right out of seminary. A novice in ministry, I was facing the challenges of holding a disparate congregation together while forging a ministry aimed at serving both halves of the congregation. Half of our members lived in the High Point housing project, home to approximately five-thousand individuals with low income, many single-parent families on public assistance and elderly citizens whose sole source of income was their monthly Social Security checks.

The other half of the congregation lived in West Seattle proper, a typical middle-class community, whose citizens had on average a higher level of education and a higher level of employment. Many were Boeing employees and the average income was four to five times greater than their fellow members on the east side of 35th SW. With half of our members below the poverty level, we were engaged with what one of our leaders branded as "constant crisis." In addition to the usual worship and education opportunities, we also created a pantry to assist those who ran out of food before the end of the month; a large "clothes closet" stocked with used clothing; cooking classes to help moms learn how to use surplus commodities; and a pre-school for four year old children in the project. On the other hand, Rev. Loren Arnett, an associate minister in the Regional office of the Christian Church in Washington-North Idaho, was inviting me to consider applying for a newly opened position as campus minister at the *University of Washington*.

I must admit that although I knew our church combined their support with other denominations to employ campus ministers at our various state universities and colleges, I really had no idea about what kind of work campus ministers actually carried out. My only firsthand experience was from my own college days attending Northwest Christian College and the University of

Oregon in Eugene, where the campus minister organized Sunday morning Bible study classes and various fellowship events and service projects involving students.

I resolved to visit the UW campus and talk to students, faculty and a few administrators that I had previously met to discuss what campus ministry might entail in the mid '60s. In hind-sight, my investigation was quite limited, just scratching the surface, nothing profound. Yet, I began to become increasingly intrigued about the possibilities of a kind of ministry that would be very different from the pastoral model with which I was so familiar. Thus, I applied for the position; I was hired and began my work January, 1966. My former Iowan mentor was convinced I had made the wrong choice. When I informed Dr. Lair of my decision, he responded that I was making a grave mistake and that such a move would not further my career in ministry in the least and that he was disappointed not to have me serving a church in the Iowa region.

For years on the UW campus, the Baptist-Disciple House had served as the home of a cooperative campus ministry devoted primarily to the service of university students from these two denominations. However, recently, a restructuring brought the United Church of Christ into the mix and a more ecumenical ministry was envisioned as well as various forms of ministry to non-church-related students. The ministry was renamed the "Koinonia Center" and moved to a newly built structure adjacent to the NW corner of the campus where I joined the senior campus minister, Rev. John Ross, a Baptist. I began by assisting him in carrying out his existing programs and "learning the ropes," so that I could cover all the bases the following year when he took a sabbatical year in Japan. We had a fairly typical program with a Sunday morning coffee hour, followed by a discussion group, after which students dispersed to attend the local churches of their choosing. On Sunday evenings we offered an ongoing study group examining issues of the day. On Wednesday evenings local church women provided a fellowship dinner for students which were followed by a guest speaker and discussion. However, the board of directors had requested that during my first year on campus I should reserve time to explore what campus ministry could or should look like in the future---a challenging proposition.

In my exploratory year I began an informal investigation into possibilities for new forms and expressions of campus ministry. I reflected on the current situation where the Presbyterians had their Westminster Foundation, the Methodists had Wesley House, the Lutherans had Luther House, the Catholics had Newman Center, and it appeared to me that all of these centers were providing duplicate services, engaging students primarily from their own denominations in similar opportunities for worship, study, fellowship and service during their university years. I found myself wondering if it might be possible to form an ecumenical cooperative approach where the current activities could continue, yet be integrated ecumenically rather than segregated denominationally. Such a move could avoid duplication of effort and free up time and energy to create and engage in new and different forms of ministry. I suggested this idea to our board (already composed of three cooperating denominations) and found them enthusiastic about such further steps in cooperative ministry. I also fostered this idea in discussions among the local campus ministers who met weekly for support and limited coordination of effort. Gradually, our cooperative ministry began to emerge.

By now I had been appointed by my denomination (Christian Church, Disciples of Christ) to serve as a board representative on a national group called United Ministries in Higher Education (UMHE). At the national level, Baptists, Disciples, United Church of Christ, Methodists, Presbyterians, and Evangelical United Brethren, had created UMHE to develop programs at the national level that would provide ministries in higher education and to serve as a "think-tank" for envisioning new forms of ministry in higher education at the local level as well. I could imagine a similar constellation at the local level involving a "united ministry" at the University of Washington, as well as at the other campus ministries across the state of Washington. The spirit of ecumenism was strong and by the early '70's, with major assistance from Rev. David Royer (UCC) who joined our staff in the late '60's, the ground work was laid for these major denominations to forge a new ecumenical organization which was named "Campus Christian Ministry" at the University of Washington. But that is David's story, and I'll rely on him to contribute a chapter on this amazing story that led not only to a "common program" but to the purchase of a building that was owned in common, with shared secretarial staff and a united budget, as the other denominational centers around the campus were closed in favor of participation in this ecumenical movement.

In the meantime, my explorations into new forms of ministry led me into conversations with students, faculty and administrators at the UW, as well as on other campuses. I chose fifty faculty members at the UW who were considered outstanding in their fields and asked for an interview. 100% of these busy scholars agreed to grant me an hour of their time for an interview. Primarily, I asked each to describe their work as teachers and researchers, which they did with relish. They were doing some great things. For example, Dr. Ted Phillips had recently joined the faculty at the School of Medicine to create a new department, the Department of Family Medicine. Dr. Belding Scribner was leading the way in providing renal dialysis for patients with chronic kidney failure. Dr. Donnell Thomas was pioneering bone marrow transplants for the treatment of children with leukemia. Near the end of the hour, I asked if they could imagine any ways a campus minister could be supportive of their endeavors. From these fifty interviews, 47 said no, they couldn't imagine any ways . . . but three faculty members, all from the medical school, said yes. One said that new developments in medicine were leading to ethical issues and it would be great to have someone lead regular discussion groups for medical students inquiring into these. A second claimed that in spite of advances in medicine, all will eventually die, and medical students were largely unprepared to deal with dying patients and their families. A third faculty claimed that although students were taught the physiology of reproduction, there was no instruction in human sexuality and that such an inquiry would be a welcome addition to the curriculum. Of course, it was understood that these would be non-credit, "extracurricular" offerings. In all three cases, I was invited by these faculty members to provide leadership for the seminars, while they provided meeting space.

I found my board very receptive to the idea that I might organize informal study groups on these three topics, and cooperate with faculty in the medical school who had identified such a need. It had also become clear to me by this time that campus ministry had traditionally been an "upper campus" affair, serving students primarily in the liberal arts. There was no evidence that a campus minister had previously crossed Pacific Avenue, the dividing point between "upper campus" and entered the domain of the "lower campus" which housed the various health sciences including medicine, nursing, dentistry, etc. I was happy to forge new trails in this realm of academia and in this part of the campus that had seemingly been overlooked by campus ministers in previous generations.

In conjunction with my three new faculty colleagues, I organized three discussion groups for medical students. At noon on Wednesdays we gathered with brown bag lunches in a conference room reserved by the faculty sponsor, who also brought homemade cookies, where I served as convener-moderator for discussions on topics in medical ethics. We met for the first eight weeks of the quarter, thus respecting the pressures of finals week on student life. I also formed a discussion group on issues related to death and dying which met in the evening, after the core curriculum had ended. I was impressed that students would bring a snack and stick around for an additional hour or so at the end of a long day in the "required" class room, for this "elective" discussion.

Thirdly, I organized a seminar on human sexuality, as with the other seminars, of eight weeks duration. I discovered that over the course of three quarters, some students rotated through all three seminars, while some simply chose one seminar of interest. Both students and faculty encouraged me to offer these fall, winter, and spring quarters. The student response to these offerings was robust, and I worked hard to provide background research and reflective questions for our discussions. The outline of a teaching ministry was forming.

An unanticipated outgrowth of these seminars was a request from a growing number of students for counseling for various issues. These students saw me as a friendly ally who might help them deal with the stresses of medical school. Others sought me out because the demands of medical school were creating stresses in their relationships or marriages. Others suffered from test-anxiety or depression. Some were uncertain if medicine was the right career choice. Many wanted help in choosing which pathway in medicine they were best suited for. As time went on, nursing students also sought me out for counseling. I had majored in pastoral counseling in seminary and felt that responding to such requests was a valid part of my ministry. Sometimes I met students in a spare room in the medical school or nursing school, but most came to the campus ministry center for counseling. It was clear that my ministry was centering more and more on human values in the "health sciences."

When I was hired, the board offered to grant me a sabbatical year for study after I had served for a minimum of five years. The offer stipulated they would pay full salary for a six month sabbatical or one-half salary for a full year's sabbatical. After careful exploration of possibilities, I chose to enter a Doctor of Ministry program at Southern Methodist University (SMU) in Dallas, conjoint with a Fellowship in medical ethics at the Institute for Religion and Human Development at the Texas Medical Center in Houston. Rev. Kenneth Vaux, PhD., served as director for the bioethics program. In 1970, Vaux had authored *Who Shall Live: Medicine, Technology and Ethics*. Just a year prior to my entrance into the program, he had convened an important national conference on "ethical issues in medicine" with lectures from anthropologist Margaret Meade, ethicists Joseph Fletcher and Paul Ramsey, heart surgeon Michael DeBakey, MD, and others prominent in the newly emerging discipline of "bioethics." My sabbatical year was one of the most intriguing and exciting years of my life. In addition to the class work at SMU and the medical ethics seminars in the Bioethics Program in Houston with Vaux, Benedict Ashley, PhD, and Albert Marachewski, PhD, I also sought out opportunities to observe surgery and clinical procedures to become better acquainted with current medical practices. I watched the famed heart surgeon Michael DeBakey perform a heart valve replacement, I observed electroshock therapy, and I followed primary care physicians in their daily routines of outpatient care. I continued my studies in the subsequent summer quarters until I completed my dissertation and graduated in 1976 with a Doctor of Ministry with a major concentration in medical ethics, the first graduate in their program with such a major.

I returned with relish to the campus post-sabbatical in the fall of 1973, bringing fresh enthusiasm and insight for the seminars that had been on hold during my absence. I was excited to return to teaching and counseling on the **Health Science Campus**. My board was enthusiastic about the direction of my ministry and fully supported my work. I entertained a high volume of requests for lectures on bioethical topics in the local churches and began publishing articles in both the secular and religious press on issues in bioethics.

Shortly after my return to Seattle after sabbatical, Lane Smith, religion editor for the Seattle Times, published an article one Saturday evening on the religion page entitled "Local minister studies ethics in Texas." Lane had interviewed me because he felt my interests in this new field called "medical ethics" would be of interest to his readership. On Monday morning following the publication of this article, I received a call from Dr. Charles Bodemer, Chair of the Department of Biomedical History, University of Washington, inviting me to meet and discuss our mutual interest in medical ethics. In our subsequent conference, he expressed a longstanding interest in expanding the department beyond the history of medicine and into contemporary issues in medical ethics. Our ongoing discussions led to him hire me as a lecturer on a one-third time basis in the summer of 1974 to create elective courses in bioethical topics for the School of Medicine. Thus, in Fall Quarter 1974, I offered the first formal course in bioethics at the UW School of Medicine. In August of 2014, I celebrated 40 years as a teacher of bioethics at the UW. The name of the department changed, first to the Department of Medical History and Ethics, and more recently to the Department of Bioethics and Humanities, and there are now eight faculty members in bioethics and one historian, Jack Berryman, PhD.

In the beginning of my tenure at the School of Medicine, all of my courses were electives. Many of my students, at the conclusion of a course, would comment that "courses in bioethics should be required in medical school." One day I discussed with Dr. Bodemer his feelings about requesting a few hours for a required component of medical ethics in the core curriculum. He was very supportive of the idea, but emphasized that I would need to convince the curriculum committee of the importance of such an innovation. Subsequently, I was given a spot on the agenda of the curriculum committee where I presented a bit of the history of my bioethics teaching in the elective curriculum and presented a request that I be granted permission to teach an introductory course in bioethics as part of the required curriculum either in the first or second year of medical school. In the discussion following, the members of the committee, most of whom chaired courses in the required curriculum, spoke strongly of the merit and desirability of my proposal. I was elated. Then the chair reminded the members of the resolution that no new curricular hours be added without eliminating a corresponding number of hours of the existing curriculum. When he asked who might be willing to "give up" a few hours from their course offerings, each and every member protested vigorously that they didn't have enough hours at present for anatomy, physiology, biochemistry, etc. and couldn't possibly give up any hours, even for such a good cause.

This meeting was my first lesson in "medical school politics." Hours in the required curriculum are equated with power in this system, and no one wanted to relinquish that power. Although I came away feeling discouraged, to my surprise and pleasure, some of these course chairs began inviting me to come as their "guest speaker" to address ethical issues, (of course within the framework of *their* course.) Nonetheless, I was pleased at their receptivity and began serving as an invited speaker in several of the required courses in the curriculum, and over the years my contributing hours continued to increase. Eventually, for example, I was asked by the director of our Introduction to Clinical Medicine (ICM) course not only to provide introductory lectures in bioethics in the first year ICM course, but also to chair a two-day program on "Caring for Patients with Terminal Illness," for the ICM-II for the entire second year medical school class. I teamed with an emergency department physician, for many years, to co-lead a tutor group for students in ICM-I, assisting in their formation as professionals. Thus, my role both in both the elective curriculum and in the required curriculum increased over the years. The UW School of Medicine is a regional center, the only medical school in a five state area including Washington, Wyoming, Montana, Alaska and Idaho (WWAMI). As our ethics program grew, I was invited by the regional directors to make an annual visit to each of the WWAMI campuses to provide introductory workshops in bioethics for their students, similar to the Seattle based program. Usually, in conjunction with these visits, I would allow an additional day or two in my schedule to provide CME lectures for physicians and to lead discussions for the local ethics committees---reaching into some of the most remote and rural areas of the WWAMI region to spots such as Barrow, Bethel, and Kotzebue, Alaska.

In the spring of 1980, I did a three month Fellowship in "Teaching in the Clinical Context" at the University of Tennessee, Memphis Medical School Campus, with David Thomasma, PhD, Director, and Terrence Ackerman, PhD and Carson Strong, PhD. The faculty provided a context for the Fellows to make rounds in several clinical settings each week, in order to discuss ethical issues emerging in that context. I rounded in the NICU at St. Jude's Children's Hospital, in Family Medicine at St. Francis Hospital, in Oncology at the City of Memphis Hospitals, and in psychiatry in the VA hospital. This Fellowship enhanced my medical terminology and improved my understanding of diseases and their treatment so that I was better prepared to discuss the medical-ethical issues as they arose in a variety of clinical settings.

In 1987, under the leadership of the Department Chair, Dr. Albert Jonsen, we created a week long CME event entitled "The Summer Health Care Ethics Seminar" which has continued for the past 27 years with an average attendance of about 100 physicians, nurses, chaplains, social workers etc., offered the first week of every August. This acclaimed CME event (Dr. Dudzinski, my co-chair, and I received an award for "Outstanding CME Event-2008," from Dr. Paul Ramsey, Dean of the School of Medicine) continues to train members of ethics committees and ethics consultation teams from across the country.

Earlier, I mentioned my incidental involvement as a counselor and sometimes mentor to medical students. In retrospect, I suppose that my exposure to medical students in our ethics seminars led them to see me as a friendly and supportive individual with a natural interest in their well-being, so that when the going got tough, I was a natural choice for support. My counseling load increased. With the support of my board, I envisioned the provision of counseling without any fees as a part of my ministry in the health sciences. In an unfortunate four year period, there were three medical student suicides. The death of these students led Dean Robert Van Citters to appoint a

159

special task force charged with examining "stress in medical education." Unbeknownst to me, many of the medical students, when asked by the committee, "what do you do to cope with stress in medical school?" responded, "I go talk with Dr. McCormick." Following the committee's investigation, I received a call for an appointment with Dean Van Citters in which he discussed the work of his committee and then requested that I commence a formal counseling service for medical students, stipulating that my job description and my hours would be expanded. During these years I was balancing my work as a campus minister, my work as a lecturer in bioethics, and now I was adding a third job description as "medical school counselor." I literally had three offices and was working about 60 hours per week; most of my elective courses were offered in the evenings.

In 1985, Acting Dean, Theodore (Ted) Phillips recognized that a shift was needed and suggested that he hire me as *Director of Counseling for the School of Medicine*, a full time salaried position. This arrangement would allow me to continue teaching bioethics (as my time allowed) so that my passion for teaching and counseling could continue to find expression. At that time, I resigned from what was by then a part-time position on the Campus Ministry staff at CCM so that I could devote my full time to the medical school work. Somewhat ironically, the work that I had begun, teaching and counseling, as an expression of my campus ministry and funded by the churches, had developed into a medical school faculty position, funded by the university.

Space doesn't allow for much detail; however, I would be remiss in not addressing a connection between events at the local and national level. As mentioned earlier, I was a delegate to the board of United Ministries in Higher Education (UMHE), formed by the commitment of resources and staff of eight major denominations to work in higher education at the national level while providing research and guidance in support of local manifestations of ministries on campus. Dr. Verlyn Barker was the chief executive officer for this organization and provided committed, insightful and faithful leadership. One of the programs growing out of UMHE, the "Health and Human Values Program" was a precursor organization to the Society for Health and Human Values, led by Dr. Ronald McNuer. Another was a group simply called "Ministers in Medical Education." I became a member of both groups. The Society was devoted to larger aspirations such as support for incorporating course work in medical ethics into every medical school curriculum. At the time I started teaching, the UW was one of only a dozen medical schools that offered formal curricula in medical ethics, as reported by the Task Force for Human Values in 1972. Today, all 126 member medical schools in the American Association of Medical Colleges (AAMC) have multiple offerings in bioethics. The Society for Health and Human Values later joined with two other organizations to form today's American Society for Bioethics and Humanities (ASBH).

The Society for Health and Human Values usually met just before the annual AAMC meetings and of course in the same city. The Ministers in Medical Education (MME) group came a day earlier and members spent time sharing reports of their teaching ventures in the various medical schools across the country. Here I should mention that many of the earliest contributors to medical ethics were theologically trained and were thus more comfortable with what was then called "applied ethics" than were students from typical philosophy departments, who were more interested in issues related to meta-ethics. Ideas shared in the MME conferences often led to the formation of new ethics electives in the medical schools served by these innovators.

Through the MME group I met Rev. David Duncombe, PhD. Although well known in recent years for his 40 day fasts to bring the attention of congress to bear on problems such as world hunger and starving children, or nuclear disarmament, at that time he was Yale Medical School's first chaplain. He recounted for us how in his first year at Yale he was asked by the gross anatomy instructor to be present in the human dissection labs as a way of supporting students in this transition from layperson to medical-professional. At the end of that first year, he led a memorial service with students, honoring the cadavers from whom they had learned so much about human anatomy. He became so knowledgeable about anatomy that the course chair appointed him to serve as a teaching assistant in the course, a role he continued for many years. He left Yale to serve as chaplain to the medical school at UCSF where he continued until his retirement. Interestingly, some years later, Daniel Graney, PhD, head of Washington State Willed Body Program, and UW professor of anatomy asked if I would conduct a memorial service for the families of the donors to his program. For over a decade, I conducted such a ceremony for those who had donated their bodies and accompanied the families to a local cemetery where the UW had a burial plot with a vault containing the ashes of approximately one hundred donors each year. There were many stories like David's and mine from ministers who had a role in teaching bioethics in medical schools in those early days, before departments of philosophy reached a turning point and began preparing doctoral students in bioethics who now populate the departments charged with teaching bioethics in medical schools.

In today's world, prepared as I was then with an M.Div. and a D.Min., there is small likelihood that I would be offered a job in medical education. However, forty years ago, I was at the right place at the right time and a door opened where I could be of service. I found a niche in academia that felt right and good and I've never looked back nor had any regrets about following the path that opened before me. There is a large ripple effect in patient benefit from our work in encouraging the professional development of ethically trained, compassionate physicians who are willing to devote themselves to the service of the sick and suffering.

I now have first and second year medical students who approach me on the first day after class and introduce themselves as the son or daughter of a mom or dad who had been in my ethics classes a generation earlier, claiming they had received parental instruction, "You've got to take McCormick's ethics class!" Many of my former ethics class students are now in key positions of leadership, serving as clinicians, on medical school faculties, and as medical directors in hospitals. I have had wonderful opportunities to mentor graduate students and junior faculty members. I've enjoyed contributing to the body of medical ethics literature through many publications. I've been able to provide lectures for professional societies across this country and participate in invited lectureships in Canada, Germany, Italy, Taiwan and Japan.

One somewhat humorous postscript to my personal story follows. In 2001, at my wife's encouragement, I stepped down to a 40% position at the UW, with the intent of transitioning toward retirement. My wife's family all live in Phoenix, Arizona, and our plan was to spend winter quarter in the sun and to enjoy time with her family. Through a variety of coincidences, after being invited to provide a lecture in bioethics at Midwestern University Medical School, Glendale Branch, I was invited to become an adjunct professor of bioethics in that school where I have taught a three credit elective on various bioethical topics every year since 2001. Further, in discussions with the Dean of Students at the medical school shortly after arriving, he was inspired by learning of the counseling services that I had helped pioneer at the UW. He invited me to take a position on his staff where I became the first medical school counselor at Midwestern---a job that I agreed to take only to get the program started, and after working at 50% time for four months, subsequently hired my replacement. As I started that winter quarter in Arizona, teaching bioethics and counseling medical students, my wife quipped, "Congratulations McCormick, you didn't really retire, you just replicated your UW positions in Arizona!"

In conclusion, from the perspective of forty years in the field, it is clear that major changes have occurred in medical education. Currently, all of the medical schools participating in AAMC, as well as most of the osteopathic medical schools across the country are offering either required or elective courses in bioethics. Residency training programs incorporate ethics conferences as a staple in their curricula. Bioethics is an important component for continuing medical education (CME) programs for physicians in practice. National Institutes of Health (NIH) now requires that doctoral students in the sciences, particularly those that might use human subjects in research, participate in required ethics training. Across the USA, hospitals have developed ethics committees charged with resolving conflicts, teaching ethics and providing ethics consultation. The Joint Commission (TJC), formerly known as the Joint Commission on Accreditation of Health Care Organizations (JCAHO) has made ethics committees in hospitals a requirement for accreditation. The American Society for Bioethics and Humanities (ASBH) is serving as a major contributor to the establishment of norms for evaluating the competence of ethics consultation services. The Report of the ASBH, entitled *Core Competencies for Healthcare Ethics Consultation*, 2011, is now in its second edition. One can anticipate that such efforts will stimulate ethics consultants to engage in continuing education and will most likely lead to the certification of those providing such services so that standards of competency remain high. Even in the face of these positive developments, much work remains to be done. Our citizens must become educated, not only in the role of individual choices toward healthy living, but also in the importance of social determinants of health so that changes can be made at the systemic level to improve the health of our nation. Finally, the principles of justice and of respect for persons imply that every person should have access to decent health care. I am pleased that local campus ministers contributed to these changes. The church should acknowledge and celebrate organizations such as United Ministries in Higher Education that had a creative hand in supporting such changes, and programs at the national level, such as the Health and Human Values Project, that played an important role in fostering work toward a better future in health care. Reflecting upon the future of health care, it is apparent that the ethical issues facing individuals, families, and society are growing in complexity and importance and will require our best critical thinking and most fair and just actions.

Currently (at age 80), Thomas McCormick continues on the faculty at the UW School of Medicine, Department of Bioethics and Humanities at 10% time. He is co-director of the Annual Summer Seminar in Health Care Ethics and directs a weeklong "short course" in bioethics for students from Hyogo College of Medicine, Hyogo, Japan on the UW campus. McCormick also continues on the adjunct faculty in bioethics for Midwestern University, Glendale Branch, AZ where his current course is entitled: "Ethical Issues in Death and Dying." When not working, he enjoys fly fishing for steelhead, salmon fishing and crabbing in the NW, and wood working in the shop in Arizona.

Catching the Ecumenical Spirit in 1968
By E. Thomas Miller

The several campus ministries at *West Virginia University*, Morgantown, West Virginia met together in 1968 and developed a covenantal relationship with one another, representing nine denominations, and endorsed by their several denominational local committees. These included Roman Catholic, Episcopalian, United Methodists, Presbyterians (PCUS and UPCUSA), Baptists (SBC and American Baptists), Disciples of Christ, and Lutheran (LCA and ALC). We agreed at that time that we would serve our own constituencies with our separate religious, worship, study and church relations. And at the same time we developed a division of labor for the University pastors and chaplains along with local pastors involved in ministry to and in the University. I was elected chair of the new ecumenical counsel to coordinate our strategy for ministry.

Several chaplains were deeply involved in relationship to those protesting the Viet Nam war as well as a team of chaplains and others who counseled students who were exploring conscientious objection, some of whom completed their applications for 1-0 or 1-AO status for their draft boards

Another group, headed up by a campus pastor and joined by persons concerned about the use of drugs, developed the Drug Education and Crisis Intervention Hot Line (24/7), and provided seminars in several dormitories. The group of nine ordained clergy of our covenantal group divided up the residence halls and provided Chaplaincies in cooperation with the house parents and resident assistance.

Student Action for Appalachian Progress

Several outreach ministries were developed, including Student Action for Appalachian Progress, a tutorial program for school children in the coal camps in Monongalia County, which at the time was one of the largest coal producing counties in the nation. At the height of this SAAP program, students logged 30,000 hours of tutoring by 200 students who had been trained by university faculty in the best tutorial techniques. This program, supported by the Mountaineer Mining Mission, sponsored by the United Presbyterian Church, USA, Tutorial programs were conducted in the neighborhoods. Faculty and staff conducted training weekends before each semester. Each weekend was concluded with an "altar call" from yours truly to sign on for a semester and definitely not to poop out on their "tutees" which would be more disappointing than not at all.

Women's Center

The first female campus minister (a United Methodist deacon) staffed the Women's Center which provided rape counseling , problem pregnancy counseling and lively discussions for University coeds. A vigorous support group of 25 coeds functioned and a hot line was established.

Shared Program and Work Space
Another significant innovation was the sharing of office space for a number of the denominational campus ministers. The Newman Club shared their office space with a United Methodist and a Presbyterian campus pastor, renaming their center "Ecumenical Campus Center." Another ecumenical center was established on the second campus of the University where three CM's shared – Catholic, (Paulist Order) United Methodist, and Presbyterian. The Center was later renamed Bennett House in memory and in honor of the chair of the ecumenical student group on campus, who had become a CO and served as a non-combatant soldier, and who was mortally wounded while rescuing a fellow soldier from the battlefield. He was posthumously awarded the Congressional Medal of Honor, reportedly the second CO to be awarded such an honor in the USA. A third center was established near the main campus which was shared by CM's: United Methodist, Presbyterian, Catholic , and Episcopalian.

The Last Resort
A Coffee House Ministry, begun by the Presbyterians, was staffed by the campus ministers on Friday and Saturdays. The downtown facility was called "The Last Resort" which seated over 100, featured student folk singers, poets, comedians, and dramatists who staged three plays a year. The Resort was open to all students, faculty and staff of the University. A downtown basement seating 100, featuring, of course, coffee, grill, and tubs of peanuts on Friday and Saturdays during the school year. The outstanding Drama Department "adopted" the Resort for three dramatic productions each year, including musical reviews, plays. Folk music was standard as well as original poetry readings, and a hilarious comedy team, mimicking the Burns & Shriver duo. Tony and Rune later went on to star in Godspell in Washington DC. after their graduation. (Ironically, both were Jewish).

Other joint programs in Morgantown included a Telephone Reassurance Ministry (for shut-ins), MonVac (a voluntary action center), a Simulation Games program for students and faculty, a citywide campaign which was a referendum for a youth center with an ice skating rink which was passed by a 75% community election, and a local chapter of the Consultation on Church Union (COCU).

Our Ecumenical Campus Ministry was written up as an effective ministry by a national Episcopal newsletter published at the Episcopal Seminary in Cambridge, MA.

Following a decade of ministry in West Virginia, I was called to be the Minister to the Campus and Assistant Professor of Humanities at Austin College in Sherman, Texas. There I was campus chaplain to 1100 students and

250 faculty and staff. Following my earlier practice of ecumenical ministry, I conducted weekly chapel on Tuesday evening (during Coffee break @ 10:00 p.m. The college had hosted a summer high school Hillel conference on campus, and as a result several dozen Jewish students who had fallen in love with the campus matriculated at the College. We tried to get the national Hillel Foundation to form a Hillel and were turned down because there was not enough to form a group. Our response: We formed a Havarem (Friends), and the chaplain was nicknamed "Rabbi." Episcopal eucharist was also offered in the Wynn Chapel as well as Catholic Mass and a Baptist Student Union. Due to our Jewish contacts we were able to host Elie Wiesel for a series of lectures. Other luminaries included in the endowed lectureships were Fr. Henri Nouwen, Fred Rogers of "Mr. Rogers' Neighborhood, and Dr. James Forbes, senior pastor of Riverside Church, NYC.

After retirement Tom Miller also helped create a Presbyterian Higher Education non-profit organization in North Carolina which functioned for ten years (2003-2013) in support of and encouragement of 21 Higher Education Ministries in the five NC presbyteries. He is now retired and living in Davidson, NC, home of his alma mater, Davidson College, and has been appointed to the alumni Board.

The Work of the Spirit
By Philip Harder

One of the least understood (and sometimes most difficult to justify in a campus ministry report to the sponsoring churches) aspects of our work is how we campus ministers weave our strands of ministry by walking and listening—yes, and sometimes responding. This style of ministry takes patience, persistence and a faith in the work of the Holy Spirit.

During one of those memorable walk and talk moments with a faculty member, whom I have known with growing trust and mutual respect, I received a "pregnant question" that has enlivened my ministry for well over three years. This non-churched and alienated United Methodist, an African scholar and chair of our **University of Portland** Black Studies Department, had just returned from doing research on the West African migration in the Caribbean Islands before and after the colonization period. The key to open up fresh knowledge about this important "lost" cultural artifact was revealed hidden in the spiritual richness of the old African religion practices still in today's Caribbean cities and country sides. After this friend-professor participated in one of these religious services—highly ecstatic and spiritualized—her research took on new meaning and insight. In telling this story, her concluding remark and question to me was, "I can no longer do my scholarly research without including the place of spirituality in my search for the truth, and I wonder if there are any other faculty in this University who feel the same way?"

On a practical level this conversation resulted in finding out who those other faculty are who are integrating spirituality and scholarship; and in a more fundamental sense, the topic has led to challenge the entire epistemology and narrow ways of knowing at our University. Under the rubric of "Expanding the Boundaries of Knowledge," College of Liberal Arts and Sciences, along with Campus Ministry, has hosted a whole series of speakers, panels, in-house discussions on the subject. Douglas Sloan and Parker Palmer have been invited scholars to highlight the importance of this quest. Conclusion: nothing short of metanoia in our thinking is required for real personal and social change.

(This piece was written in 1998 for a potential collection of NCMA stories.)
Anita and I live in Camas, WA where we attend the local Methodist church; I sing in a small choir and help lead a men's group. We lived in a retirement/golfing community for 9 years after Anita's retirement. I was president of the men's golf club, the democratic forum, and sang in the community choir while Anita was president of the home owner's board of directors. We traveled with grandchildren and children to many parts of the world. When our youngest grand-daughter needed a place to live, we sold our house and moved to Camas. We are pretty domestic and will be for a couple of more years when high school graduation will give our grand-daughter more choices.

Remembering the Story of Campus Christian Ministry at the University of Washington: An Ecumenical Journey
David B. Royer

I tell this story as a participant in events that ran from the mid- sixties into the early nineties. I came in touch with campus ministry in my first weeks as an associate minister in South Pasadena, CA. The senior pastor and I had just arrived there and on our desks was an announcement of a meeting where the campus minister at Los Angeles State would be asked to defend himself against charges of being a radical if not a communist. When I arrived at my job as associate minister at University Congregational (UCC) church in Seattle, I was told my first meeting was across the street for a board meeting of Koinonia Center (the Baptist, Disciples, UCC campus ministry). So I've been involved with campus ministry from my first job in 1965 until I left CCM in 1991.

While I once had stacks of documents that detailed the history at the U.W, I long ago turned them over to those who followed me in that ministry at the University. What was stored on my computer disappeared with a hard drive crash and I saw no reason to try to resurrect that mass of documents. I have found a couple of newsletters and a ministry review from 1989 some of which I have used and adapted for this story. It is well over twenty years since I left CCM and at seventy five, some memories come more slowly. I share here in broad brush strokes my recollections, reflections and musings on how a unique ministry was established and lasted for nearly a quarter century. Throughout the life of CCM there was always some pressure to return to a denominational "foundation" style of ministry or to move toward a campus chaplaincy model like the ministries at our denominationally related colleges and private universities. But, CCM found another way to journey for quite a while.

The roots of Campus Christian Ministry at the *University of Washington* were nurtured from several sources. By the mid sixties the American Baptists, the Christian Church (Disciples of Christ) and the UCC were funding a common ministry at Koinonia Center with two staff. About this time the Methodist Wesley Foundation hired a new staff person very dedicated to ecumenical conversation and programming and a new Presbyterian staff member of the same bent came to the Westminster Foundation. These two immediately joined in weekly conversation with the staff members at Koinonia, the Priest at the Newman Center, and two staff representing the Lutherans. So ecumenical conversation was alive and well.

Add to this mixture several associate ministers from the churches in the University District who met weekly to plan joint adult education ventures and youth retreats. I sat with this group as a staff member at University Congregational (UCC) responsible for youth and adult education. We also met with the campus ministers from time to time. Conversation often turned to mission, and the seeds of joint ventures and collaborative ministries to serve the U. District community and the University began to grow. There were also

168

two Senior Pastors (a protestant pastor and elderly Catholic priest) who truly enjoyed conversations with the "young Turks" and met with this group with some regularity. The Dominican priest said he needed a place to "explore contemporary theology" with these recent seminary graduates. Through this group we influenced some of the speakers at the University District Lectures sponsored by several congregations. Amongst speakers during the mid-sixties were Samuel Miller, Harvey Cox, William Stringfellow, and Krister Stendahl. We lobbied for these and others who were Christian educators and scholars, policy makers, folks in governance, and who were involved in prophetic inquiry. This stew pot was almost ready for a banquet, and conversation moved toward further action.

Another voice in the late sixties was The Danforth Foundation. They published a study "The Church, the University, and Social Policy" authored by Kenneth Underwood which advocated ministry to the University which went well beyond the pastoral and priestly modes of ministry - the ministry to individuals and the proclamation of faith. He said the other modes of ministry were those of the prophet and king. We were called to prophetic inquiry, studying and judging the level of humaneness of the social order moving it toward change required for approximate justice in our world. The kingly role takes up governance and the expression of neighbor love through responsible corporate action in the shaping of social policy. He also strongly advocated an ecumenical approach to ministry in higher education. The national higher education staff of our denominations brought this study to our attention. They widely distributed copies of "New Wine," a summary of the Study, and encouraged campus ministers to share it with parish colleagues as an opportunity for continuing dialogue about the nature of ministry. The seeds from "New Wine" also fell on fertile ground in the U. District of Seattle.

I believe the next event that nurtured the possibility of establishing an ecumenical campus ministry was a convocation co-sponsored by Koinonia Center and University Congregational Church. The convocation was designed by the Christian Faith and Higher Education institute and staffed by H. Lynn Jondahl (some may recognize him as the campus minister at LA State). This event brought together all possible participating denominational executives, campus ministers, students, and faculty and representatives of local congregations to consider issues of ministry. It was three days of exercises, discussions, and brain storming, ending on Sunday morning where Jondahl was the preacher at University Congregational Church.

Soon after, there were a series of self- studies and reviews of the existing ministries and the visit of a national review team. All ministries agreed to participate, including some participation of the Newman Center although they weren't represented on the review team. I believe the team included Sam Kirk (Methodist), Verlyn Smith (NLCM), William Hallman (Presbyterian) Richard Bolles (Episcopalian), Bill Shinto (American Baptist) and Verlyn Barker (UCC). Perhaps the convocation was in 1967 and self studies and reviews were

1968. They reviewed the self study documents, interviewed denominational executives and bishops, talked to faculty and students, and had individual conversations with all staff.

The review teams recommended that the ministries explore a common mission, board and staff. They believed that "a shared vision, a shared ministry, allowing still for diversity can best find strength and focus within the bonds of ecumenicity, lived out under the same roof." The review team pointed out areas that needed the attention of the ministry at the University of Washington: a) the Med School and Law School (their faculty and student needs and ethical explorations in those fields) b) more creative involvement with minority students, c) the street scene in the University community with its homelessness, drug issues, conflicts between businesses and the counter culture. d) addressing the needs of the gay and lesbian communities and their isolation. e) exploring the issues of career, life work planning and vocation and f) marriage preparation and counseling. This was to my mind very exciting, and within the year I resigned my positions at University Congregational and Koinonia Board, applied for the open position at Koinonia, said "yes" to a call and moved across the street to Koinonia Center.

The year was 1969 when a new ministry at the University of Washington meant to give expression to the prayer for the community of faith, "that they may all be one" came to fruition. Nine denominations including Roman Catholics (as represented by the Dominican Order with the approval of the Archbishop), Episcopal, Lutheran (ALC/LCA), the United Church of Christ, Christian Church (Disciples), American Baptist, Presbyterian, and United Methodist joined together in a common ministry. The effort was spearheaded by local campus ministers, district clergy, faculty board members, student participants, several denominational executives. Final decisions about staff were to be retained by denominations or UMHE . CCM was to have a common personnel committee with which denominations were to consult about the needs of the ministry. In practice personnel decisions were always made with broad ecumenical participation and at least on one occasion as coordinator I was asked by a Bishop to interview a candidate on the East coast.

At the beginning our staff included four clergy representing the UMHE denominations, three Catholic staff of two Dominican priests and one Dominican sister, one Lutheran pastor, and one Episcopal priest. And we operated out of three centers --Koinonia, Newman Center and the Lutheran Center. The new board was committed to a single location where staff, students, faculty and board members could share life together. The process was hurried along when the ancient Wesley Foundation building was in such bad shape that its board made a decision to demolish the building and not rebuild at present. The Westminster Foundation building was in a very poor location. Under the leadership of their new staff member a decision was made to try to rent out that space. The Methodist staff member moved into Koinonia. There was little more room available in that building.

We continued to discuss the possibilities for common space. Buy? Expand the Westminster facility? Build on the Wesley lot? Then the University YMCA building became available to share with the Y Director. We decided to lease the space with the agreement if we decided to purchase that building, the lease money would apply to the purchase. So we all moved into that building in steps. I believe it was in the 1972/73 school year just as I was asked to become Staff Coordinator. This architect designed building was very beautiful and a wonderfully humane space. There were office space for all staff, a common room for worship, and two lounge rooms for classes and meetings. There were a few changes that had to be made, dividing two larger spaces into two office each. We finished the ceiling in the worship space as per the architects original design.

We finally purchased the facility and celebrated the purchase of the building in October of 1977. In an address at the dedication I enumerated what had taken place over the prior twenty four months. We had been through a wilderness to get ourselves to the place we wanted to be. "Our denominations, our families, truly put us through their hoops, through seventeen boards and thirty three decision making processes by Bishops and Denominational Executives, commission, committees, lawyers and bankers. (That is by actual count and doesn't include the hours of debate, informal meetings, discussions, arguments, meeting to rewrite our bylaws, and going over architect's drawings, walking the district to look over properties.)"

We figured and negotiated the appropriate denominational capital investments in the facility and buy-back arrangements were written with agonizing care from the very beginning. Many details had to be fussed over. Several staff and board members wanted data about program support and costs for building and support expenses. Our wonderful administrative assistant offered to keep track of such information for a while. She kept counts to build a common budget. After much counting - of participants, of paper use, of demands on secretarial help, of use of paper clips, toilet flushes, flips of light switches, etc, etc, etc., we gave up that task and she was quite relieved. After discussion and careful review of every financial resource available, we agreed that we would use for program costs the same percentages used for investment in the building. Basic support of program for UNHE and the Roman Catholics would be one third each, the Lutherans and Episcopalians one sixth each. Program monies were supplemented for UMHE from the sale of Koinonia Center, Westminster Foundation and from the parking lot where Wesley House was torn down. The sale of the Newman Center and rental of the Lutheran Center also provided income.

What did all this mean in terms of mission focus and program development? Immediately after the formation of CCM some staff specialization began to take place and staff diversity increased. Over the next twenty years these new inquiries and programs took shape. Below are departments at the University we addressed, issues and constituencies of

171

special concern and programs established with special attention from CCM staff. I can only briefly address each. You can find fuller explanation by Thomas McCormick and Susan Y. Morris of their program involvement in what they have written for this project.

1. The Medical School – inquiry into needs and issues. First, we established discussion groups with medical students. That led to counseling med students which led to the Med School realization of the need for a new student counseling program. The new program hired our staff part time for counseling. Medical ethics issues were engaged and over time a new Department of Bioethics and Humanities was established, and again our staff became part of the faculty. Cancer Life/Line cancer support group established with its roots in the medical school and our staff. The ministry supported the staff salary for this work in the early years. As his work became established he moved from part-time to full salary and became adjunct staff without pay at CCM. He is still busy at the Med School. (see article by Tom McCormick)

2. Inquiry into university governance and issues related to religious studies and the establishment of an environmental program were both carried by one staff. These were two thorny issues. Religious studies was in trouble because of a law suit against the University by conservative religious groups for the "Bible As Literature" course. They believed the University was teaching religion and that violated the separation of Church and State. The suit was slowly moving to the State Supreme Court. Once settled in favor of the U., our staff became an advocate not only the course but for a Department of Comparative Religion. Working with the professor of the Bible as Lit course, the two of them gathered support for the department, which was established. The environment issue was thorny because there was jealousy and competition among departments as to which was the appropriate department to recommend a Department of Environmental Studies be established. It is now a College of the Environment with co-opted faculty from several departments. Work in this area also led to a foundation grant to CCM to aid student establishment of the Washington Public Interest Research Group (WASHPIRG). It was one of the early PIRGs and is still a major factor in the environmental field in our area.

3. Exploration of Campus/U. District scene – In 1969, I was the newest staff without any defined portfolio. In light of unrest and violence in the district, toxic relationships between activist and the police, the board asked that I get on the street to investigate possibilities dealing with homelessness, hunger, drug abuse, student unrest and demonstration, relationship between businesses, the U., students, and churches. I established relationships with the two most recent ASUW presidents, a local attorney, several shop owners, the editor of the *Helix* (underground newspaper), several faculty, two or three clergy. This group became a coalition that incorporated the U District Center, which established

programs including, a meal program and health clinic, encouraged a Community Service Bureau (attached to the office of the mayor), emergency housing for minors, etc. Funded by church and business donations and a Federal Law and Justice grant, the Center became a neutral ground where diverse constituencies could meet to talk and negotiate. The weekly feeding program has been taken over by a new non- profit and, in cooperation with U District churches, has support for a daily meal. Housing and health organizations in the area trace their roots back to our effort.

4. Ministry with International Students – staff continued support for English Conversation Class which had a long history in the ministry. This served the wives of international students who needed help with language skills and also needed a community of support. The class was taught by the 50 volunteers and childcare was provided. While originally formed by Baptist church women, the CCM Guild took on the volunteer task and owned it as an ecumenical program. Later we received a Presbyterian grant for a 1/2 staff position to expand programs with international students, which led to gathering students for meals, discussion and support. Our staff person became an advocate for international students on the campus and in the community and also helped students and families with visa and other immigration difficulties.

5. Peace and Justice Issues, Native American and Prison Ministry – The weekly program for inmates at the Monroe Correctional Center was begun by Lutheran staff. A group of students and church volunteers met with up to forty prisoners each week for discussion and support. Several education classes were established and continuing education and training was encouraged. The prison program continues to exist today carried out independently by volunteers. This staff member was also our contact with anti-nuclear and anti-war activists, gave leadership to the Peace Action Coalition (with roots in the Lutheran and Methodist ministries), Washington Association of Churches. In solidarity with the Roman Catholic Archbishop, he was involved with the anti-Trident demonstrations. Both he and the Archbishop were involved in civil disobedience. A core group of students were active in this work. The staff member was also our contact with the Native America students and communities and garnered support for Treaty Rights. The U.S. Supreme Court Decision upholding the Boldt decision granted the tribes access to half the available fish quoted almost verbatim an AMICUS brief written at CCM under his staff leadership with students and faculty from the Law School, School of Fisheries and participants from the Native American community.

6. Marriage Preparation – This priority in ministry came about first by the demands on staff time in counseling couples approaching marriage and the Protestant interaction with Catholic priests who were leading Pre- Cana classes at the Center. The priests began to consult married staff and ask Protestant staff

to lead sessions on marriage communication skills, issues of dealing with anger management, and other relational issues. Thus, marriage preparation became a matter of discussion, with the hope to develop a program useful to all denominations in the ministry. We soon hired a 1/2 time staff to lead in developing a marriage preparation program. She, working with other staff and lay volunteers, developed a full blown program. The program authored its own curriculum, and once it got fully going it served more than 250 participants a year in weekend retreats for marriage preparation. Many area congregations sent their members to our program. The Roman Catholic Archdiocese approved the program for Pre- Cana requirements if a priest would follow up with a session on Catholic theology. The program also made available couples enrichment events for local congregations. The curriculum has been used as an ecumenical and interfaith model at other universities and churches across the nation. We also adapted the materials for gay and lesbian couples. (See article by Susan Y. Morris)

7. Work with Minority Students – Expanded involvement started with international students and expanded more when we hired two new staff who were minorities. Work with the Black Student Union and the Associated Students resulted in further new programs with indigent and disenfranchised students at the U. and broader community. One staff became involved in the national UMHE committee on Community Colleges Ministry. He worked with Central Area pastors to encourage their involvement with community colleges in their neighborhood, was involved with a Seattle Housing Authority low income housing project, and helped students gain access to that resource. Both staff became informal advisors to the BSU and provided stability to its efforts.

8. Career, Life/work Planning – After implementing the street ministry, I was assigned to inquire and explore what was happening on the campus related to vocation, choosing a major, and career choice. I discovered a very small staff for a student body of over 30,000 at the career center used more by graduates looking for work rather than students seeking help with vocational choice. Ninety percent of its effort was job placement, with a limited testing regimen for those seeking career advice. Our son was entering North Seattle Community College at this time and I was interested that students entering a degree track were required to take a Career Center course which focused on choice of major and future career. The same was true for all community colleges in the Seattle system. In response, the Board decided to begin a program in Life/work planning and I was supported to attend an extensive workshop led Richard N. Bolles of *What Color is Your Parachute* renown. I began a program modeled on that experience using the resources authored by Bolles then partnered with our marriage prep coordinator to develop a specialized program for couples, for use in local congregations, for those

planning for retirement etc. The Career Center began to take notice and some progress could be seen in programs there to help students with future choices.

9. Ministry to Women – As staff came and went, more women entered our mix; at times there were as many as four women on the staff. Several Catholic women religious were present along with as many as three women representing other denominations. Programs were developed to attend to special interest and needs of women, and relationships were established with the Center for the Prevention of Sexual and Domestic Violence. The Marriage Prep program addressed more clearly the need for anger and conflict management skills and other areas dealing with violence. In response to this effort there was also a men's group established for conversation and support.

10. Pastoral and Liturgical Ministry – Of course, pastoral care for students and faculty continued as before. All staff carried responsibility in this area. There were weddings and funerals, personal crises, couple facing possible divorce, and all other manner of human need.

We began the ecumenical ministry with three opportunities for weekly worship. There was Sunday Catholic Mass, The Table of the Lord led by Protestant staff on Thursday (meal, discussion, & liturgy), and an Episcopal Eucharist each week. There were also great ecumenical moments in worship: the celebration of the building purchase, the consecration of the Roman Catholic altar, the celebration when the anti-Trident demonstrators were released from jail to name just three. In planning this last event, I said to the Archbishop that it was too bad we couldn't have a Eucharistic service. He suggested having the service including all the words of institution, but without the bread and wine present. He said everyone would understand our meaning.

We were dedicated throughout the ministry for the development of inclusive language for all our liturgies and even wrote a paraphrase of the Lord's Prayer which was used in common worship. For six years we held a common Catholic/Protestant liturgy (inclusive in language but with separate stations for the Eucharist), which was a focal point for the ministry, but it could not be sustained-- even after months of study of our different traditions. Students were pained by the separation caused by one exclusive rubric or another which we attempted, with occasional exceptions being made so we could come together. So we took a step back to our original style of worship.

An Afterword

This ministry is now a shadow of its former self. In the late 80's's and early 90's two denominations terminated their membership in CCM. The Dominican Order faced a Province-wide financial crisis. The withdrawal was followed by a decision of the Episcopal Bishop to discontinue funding of all chaplaincies in the diocese. At the very same time, the Roman Catholic Bishop had been under investigation by the Vatican, some of it from questions about inclusive language or other issues at CCM. The investigation began in 1983 and in 1986 the Pope appointed an auxiliary bishop who was given authority above the present Bishop in five liturgical and administrative functions. That status lasted about three years. The two withdrawals and the changes in the Archdiocese were devastating financially and ecumenically. I know little about the details of the present campus ministry at the University other than it is once again going through change. The Lutherans are purchasing Covenant House and the Dominicans have established an independent ministry. There is a one Methodist staff member operating out of a Wesley facility. The one UMHE staff is operating out of donated space at University Congregational Church.

Corita Kent in her book *Footnotes and Headline, A play-pray book*, which was written just about the time of our early conversations about ministry, affirms the need to celebrate together and to recite our history, our stories, our crises and successes. To paraphrase her: If we are unable to express or remember together whence we've come, we will do the opposite of remembering. We will dismember and dissolve in confusion.

Those who were around at the beginning are no longer around to recite the history and the covenants and promises made. The denominational staff, executives and bishops have gone in a passing parade. The clergy in the district have moved on or retired. A significant number of those committed to the ministry have died. Of staff who served in the first ten years of CCM, at least six are now deceased; others are spread coast to coast. But we celebrate the growth of the seeds planted in fertile soil over the years.

Following his years at the University of Washington, David Royer became Northwest Regional Director for Joint Action in Community Service, which provided volunteers for the Job Corps Training program in Alaska, Idaho, Oregon, and Washington . He is now retired with his wife Marcia and living at Panorama, a continuing care retirement community near Olympia, WA. He enjoys growing his orchids and roses, having time with nearby grandchildren, walking or hiking daily, participating in the many activities sponsored by the community, including volunteering for occasional worship leadership, and coordinating a neighborhood emergency readiness group.

40 Years and Going Strong
By Thomas J. Philipp

In the fall of 1960 I took an Intern Year while at Union Theological Seminary in New York to serve the First Presbyterian Church in Canton, New York and serve also as Minister to Students at both *St. Lawrence University* and *NY State A and T College*. It was a joy to serve with the Pastor of First Presbyterian, The Rev. Jack Wells. Jack played a significant role with United Ministries in Higher Education in New York State. After serving that year in Canton I knew I wanted to go into campus ministry. At that time the Presbyterian denomination required that a person serve three years in a local congregation before being certified to go into campus ministry.

Upon graduation from Union in 1962 I served as Assistant Minister at Jermain Memorial Presbyterian Church in Watervliet New York for three years and then accepted the call to a newly created position of Protestant Campus Minister at *Oswego, New York*. I was approved for campus ministry by Rev. Arnold Nakajima a General Assembly staff person.

I served in Oswego from 1965 to 1972. From 1968 to 1972 I was also on the faculty as Assistant Professor of History, team teaching a course in Western Civilization titled "The History of Ideas and Movements." This was the great era of student involvement in civil rights, anti Vietnam War demonstrations, and protests against certain university policies. I, and most of my colleagues in campus ministry during this period became very much involved in these movements and these movements shaped our style of ministry. We were out there with the students in their protests. It was also the time of the emergence of the drug culture and the development of gay/lesbian groups often turning to the campus ministry for support. The gay/lesbian group at Oswego met in my home for their weekly meetings and soon included several persons from the town community as well. It was wonderful to have the full support of my campus ministry board for my involvement in all these various aspects of my ministry.

In 1968 I helped to form the New York State Campus Ministers Association and served as President from 1968 to 1972. The Association developed a number of seminars that included not only campus ministers but also faculty members and local pastors and lay people wishing to develop a mutual ministry addressing the issues and concerns of the day. New York State United Ministries in Higher Education (a joint enterprise of the United Church of Christ, American Baptists, Presbyterian Church (USA), and the Reformed Church in America with support from the United Methodists) was the vehicle for providing denominational support for the twenty-two various ecumenical campus ministries around the State. In some cases there would be two or three UMHE supported ministries on a single campus (Cornell and Syracuse) and other campuses receiving no UMHE support. In 1967 UMHE produced a two-page document that suggested experimenting with a team approach covering a geographical area rather than funding individual campus centered ministries.

By 1970 the State Commission of UMHE was ready to act on this new strategy. New York State was divided into nine geographical areas. The twenty-two campus ministers were assured of being funded through June 1972. The positions were then to be cut to seventeen and each campus minister needed to be committed to an "area ministry" and be shifted to a different area from the one in which they worked. This strategy meant the end of my ministry in Oswego and I was called to serve with Rev. Hugh Nevin in a ministry on Long Island covering the two counties of Nassau and Suffolk. I remember well the brief job description I had. "There are twenty-two institutions of higher education on Long Island. You are to relate to them."

I came to Long Island in July 1972 to serve with Hugh as staff to the newly created **Long Island United Campus Ministry**. We developed a "project approach' for LIUCM. Each project drew people from campuses, local churches, and the community at large, to address particular issues. Some examples were:

(1) The Peace Education Project which brought together faculty from both high schools and colleges to develop a peace education curriculum to be used in the high schools. This project was aided greatly by staff from the American Friends Service Committee New York City Office.

(2) Gay Community-Religious Community. This project provided for a dialogue between the gay community and our religious communions. Students and staff from five colleges participated and I assisted in the development of two organizations that address the needs of GLBT youth (Pride for Youth in Nassau and Long Island Gay and Lesbian Youth in Suffolk). Both of these organizations continue to exist and have served hundreds of GLBT youth and their families on Long Island.

(3) A most significant program was our Vietnam Veterans Service Project. This project was developed to identify the needs of the returned Vietnam veterans and to assist these veterans in developing structures and strategies to address those needs; and to sensitize the university, the church and the community at large to address those needs and find ways to harness resources to address them. Before this project came to a close, over 16,000 Vietnam Veterans were contacted and served in some way.

(4) The Nassau Coalition on Family Planning. A New York State-wide study on adolescent sexuality indicated that Nassau County had the highest rate of teenage out-of-wedlock pregnancies of any other area in the State excluding New York City. I was asked to assist in putting together a coalition of university personnel, religious leaders, and community leaders. Representatives from four Nassau County colleges and several local pastors and community agencies produced a study titled "Children Bearing Children. The Coalition formed a Board and with various grants was able to hire a

Director and Assistant Director. Out of this developed the Center for Family Resources. I served as its president for several years.

This is a sample of projects that developed interaction between Campus, Church, and Community.

In 1982, I cut back my position as Executive Minister of LIUCM to provide for part-time staff on certain campuses, and became Pastor of Community Presbyterian Church in Merrick and served also as Protestant Chaplain at CW Post College of Long Island University, serving in this dual role for 25 years until I retired from campus ministry in 2005 and from the Merrick Church in 2006.

From my first years in Oswego up to and including the present time I have been a member of NCMA, serving for a few years as representative of the Northeast Region and from 1979 until 1982 as Secretary of NCMA. I have attended most of the annual conferences and received the GNOME Award in 2000. In 2001 I received the Presbyterian Church USA Higher Education Honor Roll Award. I have found NCMA to provide stimulating conferences, a fellowship of colleagues in campus ministry, significant resources and a vehicle for keeping this ministry on the agenda of our denominations.

In my retirement I have been serving for the past eight years as the Pastor of Old South Haven Presbyterian Church in Brookhaven New York. It is a wonderful little congregation of 50 members, probably the most liberal of congregations in the Presbytery of Long Island. I am 78 years old and will need to make a decision soon as to when I 'fully retire' and move into 'independent living' quarters with continuing care as needed.

Campus Ministry and the University of the Earth
By Ted Purcell

Perhaps it all began in the Genesis command to "tend the garden" of creation, or what I have come to call "the original human vocation," the responsibility to care for the earth, living in a sustainable and mutually-enhancing relationship with the planet and all beings with whom we share the on-going creation. As Thomas Berry reminds us, the earth is not a collection of objects, but a communion of subjects. The earth, our shared home, is not just a commodity to be consumed, but a community to which we all belong.

It is this inspiring reality which has been the basis of the emerging sense of calling that eventually led me into campus ministry, expressed through a series of contexts including a pastorate in a campus church (Cullowhee Baptist Church at *Western Carolina University*, 1970-74), and Baptist campus ministries at *N.C. State University* (15 years, 1974-89) and at *Duke University* (22 years,1989-2010). Fifty years!

While at NCSU I followed my long-time practice of auditing occasional courses that continued my education for ministry and allowed me to relate to students in their world. Once I took a course in environmental ethics in which we were required to do a project in which we related our vocations/majors to our environmental ethics. Up to that time I had never systematically studied what that would mean for my vocation or for institutional religion. At various times my campus ministry role has allowed me to lead retreats, facilitate vocational discernment groups, and to enjoy class room teaching (Human Sexuality, Spirituality and Ecology, and inter-faith dialogue). Although the obvious relevance of each topic for campus ministry is abundant (I completed my D.Min.in conjunction with co-teaching a course in Human Sexuality), nothing has enlivened my own spiritual journey so powerfully as the experience in myself and others of the sense of the Holy, the presence of the sacred in the natural world, and the throbbing awareness that the ecological crisis of our time is a spiritual and ethical issue of such magnitude that we ignore it at the peril of countless forms of being, including the human.

These brief reflections invite me to trace the thread that leads throughout my life, so that I enter into a long path that echoes the same refrain at every turn, often voiced by the science of ecology, with its focus on the interconnectedness, interdependence, and the interrelatedness of everything, and the distilled wisdom of the great spiritual traditions of the earth. With resounding insistence they seem to say to all who will listen: There is no such thing as "my life." We are inseparably bound together, making the necessary journey from "I" to "we," responding to the community of life which requires us to put the deepest love of which we are capable into action for the sake of the earth and all her creatures. We can love with heart, soul, mind, and strength. And we can love our neighbors as ourselves.

The great privilege of campus ministry often includes extending relationships with students after they graduate. As I write these words, I am in northern California for an immersion into the great beauty of Yosemite and surrounding areas and a weekend of the Bioneers conference, as well as to greet a new baby in the family. I am also very excited about sharing time with several former students who participated in my classes and/or the vocational discernment groups I facilitated through the Duke Chapel's Pathways program.

One of the courses I taught, Spirituality & Ecology: Religious Perspectives on Environmental Ethics, was designed to help students examine their values, attitudes, beliefs and practices as these may affect their own environmental ethics, as well as to increase their understanding of the teachings of various religious traditions. In addition to reading texts, students kept weekly journals and wrote a paper on the process of their evolving environmental ethic and how it connects with their own vocational work. Some of the impetus for the course came after I was invited to submit a proposal to the Dean of the Nicholas School of the Environment following our joint sponsorship of a campus series of lectures by Thomas Berry on The Role of the University in Earth-Human Relationships.

My interactions with the students also included some counseling, weddings, continuing correspondence, and some informal spiritual direction, another aspect of my vocation, which I have been practicing for many years.

But what about campus ministry? Knocking on the big 80, I'm still doing it, only now my campus is the universe, which, by the way, is what the University is supposed to be teaching about, right? Not just how to serve the extractive economy, but how to be in a relationship of intimacy and wonder with all that is.

And the students? They are still with us, here and now, often ready to lead us into the future. At least the ones I know are ready to chant: "It hasn't all happened yet!" It's about something called hope. As one of my favorite writers, the poet-farmer Wendell Berry, suggested, be joyful even when you know the facts. I believe it's good counsel.

So here I am, four years after my retirement from the Religious Life staff at Duke, somewhere in between the way it was and the way it is. Lately I've been learning to live with Parkinson's disease, which is clearly, for me, another dimension of the spiritual journey. One of my most fascinating activities is some recent interaction with the Duke Center for Integrative Medicine, where I spoke recently on a panel addressing a group of professional yoga teachers on Aging and Spirituality.

The Duke Vigil
By Clyde O. Robinson, Jr.

It was about seven-o'clock when the telephone rang. I remember because the early Saturday morning Horror Show, featuring Boris Karloff as Frankenstein, had just run the title screen, and I was settling in for a quiet two hours before mowing the grass. The caller, my grad student assistant, yelled into the phone "Guess where I am!" I muttered something about my movie, and he rushed on to say, "I'm sitting on the piano in Doug Knight's living room." That got my attention. Doug Knight was the president of Duke University.

"What in the world are doing in Knight's house?" I asked frantically, Frankenstein completely forgotten by now. The story came tumbling out. Martin Luther King, Jr., had been killed the week before, and Duke students had been searching for some appropriate University response. Their leadership had quickly come to the conclusion that Duke should raise the wages of non-academic employees, many of whom were black, to the lofty level of $1.60 per hour. They had presented the proposal to the Administration who, of course, temporized. The students pondered ways of encouraging them to act. Flushing all the johns on campus at once to destroy the sewage system was considered; a night time march into the area where many Duke faculty lived to discuss the issue was finally decided upon. When President Knight realized what was happening, he feared the consequences, especially if some of the town's red neck bullies learned what was taking place, and quickly invited the students into the President's palatial home, where they proceeded to spend the night. Jamie Little, my colleague, had been with them, trying to encourage them to moderation.

Before the day was over, the students had transferred themselves to the main quadrangle and had grown in number to over 1,500. They camped there in front of Duke's lovely Gothic chapel for the next two weeks, persistently insisting that Duke respond to King's death by paying their cooks, cleaners and gardeners a living wage. Prominent faculty did not join their ranks publicly but did press their case in the faculty senate with the Administration, and finally with the Board of Trustees. On Easter Sunday, James Cleland, Dean of Duke Chapel, unexpectedly swung open the massive Chapel doors, bread and wine in hand, and served the Lord's Supper to the student encampment. Perhaps the most dramatic moment in what came to be called the "vigil," occurred when the Chair of the Board, a corporate officer of a major automobile manufacturing company, arrived on campus declaring that he had come to fire the President for not expelling the students. Cooler heads prevailed, and that same corporate magnate was later to be seen, arms crossed, linked into a giant circle of students and faculty that surrounded the Quad. He was singing "We Shall Overcome" at the top of his lungs!

The trustees finally met the demands of the students and increased the wages of the "non-academic employees" to $1.60 per hour. The students broke camp and returned to their dorms and classes. It took those self- same employees days to remove the debris from the Quad and restore its manicured lawn. Two sleeping bags, my meager contribution to the vigil, were never seen again. The task remaining to some of us was to interpret the Vigil to a hostile community that included congregations and denominational agencies.

The Presbyterian campus ministries at NC State, the University of North Carolina in Chapel Hill, and Duke had over the years sponsored symposia for North Carolina ministers and lay leaders. My colleagues, Don Shriver and Harry Smith, together with our ecumenical team at Duke, quickly decided to sponsor a day on campus for church folk who wanted to understand what the Vigil was all about. We arranged for them to visit with students in their natural haunts during the early part of the day, their task being to listen to what students had to say about what had taken place. We brought them back together to report their findings in the presence of a panel of students who then were given the opportunity to have the last word.

Genuine dialogue took place that day. Stereotypes were shattered literally left and right. One moment is engraved forever in my memory. Doug Adams, a senior that year and now a professor at Pacific School of Religion, expounded at length as he analyzed the Vigil economically, sociologically, politically, theologically and—as only a serious minded senior can do—tried his best to help us understand his motives. When he had finished, he bounced once or twice on the soft sofa where he was seated and said, "And besides it was Spring!"

It was my privilege to be a part of the religious community at Duke in 1968, when that community provided major leadership in helping the University respond to the social ills that had cost Martin Luther King, Jr. his life.

Walking to Work

People sometimes chuckle when they notice that a staff person for United Ministries in Education lives on a rural mail route. "How can a person live in the country and relate to the sophisticated intricacies of the church's interface with higher education in urban America?" they query. And my answer says much about who I am discovering myself to be.

Week in and week out DC-9's, Holiday Inns, university campuses and issues in higher education, and church buildings and ecclesiastical politics outline my life and consume my energy. Planning, evaluating, consulting, developing organizations, listening, intervening, newsprint, magic markers— they are my world. Weekends, holidays, hunks of the summer and whenever else I physically can, I get back to "Route 2, Box #340" to the land and blood that nourish my roots and restore my soul!

The Steele Creek farming community where we live is some ten miles and twenty minutes from the heart of Charlotte where Louise works as a counselor in a large, urban community college. It is three miles and six minutes from the Charlotte airport so that I can almost walk to work. But the meaning of living here lies far deeper than convenience.

Living on Whispering Pines Lane has to do with family, earlier generations of whom lie buried in the old church yard a half mile away and dozens of whom are within a few minutes' drive from our home. It has to do with three acres of oak, cedar, gum and hickory; with firewood, sawed, split, stacked and with blisters to prove it; with a compost pile and a garden that awaits it; with camellias, nandinas, rhododendrons and even Monkey Grass destined to grow naturally and not to be coiffured; and it has to do with living with people in the space of the house.

There's a living room fireplace, lit with wood we cut and surrounded by big soft chairs for reading theological tomes, personnel and guidance periodicals, and contemporary novels. The stereo offers a little bit of everything from Loretta Lynn, to the Goose Creek Symphony and Three Dog Night, to Beethoven and Purcell. But the chairs are mostly tor talking, talking, talking—and keeping our worlds in touch. There's a big kitchen that sees lots of pinto beans, turnip greens, cornbread, raw vegetable salads, soups and strews (some of which often simmer in the iron stew pot that sits by the side of the living room hearth). There's a shop off the garage where bottles are cut into glasses, lamps are repaired, lumber is sawed and sanded, furniture is refinished, and Christmas gifts are made. There's a special room for the friends, colleagues and family who delight our lives by their frequent visits.

Off our bedroom, there's a study with a dictating machine, an airline guide, a telephone answering machine, some file cabinets and a huge oak roll top desk where I now sit. Corita prints, an Arizona landscape, a Jacques Brel quotation and pieces of newsprint catch my eye. Sitting here today, I have played consultant to a community college counselor who wanted help in designing a training event for his local church, I've been pastor and political strategist for a key figure in a UMHE state commission, I've helped a colleague develop an instrument through which our Eastern Regional Team might come to use our skills and resources more effectively. Today I've read about the current attitudes of Black students, I've discussed a continuing education event for campus ministers in the area, and I've opened a pile of mail and shed some tears over the next three weeks' travel.

But what I'll be doing out there from San Francisco to Florence, Alabama, and Gainesville, Florida, I like to do. It uses my skills in areas of work I care about. I'll be looking for models of ministry in community college settings in the hope that they may be shared throughout our network; I'll work on planning for a more effective strategy for relating the church and Black higher education. I'll do a workshop to help a university develop its helping services for students and others; I'll visit a new city to open conversations about an

184

ecumenical ministry; I'll see bunches of judicatory officials who have responsibility for ministry in higher education; and I'll be eager to get home again!

(These two pieces were written in 1998 for a collection of NCMA anecdotes.)

Clyde Robinson, beloved mentor to so many of us, is currently living the good life in Rock Hill, SC. He says, "I relish news of continuing projects such as Steve Darr's work in Vietnam, close friendships developed in the Asia Pacific region of WSCF, and memories of colleagues on campuses across the country. I fondly remember the wedding vows for Betsy and Mark that Helen Neinast and I heard many moons ago with dear friends such as Earl Lowell cheering us on. We love visitors; come on down."

Having His Say: Forty Years of Ministry in Higher Education
By Robert Thomason

I was 31-years-old before I discovered what I wanted to be when I grew up. I had known since my late teens that I wanted to be in full-time Christian service. For ten years, I thought that God's calling for me was a career in law. But after following that path to a coveted position with a large Atlanta law firm, with a new baby and a new house, I began to have doubts about whether I was fulfilling my calling. When I finally discerned that my passion all along had been for the ministry of the church (as some of my elders had already tried to tell me), I took the plunge into those murky waters of theological study and ordination. During my seminary days, I worked as a youth director, first in a local church and then for an annual conference, but, upon graduation, I followed the normative path of pastoral ministry, first as an associate in a large church and then as the pastor of a small congregation. Still, I sensed I was in the wrong place of service.

Sometimes (certainly not always) the Methodist appointment system actually works. In 1966, when I was sinking in the quicksand of the Oakwood church, for which I was not the appropriate pastor, my district superintendent called and asked, "What would you think about going to be Director of the Wesley Foundation in Milledgeville, Georgia?" Without much enthusiasm but desperate to get out of that quicksand in Oakwood, I agreed to give it a try.

Exactly 40 years ago today, my wife Rose, our two pre-school sons Mark and Bryan (as well as our pre-school nephew Allen who was spending the summer with us), and I moved into the tiny four-room apartment inside the Wesley Foundation House. I soon learned that God really did have a place of service just right for me. And throughout my forty years in five ministries in higher education, I have felt that I was truly in the place God had called me to be.

The Milledgeville Experience

The Milledgeville Wesley Foundation served three campuses. The "premiere" institution was the Woman's College of Georgia, one of the last remaining state female colleges. (It became coed while I was there.) A few blocks away was Georgia Military College, a prep school and junior college situated on the grounds of the old state capitol. And just outside town was Milledgeville State Hospital, with an Affiliate Program in Psychiatric Nursing for student nurses from hospital-based training programs. The State Hospital was the only state mental health facility and had three times as many patients as the town had people.

Milledgeville, in the summer of 1966, was still very much the old South and, of course, a racially separated community. I could stand at the front of the Wesley Foundation House and see a college residence hall just behind me, a decaying mansion built by a former governor in 1836 next door, the former governor's mansion (now the home of the college president) across the street, and, next to that, the Cline home, where Flannery O'Connor's mother still lived and where Flannery had lived until her death two years earlier. Rising above those, I could see the spires of the college and the First Methodist Church, where I had my office. Looking in the other direction, only another block away, I could see where the African American community began and, not coincidentally, the curb and sidewalk ended, and some of the houses were without electricity and running water.

The first January I was there, we celebrated the twenty-fifth anniversary of the ministry, and I wrote these words for the occasion:

A ministry for the future will require authentic listening to the college communities and to what they are saying to the church... A ministry for the future will find The Methodist Church losing its identity as such on the campus so that it can more adequately be the Church of Christ—the One who freely gave up His life for all [people].... A ministry for the future will require serious study of theology and related fields.... A ministry for the future will involve students and others in significant and responsible action to alleviate suffering, rectify injustice, and make life more abundant.... A ministry for the future must be radically open to the future and to the God who calls the church into being, not simply out of the past but out of the unknown that lies ahead.

And then, almost as if I could really see into the future, I concluded:

A ministry for the future demands obedience to that call, even when it requires bold new steps that may prove to be unpopular and even unsuccessful. A ministry for the future requires faith, for, like Abraham [and Sarah], we cannot know where we are to go, what things are going to be like when we get there, nor even why we must go, until we take our first, fumbling steps.

Emerging Themes of My Ministry

As I read those words in preparing for My Say, I realized, perhaps for the first time, how much certain beliefs about ministry have shaped all that I have been and done. I want to highlight those beliefs throughout this reflection in the hope that they might be of some value to you or, at least, a basis for dialogue about what the church's ministry is all about. I'll start with a few from my Milledgeville experience.

First, ministry is mutual. We do not bring God to the campus. God is already there in so many amazing ways. Our initial task is to discern God's activity. Higher education is not "the enemy," but, rather, one of God's means for disclosing Godself. I didn't get much further with that theme in Milledgeville than listening, but it shaped my attitude from then on.

Second, ministry seeks to realize the unity Christ intended for the church. Yes, I confess that I'm a hopelessly incurable ecumaniac. I view ecumenism not as a pragmatic strategy for some situations but as a theological imperative for the whole church. In Milledgeville that imperative led us to be more than just a denominational student club, and to reach out to a larger constituency through our weekend coffee house. It led us to join our efforts with four other religious groups to reach out to the whole campus with such programs as a feature film series and dialogue held in a campus auditorium.

Third, ministry is more about asking questions than about supplying answers. When I was in college, I attended the quadrennial National Convocation of Methodist Youth at Purdue University. I will always remember the huge backdrop across the stage of the auditorium where our plenary sessions were held. It was a panorama of all sorts of questions—mostly the "why" questions. The convocation theme was "Living the Questions." That's what the Bible encourages us to do, isn't it? In Milledgeville, we provided many opportunities and settings for struggling with questions—weekly programs for student nurses, a Sunday school class at the local church, a Sunday night supper discussion, the Saturday night coffee house.

Fourth, ministry is inescapably about social justice. I can't imagine how anyone can read about Jesus' understanding of his call to ministry and not hear the summons to actively seek social justice. In Milledgeville in the late sixties, that imperative clearly demanded action to address racial injustice. The Woman's College had, just the year before, admitted its first two African American students (two local young women living at home). The town was still rigidly segregated; the local movie theater had a separate balcony for African Americans, for example. The public schools began a slow integration process while I was there; my son Mark was in the first integrated class. And, of course, the churches were racially divided.

One of Wesley's first steps to address racial injustice was to respond to a white teacher's request to provide a tutoring program for 20 African American children in her first grade class needing special help. They came to the Wesley House every week, where tutoring was often followed by a meal and other activities led by Wesley students. At the same time Wesley became the monthly meeting place for a local community action organization I helped to form called Concern. Composed of 100 members, equally divided between black and white, Concern provided an outlet for concerned citizens within and outside the college to address community needs and issues.

Because Wesley had become known as a place where blacks and whites met as equals, it was natural that, as the numbers of African American students on campus increased, Wesley became their gathering place—on Saturday night at the coffee house as well as throughout the week.

After three years in Milledgeville, I was offered the Methodist Campus Ministry position at my alma mater, Emory University in Atlanta. I was reluctant to leave. I had never before felt more alive. My continued ministry in

Milledgeville, as you might imagine, was always precarious. However, the Board each year voted to ask for my reappointment, albeit by a small majority. I survived, I think, because I had learned two important survival skills. (1) My Board always knew what I was doing, even when I knew they would not all support it. (2) Our ministry was always interpreted in a theological framework. It was not just me "doing my thing." It was us doing what God had called us to do.

Finally, though, I decided to leave, largely because maintaining family life while living in a student center had become too difficult, especially for my wife. (I would probably not have been married to the remarkable woman who was my partner and soul mate for 42 years if I had not.)

The Emory Experience

Emory University in 1969 enrolled many of the brightest and best students the Southeast produced. Still church-related but by no means church-dominated, it educated many of the leading professionals in the South—lawyers, doctors, preachers, business leaders, educators. Just before I began my ministry there, the African American students had confronted the University with its racism and had been rebuffed by the administration. A remarkable young man, Charles Haynes, just a sophomore and newly-elected President of the Student Government Association, had responded by organizing seven-week-long Seminars on White Racism for the entire University community. I began my ministry at Emory by becoming part of his team.

The Methodist ministry at Emory was part of a loosely-bound United Campus Ministry, led by the University Chaplain Dick Devor. Insofar as possible, each denominational ministry did its work through cooperative planning and on behalf of all. Housed in University facilities, our focus was the total life of the University, including its many graduate schools.

It was a "season of discontent" at the University. Not only were there tensions over racial discrimination, but the anti-war movement was reaching its peak as well. The women's movement was raising consciousness about the status and role of women in the University, and the mission of the University itself was being examined.

It was also the year that the results of the monumental Danforth Study of Campus Ministries were released with the publication of Director Kenneth Underwood's volume *The Church, The University and Social Policy*. Our ministry throughout my five years at Emory was shaped by those findings. We were especially led to affirm our role in helping the University to reflect on its calling and to examine its values and practices. We wrote and circulated papers, such as the one on "Discrimination Against Women in the University." We organized forums, such as the six-months-long weekly luncheon discussion of "The Role of Emory in the Seventies." We served on University-wide committees, helping to address the issues we were raising, such as my service on SGA's Racism Commission. Former colleague J Springer of the NE

Pennsylvania Higher Education Ministry captured graphically what we were trying to do, and it's my next statement of belief about ministry.

Fifth, ministry is about "seasoning the center rather than hustling on the sidelines."

In 1970 the University Chaplain, our team leader, went off to do a sabbatical, and I was named Acting University Chaplain in addition to my role as Methodist Campus Minister. One of the new duties I assumed was responsibility for the Sunday morning service of worship for the University community. That service took many forms, but there was one continuing expectation. It must be original, creative, and authentic. Many preachers filled the pulpit during my two years in this leadership role. Numerous liturgies were composed, worship settings designed, forms of music and dance employed, themes explored, and media tried to enable the gospel to come alive for the diverse congregation of worshippers.

Sixth, ministry is proclaiming the gospel in language and other symbols that can be heard by the contemporary culture.

The anti-war movement at Emory, as on many campuses across the country, reached new heights with the killing of students at Kent State University and Jackson State College in the spring of 1970. The most difficult "sermon" I have ever preached was the one I was called on to offer at a rally on the quadrangle organized by student leaders following those tragedies. Two of the most meaningful ritual acts I have ever participated in were the sharing of cups of water during a peace fast in front of the campus food service center and the making of paper cranes during a peace rally.

Seventh, ministry is the response of Christian faith in non-traditional settings with ritual acts in response to current events.

Two urgent pastoral issues for students in the 70s were the draft and problem pregnancies. Most college counseling services were ill equipped to respond to these issues. At Emory, the United Campus Ministry secured needed training and provided such specialized counseling, eventually assisting the College Council to establish a Draft Counseling Center and coordinating a network called the Clergy Consultation Service to assist young women with problem pregnancies. Recognizing that student advisers in the residence halls are the "front-line" counselors for most undergraduates, our team of campus ministers negotiated chaplaincy roles in each residence hall and focused primarily on assisting the student advisers in dealing with the problems they encountered.

Eighth, ministry is providing pastoral care for a community by identifying, enlisting, equipping, and supporting a team of caregivers.

In 1972, when we learned that the University Chaplain would not return and that the future of the position was in jeopardy, our "united" ministry began to fall apart. The Presbyterian Campus Minister Emmett Herndon and I, though, continued to be a team, sharing almost all our programming and creating new ministries together.

One of those new ministries that emerged came to be known as the Emory Committee on Biomedical Ethics. It came about from a casual conversation with an anatomy professor one morning in a campus parking lot. He talked about the ethical questions with which he was struggling in the basic brain research he was doing. We asked if he might be interested in sharing that struggle with others from a variety of disciplines who might help to clarify the issues and options. We assembled a team of dreamers and planners and eventually more than 200 persons from across the University and community joined us—folks from theology and law, administrators from the Center for Disease Control and the State Department of Health, liberal arts professors and nursing instructors, graduate students and full professors, faculty from Emory and from other local institutions, local pastors and social workers. We met about six times a year to hear a presentation, like the initial one presented by the anatomy professor, and to engage in dialogue about the ethical issues raised. That program is still alive and well today.

Ninth, ministry is opportunistic, connecting folks with similar concerns and enabling them to minister to one another.

MAHEM

Partly growing out of this experience transcending campus boundaries, we decided to do a survey of campus ministry in the whole metropolitan Atlanta area. The pattern was clear. The churches had concentrated almost all their ministry resources on two campuses—Georgia Tech and Emory. The institution with the largest enrollment in the state, all commuters, was Georgia State University. It had almost no ministry presence. The Atlanta University System, a consortium of traditionally African American schools, was likewise neglected. Needless to say, the recently-established community colleges encircling the city had not even appeared on the radar screen of most churches' concern.

Shocked by this basic unfairness in the allocation of ministry resources, Herndon and I developed a proposal for addressing the inequities and expanding the scope of the churches' ministry. The proposal was to create a Metropolitan Atlanta Higher Education Ministry. Its acronym was MAHEM. That alone may have been enough to seal its fate from the beginning.

Knowing that additional funds would be difficult to obtain, Herndon and I proposed that our ministries re-deploy us part of the time to develop this new ministry and funding for it. We envisioned a four-fold thrust: (1) Development of new ministries; (2) Training volunteers within institutions for the task of ministry; (3) Conducting research to discover the most effective ways of doing ministry; and (4) Hands-on ministries, particularly ones that seemed appropriate for an area-wide approach.

While our local ministry boards at Emory and the Presbyterian judicatory were willing to provide our services to launch this new work, the Methodist judicatory was not. By this time, I had become so strongly committed to the project and was so "psyched up" for trying something new, that I could not simply file our proposal away. Providentially, I believe, at about the same time, I read a notice in the Chronicle of Higher Education seeking a campus minister to launch a metropolitan ministry in Jacksonville, Florida. It sounded strikingly similar to what Herndon and I had proposed for Atlanta. So I applied, was called, and appointed.

The Jacksonville Experience

For eighteen months, a group of church and college leaders in Jacksonville had been meeting to explore the establishment of a ministry with the higher education institutions in the city. Schools initially represented were Jacksonville University (private, independent, largely residential) and the University of North Florida (an upper-class and graduate state university, wholly commuter, only 10 years old). The vision, though, was larger, and included the several campuses of Florida Junior College at Jacksonville and Edward Waters College (a traditionally African American four-year college related to the A.M.E. Church). Participating local churches and judicatories represented six denominations (you could guess which ones, except for one surprise—a Missouri Synod Lutheran congregation). Official representatives of both churches and colleges had created a structure and secured funding for a creative, new approach to ministry designed to address the new realities of higher education—commuters, many of whom were non-traditional students, inadequate church resources to provide ministers for each campus, etc.

When I arrived in Jacksonville the doors immediately began to open for me, and I began to reap the benefits of the careful developmental work, led by Ed Albright, which had prepared the way. Two campus offices had already been arranged; twelve participating local churches already viewed me as their minister on campus; and a committed group of representative Board members were ready to provide their services for the work of "our" ministry.

Tenth, ministry is best when done as a partnership between church and college.

During my ten years in Jacksonville, I learned to think in a whole new way about ministry in higher education. I managed to shed the "lone ranger" model and found the joy that comes from being the enabler of a host of "ministers" from church and campus. A few examples will illustrate. A local pastor and members from his congregation provided Divorce Rap on campus for those struggling with the pain of that experience. A team of students, college administrators, and church youth leaders provided a city-wide Going to College Seminar for senior high school students. Several local clergy team-taught a college religion course. Families from local churches "adopted" local international students, and hundreds of church volunteers hosted 50 students from across the country at Christmas International House. A student and faculty team organized Student/Faculty Dialogue Groups, meeting in faculty homes.

192

Eleventh, ministry is multiplied when volunteers are enabled to carry out a variety of ministries.

While we never managed to provide ministries on every campus in the city, we were able to add Edward Waters College and one of the FJC campuses to our partnership, as well as churches of two additional denominations.

The Northern Virginia Experience

By 1984, I was ready for a new challenge in a new place. United College Ministries in Northern Virginia, committed to serving George Mason University and the five campuses of Northern Virginia Community College, was seeking new leadership. I was called to be their first full-time Minister Director. Located in the Virginia suburbs of Metropolitan Washington, UCMNV had an 18-year history of struggle and endurance. Their vision was much like that of the Jacksonville ministry. One of the unique challenges they faced was the multi-ethnic, multi-racial, multi-faith, multi-national, multi-everything character of the student bodies. Early on, we determined that faithful ministry for us required that we find ways to connect to that reality.

Metro Washington has unique resources for ministry. It's home for several theological schools and scores of underemployed clergy. We devised a plan to link those resources to that multi-everything reality by employing part-time chaplains to serve particular campuses and/or particular racial ethnic populations. Our chaplains were sometimes seminary interns earning field education credit; other times, they were underemployed local clergy, doing our ministry along with another. During my thirteen years at UCMNV, we employed 37 different campus chaplains. We were convinced that the best way to demonstrate that we were serious about ministry with a variety of racial ethnic groups was to reflect diversity in our staff. Half of our chaplains during those years were persons of color--from four different racial ethnic groups. In the latter years, we often had four chaplains, each from a different racial ethnic background.

Twelfth, ministry is most clearly identified as ministry for all people when there is racial ethnic diversity among the staff.

As our chaplains began their work each year, they would initially identify those on campus who might be thought of as "outcasts." After all, Jesus, in his ministry, seemed to have a particular affinity for those members of society. The outcasts might be the LGBT students or the Muslim community or particular racial ethnic populations. They would establish a relationship with those groups, usually through their organizations. Specific ministries would develop from that relationship.

Thirteenth, ministry is especially attentive to those who might be considered "outcasts" in the campus community.

Our chaplains would also identify key campus organizations, such as student government or the campus newspaper. After establishing a relationship of trust with those organizations, opportunities for cooperative programming would often emerge. An example was our region-wide sponsorship of lectures about peacemaking, featuring a Nobel Peace Prize recipient, held on each of our campuses and in a church setting, funded jointly by a variety of campus organizations.

Fourteenth, ministry is best offered, where possible, in coalition with other campus groups who share the vision.

On commuter campuses, it is particularly challenging to find a way to connect with the lives of students. Two ways that proved to be particularly effective for us were projects borrowed from other places: The Listening Post and the Praxis Project. The Listening Post, staffed by volunteers, provided a table in a busy place on campus (usually near food) where a friendly listener offered peanuts and non-judgmental conversation. Available several hours each week on multiple campuses, the Post attracted hundreds eager to be heard.

The Praxis Project enabled students enrolled in certain classes to perform community service for course credit. The chaplains negotiated the service settings and led reflection groups processing the experience.

Fifteenth, ministry is most effective when it can find a way to "infiltrate" the busy lives of students.

Beyond the Campus

When I decided to retire in 1997 I was not yet ready to sever my ties with campus ministry. The National Campus Ministry Association had provided a vital network throughout my years of ministry. I had been a member almost as long as the organization had existed. I had served a three-year term as a Regional Representative of the Southeast in the early 70s. I had initiated and planned Southeast Regional Conferences for ten years. I had helped plan national conferences in Fort Worth, in Durham, and in Washington in the 80s and 90s. I had been the Partnership Program Coordinator throughout the 90s. Knowing that George and Sally Gunn were seeking to relinquish their responsibilities as Membership Secretary and Newsletter Editor, I offered my services. (You don't have to wait to be asked. Just volunteer.) My offer was accepted and here I have been, gladly, for the last nine years of my higher education ministry—minding the store, so to speak. I've been paid a small salary to do it, but I would have happily done it for nothing. Helping this organization fulfill its mission and maintaining the network of relationships among all of you have been the joy and delight of my retirement.

Fifteen years ago, when the Northern Virginia ministry celebrated its 25th anniversary, I wrote about the challenges facing us. To my amazement, they seem to me to be the same challenges that face us today. There are four of them:

(1) A higher education community which is increasingly multi-ethnic, multi-racial, multi-cultural, and multi-faith. I ask: Can we, ministries rooted in a Christian faith shaped largely by Western culture and the

American experience, overcome our cultural chauvinism to allow the God of all creation and all peoples to be seen and experienced?

(2) A mainline Protestant community which is increasingly anxious about its future and constantly tempted to care more about institutional survival than the needs of the world. I ask: Can we, ministries of service to the world, in particular, the world of higher education, totally dependent on the "missionary" vision and generosity of the church, continue to be a priority on the church's agenda?

(3) A higher education community, which continues to grow in enrollment, in diversity, in numbers of institutions, and in "campuses" (virtual and otherwise) where courses are taught. I ask: Can we, ministries still struggling to be fully present on the campuses we already serve, find ways to extend our outreach beyond its present scope?

(4) A society (including both church and campus) which is increasingly secular but which continues to hunger and thirst for meaning. I ask: Can we, a ministry which values loving God with our minds, discover new ways to engage people in the church and on campus in the search for truth and meaning?

I'll sign off now with the words that have concluded my ministry in at least three places. This will make the fourth. They're words of Dag Hammarsjold, the late Secretary General of the United Nations: "For all that has been, thanks. To all that shall be, yes!"

The preceding speech was presented on June 30, 2006, to the annual conference of the National Campus Ministry Association, meeting at Lewis & Clark College, Portland, Oregon. It concluded my nine years of service as Administrative Officer/Membership Secretary/Newsletter Editor of the Association, my "retirement" job.

Robert Thomason is living at Westminster Woods on Julington Creek, a continuing care retirement community just south of Jacksonville, FL. His days are filled with tennis, horseshoes, swimming, singing in two choirs, coordinating a weekly Seekers book discussion, leading a Food 4 Kids program, and chairing the Residents' Council

Three by Thad
By Thad Holcombe

The following "blogs" were written by Thad for the NCMA Online Newsletter in 2012 and 2013.

Discerning Priorities of Campus Ministry at Your University/College

These comments are in response to questions asked in the workshop I facilitated at the 2013 NCMA conference in Georgia. While presenting "Seeing the Forest Before Identifying the Trees: University Ministry as a context for Campus Ministry," I suggested an approach to discerning what are the particular concerns of the college/university culture that might be addressed. The process I am suggesting is, in addition to other resources, available in books/articles, which includes Sharon Park's, *Big Questions, Worthy Dreams: Mentoring Young Adults in Their Search for Meaning, Purpose, and Faith* and Eric H. F. Law's *Holy Currencies: 6 Blessing for Sustainable Missional Ministries.* .

This approach entails interviewing faculty, administration along with the ministers, priests, pastors, and rabbis that are staff for your partner congregations. The results of interviews would then be shared with your board, leadership team and/or a group you especially organized to give you feedback. It is important to have several conversations with students who are diverse in academic interest, age, and classification, as well. All responses in interviews need to be kept confidential. These interviews may take several months or a semester and can be done when beginning a ministry or as a way to keep "updated."

The questions I am suggesting can be amended, but need to be asked of each individual you interview. It is important that the interviews be held on the "turf" of the person you are asking. It has been my experience that a forty-five minute limit can be difficult to keep. It may be the first time you have met with an individual and so getting acquainted entails sharing with him/her who you are and why you are doing an interview. This is in addition to the initial setting of an appointment. What I discovered is that the time together is shared in the university "grapevine" within the department and/or friends. Emphasize that the conversation is confidential as to particular responses, but will be shared along with other responses so you can get a perspective that is more accurate than your making assumptions.

The questions that I am putting forth come from my experience in the 60's/70's while being on site review teams that spent two days on a campus for purposes of support/evaluation of a ministry. They were made possible by having higher education staff employed by denominations who regularly visited campus ministry sites. Some of you reading this may remember Clyde Robinson, Abby Abendroth and others.

Again, amend these questions as you see fit, add some if you feel something is lacking, but be consistent in asking same questions:

1. What are the crucial issues or problems to be dealt with, the opportunities to be taken, the accomplishments to be celebrated in your particular university? (You might add a follow-up to this as to how is the university dealing with any/all the matters described?).
2. Where in the university do you find serious conversation about the purpose of higher education?
3. Describe and evaluate the support services provided by the university (personal and career counseling, health services, support groups for gender/racial ethnic groups, etc.) Are additional services needed? Are there reasons the institution is not providing them?
4. Describe the life of the typical student as much as possible. What do you think are their apparent values, life styles, living patterns, social configurations, study habits, etc.
5. How would you describe what is needed to nurture ,encourage, and enhance students to be "engaged" learners and not focus on just grades and faculty expectations?
6. How would you describe the morale of faculty/administrators and their relationship with each other?
7. What keeps you excited/motivated about your position as faculty/administrator?
8. (If time allows.) How do you perceive (insert the name of the ministry you staff)?

How do you identify who to interview? Administrators are best done by position, i.e. Provost, Dean, Head of Department, etc. Faculty can be identified (besides ones on your board) by asking students and looking at faculty who have received teaching awards – also, if you have a particular interest and want to become acquainted with faculty in a particular department, it would be worthwhile to set appointments with those faculty.

When interviewing those on staff with partner congregations, the questions could include the following:

1. What has been your experience with the ministry?
2. How is the best way to communicate with the faith community you staff?
3. What do you expect of the ministry?
4. (Add appropriate questions as you see fit.)

The question may arise, "What about the students?" This is where your understanding of faith development comes in along with what you glean as you share the results of your interviews with students. It is also important to ask of yourself what you think is the purpose of higher education, given the context of today's culture and the history of the university. Above all, the process I am suggesting is a way to practice one of the most important aspects of ministry – listening to what is said and not said and carefully listening to yourself.

Campus Ministry – InterCollegiate Athletics – Mission of Higher Education

...when football and men's basketball programs cloak their vigorous commercial activities as educational endeavors, they are deceiving tax payers and their own universities. (Nancy Hogshead Makar, "Tie Money to Value"', *Chronicle of Higher Education*, December 11, 2011)

A six million dollar football coach "buy out" and ticket scandal at University of Kansas; the Penn State controversy; and my being at the University of Oklahoma when weapons were found in an athletic residential hall and...the list goes on and on. While being at KU, I have listened to an increasing number of faculty express anger at not having any influence on the direction and quality of athletics. It was not the student athlete that was prompting this frustration, as much as the increasing systemic influence of the athletic corporation in the "commercialization" of the university that occurs through sponsorship of a major entertainment industry, i.e. football and basketball.

At the suggestion of a faculty member, I contacted Amy Perko, Executive Director of the Knight Commission on Intercollegiate Athletics. This commission continues to be the major force in asking for reform of the NCAA. This set in motion what is now given the title "ECM's University Community Forum on Higher Education and Athletics: which coordinated Amy Perko's visit. She did two excellent presentations early in the semester, followed by a UC Forum ECM sponsors on a weekly basis. It was a panel of two faculty and a Chancellor Emeritus. Since then we have had two more panel presentations. These were suggested by the members of the UC Forum composed of 24 members, who are faculty, athletic corporation staff, and students.

Many faculty are frustrated, others disillusioned, while others could care less,-- or see any challenge to the coming "tsunami" of money similar to "tilting at windmills". I think the consequences of a major Division I reseach university, such as KU, not challenging the growing acceptance of sponsoring a multimillion dollar entertainment industry are detrimental to the mission of higher education.

I watch the basketball and football games and read the sports section in the Kansan, KU's student newspaper. This section seems to grow larger, so much so that I wonder if it is not analogous to the priorities of many students at KU, who experience their classroom education as another commodity to be consumed along with sports?

It is complicated. Why should ECM at KU even be involved? Our stated purpose of the UC Forum on athletics is "to coordinate and facilitate, during the Spring Semester 2012, dialogue for examining the compatibility and improvement of the relationship between higher education and collegiate athletics at KU." Our hope is to have a dialogue and not a debate.

The ministry's involvement is in keeping with the stated purpose of the UC Forum, a tradition at KU since the 40's, which is to facilitate dialogue that can build bridges between different perspectives within the university, especially pertaining to the important issues of the mission of higher education.

I encourage any of you reading these comments, especially if you are having a ministry with a Division I school in athletics, to consider initiating such a dialogue as a way for faculty and others to speak freely on how they are feeling about this issue.

As one faculty member said "What the university pays our janitorial staff is inadequate, while our athletic salaries and expenses increase exponentially." It is an Occupy issue and an issue of justice that we in campus ministries can attempt to address.

March, 2012

Alternative Breaks: A Ministry of Praxis

Alternative Breaks are often opportunities for university students and others to understand themselves, society, and their interdependence with the earth, in new ways. The alternative breaks sponsored by the Ecumenical Campus Ministries at the University of Kansas are open to persons of all faith traditions and those who have none. They are influenced by the "critical pedagogy " of Paulo Freire, an important educator of the 20th century, who was an education adviser to the World Council of Churches.

"Praxis" is therefore encouraged. It is a process of reflecting on the experience of the alternative break. This is done recognizing that the participant needs to be open to rethinking his/her own way of life as they experience another culture or context than the one in which they had been raised.

Alternative breaks can be very affirming. Participants can learn that they are not "empty vessels" to be filled by the expertise of an authority figure in a classroom. Freire challenges such "banking education," where students answer questions that have no relevance to their own experience. Unfortunately, at KU, not all classrooms are like this; in contrast, questions raised from alternative breaks are welcomed. Both student and professor are recognized as having expertise.

As I listen to evaluations of alternative break participants, I am often struck by how the learning experienced becomes connected to the possibility that they can effect change in society. A new or deeper understanding of their life story gives impetus to this possibility. The past becomes connected to the present in a way that a new narrative empowers them to explore their life as one where "their great joys (gifts) can meet the world's deep hurts" (A paraphrase of Frederick Buechners's definition of vocation).

The aspects of faith that are reinforced are numerous. In addition to possibly discerning their "call" or vocation in life, justice is understood as systemic and as in contrast to charity; thus, love becomes a way to publicly affirm social change with compassion – an ability to "suffer with others." Faith becomes a verb that describes how one makes sense of life. It changes as one understands one's life as a faith, and with a sense of "grace" can accept the past as a way to learn and not be thwarted by mishaps that have occurred along the way. Often a sense of gratitude is evoked as the ability to be in solidarity with others who are different is experienced and the hospitality extended by the stranger is celebrated.

"Journey" as a metaphor may be discovered as they have a change in perspective on social and political issues, or as a new appreciation of living interdependent with the earth is acknowledged. Our own story of liberation, i.e. Exodus, gains new relevance. One can be "reborn," not in the sense of suddenly being "saved" and protected from life, but in being drawn into the very midst of living where the Holy is present in the mix of the sacred and the secular.

I am retired in Lawrence, Kansas. I continue to be involved in Presbytery of Northern Kansas, am Moderator of the First Presbyterian EcoTeam, which is the first Earth Care Congregation in the presbytery. I am also Moderator of Lawrence Ecology Teams United in Sustainability (LET-US) - an interfaith network of faith communities green team for education and advocacy on earth care/climate change. My wife, Linda Watts, continues part-time as a School Social Worker, along with involvement in local to national issues regarding hunger/poverty. I volunteer at Just Food, a central distribution site for food pantries and cooking classes. In addition, along with taking naps, I collect regional art found at estate sales and auctions in area. I am involved in two book groups, one with mostly clergy and other one sponsored by LET-US. One daughter is with AmeriCorps at Lawrence Homeless Shelter and the other one is living/employed in Chicago.

The Thing Itself: The Tapestry of a Ministry in Higher Ed
By Thomas Mainor

An interesting and varied cast of characters provided material and the looms that helped to weave a curious tapestry of campus ministries in Virginia in the late '60s into the '80s. Beyond traditional student ministries, there was a slow evolution, a journey that led to new understandings of the *Thing* itself. What developed was not a carefully conceived and fabricated design or vision. What did emerge was an interesting opportunity to take part in campus ministry during a time when national, regional and local governing bodies shared the costs, and when Campus Ministry shared ideas of ministry shaped to the times.

Following Seminary, I was called to a rural/labor parish, Falling Spring, in the 'forks of the James' 'twixt the Shenandoah and Roanoke valleys of Virginia—a wonderful congregation in an historic setting. The view from the front steps of the Church was idyllic, rolling foothills, Blue Ridge Mountains, homes and farms. Great folks. Good things were happening.

With uncertainty, I accepted a call in1967 to be Presbyterian campus minister at **William and Mary** and Associate Pastor at Williamsburg Presbyterian Church. The call came from three agencies; the Synod of Virginia, Presbytery of Norfolk, and the Williamsburg congregation.

At William and Mary, with an interesting array of colleagues, we soon formed CaMU, Campus Ministries United, enabling us to work together ecumenically and interfaith with students, college faculty and administration in ways not otherwise possible. Our joint efforts helped provide access to college resources and venues that might otherwise be unavailable. For example, we co-sponsored with the art department an on-campus exhibition of the linoleum block print art of Robert Hodgell, of then Florida Presbyterian (Eckerd) College. We featured a Wesley/CaMU Coffee House performer, guitarist/vocalist, Cleveland Francis, in standing-room-only crowd in Phi Beta Kappa Hall, space provided by the college.

Engagement with the Honors Program, Student Affairs, and a newly formed Department of Religion was well received. We created a joint office through the facilities and resources of the Wesley Foundation, where United Methodist campus minister Braxton Allport and I shared space and secretary. CaMU met regularly to plan programs and provide mutual support for seven denominations including Catholic, Christian Scientist and Jewish communities. Each of us worked with denominational groups with students, providing pastoral and liturgical support opportunities, and together on campus with a variety of program efforts.

In 1969, the Danforth Report, *The Church, the University and Social Policy*, was published. It made significant impact on my own understanding of higher education ministry. Focused on mainline Protestant ministries, director of the study Kenneth Underwood identified four principle modes of ministry considered most influential: those of pastor, priest, prophet and king. That is, ministry to persons, the speaking forth of the essentials of faith and provision for liturgical occasions, focusing on justice and mercy in society, and the governance structures of society—how love of neighbor is expressed practically where we live.

The basic assumption in the Underwood Study was that the university is a key institution in our society. The role was one of working with faculty and developing student leadership who would have significant opportunity to become competent in a variety of disciplines, to shape social policy and influence legal, science, business, political rhetoric and the social fabric of society. The university also greatly influenced those who would eventually become leaders in religious communities. Universities enabled society to remember and reflect on its history and values affirmed from founding documents and events that challenged those values through the years. The poetry and literature of cultures provided introductions to the meaning of life in a larger commonwealth. Study of new developments in scientific research about the world around us, about the human imprint on the earth and negative influences upon it, how to think about the order of things, and how to govern and be governed--all were fundamentally important. Also significant was the nature and provenance of the values that prevail in academic inquiry and in society's economic and legal frameworks. Underwood felt that too often, the university operated under values-free research while church efforts on behalf of social and corporate ministry lacked competence. Both aspects, he felt, were critical and significant to society. Linkage of well-informed, and knowledgeable ethical reflection was essential to a healthy society—thus the Church (writ large), the University and Social Policy.

The role of the church—I understood—was not only to be a pastor to students, but also at least as vigorously and competently, see faculty and administrators in a pastoral and collegial light (many sat in our congregations). We were to seek—among many voices present—to reflect a responsible prophetic voice in the community. We had no 'right' to be heard. We did have—because of the roles religions play in the world, for good or ill—a significant opportunity to be responsibly engaged as congregations around campus and in programs we might co-sponsor as partners within the College. Indeed, religious communities had a long history of founding schools and colleges, not least in the early days of our nation—Harvard, Princeton, Davidson, Duke, to name but a few. Our engagement within education had a long history and no less in publically funded higher education.

At William and Mary for CaMU, the Honors Program was willing to partner with us in occasional programs. In the Viet Nam era, a Peace Research academic focus was initiated, primarily by the Honors and Project Plus faculty with CaMU staff as part of the faculty. It was significant, given all that was happening on campuses across the nation, such as Kent State. Under the leadership and resources of the Honors and Project Plus program, we worked in the creation of a yearlong *Conflict and Conflict Resolution* emphasis. There were 85 students and 15 faculty selected across disciplines—including military science—in the program. The co-ed dorm, innovative in those days, housed all 85 students, providing opportunity for non-structured exchanges. The course represented one-quarter of a student's academic load. There were weekly evening seminars for the program that included guest participants. One evening seminar on the Palestinian-Israeli divide included a representative of the Israeli Embassy in Washington, and a Palestinian envoy—also from D.C.—who engaged with one another and with students and faculty.

On one occasion, we were able to co-sponsor Marvin Kalb, then CBS Diplomatic Correspondent, for about 500 in a Parents Day program. Honors at W&M helped with the costs and he spoke to two classes, in addition to an evening presentation. In that period during Viet Nam demonstrations and the Kent State tragedy, such was a strong positive dialogue on campus.

Meanwhile, Synod-wide in those 'thrilling days of yesteryear,' the Synod's executive, James A. Payne, Jr., played a strong partnership role in support and development of a Synod-wide Campus Ministry Staff Team. Presbyterian team leadership included campus ministry Sage, Woody Leach, serving Virginia Tech. His campus ministry focus on justice ministries and his long presence at VPI was strong and a significant. His associate was Jim VandeBerg, an insightful and thoughtful colleague, whose talents provided important leadership then and in future years to the denomination. They were especially involved in a host of issues related to Appalachia and the social issues that grew out of the exploitation by the coal industries of the region. *Night Comes to the Cumberlands* and *Yesterday's People* are examples of the books focusing on the times. Both Jim and Woody played major roles in leading and interpreting the campus ministries that evolved across the Virginias, and in my own understanding of what ministry in higher education was all about.

Synod executive, Jim Payne, worked actively and supportively with us and helped higher education ministries evolve, including guiding us in dealing with funding issues. Each of our campuses had different styles of ministry, and the staff team seemed to come together to breathe fire into the larger strategies for the new Synod of the Virginias (including West Virginia and Pennsylvania's Trinity Presbytery) and local campus ministries across the area. This particular team also included ministries on campuses large and small. "Flash" (Howard) Gordon at UVA and others included ecumenical partners on campuses, such as Jim McDonald, United Methodist Minister at THE University. The ecumenical team partners grew in importance and included Catholic Campus Ministry coordinator, Cosmos Rubencamp, and John Coffey of the United Methodists. Throughout this time, denominational staff such as Clyde Robinson of the PCUSA and others were significant and supportive colleagues.

Importantly, we were enabled to envision and plan campus ministry across Virginia in a larger context with our supporting agencies than might otherwise be possible. Pastoral concerns joined Jim VandeBerg and I with the national

Clergy Consultation on Problem Pregnancies. which dealt with the issue of abortions and alternatives prior to Roe v Wade in 1973. This evolved into denomination-wide pastoral efforts on the issue, which later began to focus on larger health ministry issues.

Our campus ministry team approach also involved the expansion into northern Virginia—George Mason University and Community Colleges in the area—where we gained yet another United Methodist Colleague. Robert Thomason provided significant leadership in the years ahead. He later became staff to the Virginia Council's Campus Ministry Forum. Jim McDonald, formerly UMC Campus Minister in Charlottesville, became Executive for Virginia Council of Churches. This mirrored national trends, as Campus Ministry tended to transition from denominational to ecumenical efforts. Significantly, funding was available from denominational leadership on the national stage. Presbyterian national staff was deployed regionally as well as UMHE. It was also a time when social issues—especially civil rights and the Viet Nam war—played out with powerful campus impact. The Church asked what it meant to be Christian in such a time, and controversy swirled around ways in which ministers on campus understood their role. Pastoral and Prophetic intertwined. The support of UMHE and the National Campus Ministry Association were significant, especially providing support and perspective. So, too, was the influence of national denominational leadership, who provided funding.

At UVA, Jim McDonald, a supportive colleague over many years, was part of a team approach through the Virginia Council of Churches called the Virginia Campus Ministry Forum. In the early '70s, Jim and I had attended at least two or three annual conferences of the American Association for Higher Education in Chicago. There we were immersed in issues and trends in higher education and, we thought, important to campus ministry. For me, one workshop, sponsored by Nursing Educators, featured one whose leadership would prove significant in future bioethics and health ministries. Introduced to the insights of Dr. Edmund Pellegrino—then Chancellor and VP of Health Sciences at the University of Tennessee Medical Center in Memphis—fresh notions began forming of what 'campus ministry' might involve and what types of campuses might be part of the scene. It proved to be important in years ahead as health care and ethics issues continued to grow in understanding the relevance of higher education ministries—not only to campuses, but—to the ecclesiastical communities own concepts.

In the late 60s and early 70s, Presbyterian higher education ministries in Philadelphia, under contributed staff, campus minister Ron McNeur, performed administrative support for the Society for Health and Human Values. Verlyn Barker wrote for United Ministries in Education a report in 1987 entitled *Health and Human Values.* In it he provided a historical record of the Health and Human Values and was to "lift up the learnings of the program for the churches." He noted that we become involved in addressing pain and suffering, and risk being consumed by it. *We can become so involved in addressing the hurt that we do not have time to help persons and communities understand issues and needs in order to anticipate decision-making and participation in our complex world.*[1] A listing of colleagues mentioned demonstrates a depth of commitment from across the nation.

During these days, biomedical ethics grew from an early 'nascency' to become a critically important dimension in medical and nursing education. As well as, it attracted a significant core of philosophers and lawyers. The Society was officially established in 1969. It was an entity of United Ministries in Higher Education. Part of its early funding came from the National Endowment for the Humanities. Again, engagement at a national and regional level was significant in obtaining needed finances. SHHV sought primarily to be a membership organization for those engaged in studying and promoting values in medicine and medical education. The primary objective promoted informed concern for human values as an essential dimension of the education of health professionals.

The first Department of Medical Humanities was formed at Penn State University Med Center in Hershey, PA. Bioethics emerged as a new discipline. Dr. Pellegrino and others visited over 80 medical schools to introduce faculty and students to the new discipline and to set up an educational program for future generations of doctors. They intended that bioethics move from literary texts, reports and commissions to changes in the clinical practice of ordinary physicians and health professionals and clinically based bioethics committees. One cannot peruse the lists of SHHV leaders from the early years without noting the frequency of Dr. Pellegrino's involvement.

An Internal Medicine specialist, Dr. Pellegrino, in 1975, led Yale-New Haven Medical Center. In 1978, he became President of Catholic University, then Director of Georgetown's Kennedy Institute. Dr. Pellegrino strongly felt that Medicine was a moral enterprise. He told *Georgetown Magazine* "if you take away the ethical and moral dimensions (from medicine), you end up with a technique. The reason it's a profession is that it's dedicated to something other than its own self-interests."

Departments of Medical Humanities and Bioethics committees slowly came to be recognized and organized in medical education and health care settings. Committee members needed education in a field that saw the growth of an extensive literature. Attitudes of resistance and skepticism slowly gave way as medical faculties recognized the importance of a humanities component in scientific medicine. Medical curriculum came to include substantial time and content in ethics, law, humanities and the social sciences.

In 1998, SHHV, along with the Society for Bioethics Consultation and the American Society for Bioethics, merged to form the American Society for

---

[1] Thomas Carson, *Health and Human Values: A Ministry of Theological Inquiry and Moral Discourse* by Verlyn l. Barker, p 142, United Ministries in Education, 1987.

Bioethics and Humanities. Many of the early leaders provided a core for both organizations, and the academic depth was sound and impressive.

In the early 1970s, as *Campus Urban Minister for the Presbytery of Norfolk,* with the support of the Synod, the work expanded. Not only did this continue to involve the College of William and Mary, but Old Dominion University, Norfolk State and nine other schools across the region. Soon, however, Eastern Virginia Medical School and ODU were a heavy focus for me on the other side of Hampton Roads. *Eastern Virginia Medical School* (EVMS), a community-based medical school being developed in Norfolk, became for me a primary campus among those in our region.

Dr. Donnie J. Self was hired as shared faculty with Old Dominion and EVMS, including financial and staff support from Synod and Presbytery Campus Urban resources. Don received a B.S. in chemistry and a B.A. in philosophy in 1965 and 1967 from Furman University. He worked two years as an industrial chemist. In that period, he pursued graduate studies in philosophy. He gained his M.A. and Ph.D. degrees in 1969 and 1973 from the University of North Carolina at Chapel Hill. For six years, he did cancer research in neuropathology at Duke University Medical Center. When he came to Norfolk, he began an active focus in Bioethics. His area of special interest concentrated upon cognitive moral development theory and its application to the field of medicine.

Over the years, Dr. Self taught bioethics at ODU and EVMS, then became full-time at Eastern Virginia. It afforded me an exceptional opportunity to work with Dr. Self and others in the context of medical education. King's Daughters Children's Hospital, Norfolk General and Leigh Memorial Hospitals provided for me the clinical context to work in the area of neonatology as chaplain/ethicist. Other hospitals came on board and enabled a remarkable array of opportunities for the Human Values program and its students. For me, as a campus pastor interested in bioethics and health care issues, this was a significant gift to efforts in understanding how religious communities could be constructively involved—getting educated on the issues as well as engaging in and contributing to the dialogue from a religious values perspective. We were exploring the interfaith with medicine and religion. Around the country, these programs began to grow and find a place in medical and nursing education. Dr. Granger Westberg was one among those in Chicago with whom we worked over the years.

During the late 70s, with the advent of in-vitro-fertilization in England, the EVMS-based Jones Institute for Reproductive Medicine gave significant opportunity for Dr. Self and the program to engage with doctors Howard and Georgiana Jones, of the EVMS Department of Obstetrics and Gynecology. The challenges of and resistance to the idea of in-vitro fertilization at that time were significant. Before the birth of the first In Vitro Fertilized baby in the U.S., Elizabeth Carr in 1981, there was not only the challenge of starting such a program, but through Drs. Jones' efforts and those of Medical Humanities, discovering how to helpfully engage with the larger community, the Catholic Diocese of Virginia and others. The department assisted in helping communications with Bishop Walter Sullivan and others in exploring issues, the science and moral concerns inherent. Bishop Sullivan was engaged in the discussions.

Don Self put the department of Medical Humanities at EVMS on a remarkable course through the years. He led annual Human Values retreats for the entire school, students, administrators and faculty. He invited a strong list of national leaders in Bioethics to monthly discussion groups with faculty and students. Genealogy studies and patient interview skills were emphasized. Among others, he published numerous articles in ethics and moral development theory. In the area of moral reasoning among medical students he published several articles on their research with the Rev. Dr. Joy D. Skeel of the Medical University of Ohio in Toledo. He has to date written and published over 100 articles and published three books in important areas in the medical humanities. Around 1982, he moved from EVMS and became faculty in Medical Humanities at Texas A & M University College of Medicine, continuing his creative approach to health care issues, detailing issues concerning care and cure. In recent years he has become editor of the Journal for Theoretical Medicine.

Clearly, we were quite fortunate to be able to share in the growth in the area of medical humanities. In no way could ecclesiastical budgets have afforded us the resources to design such, even had we the brains or skills to do so. But allowed to partner with the new medical school, physicians and others enabled an involvement that exceeded expectations. At least mine. Study opportunities for me afforded included two visits to the University of North Carolina Med School to work with Dr. Larry Churchill, in the Department of Medical Humanities, with clinical opportunities provided by Dr. James Bryan II, who was professor of social and community medicine. Larry Churchill and Dr. Bryan made it possible for me to take part in daily rounds with physicians, medical students, nurses and clinical pharmacists—a model which was found to be an effective and sound way to learn and practice patient care. Grand Rounds on Morbidity and Mortality also provided powerful insights. The manner of teaching and the results repeatedly won Dr. Bryan with accolades from medical students. Students and alumni praised Dr. Bryan for demonstrating the importance of getting to truly know patients and then to care for them as individuals. On home medical visits with Dr. Bryan, I learned a lot about pastoral care. Student after student, when he receive a Mentor Award for Life-time Achievement said, essentially, "Dr. Bryan taught me to be a 'real doctor,' one who can talk with patients, one who combines intelligence with compassion." The clinical model experienced in those study leaves made a powerful impression over the years, which translates well for chaplains and pastors in medical settings.

Dr. Larry Churchill, who later moved to Vanderbilt University, explored among many issues, the ethics of the justice issues in health care reform, as well as the basics of *What Patients Teach: The Everyday Ethics of Healthcare.* He remained an invaluable and accessible colleague over the years. He has written numerous articles and books. One on *Rationing Health Care in America* grew out of both clinical observations and moral reasoning.

Having served on an advisory member of the Human Values Committee of EVMS for several years, I became in 1980 for two years a part-time member of the EVMS faculty in Medical Humanities and Religion. At the same time, I served as part-time staff to the Virginia Campus Ministry Forum, with attendant duties. At EVMS, the clinical area in which I was able to serve for two years was the Neonatal Intensive Care Unit at King's Daughters Hospital for Children.

Joining the faculty of EVMS in 1980, Dr. Thomas Pellegrino, oldest son of Edmund Pellegrino, who brought to his practice and teaching in Medicine and Neurology the passions for human values in medicine we saw in his father. He was an immensely popular professor and a highly regarded physician, as well as a colleague in programs on Ethics and Health Policy across the region.

From a 'campus ministry' perspective, things changed dramatically in 1983 when I was asked to become the first hospital chaplain for **Norfolk General and Leigh Memorial Hospitals,** consisting of two hospitals with 900 beds. Concurrent with that move in about 1983, Norfolk General became Medical Center Hospitals and founded its first medical helicopter trauma team. They had a crew of about 26, a state-of-the-art flying intensive care unit with a staff second to none. Not complaining, you understand, but I had a wonderful secretary to assist me in serving the two hospitals. In time, we were able to engage about 40 volunteer community clergy as volunteers to give a semblance of full coverage. The major clinical areas covered, in addition to the Operating Rooms, were the Trauma and Burn Unit, some step-down units and especially the newly developing hospice unit. We provided chaplaincy services across the religious spectrum and sought to engage in a 'medicine and religion partnership' method of approach developed in the EVMS human values program, where I continued an adjunct faculty status. We conducted sessions with community clergy on a regular basis and with medical and nursing staff around *Issues in Patient Care,* which covered a host of subjects dealing with staff, families as well as patients and occasionally in congregations.

An area of persistent concern remained access to and the provision of quality health care for all persons. Then as now, health costs were soaring. This had been a focus--not only of denominations during the 1960s and 70s—but across the U.S. I served the Presbyterian Church U.S. (southern) as part of the Committee on Therapeutic Abortion, which (after Roe v Wade in 1973) then was melded into the Presbyterian Health Network (PCUS), recognizing the larger health care dimensions of the day, staffed by Patricia Turner from the Atlanta office of the denomination. We focused on assisting congregations with locally based church health centers and advocating for health care reform. We partnered before the reunion with the United Presbyterians with the Presbyterian Health, Education and Welfare Association (PHEWA) of UPCUSA. There we sought to increase the focus on health care issues in their annual conferences. They reflected significant aspects of the Underwood Report of years earlier concerning the Church, University and Social Policy. Many were from colleges and universities.

Vice President Hubert H. Humphrey, at the dedication of the Health and Welfare Building in the nation's capital said that *the moral test of government is how that government treats those who are in the dawn of life, the children; those who are in the twilight of life, the elderly; and those who are in the shadows of life, the sick, the needy and the handicapped.*

In 1976, a report of the Presbyterian Health Network, authored for the Health Network by Albert Keller—a pastor and minister in medical education"[2] in Charleston, S.C—went to the General Assembly. Its preface:

> Health and the provision of health are priority concerns... The issue of health points to the basic assumptions about the nature and value of human life. For this reason the Church has a compelling interest in that debate: at a fundamental level, that debate is theological. In giving serious attention to the meaning of health and to the social structure by which health care is delivered to people, we, the Church, acknowledge our unexcelled opportunity to declare the Gospel at a level of deep personal concern to our communities.[3]

That theme, of health and healing being an "unexcelled opportunity" stuck with us and with many elements of the church as we worked together in the '80s to address the need for controlling health care costs and assuring access to quality health care for the nation. We knew the costs kept soaring far above the inflation level, and the issues were fundamental to ministries of the Church of Christ. A stimulus was the increasing costs to the Church's Board of Pensions, with the medical coverage included. But it was not the only reason. In 1980, the national health bill was $248.1 billion, 9.1% of GDP. In 1986 it was $458 billion and 10.9% GDP. As this is written in 2014, national expenditures approach $3 Trillion, and 20% of GDP. We still spend twice as much per person as other industrial nations without arranging as they do in assuring every citizen the care needed.

---

[2] Albert Keller was pastor of Circular Church in Charleston, S.C. He was also Associate Professor of Ethics in the Department of Family Medicine at Medical University of South Carolina. He was active in SHHV and wrote articles on healthcare, healing, and bioethics issues as they unfolded in those years. He recently retired and still lives in Charleston.

[3] From the Preface of the statement on "Health Care: Perspective on the Church's Responsibility, "General Assembly, Presbyterian Church U.S. (1976).

The Presbyterian Church along with other religious communities over the years had continued to provide health and healing ministries through medical services. As in years past Catholics, Presbyterians, Lutherans and Methodists, 7th Day Adventists and others had many hospitals bearing their names, nationally and internationally. Many bore the names but were no longer denominationally connected. The tradition continued. As example, Rush Presbyterian St. Luke's in Chicago, or Lutheran General, Presbyterian Hospitals in NY, Pennsylvania and California. We recognized, too, that such modest services by religious communities could not accomplish what the nation required. We knew we had to support national policies and programs that met the needs of the larger society on a just and humane basis, and issued six position papers on health issues from 1960 to 1983.

In 1984, the General Assembly of the Presbyterian Church authorized and began work through a Task Force on Health Costs and Policies, which was overseen by three agencies: the Advisory Council on Church and Society, International Missions and the Board of Pensions. I was appointed national staff to the Task Force in the spring of 1985, necessitating a move to Philadelphia for three years. Not your grandfather/mother's campus ministry any more.

The Task Force consulted many policy analysts and authorities. During our three years of study and research, we traveled to Toronto and became informed by the Canadian Health System, met with experts from the School of Public Health at Macalester College, Toronto, and looked at health systems of other nations. As well, we engaged health policy experts and lobbyists from Washington, D.C. We had solid research from university departments and obtained details on health indices from across the nation. We enlisted the partnership of seven presbyteries and four theological seminaries in special projects. The question asked all of us: *What would it look like if, at every level of its life, the Presbyterian Church took seriously the health and healing dimensions of the Christian Faith?* We conducted surveys of 1835 congregations seeking to discover what was happening in local congregations.

We published in 1988 a book of essays reflecting our efforts, edited by Walter Wiest of Pittsburgh Theological Seminary; *Health Care and Its Costs: A Challenge to the Church.* Fifteen contributors from across the spectrum contributed to the book. Authors came from many higher education institutions: Boston University, Franklin and Marshall College, Pittsburgh Theological, United Theological in New Brighton, Minnesota, Union Theological in Richmond, Colgate Rochester, Medical University of South Carolina, and LSU. Other authors included Dr. Granger Westberg on the role of a congregation in health ministry (who played an important role in our Medical Center Ministry in Chicago), a nurse practitioner and minister, as well as staff. University Press of America was publisher. The Report itself, *Life Abundant: Values, Choices and Health Care*, was submitted to the 1988 PCUSA General Assembly. (Historic Note: Sometime in this period, UMHE colleague Clyde Robinson staffed the merging of the campus ministries of Betsy Alden and Mark Rutledge. The deed was accomplished in Albuquerque, New Mexico, in a nuptial ceremony that registered 5.2 on the Richter scale.)

As contract staff, responsibility with the Task Force ended in mid-1988. That left me scrambling to discover what lay in the future, as the time up until mid-year was filled with completing Task Force responsibilities. A professional colleague who lived in Albuquerque, Joan McIver Gibson, then Senior Program Director of the Institute of Public law at the University of New Mexico, suggested an opportunity to "go west, old man." She also lead annual summer seminars on bioethical and health policy issues at the Presbyterian Church's Ghost Ranch in northern New Mexico. These seminars were a regular feature at Ghost Ranch from the mid-eighties through the nineties. In 1993, Joan served as a member of the White House Ethics Working Group on the Clinton Health Policy Task Force. Dr. Gibson invited me to come to Albuquerque (to take the opportunity available) as a study opportunity with law and med students at the **University of New Mexico's Institute of Law and Public Policy.**

Betty and I sold our house in Philadelphia, and moved to Albuquerque (with no guarantees of anything). During this time, I served an interim as Chaplain to the New Mexico *Center for the Severely and Profoundly Retarded* in Los Lunas. I was later called as part-time pastor to New Life Presbyterian Church—a really interesting and challenging time and a unique congregation. Other involvements involved serving as secretary to the board of Albuquerque Health Care for the Poor and as a member of the Institutional Review Board of St. Joseph's Hospital.

David McGowan, long-time NCMA/UMHE campus minister at the **University of Illinois Chicago** developed a nascent **Medical Center Ministry** supported by the Presbytery of Chicago and the United Methodist Northern Illinois District. In 1990 I accepted a call to become director of the Ministry. A United Methodist pastor, Judith Kelsey Powell pastored the United Church of the Medical Center. The Director of the Medical Center Ministry was to lead ministry at University of Illinois Chicago (UIC) Med School and School of Pharmacy Administration, Rush-Presbyterian St. Luke and Cook County Hospitals. Both the congregation and the Ministry were in the same building in the shadows of the West Side Medical Center complex.

The next five years were a wonderful opportunity to explore what was possible. Health reform was on the national agenda. At the time, there were known to be over 5000 parish nurses across the nation, and was part of a vision led by Dr. Granger Westberg. Dr. Westberg became a member of our MCM Board. Primary and preventive care was emphasized. Lutheran General was a center for the Parish Nurse Network. The University of Kentucky had such emphases. Congregations (such as Fourth Presbyterian in Chicago and Central Presbyterian in Atlanta) were already deeply involved in their own full time and well staffed health ministries.

Our presence in the shadow of the Med Center afforded wonderful and significant opportunity to work in clinical areas with physicians, nurses, and chaplain/bioethicists in Cook County, Rush Presbyterian St. Luke and UIC hospitals. Dr. Homer Ashby—who worked with us on the Task Force on Health Costs—was instrumental in opening doors with McCormick and Lutheran Seminaries, located on the University of Chicago campus. Dr. Ashby and I co-taught a course, *The Church as Health Resource*, over a period of four years, with a total of 53 students. Many were dual degree students in nursing and ministry or law and ministry. 18 students took fieldwork with us at the West Side Medical Center.

Medical Center Ministries also shared planning and teaching in dual degree efforts at West Side Medical Center and Park Ridge Center. We developed a ten-week multi-disciplinary integrative seminar on the Health Minister/Parish Nurse dual degree with nursing schools at Loyola, North Park, Rush Community Nursing, St. Xavier, McCormick and the University of Chicago Theological Seminaries. With partnering, we were able to utilize a widely diverse and talented faculty for the courses, Including Mary Ann McDermott and Robert O'Gorman of Loyola, Homer Ashby of McCormick Seminary, Linda Edwards of Rush, and important other partners.

Among our interns, Barbara Sittler worked a year with Dr. Dan Brauner-an MCM Board member—in the Geriatrics team at UIC. Dr. Brauner provided preceptorships for two additional students. Kimberly Hawthorne (a dual degree in law and Divinity) worked with First United Church in Oak Park. Her Senior Ministry Project was entitled *Sisters in Healing: Patient Stories and Histories of Healers*. Stacy Kitahta wrote an excellent reflection from an international perspective, part of which was the Christian Medical Commission of the World Council of Churches. Among the things Elizabeth Robinson took from our course at Seminary was: *At the very least, we should emphasize that the community is instrumental in helping the individual to maintain her health.* Quoting Albert Keller from *Health Care and Its Costs*, she writes, as *sickness changes everything, healing, as well, changes everything.* She concluded: *Healing is a relationship event. Healing places a person back in community... In Biblical faith, the creation of community—truthful community, embodying justice, mercy, and centeredness in God—is perhaps the ultimate act of healing.* Amy Fleischauer worked with the Park Ridge Center (Second Opinion Magazine) on the issue of physician-assisted suicide. These students had opportunity to minister to patients, and discover the importance of colleagueship with and ministering to medical and nursing staff. We engaged with faculty and students at the UIC School of Pharmacy Administration with Dr. Jack Salmon and others and presented to pharmacy students on ethical issues.

Health Policy issues remained a strong, persistent and divisive issue. Invited to be a member of the Health and Medicine Policy Research Group, which provided a significant opportunity to continue to explore issues in health reform and health financing issues. Close proximity to the Canadian Health System enabled the group to engage Chicago political leadership in exposure to Canada's approach to health financing, resulting in a visit by a group of leaders to Toronto to meet with Canadian Public Health experts. Later a Canadian legislator from Manitoba came for a program offered describing the strengths and weaknesses of the system. Dr. Quentin Young, a physician at Cook County and in private practice, led health and Medicine Policy Research. He was an advocate for comprehensive health care reform. He still is at it with a sterling group of colleagues through the work of PNHP, Physicians for A National Health Program, with over 150,000 physicians across the nation. They advocate a Single Payer approach to health reform.

The 1993 205th General Assembly of the Presbyterian Church endorsed the principle of a universal health plan for all, giving priority to a single payer system. That system was described as:

> ...a publicly funded system of privately delivered medical care that includes the establishment of a public financing system, a definition of universal benefits, the establishment of prospective capital improvement budgets, caps on financial expenditures, and oversight of quality control while maintaining the private delivery of direct medical services.

The Church's task regarding health was seen to affirm and serve the values of compassionate justice in the political economy, as well as a model that leads by example in its own heath ministries. *Life Abundant* (1988) was noted as supplying theological and biblical roots for such being and advocacy. As in the assumptions of Kenneth Underwood decades before, this was "the responsible community" inventing and evaluating itself. It did so in addressing health care and social policy.

> The nurse, physician and health professional are co-ministers and healers, their interventions occurring at some of the most sacred moments in life— birth, death, trauma, even conception... The Church must clearly affirm the ministry of these health professionals within the worshipping and ministering community of faith... Technical competence and human compassion belong side by side in both the religious and secular arena.[4]

In 1995, Medical Center Ministries—at least my part in that era—came to a close when Rush-Presbyterian bought our building and property for its own expansion. The congregation of the United Church of the Medical Center moved a few miles west to the suburbs. After repeated attempts to find a way

---

[4] Thomas F. Mainor, A Biblical and Theological Basis for the Church's Health Ministries, in Walter Wiest, Editor, *Health Care and Its Costs: A Challenge to the Church*, University Press of America, 1988, p.226.

to continue—MCM was terminated. We explored alternatives with Evangelical Health Systems and other partners, as well as foundations. The share of funds from the sale of the property was to be used only for new property, not programming or staff. We lost our support.

Kenneth Underwood's recommendations of the '60s and '70s—that is for campus ministries to receive increased funding from foundations and governing bodies—special ministries across the board were nevertheless truncated. The imperative to integrate the four historic modes of ministry into a comprehensive concept of the Church's mission still was 'a work in progress'. We have focused well on providing persons with a faith perspective from which to cope with life's enduring challenges. We have not done so well in corporate and social ministry. Integration of the four modes of ministry is, as Leo Sandon wrote, "the necessary prerequisite for meaningful mission…"[5]

Called to pastor **Shady Grove Presbyterian Church in Memphis, Tennessee**, beginning in 1996, seemed to be an admission on my part "at last," some said, to return to the congregation: "the congregation is where the real action is!" As Verlyn Barker has written in his own reflections, there was always much discussion about congregation-based ministry. That was the mantra heard over and over. But the question repeatedly arises, "*What would it mean if at every level of our lives we took seriously the implications of the gospel in every setting and situation in which we find ourselves*—especially and including those educational centers, medical, nursing and law schools— even schools of business administration—where the 'best and the brightest'— as well as the least of us—seek to learn what it means to serve the commonweal with their whole being?"

Never one to totally agree with the foregoing, nor to discount the centrality of congregations in moving the church forward, it seemed that institutional ministries for me were now in the rear view mirror. Now, my intention was to be a good pastor and finish out my remaining years before retirement with a wonderful group of folks at Shady Grove. But out of that call grew a number of interesting developments. And with the support of the congregation, things happened.

The Memphis Church Health Center, led by clergy/physician Dr. Scott Morris, was a growing health ministry in Memphis directly providing care to those who were the working poor and without health insurance. The Center provided excellent primary care, pastoral care and excellent referral services provided significant access to specialists across Memphis. Methodist Hospital contributed important resources and support, both physical and human. Dr. Morris was an enthusiastic and convincing leader for the Center. A member of our congregation proposed for Shady Grove to support the ministry through a "Race for Grace". A 5-K run, begun upon the Congregation's 40th Anniversary, and continued over the years. The Race was a success. Another resource we

---

[5] Leo Sandon, Christian Century, February 7-14, 1979, p.128.

were able to provide was for the National Parish Nurse Network out of St. Louis, who needed a place to gather parish nurses in Memphis for education and certification. We did that. I was invited to serve as a faculty member in Bible and Theology for the annual sessions. The commissioning was held in the Sanctuary.

An opportunity arose to teach with a physician colleague at Memphis Theological Seminary entitled, "Health Ministries and the Church". Dr. James H. Ericson and I did this jointly for two years. Dr. Erickson, an MD, MPH and MS worked with the Civil Air Patrol National Health Program.

The third important area was the ability to encourage and be part of Dr. Tom Feagin's efforts at Methodist Central Hospital, who led in formation of a Bio Ethics advisory committee for the area. We met regularly at various hospitals, but mostly at Methodist. Over time we formed what was called the Memphis Bioethics Consortium. With the collaboration of many in area hospitals – including City of Memphis Regional Hospital, a strong Veterans' Administration hospital, St. Jude's Children's Hospital, Baptist and others –the Consortium began symposia on various topics that were held, not only in various local hospitals, but also annually at the University of Memphis and Rhodes College. At the University of Memphis, the Consortium sponsored Dr. Larry Churchill (newly arrived at Vanderbilt Med School) for a focus on justice issues in health care reform. In the year 2000, at Rhodes College, the Consortium featured Dr. Al Jonsen, emeritus professor of medicine and ethics from the University of Washington. Dr. Jonsen presented two addresses, the first tracing the history of medical ethics beginnings, "God committees"— dialysis anyone? And another on how to analyze clinical cases. Dr. Robert Llewellyn, Vice President for Academic Affairs at Rhodes was both and member of the Consortium, hosting us on many occasions, and finally assumed responsibility for leadership. Dr. Feagin retired. So did I. Dr. Rob Llewellyn, at Rhodes College carried on.

The journey – The Thing Itself; the Tapestry of but one aspect of ministry in higher education – sought to be one of responding to both demonstrated need and opportunities presented, inspired by our understanding of what we understood as faithfulness to the task. It reflects a conviction concerning how we practice conveying the Good News, how we show the ways in which values are conveyed in our society beyond the sanctuary and into our schoolhouses and the communities in which we live. For me, it seems to fit what it means to be *doing justice, loving mercy, walking humbly with God,* discovering the responsiveness of the Samaritan *not* passing by the one wounded, and of learning and forming life around what love of the neighbor requires.

Post Retirement, Betty and I returned to Williamsburg in 2002. An early opportunity to 'fail retirement' was the invitation to teach a course in ***William and Mary's Christopher Wren Association's courses for life-long learning.*** Partnering with two colleagues in Williamsburg—one was director of Olde Towne Medical Center—Judy Knudson—and the other a physician who taught at Yale Medical School for over 20 years, Dr. John Marsh. Our focus was essentially to discuss the issues and advocate for comprehensive health care reform. We felt the nation needed to move toward a "single payer" method of health care reimbursement. We were extremely fortunate to have Neurologist Dr. Thomas Pellegrino of Eastern Virginia Med School join with us for the course for three years. His presentations with us were a wonderful example of a practitioner who combined his understanding of patient advocacy with powerful analyses of health care costs, policies and procedures in very helpful and compelling ways. We were enriched by his wisdom and instructed ourselves by his willingness to teach with us. Those in our classes were quite responsive.

This journey in higher and medical education ministries made possible introductions to many outstanding faculty, scholars and students. In this journey, I found religious and faith perspectives operative in some of the most difficult and painful moments in the lives of patients and families. The privilege of being allowed to engage in the paths that emerged was one for which I shall always share enormous gratitude. Thanks be to God.

Life now--I have been active as a Williamsburg Elections Officer for over 10 years, am a member of the Colonial Group Homes Commission which deals with youth who have come afoul of the law but for whom we seek to provide alternatives to incarceration. I'm still with Physicians for a National Health Plan, and have stayed active on that front. I play tenor sax in the Dog Street Rhythm Kings for around ten gigs a year. Lots of fun. Then, let me tell you about our 3 grandchildren.... our trips to London, France and Italy, and back to Santa Fe. Tennis is a regular thing, about 4 days a week . Oh, oh, oh... and did I tell you that Betty retired from cooking when I retired. That means that I have had to upgrade my skills learned at my mother's knees, but without all the fattening stuff. So, I'm cooking for the household on NORMAL occasions. But when company comes, the professional takes impressive charge of the kitchen.

Reflections, Memories and "Burnt Offerings"
By Jim Davis

Upon receiving the gracious invitation from Betsy Alden to share my reflections, memoirs, and stories about my experiences in campus ministry I was deeply touched to be included in this meaningful project to celebrate NCMA's 50th Anniversary. I was, however, humbled because of the pioneers and stalwart leaders of the campus ministry movement that preceded me, those upon whose shoulders I have stood and by whose visionary leadership I was inspired and privileged to follow.

My story begins with a start and stop journey of feeling a call from our Creator God to ordained ministry in the United Methodist Church. The confirmation of this call came as an undergraduate student at the University of Minnesota in Minneapolis under the creative and profound ministry of several persons that I will never forget. I wish to be clear that it was because of these campus ministers and the programs they led that it became imperative for me to pursue ministry on campus, myself. It became my conviction to try my best to pay back what was given to me. I give thanks for the opportunity to have given my entire post seminary ministry of 38 years to three distinct types of ministry in higher education: Wesley Foundation and UMHE Ecumenical Campus Ministry at the University of Minnesota, Duluth, and College Chaplaincy at the University of Puget Sound.

Tom Payne was the pastor at the University Methodist Church in the university business area in Minneapolis called Dinkytown, and the Wesley Foundation shared a building that included the sanctuary of the church. As a junior taking courses in history and philosophy and reading and studying such philosophers as Camus, Sartre, and Kierkegaard, I had my socks knocked off by Tom Payne's sermons as he connected his exegesis of biblical passages to the writings of these great philosophers. It was to be my first concrete example of how the mind and the heart could engage each other in the development of the faith of young adults. This blending of reason and scripture as they joined with tradition and experience fed my own soul and excited me with the possibilities of how I might be part of such a church and ministry!

Two campus ministers from that setting that also engaged my mind and heart were Bob Ouradnik and Carl Caskey. This was the time of the primacy of the teachings of the Ecumenical Institute (E.I.) out of Chicago, which was created and led by Joseph Matthews and Joe Slicker, who came to Minnesota to speak and teach about how God was breaking into our lives and "cracking open" the wombs of possibility. I recall van trips to the West Side of Chicago, where E.I. had established a teaching/worshipping/mission community in the midst of great upheaval and social change in that neighborhood. Back at the U of M Wesley Foundation I vividly recall Bob and Carl leading study groups based on the same theologians and texts that E.I. used, such as Tillich, Niebuhr, Bonhoeffer, John A. T. Robinson, and others. These "radical" studies excited my mind and heart with the call to act for societal and ecclesial change and social justice.

Jeanne Audrey Powers, campus minister at the St. Paul campus and director of the Minnesota Methodist Student Movement, was instrumental in bringing outstanding theologians as keynote speakers at our state wide conferences and also getting other students and me excited about going to regional conferences where we met the likes of Clarence Jordan and James Lawson. Jeanne Audrey was the key, as well, to sending a group of us to the South in 1964 for a Spring Break trip to Rust College. It was there that we had the incredible opportunity to join Rust students in a circle on the campus green to sing *We Shall Overcome* like I never had before. This followed having tasted the strong anti-black prejudice of Holly Springs, Mississippi, as death threats were directed at me and another Minnesota "white kid" as we walked around town to look at antebellum houses. I believe these threats were directed at us because we were staying at "that black school", symbolizing our support of Rust, and being perceived as meddling northerners. This experience taught me about the ugly reality of deep-seated racism, something that African Americans faced in their lives daily, something that I realized I could escape from merely by traveling back to my home state.

As I write this reflection I recall again how pivotal these campus ministers and the experiences they provided were in my own formation, one which put me on the path to develop my mind, feed my soul, and live out the Gospel to act for justice. It was this that drove me to declare my intention to enter the ministry and to vigorously pursue campus ministry as my own calling.

My first appointment following seminary was at the **University of Minnesota, Duluth**, serving as a half-time Wesley Foundation Director and half-time co-pastor with Richard P. Mathison, an outstanding preacher at University United Methodist Church. Evelyn Dack was an experienced, committed laywoman who continued to work with Wesley Foundation there and provided a good foundation for my initial attempts to figure out how I would actually go about this ministry! It was a good place to get my feet wet in both campus ministry and local church ministry. The realities of fiscal limitations became obvious when, in the spring of 1969, the church board announced that they could not afford two pastors and also pay for the new organ's loan! Guess what stayed and who had to leave!

At that precipitous time, Richard E. Nelson, the Presbyterian campus minister who worked with the United Campus Christian Fellowship, came to me and the Wesley Foundation Board to offer a collaborative partnership in what would become the United Campus Ministry of Duluth-Superior. I shall never forget his generous offer to step back to ¾ time so that I could become a full time campus minister with the UCM. As a young recently married campus minister who would have an equally young family in the coming years, I was forever in awe of Dick and his graciousness. I thoroughly enjoyed working with him for the ensuing 8 years as part of the new ecumenical campus ministry organization, United Ministries in Higher Education. A patient mentor to me, Dick was a visionary thinker and creator of new ministry efforts and walked delicately into the field of creating a curriculum for educating medical school students on issues of faith and ethics at the new medical school at the University of Minnesota, Duluth. In working with the Dean of the Medical School, Dick adroitly arranged for Ron McNeur to come as a consultant for setting up such a curriculum on ethics and values for future physicians.

The importance of working effectively with the United Campus Ministry Board was clear. As the role of campus minister had evolved from being a "student worker" for a specific denomination into working collaboratively with professionals from various denominations and religious organizations, we recognized the critical importance of engaging the campus enterprise as a whole. This, of course, led to embracing the development of relationships with faculty, staff, and administrators.

We were extraordinarily blessed with an organization named the Council of Religious Advisors (CRA), which was composed of various Protestant campus ministers, an Episcopal priest, a rabbi, a Catholic priest and Benedictine nun, and a Christian Science practitioner. The university recognized us as advisors to registered student organizations, which gave us the privilege of being on campus. While recognizing our traditions' differences in practice and issues, the CRA became a remarkable ecumenical team that was effective in developing significant levels of trust with the university administration. Of course, there were limits! Worship could be held on campus, but only in buildings that were not funded by legislative money. In fact, I vividly remember the Academic Dean coming to a meeting of the CRA to apologetically request that we not continue to conduct Lenten prayers in the Art Gallery. The student government president, a Jewish student and nephew of the local president of ACLU had lodged a complaint! I also recall how Father Selman Threadgill set a meeting with the Provost to object to the Provost's plan to bring a retired battleship to the Duluth harbor. Selman later reported to our CRA team that he had not been received warmly and was summarily asked to leave the provost's office!

Many of our "ecumenical team" members were involved in efforts to be peacemakers during the escalation of the Vietnam War. Lutheran campus minister Brooks Anderson participated in marches in the South and several of us participated in organizational meetings of students and other activist oriented young adults from the community to plan protest marches. It was a pivotal strategic presence for us being there to encourage non-violence as protests were planned, including two large marches through the city. These activities involved a large number of students, and it was clear to us that our roles were important as witnesses to our belief that God called us to be peacemakers. We were deeply aware of the possibility of escalation and violence even in Duluth because we knew of the bombings in Madison at the University of Wisconsin. Newscaster Charles Kuralt determined that it was worthwhile to cover the protests even in the small city of Duluth that would show the extent of the antiwar movement in America.

I was always struck, however, even in very serious times, by the humor of God and the complexity of humanity. I recall well a favorite story from this time, one which involved the sole campus policeman on the UMD campus. Officer Ole was a friend to many and all of us in the campus ministry. He did his best to "educate us" about the foibles of pot and started each September by coming by the Student Religious Organizations office to light some up for us all to smell and "make us aware" of how it was a dangerous and nasty habit. Prior to one of the two large anti-war marches in downtown Duluth a rumor spread around the campus that students were planning to burn down the ROTC building. The administration assigned Ole to guard the building and we later learned that he had taken a portable television set with him to camp out in the building ostensibly "to protect it from violent students". The march concluded successfully and peacefully, and upon our return to campus we learned that some students, in fact, had tried to burn down the ROTC building. The irony of this story is that the building was constructed of corrugated steel walls and the students had used highway flares to try to accomplish their ends! There are times, indeed, for laughter and relief in this world of conflict, anger, and injustice.

The CRA was consulted regularly by the Dean of the University and the Dean of Student Activities, Dean Kjolhaug. The importance of building trusting professional and personal relationships with administrators, staff, and faculty was apparent on many occasions during those nine years that I experienced with them. This was visible through invitations from the dean for us to attend Student Affairs staff meetings, even as the university was deeply aware of the constraints of separation of church and state. These relationships of trust led to invitations to Sister Claudia Riehl and me to teach a freshman seminar for credit and to Father John Husband, Sister Claudia and me to participate in staff training for resident assistants in the dormitories. This group became a prototype for me for the possibilities for interfaith and interdenominational cooperation and collegiality. We held retreats together, did planning meetings together prior to the beginning of each academic year, and attended each other's family events and personal celebrations. This deep collaborative spirit led to such remarkable occasions as my spouse and me being invited by Bishop Anderson of the Diocese of Duluth to present the elements during mass at the College of St. Scholastica, where our CRA team member Sister Claudia, "happened" to be a member of the faculty and the Benedictine Order.

It was during these early years that I became an active member of the National Campus Ministry Association. Attending national conferences became an important part of my life. These conferences, starting with one in Denver, gave me opportunities to meet other colleagues in campus ministry from around the country. Hearing dynamic speakers and theologians was highly significant in enabling me to "do my ministry" back at UMD and in the Duluth community. A regional conference held at a retreat center near Stillwater, MN, on the banks of the St. Croix River, brought together campus ministers from all over Minnesota, Wisconsin, and Iowa. The keynoter was Sam Keen, author of *Fire in the Belly* and *Faces of the Enemy*. That is where I met several colleagues who impressed me with their deep commitment to a cutting edge ministry on campus that my own denomination used to call a "special appointment" until it became defined as "ministry beyond the local church."

The 60's and 70's were also times often filled with distrust and disrespect from local church members and pastors and those in the communities in which our universities resided. Sarcastic comments such as "When will you enter the REAL ministry?" were often hurled at campus ministers, and funding from denominational sources was regularly jeopardized. Often small campus ministries were pitted against larger programs at major universities, a factor which at times put stress on collegial relationships. I recall well the deep anxiety created by state commission budget meetings when we never knew whether we would go home with a job or not. Shortage of funds led to calls for detailed evaluations of campus ministry programs and campus ministers.

I personally recall my own angst when I learned that our campus ministry program in Duluth-Superior was scheduled to be evaluated by two regional staff members from UMHE. In fact, we hosted two such evaluation processes during my tenure in Duluth.

It was through these processes that I learned the importance of completing thorough evaluative processes conducted by outside consultants. The UMHE regional staff members who came to our campuses were Dale Turner (AB) and Cecil Findley (UMC), who conducted in-depth interviews with university staff, administrators, students, faculty, campus ministry board members, and various clergy from congregations near the universities. These evaluations were extraordinarily valuable to Dick Nelson and me and to our board. I was surprised to realize that such thorough, careful evaluations by established professional consultants from off-campus in effect reinforced the importance of these ministries to university and community people alike. The credibility of the campus ministry venture itself was heightened significantly by the systematic process of evaluation established by UMHE, which I hold in deep admiration for its commitment to excellence. I remain grateful also for its ability to address the need for evaluation to deal with the distrust of campus ministry in the larger church.

As the "management by objectives" quantitative movement had begun to make its presence known in all kinds of ministries Dick Nelson, our governing board, and I examined the Danforth Study on Campus Ministry by Kenneth Underwood. We found it to be a most helpful tool to refocus upon what approaches Jesus had taken in his ministry. (*The Church, the University, and Social Policy: The Danforth Study of Campus Ministries*). The much shorter summary booklet, *New Wine*, became an invaluable resource to guide us in measuring the effectiveness of our campus ministry. The priestly, pastoral, prophetic and kingly (governance) roles identified as foci of Jesus's ministry provided insights into how our campus ministry board and we as campus ministers might more effectively direct and measure our efforts in ministry. In fact, this format was most useful in writing annual reports to judicatories, commissions, and interpreting our work to local churches.

The end of the 60's and early 70's found me engaging not only in efforts to end racial injustice and the Vietnam War, but also to join women in advocacy for women's rights. Although the Methodist tradition had been ordaining women for more than 20 years by the mid 70's the majority forces continued to minimize women's leadership opportunities in the church. Women in prominent leadership positions included campus ministers such as Jeanne Audrey Powers, whom I mentioned earlier as pivotal in my faith formation. As ordination of women had yet to arrive in some traditions the Council of Religious Advisors at UMD sought to raise the bar by inviting persons such as Jeannette Piccard of the Episcopal Church to speak on campus. Prominently known with her husband Jean Piccard as world-class hot air balloonists, she sought to be ordained. "How long must I wait?" she proclaimed! "I am now 78!"

In addition to seeking approval of the Equal Rights Amendment, the movement to establish the right to choose abortion for unplanned pregnancies was a major issue on our campuses as much as elsewhere in the country. My own collaboration with faculty members included working with a psychology professor who established a counseling group of professional persons on campus and in the community who would meet with women, girls, and family members as they considered their choices concerning their pregnancy. Our group of professionals included three clergy, a professor, a community activist and a social worker. When requested, referrals were made to physicians to perform legal, medically sound abortions out of state. Many of the women with whom we met were students. Some were persons from the greater community. One of the most insightful things I did as a campus minister involved in this counseling and referral service was to fly with a group of women to Rapid City, South Dakota. An OB/GYN physician there was able to provide legal, safe, abortions because of a U.S. District Court Order. I was presented with the opportunity not only to support these women but also to become aware of the immensely tense and somewhat fearful experience for them to travel 500 miles for such a procedure with a physician whom they did not know. As our community/campus counseling and referral service became more widely known in Duluth, we found ourselves at the center of controversy. Like my experience during the protests during the Viet Nam War, I found myself receiving phone calls at all hours from persons objecting to this type of ministry.

An additional emphasis of ministry on campus included the first Earth Day observance and programs advocating for care for God's creation. Again, it was a member of the Council of Religious Advisors, Brooks Anderson, who initiated the Earth Day program, which became an annual event. Inspired by his efforts and knowing that all of creation is of God, many of us became advocates for environmental care and justice.

A very significant emerging emphasis in campus ministry was learning to understand and listen to gay and lesbian students, faculty, and staff about their lives and experiences of oppression. I am deeply grateful for a young man who was a guest speaker in a graduate school class at UMD. He shared his sexual identity with us and proceeded to talk about the deep pain he had experienced as a gay man in his church. His candor led me on a long journey of seeking to more fully understand, which in turn has become a key component of the campus ministry programs I led since that time in Duluth, particularly in my recent role as University Chaplain at a private, church related university. Campus ministry programs across the country have come a long ways in affirming lgbtq students as children of God deserving the full ministry of the church.

I left Duluth and the campus ministry at UMD in 1977 to accept an invitation to become the chaplain at the **University of Puget Sound**, in Tacoma, Washington. I continued to be a member of NCMA for several more years but eventually found that my budget did not allow me to continue to attend two national conferences each year. I give thanks for the extraordinary opportunities to continue a ministry in higher education at Puget Sound from 1977 until my retirement in 2006. I know for a fact that my years of experience in Ecumenical ministry and interfaith expressions in Duluth/Superior laid the groundwork for leading a chaplaincy program which embraced a wide spectrum of needs for students, faculty, and staff, while also seeking to act for social justice on campus and beyond.

I hold a deep gratitude for the privilege to work with immensely gifted and prophetic campus ministers, not only at Duluth-Superior, but across the nation through United Methodist Campus Ministry, UMHE and the National Campus Ministry Association. NCMA is to be recognized for its significant role in enriching the lives and ministries of countless colleagues throughout the nation. It has ably served as the right organization at the right time through periods of great change and immense challenges. Bravo to all those colleagues who gave sterling, prophetic leadership to NCMA and forged new pathways for campus ministry to be such an effective witness to ministry with students, the university, and society at large.

Jim Davis now lives a "Thoreau-like life" with his wife/life partner, Nancy, in the forests of Western Washington State, 20 miles from Tacoma. Post retirement foci for Jim and Nancy are (1) living "green" and advocating for care for the earth by being actively involved in the Greening Movement of the merged UCC/United Methodist congregation they attend and the Washington State Earth Ministry Program and (2) advocating for full inclusion of GLBTQ persons in the life of the church and society. They also serve as consultants/facilitators with congregations, religious leaders, and non-profit organizations for visioning and strategic planning and conflict resolution. Jim continues his involvement in Leadership Development in the United Methodist Church as a founding member of Advisory Committee for the Bishop Jack and Marjorie Tuell Center for Leadership Excellence.

A Particular Career in Campus Ministry
By Diane Kenney

Consider this a musing about a calling. I begin so aware of the connections, of all who, through 45 years of campus ministry, helped me to understand. I realize I was given credit for many things I did help happen, but which began as the ideas of another. We acknowledge these thoughts, but most of us don't write them down until challenged to do so by something like the 50th Anniversary of the National Campus Ministry Association. Then comes the dilemma: Is what I am remembering what actually happened, or are my thought processes improving upon reality? Another dilemma: I wasn't asked for a 500 page volume, but not including everything means persons and situations for which I continue to be thankful are going to be left out. Please accept this for what it is: a short, intensely written summary, offered in thanksgiving for a career which continually allowed me to learn. It is a "period piece" directly related to my own campus ministry experiences between 1969 and 2012. Campus ministry is currently in the midst of change as denominations struggle to retain identity and membership; possibly some of my "learnings" will be of value to others. Hopefully they will be of some value to those involved in the current denominational and institutional struggles over whether campus ministry and chaplaincy should continue to be funded at all.

A spring of 1969 graduation from Pacific School of Religion, a summer spent as administrative staff for the Community of the Great Commission camp site in Northern California, and then an August move to *Stanford University* in a position initially called Assistant to the Dean of the Chapel: this was how I began in campus ministry.

The Dean of the Chapel was Davie Napier, an extremely personable, thoughtful, poetic, intellectual Hebrew Scriptures specialist (yes, we called it "Old Testament"), who was willing to be an "activist" Dean. He reported to the President of the University and was well liked by many members of the Stanford Faculty. Sunday church services attracted students and Palo Alto community members from many faith traditions -- most seeking valid ways to live their own lives. The resident rabbi approved Jewish students taking Davie's Hebrew Scriptures course. My initial involvements were (a) providing some administrative leadership (the University Administration would have called it "supervision", but...) for the many religious leaders credentialed to work on the campus, (b) slowly taking on responsibilities for creating liturgy to resonate with the congregation that gathered to hear sermons preached by Davie and invited guests, (c) serving as teaching assistant for the Hebrew Scriptures course, and (d) "hanging out." I was initially assigned to live on and serve a floor in a residence hall; somewhat introverted person that I am, I was a complete failure in the dorm even though I had worked in Res Life at my own undergraduate institution, and a very kind Head Resident and a very kind Dean thought it would be best if I moved off campus at the end of the first academic year.

Senator George McGovern was our initial guest preacher in the fall of '69. First major learning: in a setting like Stanford you quickly become accustomed to being around highly respected people - those from within and those visiting the campus. It was the "Vietnam Era" and many Stanford students and faculty were involved in anti-war activities. The Chapel (locally called Mem Chu) welcomed being a location for some of those activities. We were blessed to have two staff persons within the Division of Student Affairs who, out of their own strong Quaker traditions, believed that students who opposed war needed to carry their beliefs beyond "anti" into choosing and developing careers which respected the earth and all that lives upon it; those two worked at creating the seminars and volunteer situations which helped students do that.

It wasn't that we "all got along." We didn't. There was a strong and much appreciated Non Violence House on campus; there were also faculty and students who believed revolution was the only way, while others believed you do what your government requires. Some students were struggling to establish their own identity which, not unusually, often conflicted with the value systems of the families from which they came. But there was also a great deal of respect. At my first Stanford sit-in I stood in awe as the student leaders completely cleaned up the area they had been occupying. No one ordered them to do so; that was just appropriate behavior.

In contrast, moving freely around campus as most of us did, I went to an on-campus demonstration in front of the Hoover Institution on War and Peace, a public policy think tank. I soon knew what it feels like to have a bayonet held against my backbone as I was personally ordered out of the area.

One evening, members of a self-defined "revolutionary group" announced a "take over" of Mem Chu (a 2000 seat facility) at the end of a campus anti-war teach-in. How do you handle it? It was solved as two great students, Pia and Tom, well known in the non-violence community and a part of the Chapel student leadership, picked up brooms and went into the middle of the sanctuary. They calmly announced they were the custodians for the evening and it would be appreciated if those sitting-in didn't create any more work for them. The group was welcome to stay as long as they wished, but please, be respectful of the custodians. The group disbanded shortly after midnight.
We were all learning; most of us were learning all of the time. Our teachers were one another.

There were eighteen and nineteen year olds much wiser than I; there were students of different colors willing to educate me about the realities of their experiences. I continue to be grateful for casual invitations to go bowling with members of the Black Student Union. After the Kent State debacle a very generous African American professor quietly suggested we never mention Kent State without mentioning Jackson State. Thankfully he made the suggestion prior to our making any great mistakes.

226

Of great importance to me and the larger community was an informal volunteer network of creative women, some of whom were identified as "faculty wives;" many of them were highly credentialed but were in families where the husband was the designated bread winner. These women went way beyond "volunteering." They developed alternative employment agencies, partnered with women from East Palo Alto to work cooperatively on eliminating racism, opened their homes and hearts to any of us in need of their wisdom, and willingly participated in groups some of us designed.

Colleagues! YWCA Directors, United Ministry in Higher Education clergy, leaders of the Catholic Newman Center and interns; I think we experienced what it was like to be "collegial." The group expanded to include individuals representing several denominations as well as para-church staff willing to engage in theological discussion and participate in co-sponsored events. I learned this was not the usual model. Campus ministers in other settings often worked alone or in competition. Why was Stanford this way? During the "Napier" years, I'd attribute it to the Dean, to the presence in the Religious Studies Department of people like Robert McAfee Brown and Jerry Irish, who appeared to move easily between the academics and the practice of religion, and to the women referred to above.

I was sometimes confronted by people who had "never met a woman clergy before," or "weren't certain women could be clergy." Forty-five years later those kinds of encounters continue.

My title changed to Assistant Dean, and Davie Napier left Stanford to become President of the Pacific School of Religion, while I worked with a series of short term interim Deans: Wayne Rood, Bob Brown, Brad Abernethy (previously Chaplain at Rutgers}.

The extensive work of a search committee, commissioned to provide three names to the President, and the subsequent calling of a new permanent Dean of the Chapel, meant Religious Life at Stanford was moving in a new direction. Two names that had been submitted were of nationally well- known activists. The President made it known to the committee that no matter his own feelings, administratively he could not extend an invitation to either of them.

After a year with the new Dean, with the urging of visiting preacher Beverly Harrison, I applied for an Underwood Grant from the Danforth Foundation and spent 15 months at the Graduate Theological Union in classes focusing on the relationship between liturgy and social change, a time for which I will ever be grateful. I learned from others that Bev, a member of the Underwood selection committee, didn't leave the room until several persons she wanted to receive the grant were so honored. And receiving the grant meant that Bob Rankin, Underwood administrator, involved several of us who didn't fit the historic depiction of campus religious leaders, in a variety of national gatherings. My unending thanks to Bev and Bob!

As the Underwood grant came to an end, Roy Sano, then Chaplain at Mills College, Oakland, CA, asked if I'd be one of several applying and interviewing for a temporary position at Mills, as he was going on sabbatical. It seemed viable. I was familiar with private institutions, Mills was in the Bay Area and it would allow me to finish the academic work I had undertaken. I had heard privately that some women faculty, staff and students were intrigued with what a female chaplain might bring to the setting. The position was listed as half time (Dr. Sano was also a part of the teaching faculty; I would not be in the classroom but could sign off on independent studies for students). Some female faculty were very welcoming and I sensed community as students, limited to women at the undergraduate level, chose the campus chapel as a place to gather, talk, share their lives. But a power struggle was also underway.

Some long-term male faculty, not comfortable with women in leadership positions, made their concerns known in many ways. There were also concerns I simply couldn't grasp, again expressed by some of the long-term male members of faculty and staff. Women's dances were questioned; wouldn't they create "illicit" relationships? At the same time I was told of a male faculty member who used his authority to initiate a sexual relationship with a student. My mistaken notion of "confidentiality" kept me from finding an appropriate way to intervene. Just across the Bay in Palo Alto I had friends I could have approached for counsel, but my lack of confidence kept me quiet.

As the academic year came to an end, Roy made it known he would not be returning to Mills. Several students approached the administration asking that I be kept on, but were not responded to - and soon Diane Kenney became the focal point of student-led demonstrations as banners and leaflets appeared demanding my retention as the choice of students. Then finals hit, as they always do, and the year ended.

One of my errors was in not asking, before Roy left, that he name an advisory group to serve at my request. I continue to think of a short list of students I know I did not serve well, even though my very occasional Googling of their names tells me they are creative, talented, much-respected and productive women.

The job search began! I belonged on a campus. The National Campus Ministry Association was highly respected for many things, but of importance to many of us was the information it provided on positions that were open. A few months of looking for direction, and I faced a choice. A congregation in Austin, Texas was seeking a staff person to direct ecumenical campus ministry. I was having trouble deciding whether Texas was where I should be. The lovely search committee wanted me and wooed me with weekly shipments of Texas Pecan Pralines, but I was intimidated by the "church-based," although ecumenical, nature of the ministry to be created.

Youngstown State University, in Youngstown, OH seemed a better fit. No, this Californian had never faced a true winter, had no experience with public higher education, and knew next to nothing about communities based on industry. I did know people from Ohio. One family from Stanford was now living in Ohio; another was now at Union in NYC, and therefore not terribly far away via the Pittsburgh airport. I thoroughly enjoyed the interview. The campus ministry was independent, but was affiliated with the Mahoning Valley Council of Churches. The University was perpendicular to Wick Ave, and Wick was home to a series of congregations (Disciples, Presbyterian, German Congregational, Greek Orthodox, and Episcopalian) committed to and involved in the single campus ministry. The congregations had learned to work together in service to the local community. Anyone entering a congregation to ask for food or money was sent across Wick Avenue to the Council of Churches, where a social worker was on duty during regular business hours. An intake interview was held, clarity was reached about the resources that would be most helpful, an agreement was signed listing responsibilities of the agency and the client, and initial resources were distributed.

The Catholic Newman Center was a block away from where my office would be. The Catholic Diocese was a very few blocks away. The campus ministry board made an offer; I replied affirmatively, and arrived to temporary housing having been arranged and to a fully functioning board with funding in place. The Board consisted of very nice and competent persons who knew the area and its cultures.

Some were strong members of the University Community; others were clergy and laity in local congregations. Almost all treated me as a friend - and the learning began.

The initial learning: through the Department of Religion I was to teach two or three sections each semester of "Intro to Religion." There were no approved guidelines for the course; one or two local pastors would teach additional sections (the tenured faculty didn't want to do it) and it hadn't been decided that it would be of value if we worked out a joint syllabus. Students flocked to the course because it fulfilled a humanities requirement. Many had been raised in the Catholic Church and, as was normal for the era and the place, "knew what religion was." So it must be easy. Registration was limited to 30 in each section. I spent the five years I was there modifying content and methodology. Whatever I did, some were hooked; others sat through. I confused some by making extensive comments in red pen on their essays and then giving good grades.

An on-going program was a Wednesday lunch in the Episcopal church, complete with tablecloths, cloth napkins, full place settings and candlelight! The site, setting, food and clean up were contributions of the Episcopal congregation to the campus ministry. Those who chose put $3 or so in the basket. Faculty, staff, students appeared, often numbering 70 or 80. It was an extremely gracious hour made available to a very diverse crowd, and it was the idea of the congregation's administrative assistant as to how they might serve the university.

Soon a retired nurse, a member of First Christian, approached me with her idea. She had connections at a local hospital; the medical records chair and several physicians and residents were willing to offer free services one evening each week if we could find a location for a free clinic. The nurse thought the basement of First Christian, complete with stage, dressing rooms and restrooms would make the perfect site. Was I willing to pursue it? She also put together a system where physicians donated their not-needed or soon-to-be-outdated pharmaceuticals. We sorted through them, and an appropriate company came to make certain those that would not be dispensed would be properly disposed of. We presented the idea to the governing board of First Christian. The one awkward but sincere question, which she handled magnificently, had to do with whether V.D. could be contracted through toilet seats.

We were up and running. Students liked the Free Clinic because, as most continued to live with their families, they could now see someone other than their family doctor. Interns, physicians and nurses liked it because they saw and treated things they might not normally encounter in their local hospital. Soon faculty were using it for the annual physical their benefits provided (and their insurance was billed as a contribution to our clinic operation), and the R.O.T.C. found it a great way to get necessary physicals for their recruits. That is how one lay woman, with connections, envisioned and helped provide something of great value to the broader campus community.

During the clinic time, relationships were built and some very practical, hands-on, theology was shared. After the clinic closed each Wednesday evening, all professional staff and volunteers met at the local beer joint and very honest conversations continued. A good friend and member of a religious order volunteered each week but did not join us at the after session. It took time before I deciphered the cause: the issue was not beer, but not having cash to pay for it. Soon a different volunteer was inviting her each week to come as their guest. The clinic idea was the product of a lay woman with connections; the stable presence was the woman from medical records who knew and was respected by the hospital staff. The campus ministry and the campus received the benefits.

The size and historical stability of Youngstown made things possible I had not experienced before. It was normal for us to do meditative moments on the local radio station. The University President asked for help because the young adult child of a trustee was participating in what we then called a cult. This young adult was no longer in contact with her parents, could I help them understand what was going on? I have to wonder why these connections appeared in my life. The director of the campus career center was a long time Youngstown resident and highly respected on campus and in the community. People in important places knew she was totally committed to the campus ministry. We had access because she was always recommending us.

Youngstown was a steel town. Resident families had been there for generations. Then US Steel and other facilities decided there was more money to be made in other fields and the plants began closing, leaving thousands of families without income. A coalition of religious persons was formed to work against the closures. Someone suggested that a Protestant female and a

Catholic female needed to be part of that coalition. I was asked; my campus ministry board decided major changes in employment always affected universities; therefore, I was to spend approximately 25% of my time with the coalition. Similar decisions were made in the Catholic diocese and Protestant denominations. I'm not certain how this happened, but I became the official designer of liturgy for this body. Eventually the very kind Catholic Bishop got used to Protestant me telling him that something liturgical he was suggesting for a community- wide meeting just wasn't going to work. We all were learning! My California roots had taught me ethnicity was often related to skin color, but in Ohio ethnicity was related to what part of eastern Europe your relatives had come from. Those communities differed strongly from one another, but they all had the same hopes for the next generation. The shutting of steel plants was shattering those hopes.

The Ecumenical Coalition of the Mahoning Valley came into existence in response to the announced closing of the Campbell Steel Works, eliminating the well paid employment of 4000 persons. This was the first of several plant closings. The Coalition began with a phone call from the Cleveland office of the Episcopal Bishop, John Burt, to the Youngstown Catholic Diocese Bishop, James Malone. Within days the Bishops called a meeting with other religious leaders and Dr. Richard Barnet of the Institute for Policy Studies (a research organization based in Washington, D.C.}. The Institute recommended to the soon-to-be-named Ecumenical Coalition of the Mahoning Valley that work with the Exploratory Project on Economic Alternatives, headed by Dr. Gar Alperovitz, should be undertaken to address the economic problems facing the Mahoning Valley. I know that most major decisions concerning direction were made in small closed-door sessions or on the telephone, but since it had been determined that two professional female faces needed to be present in all public and press related gatherings, I was involved.

For flights to Washington the plane was provided by John Glenn. As the "worker ownership" concept grew, my interviewing skills were tested as several from the Coalition would meet late night hours in a quiet hotel room with workers willing, without the knowledge of their employers, to help us create a financial plan for the reopening of the plant. Staughton Lynd, a former American History professor at Spelman College and Yale University, provided legal counsel to the Coalition. For some of us Staughton was much more than a legal mind. A committed Quaker, he functioned as though everyone, regardless of title or education, was of equal worth. He never appeared to be rushed. In continuous, informal conversations he provided an on-going education on everything from social analysis and worker history to Quaker belief systems. His affirmation of persons meant connections grew between individual clergy and local steel workers. I enjoyed continual conversations with several steel workers who, having no interest in a degree but committed to learning as much as they could, had taken every possible history course at the University. Lynd and Alperovitz were well acquainted with each other. A joint publication prior to their Youngstown involvements explains how through "public ownership and coordinated economic planning, popular participation in decision-making can be increased and power can be decentralized." However, decentralized power was not what corporations were seeking. Soon the local union leadership discovered union headquarters did not consider it in their best interests, either. On a trip to Pittsburgh, to union headquarters, Youngstown union leadership discovered the goals which led to corporate decisions paralleled the goals of international unions. The personal tragedies began: heart attacks, strokes, accidents. We attended far too many memorial services and kept tabs on many workers then on medical leave.

Ramsey Clark signed on as a *pro-bono* advisor and the young and committed leadership of Northeast Ohio Legal Services entered the arena. We had proven, at least to our satisfaction, that worker ownership was feasible. Could corporations be forced to make available their plants to a worker-community cooperative? Funds were in personal bank accounts ready to be used for the purchase. Companies refused to sell, preferring to close. The decision of the court was they could not be forced to sell. Additionally, attorneys with Northeast Ohio Legal Services were advised by the judge to refrain from involvement in any further cases. Strategy sessions continued on many levels, but for many of us living in Youngstown, the time we were committing to the Coalition now focused on pastoral care for residents of a city in despair.

That summer my roommate at a denominational meeting was Beverly Harrison. She asked questions, listened, and eventually told me I had most likely done everything I could in Youngstown, and it was time for me to leave. I hadn't considered it. The multi-generational residents of the area had nothing to leave for, so how is it that I could leave?

A few months later I asked family members if I was welcome to come back to California without a job. They responded affirmatively, and I submitted a resignation to the campus ministry board for the end of the 1981-1982 academic year. One week later I received an announcement of an opening for "Ecumenical Campus Minister, *University of Southern California*."

I arrived in Los Angeles on a Wednesday, interviewed for the USC position on Saturday morning, and spent the rest of the day at a Dodger game. I was offered and accepted the position that Sunday afternoon.

The University Religious Center (URC) on the USC campus was built in the 1960's on land provided by the University and with funds from the denominations involved and the University. The organizers of the project were leaders in Protestant denominations. They had invited all religious organizations then practicing ministry on the campus to participate in building a joint facility. Hillel, the Catholic Diocese and Latter Day Saints chose not to participate in a joint project, but to create their own facilities. The Evangelical Lutheran Church in America, Episcopal Church, American Baptist Church, Methodist Church, and the Presbyterian Church were a part of the building project. The name of the facility was chosen by the Trustees of the University. Denominations and funding continued to evolve. In 1982 the United Methodists, Presbyterians, Disciples, Church of the Brethren, and United Church of Christ were working together at USC under a regional United Ministries in Higher Education (UMHE) design, and it was this local consortium that was hiring me as the campus minister. Each campus had its own denominational configuration.

United Ministry had been in place for a long time. All involved in campus ministry know there are many more possibilities for design and implementation than any one ministry can engage with integrity. Although previous United Ministry directors had worked in peace with justice activities and small groups, the emphasis had been on counseling. The Board wanted to move to a new model. Faculty had long been involved. Were there emphases that would help additional faculty and staff with what they were attempting on campus? Additionally, United University Church (technically Presbyterian and Methodist but welcoming all) was next door, so we were asked to not provide Sunday services. All ministries in the URC worked together under a Gift Agreement that would serve a minimum of 40 years. None of the ministries housed in the URC paid any expenses for facilities; one representative of each organization served on the governing board; we had individual suites of offices and shared several rooms in common. We worked in conjunction with the Office of the Chaplain, also housed in the facility. It seemed to be the best of all possible worlds!

In addition, USC was going to be an Olympic Village in 1984, and the URC staff, Roman Catholic Staff, Hillel Staff and LDS staff, with a few added to meet the needs of those severely under-represented, were to be the Chaplaincy staff for the Olympics. The URC would be inside the village, and we would keep our regular offices during the Olympics. The common spaces would serve as a television room, a snack bar, and a place for meditation. We were free to program any way we chose. Much of our cooperative time that first 18 months focused on creating possibilities for Olympic realities. In the Olympic setting as well as in our regular programming I was never quite prepared for my own intensive learning. One afternoon as I was sitting in front of the TV with athletes from several countries, one of them asked me why US television always switched event coverage to whatever it was a US athlete was currently winning. I was silenced by my own stupidity, for I hadn't even noticed!

The URC governing board had long agreed that groups which found it difficult to obtain space on campus but represented our own somewhat undefined values would be welcome in our common space. That meant that, in 1982, GLBT rap groups were already meeting several times each week. The United Ministry Lounge welcomed Health Center staff during the middle of each work day, as they had no adequate staff lounge in their facility next door, and that provided me a tuition free education on the realities of student mental health, viruses affecting the football team, additional AIDS information, and material on other relevant topics. Mary Kurushima served as administrative assistant to Paul Kearns, the regional UMHE Secretary, who was also housed in the facility. And Mary was a gem! Within a very few weeks I was acquainted with most Asian Pacific women working on the campus and began to understand how women would take positions which were underpaid and without appropriate regular benefits because, if they stayed on the campus for 15 years, their children would have tuition remission. Mary's husband, Eddy, was an artist who came by to pick her up from work every afternoon. He brought me sketches from his World War II internment camp and military experiences. He would say it was partially "because of my urging" that he began painting from these sketches, and his art work was the first of an informal series of art shows we hung in the United Ministry Lounge over the years. Corita Kent posters, John August Swanson's work and African History Month displays helped to build an image of an informal setting committed to diversity and ethical development.

In May of 1985 my life changed wonderfully. DarEll Weist and I were married in the patio of the URC. DarEll was the United Methodist representative to the group that hired me. His question of me the day of the interview had centered on things I had attempted in campus ministry that had failed. I knew then and continue to know what it is like to have someone who always has your back, is a risk taker, and responds to each "Geez, I'd really like to but it won't work" with a "Why not?"

A casual grouping of staff people from the Division of Student Affairs, a few faculty and several students began to gather every other week, struggling with ways to aid faculty and staff to develop broader understandings of what diversity might mean. The United Ministry lounge was the safe place for such things; my office took responsibility for inviting staff and students to be honest with one another and to commit to holding comments and concerns in confidence. We named ourselves PROACT (Push Racism Out, Accept the Challenge Today). In classes and group meetings we distributed hundreds of sheets asking students to self-define and then describe what it was like to be "that" on the USC campus. We grouped all responses and put them on large boards in the middle of campus. An administrator from the business school walked by, read them all and then quietly stated that this information had to be put in the hands of the faculty and administration. The only way it would get there is if we put it in an inexpensive publication and placed it directly into faculty mailboxes. Work-study students designed the booklet; a small grant from a denomination paid printing costs, and into campus mail it went. A highly respected professor of journalism was subsequently asked by the Provost to chair a campus-wide committee to address these issues. He was willing to do so if I could be on the committee (which bent the institutional rules). My participation was agreed upon, and in very intentional ways USC began working, indeed struggling, with course requirements and other ways of broadening the experiences and understandings of students, staff and faculty.

Work Study Students! We were totally dependent upon them for most of what we attempted. We struggled for that initial contract. Dr. Alvin Rudisill was University Chaplain and Director of Civic and Community Relations. He had begun at USC as Lutheran campus minister, taught in the Schools of Religion and Medicine and was respected as an administrator. I carefully considered the government regulations on work study students and knew that much of the work campus ministry offices were doing could legally be served by students on the work-study payroll. I presented the information to Dr. Rudisill, and together we made an appointment with the appropriate financial aid administrator. The informal hearing did not go well. The administrator could not get beyond "separation of church and state." We left. I was horrified; Al then gave me lessons in how to go beyond and above certain administrators while apparently giving them credit for administrative boldness. Our contract appeared and at the next Religious Directors meeting the guidelines for employment of work-study students were shared with all Religious Directors.

During the 80's and early 90's denominations were making program grants to campus ministries. The funding was not excessive, but creativity was prized. I served on an informal committee out of the Joint Educational Project, a campus office that worked with students and faculty interested in service learning components as a part of their classes. A counselor from Manual Arts High also served on the committee. I approached a denomination for funding, hoping to place approximately 12 undocumented high school students in university, museum or school board work settings during the summer. Technically these people would not be "employed," but would be receiving leadership development grants from United Ministry. Each work contract would be developed with the particular supervisor. The funds were received. Now I needed the high school students. The Manual Arts High School counselor chose about 15 students for interviews. I had approached various settings about their willingness to take an "intern" for the summer at no financial cost. Now the task was to match the student with the setting. I knew the students were not adequately documented; the counselor knew the same, but it wasn't information that needed to be shared. The response? The students were spectacular! Their supervisors called throughout the summer to praise them and ask how I had found these wonderful high school students. The students were happy for good summer work and impressive additions to their resumes.

Most of them had come to the US with their parents when they were very young. One of them, at the age of 14, was sitting in a movie theater on a Friday night when a raid took place. She was rounded up and sent back over the border. Nine months later she appeared in the office of her Manual Arts counselor. She had worked her way back across the border and to Los Angeles.

Each campus ministry runs its own series of "regular" groups. They vary: traditional weekly gatherings with food, a coffee house, women's groups, retreats, film series, invited guests, anti-war activity and "The Last Lecture Series." Then there is the serendipitous; for example: the squirrel that came in the office each day to receive a part of a granola bar from my hand. When church people ask about your ministry, they are often referring to these groups. Ours changed on almost a yearly basis as we worked hard to have students take leadership and responsibility for how and why they wanted to gather together.

Then we developed "A Community Place." USC is located in a central part of L.A. called University Park. Like most very urban situations, there are many levels of poverty. United University Church was handing out sack lunches to the homeless during regular working hours. The administrative assistant, creator of the program, decided it was interfering with regular church programming. We talked informally about possibilities and I said I'd think about what might be done. I began a conversation with the campus director of security, and in the process learned his story. He was headed for the ministry when a Vietnam War experience redirected his commitment. He needed to answer a call to help people be safe, and subsequently earned graduate degrees which prepared him for major roles in campus security. I had come to him to see if he could help United Ministry find a place on or near campus where a food distribution program could continue without disrupting others. He told me he'd watched me since I'd arrived, because he was intrigued with the tasks we initiated and the positions we took. I had a friend I hadn't known about. Soon we had a patio site in a local Lutheran church directly across from the campus. The site was historically understood to be a safe place by neighborhood people in need. We had campus police on call should we ever need them - with the understanding that if called no force was to be used and their task was to help solve problems, following my direction. Additionally, all officers under his direction carried "A Community Place" business cards. If they found a neighborhood person seeking handouts on campus, they directed them to A Community Place.

A student leadership team pulled together; we worked on funding and involving volunteers. Three days a week, from 11-1, sack lunches were handed out following specific guidelines, and the first week of every month bus tokens and taxi vouchers were distributed to those who registered and qualified. I was present most of the time to problem solve, but constantly stood in awe as students addressed every client (and often there were more than 100 in the two hour period) by name, asked about family members or the job search, and helped them with other needs. Often those needs included filling out forms for someone just released from jail who was not literate, or talking with seniors about possibilities for housing. International students often volunteered with A Community Place because they wanted to get over their fear of the neighborhood. Thursdays at 5:00 volunteers met to prepare lunches for distribution. The program has now been running for 15 years.

236

As a member of a Presbytery I helped lead three groups to Nicaragua on work teams under the direction of CEPAD, the evangelical or Protestant churches of Nicaragua. Our on-site experiences were facilitated by a Presbyterian clergyman from Pennsylvania, working with CEPAD. After the second trip he asked why I wasn't bringing students. The reality? I hadn't thought of it. Presbytery experiences were so distant from campus experiences, I wasn't certain I could find appropriate students. The conversations began. He was very interested in discovering more about women's leadership in Nicaragua. I was very interested in grass roots organizing. We put together a ten day program for USC students in Nicaragua focusing on "Women's Issues," open to males and females. The second year we added some conversations with Nicaraguan GLBT groups, because of the interests of two students traveling with us. The third year we began to have conversations with persons who had attempted to come to the U.S. illegally, and our new title was "Women's Issues and Immigration Realities." Each year the agenda for the approximately 15 students was slightly adjusted. Only one or two individual students, out of the seven year total of 100 students, expressed disappointment. And I continued to learn. One year we were meeting with the appropriate person from the US Consulate in Nicaragua to talk about immigration. He wanted to know something about the group. I sat in shock as the first four students introduced themselves and indicated their parents had come to the U.S. illegally. I hope he was listening. After the first year the Dean of Social Work was pleased with the reports her students brought back and chose to fund any of her students who were subsequently accepted for the program. Women's Issues and Immigration Realities continued through 2012, when I technically retired from USC.

When I began at USC an on-going unit of the ministry was Orchard House, a rather historic building just a few blocks from campus. Through a series of exchanges it had been a gift to the United Methodist Conference with the understanding it would only be used for USC campus ministry. When I came it was occupied by student musicians who enjoyed living together because each of them understood why it was necessary to experience the practice sessions of others. The Director of International Students and Scholars called several times asking if a place could be found for a particular international student, and we made an accommodation when possible. One morning the house next door caught on fire, destroying much of that property and killing one of the next door students who was trapped in a bathroom. The fire jumped the driveway to our property, but the extreme attention of the fire crew saved our building, although there was damage to electrical systems and outside surfaces, as well as flooding. Although the Red Cross was on site to provide new housing for our students, the students decided they wanted to go through this together. With my permission, although I'm not certain the Conference would have thought it appropriate, a generator was brought in and they continued to live "in community" through the five months required for complete repair.

Then, with the help of a faculty family, we decided to make Orchard House more intentional.

At an appropriate time we transformed Orchard into a residence for students interested in living in community who wanted to maximize their urban experience. Curt Roseman, Professor of Geography, was retiring from the university but would return to campus each Spring semester to supervise continuing graduate students. He approached me, I agreed, and one large room in the house was saved for Curt and his wife, Elizabeth. Each Spring semester they led urban tours, welcomed other faculty into the house for seminars, and aided students living there with projects related to urban life. Students formally applied to live there. Continuing students and I did extensive interviews, attempting to choose additional residents who would learn from each other. The rent was fair; everyone had responsibilities. Most semesters it was a strong success.

The initial 40-year period of the Gift Agreement for the University Religious Center was coming to an end. I was serving as Chair of the Ecumenical Mission, which was the Governing Board for the Center, and asked Byron Hayes, a highly respected attorney whose specialty was Real Estate, to evaluate the legal documents related to the Center. Byron, an extremely committed United Methodist layman, was willing to provide *Pro-bono* services. Byron responded to my inquiry: "The documents were written by attorneys of diverse opinions who knew that when the 40 years was over they would not be around to deal with the consequences." And there we were. With Byron's help we did some on-going strategizing. The documents called for several ten year extensions but did not list costs or responsibilities. Several months later the Provost's Office called asking for an appointment with the Governing Board. We went over, filled with trepidation. We were met by two skilled administrators from the Provost's Office and a Professor of Religion and Law. One Provost began, "We've been evaluating the Gift Agreement and feel as though the USC Administration has not fulfilled its responsibilities. Therefore, we would like to suggest some conversations about how to fulfill those responsibilities and how to implement the extensions." "From this point on," one Provost continued, "the denominations you represent need to be treated as major donors to the University because of what you and your predecessors have provided the campus." We managed to maintain our dignity and composure until we were out of sight.

A second meeting was held with the same representatives and skilled persons from Physical Plant. Work began on improving furniture, changing carpeting, updating the kitchen, and doing necessary work in the Chapel.

Al Rudisill had retired from the Chaplaincy, and, after a search, the position was filled by a local rabbi. The position was re-named Dean of Religious Life. Dean Laemmle served a term and an extension, and then she asked to not continue. Another search was held and was truncated as the search committee announced they would be appointing the first Hindu Dean of

Religious Life in a major U.S. University. With each appointment the Governing Board was called upon to make it clear to the Dean that, unlike other appointments within the University, the facility did not come with the title.

All things change. The Provost moved on. Several candidates were considered for the Provost's position. The appointment did not go to the administrator who had convened the Governing Board. The second administrator who had been working with us left the University. The Professor of Religion and Law had to tell us he could not work with us unless requested to do so by the Provost, and he did not think either he or we should initiate that request.

Approximately four years into the term of the Hindu Dean of Religious Life, we all received a letter. He believed the University had more than met its obligations, the initial 40 year Gift Agreement period had ended a few years previously, and he was terminating the agreement. We would meet to decide how much space each of us could continue to have, and what the conditions for retaining that space would be. Byron Hayes became a very public presence in our conversations. Because of the incompleteness of the legal documents he did not think we could win the arguments over space legally. He believed they could be won ethically. Bishop Jon Bruno, of the Episcopal Diocese, in conversation with other denominational leaders, decided to take on the argument. Soon thereafter, however, he was diagnosed with a very serious illness that required existing in a tent while on chemotherapy for several months at a time. His commitment to the dilemma of the Ecumenical Mission had to be set aside.

In January 2011 the Southern California Ecumenical Council, at its Week of Common Prayer celebration, honored me with the Gene Boutilier Award for Excellence in Ecumenical Leadership. In April of 2011 the Council Director for the United Methodist Conference called and said she needed to see me. I had to pick up something from a gallery near the Conference Office, so agreed to come by that afternoon. I walked in and was asked to wait "while others gathered." We met in a small conference room and I was handed a letter which indicated the Conference would no longer provide any financial support for my salary. I could continue in the position and the campus ministry space as long as I chose, but there would be no salary from the Conference. Then a disagreement began between the District Superintendent and the Council Director. She wanted me to turn over the keys and responsibilities for Orchard House at the end of the semester. He maintained that if I was continuing under the auspices of the local board, then I could continue with Orchard House as a part of the program. She wanted to sell the property. He indicated he could not support the selling of any property at such a down time in the market. The conference had been providing 50% of my salary and had served as my employer. There was no reason given, but from information the Council Director shared with others, I learned she had told the Conference Board of

Higher Education they had to cut expenses. They had not done so; therefore she "showed" them how it could be done. The Board of Higher Education was told the Conference did not intend to be employing any campus ministers within five years. And why was I the first one cut? This has not been verified, but I assumed part of the reasoning was that I am not a United Methodist, therefore they did not need to guarantee employment, I was beyond the traditional retirement age, and a United Methodist/Presbyterian Church also existed on the campus.

I have always cherished local Boards. When I got home from that meeting a call was waiting for me from the United Ministry chair. As I left the Conference Office, the Council Director had called him to inform him of this action. He asked me to think about what I wanted and we met for dinner two days later. What I wanted was a respectable time to adequately close down the ministry. That would include several tasks: managing Orchard for one more year since we'd already chosen the residents, continuing with A Community Place for a year while I sought a new 501C3 organization to provide legal and supervisory support, deciding whether there would be life for the Nicaraguan adventure after the trip planned for May, 2011. The Board agreed. We located some funds for an intern who had participated in many of our programs and was willing to do hands-on work under my supervision. She brought a community garden aspect to A Community Place and aided in the recruitment and preparation of students for the Nicaraguan adventure. The Nicaraguan adventure continued through the summer of 2013, and it was my decision that we not continue any longer. A Lutheran urban collective provided legal and supervisory support for the student-run A Community Place. United Ministry managed Orchard House for the additional year and then happily turned it over to the Conference. And in the time between May 2011 and 2013, I stepped back a bit further each month. It has taken us until this Spring to fully close the checking account by depositing the few remaining dollars in the A Community Place account.

A few learnings from these last few years: In having my campus ministry career end this way I recognized for the first time the number of persons who, throughout the years, have had the same experience. One wonderful Disciple retired clergy said "Diane, all of this happened to everyone else 20 years ago! How did you manage for so long?" People within institutions, whether it is the church or the university, are more comfortable relying on legal or administrative decisions rather than talking things through. All of this could have been handled without the pain for anyone if open conversation had been encouraged. Ironically, those who inflict the pain then want to give the retirement parties. (I didn't accept!). And there are those whose comfort comes in saying, "But I was just the messenger!"

Some you considered good colleagues will never speak of these realities with you. You disappear. I do understand that part of it is the fear they may be next.

The "church" places people on campuses with little clarity as to what the expectations are. The materials you find to work with are situational. I understood my task in each setting to be the creation of a work of art on a canvas, much like a Jackson Pollock, filled with the lives of students, the experiences of faculty and staff, the realities of civil society, even the realities of civil unrest or 9/11 terror. It is all there to be worked with. And on the campuses I served I was surrounded by those choosing to be a part of the process and very willing to help in executing the design. When it works, the result is a ministry where power is decentralized, talents are recognized, all are learning and respected, and the Word comes alive in unexpected ways.

My thanks to those who made it possible.

Diane Kenney, with her husband DarEll Weist, is living in Pilgrim Place, a community in Claremont, California for persons whose professional lives have been in religious or nonprofit institutions worldwide. Other members of the household arc cats Christmas and Summer. Retirement does not mean the end of committee meetings; it does mean that learning to play the hammered dulcimer, vegetable gardening, Rosetta Stone 1-5 (Spanish) and international travel have made it to the top of her "to do" list.

Feisty Women Forging Life-Time Connections
By Marna McKenzie

The *UC Berkeley* Campus was in turmoil in 1969. Outside the window the CA National Guard troops were at the ready with hand grenades, helmets, boots. Across the street students were milling about, talking in small groups, waving banners. Just before noon an older man from the nearby conservative Presbyterian Church had been photographing the "filth" posted on the bulletin board outside my office. Earlier in the morning I had discovered a very young girl curled in a fetal position on the bathroom floor - a miscarriage. An ordinary/extraordinary day in campus ministry at UNITAS, the ecumenical campus ministry on the corner of Bancroft and College, Berkeley.

I was the interim campus minister of this venerable ecumenical ministry, not because of competence but to hold together a program going through the throes of leadership change, attacks by conservatives, board power struggles, and the shifting of the universe of the university (and world) - the Free Speech Movement. Details of these days is recorded elsewhere but my situation was unique.

I am not an ordained clergyperson. I had started seminary a few years before but with a newly visible feminism found the instruction and atmosphere to be toxic. Nevertheless, I was on the ministry staff as administrator, a Lay Professional in the Presbyterian Church (with no benefits). John Hadsell has written a comprehensive history of the ministry personnel changes and challenges. Three events during this time are mine to tell.

Story Number One. Joann Nash Eakin was one of the ministers when I joined the UCB team. Feminism ferment was bubbling on the campus. She and I became connected with a group of "radical" women attending the Graduate Theological Union, a consortium of seminaries north side of the campus. We began meeting together, doing "consciousness raising" about our situations as women, still hanging at the edge of leadership and influence in theological education and the life of the churches.

Our discontent moved quickly to rage and, as confidence built, we formed the Office of Women's Affairs (loving the double entendre of our name!). We organized to press our case in 3 directions-- the seminary presidents and boards, theology, and the local churches. We met often to hold together our strategies and our courage. Joann and I (and others) took on the local churches, demanding to have voice at such gatherings as the Presbyterian Asilomar Gathering, the UCC Annual Conference, the United Methodist offices in San Francisco. We pressed to be heard.

A few men came forward to publically support us; many rose to rave about "The Bible" and "history " and our "destroying the church." Women came forward to tell their stories, some shyly, some bold and angry. Anne McGrew Bennett offered powerful leadership and kept us focused on the international implications and our connection with the peace movement. The OWA base expanded to include Catholic sisters (who were way ahead of Protestant women), Unitarians, Jewish sisters, Baptists, Disciples of Christ. Networks were formed across the country linking seminarians and women theologians and scholars who were bursting with radical insights and notions and forcing the religious world to pay attention to the powerful force of women who were demanding to be heard. We scraped together money for conferences in Berkeley, Chicago, and LA. The organized religious hierarchies began to pay attention.

Over the years the OWA became the Center for Women and Religion and continues its presence and influence. Its history is well documented and its stories recorded in the archives of the Graduate Theological Union. I am considered one of the "Founding Mothers" of the OWA. It gave me a community of women to bring me to voice and action with life-changing influences.

Story Number Two. One day in the early 70's, Jan Greisinger appeared at my office door. At that time my professional world was circumscribed by the UC Berkeley campus ministry and beyond that Cooperative Ministries in Higher Education, the Northern California ecumenical organization linking campuses from Santa Cruz to Davis and Reno. Campus ministries were struggling with financial survival as denominational money was vanishing and the student population changing-- in fact the whole scene was changing! But that is another story.

Jan (an ordained UCC campus minister from Ohio) was moving about the country visiting campuses where there was purported to be women on staff. She was one of a very few women in campus ministry leadership and had gotten a grant from the National Campus Ministry Association to identify women in campus ministry—$5000 if I remember correctly. How about identifying and organizing the women? She offered to pay for transportation for a gathering, and Campus Ministry Women quickly evolved. CMW was a small group of women, each with incredible stories of struggle as women in ministry—and life. We met in homes all over the country—slept on the floor and cots, fixed our own meals, wept and laughed and plotted.

We invited campus ministry women to prepare proposals for women-related projects on their campuses. Each gathering we reviewed the proposals and after deep deliberation gave modest $$ and encouragement and support all over the country. Oh, the amazing women who gathered and who were empowered by this slight and feisty organization. Life-time connections between us were forged, and for many of us we first experienced "sisterhood." I hope the details are sacred in the archives.

Story Number 3. This story is a hodge-podge. I write this out of moments of reflections over the years now passed. My world now focuses around the arts and family and friends. When I was 38 years old, my children were fleeing the nest, and my husband was entwined in his work. John Hadsell asked me to work with him in UC Berkeley campus ministry and thus began my real adult journey as a woman. The two stories above are cherished and formative memories of events, but what was really changing was me.

My world moved from the Berkeley campus to organizing new ministries in Northern California to working with UMHE and national responsibilities to international connections. Each environment challenged, demanded, and drew from me new aspects of myself. Most significantly I came to know what working with a team requires, how linked my life is with faith journeys, what intimate friendships can transcend time and space--Betsy and Mark and Charles and Clyde and Barry and Lizann and Joann and John... and on and on. The dates are irrelevant right now. The heart memories are forever.

After 15 years in Santa Fe, NM, Marna McKenzie has moved to Sebastopol, CA an hour north of San Francisco in 2014. She has found a lively art community, fascinating area history, a challenging writers group, and is within hugging distance of family.

Change: 1969-2003
By Manuel Wortman

In 1969-70 I shifted from the rural United Methodist Church in mid-state North Carolina to try my hand for one year at the Wesley Foundation, the *University of North Carolina in Greensboro*. After a successful year there, I moved to Appalachian State University for 5 years, then to the University of North Carolina in Chapel Hill for 23 years, finishing my career as the Conference Executive for Higher Education and Campus Ministry in the Western North Carolina Conference of the United Methodist Church, appointed by Bishop Charlene Kammerer, a campus minister, former assistant and later acting Minister to the University at Duke (a position that the then President of Duke offered her fulltime, but she chose to return to the local church, and was soon elected Bishop.)

For the sake of history, here are some of my most salient memories. In 1969 when I entered campus ministry, we sixties folks remember the horrors of 1968, which may have been the most difficult year in my memory. Though it had been nearly five years, it seemed only the month before that John Kennedy had been shot, then Martin Luther King, Jr. and Bobby Kennedy were both killed in 1968! The world of downtown larger cities felt like they were in flames nightly. Spock and Coffin were indicted for violation of the draft law. The TET Offensive became a killing field; a Vietnamese security officer executed a Vet Cong prisoner with a pistol to his head. And a military politician was saying that it might be necessary to "destroy a Vietnamese village in order to save it." At the time of the "Prague Spring", the Republicans nominated Richard Nixon for their candidate, the Democratic Convention in Chicago erupted, George Wallace ran his own Independent campaign, NOW protested the Miss American Beauty contest, Eugene McCarthy washed out, more that ½ million US soldiers in remained posted in Vietnam, and Arlo Guthrie sang about "Alice's Restaurant." And it did not cease; at Kent State in 1970, Ohio National Guard fired 67 rounds in 13 seconds into anti-war student demonstrators, killing 4, injuring 9.

What a time to enter campus ministry! How could we ever forget? Or forgive?! In Greensboro, NC, where rude memories of sit-ins at Woolworths lingered, the Wesley Foundation with the Quakers and others entered into anti-war and civil rights activities. I was asked to do a weekend workshop on social change for the Presbyterian students. The UNCG group was exclusively white; we were to meet students from a historically black university, Fayetteville State, for a weekend at the beach. Though the Presbyterian ministry had informed the motel that we were a mixed racial group and had been assured that was not a problem, it turned out otherwise when we arrived. The African American students were told they could go to the next beach [a "colored beach"] for their sleeping quarters. All students voted loudly and unanimously, "NO!" We awakened the local Presbyterian minister, and students of all colors slept in every nook and cranny of the Myrtle Beach Presbyterian Church for the two nights we were there—and the next morning we had social change in the color of our faces!

From that charged environment, I moved to a quieter, mountain campus at *Appalachian State University* in Boone, NC for five years of new but creative activity. Wesley students and I, with the help of a friendly faculty, succeeded in introducing a Peace Studies minor into the curriculum. We founded a Student Volunteer Service Corp and sent 150 students to work-- mostly with children in the mountain coves. At that time, we were only beginning to work with un-planned pregnancies among our students. I can never forget that I counseled 18 students about abortion in one month. The gay and lesbian students found Wesley to be the safest place on campus. Carlyle Marney, that great Southern preacher of the time, said of that ministry to gay and lesbian students: "best damn thing he had heard about the church in a long time."

In 1975 I moved into the legacy of Bob Johnson, Banks Godfrey, and the activism on the campus of the *University of North Carolina*, with a residual remembrance of Wesley's coffeehouse where James and Livingstone Taylor had played during their high school years. Though his imprint was branded on the campus, Bob Johnson moved on. He and Mike Bloy, Nancy Malone, and Bernard Lafayette laid out our academic world with the *NICM Journal* and regular conferences. The retired chaplain from Northwestern, Ralph Dunlop, living 6 months per year in Chapel Hill, became a fortress for us emotionally and politically.

But the times, indeed, they were a' changing. After the death of Kent State students, there seemed to be a shift. As the students said: "There ain't no peace without, so we will look for peace within." Variations of Eastern Religions began to be studied and practiced, which, in turn, led the more religiously conservative students toward evangelical groups. (Intervarsity may have had the largest chapter in the US at Chapel Hill.) We at Wesley continued our activist legacy and worked, when possible, with minorities, providing the space and some support for the first African American student newspaper on campus entitled," Black Ink." And Wesley helped form inclusive residency living communities at Wesley and on campus. But the newest things for students became forms of volunteerism and more traditional student ministry styles. We even had a singing group of 50 or so students. One student, the son of a missionary, pushed us to do work mission teams. These trips were so successful and had such strong impact on students, that we did an annual mission for the next 16 years: to Mexico, the Caribbean, NYC, Atlanta, and Miami, alternating every third year working with the mountain poor in NC. Students' lives were changed. More than 50 students from this one Wesley Center entered professional ministry in the next 18 or so years.

At the national Section on Campus Ministry for the United Methodist Church, we tried national and regional conferences again with considerable success, but any notions that we could revive a Methodist or an ecumenical student movement soon went by the way.

It was years of hard work and remarkable memories. When the nights were cold and things seemed not to be going well for me personally, I developed a rhythm of remembering the "saints of Wesley," and my uncertainties about my vocation and career disappeared into the realities of the real movement of God's presence in ways I could never have imagined.

But not all was well. I moved into an administrative post and spent 5 years trying to help my younger colleagues prepare for the hard times when funds would diminish in large portions. It has been difficult to watch.

We pray that Campus Ministry, the "best kept secret in the Church," will not only survive but continue with vigor.

Manuel Wortman and his wife Karen, a former middle school counselor, are happily retired in Chapel Hill, where he enjoys playing golf, serving as an associate pastor at University UMC, and singing in the church choir.

Pioneering for Campus Ministry for Women
By Jan Griesinger

I worked for the **World Student Christian Federation** (WSCF) from 1971-1975, specifically for the North American region on what was called a women's project. I edited a book, the first FEMINIST one as far as we know, with articles by women all across the world – not things written by European travelers about what they saw but writing by actual women living in the country they wrote about and describing the status of women.

I helped form the group Campus Ministry Women in 1972, and much of my work was with that group – giving support to women working in their field, exchanging info, meeting nationally a few times. Women in Campus Ministry included women who served as office staff and wives of men working in campus ministry, as those women also often worked hard as volunteers. It continued until 1996.

From 1976 to 2004 I served as Co-Director for United Campus Ministry at **Ohio University**, Athens OH. I was privileged to work with students, faculty and staff on things like personal support and faith struggles but also on work for justice.

One of the best things was taking students on several spring break trips in several different years to the historic sites of the civil rights movement – Montgomery, Selma and Birmingham Alabama, Memphis, TN, Jackson MS, Atlanta GA. We were all inspired to see museums that had been created, attend the church where MLK preached, the church in Selma where the famous march began to Montgomery. I also enjoyed fine trips I took students to in Puerto Rico and Cuba. And we did some hurricane relief work in New Orleans. Here are some comments from student evaluations from the 2002 Civil rights trip:

- *"It gave me a renewed faith in black people, gave me a chance to put everything into perspective and filled in a lot of holes from previous information that I learned."*

- *" I came to realize the role of non-violence in standing up for what we truly believe in. The movement was for all people and not just for African Americans as I believed earlier. 1955-1968 was a small phase of what was started earlier and something that needs to be carried on by our generation."*

- *"It changed me forever. There are so many books I want to read. I want to educate people about what I've learned. This trip changed me as a person."*

- *"The trip gave me a more clear idea of what still needs to be done in human rights issues. I also was able to get the perspectives of those who were not black (those who went on the trip.) It also gave me the sense of my history as an African American.*

In addition there was the work on such things as divestment so the university would spend no funds in South Africa until after full liberation there, stopping US funds going to Central America to prop up bad rulers, working hard for LGBT justice, protesting the war in Iraq, during which a number of us were arrested sitting in the street at the main campus intersection. The peace vigil we began in 1979, one hour a week at our county courthouse, is still going on to prevent future wars and to work for justice for the 99%.

I helped start the Women Take Back the Night march in 1979 and it still continues to this day. I worked hard to get a Women's Center in the student union building, which finally happened in 2005. I helped start the battered women's shelter in 1978 and it continues.

We did good interfaith work through a campus ministerial association. I served on the statewide board of Ohio Campus Ministries from 1989 until the present.

I have a story written in *Journeys That Opened Up the World,* edited by Sara M. Evans, 2003, about our involvement in the WSCF and the connection between church-related experiences and the movements for justice. Also my work appears quite a bit in *Feminism in the Heartland* by Judith Ezekiel, 2002, on the women's liberation movement in Dayton OH, which I co-founded in 1969.

Jan served as the Co-Director for Old Lesbians Organizing for Change, a national organization founded 25 years ago, from 2004 until the end of 2014 and currently serves on the board of the Appalachian Peace and Justice Network. She lives at the Susan B. Anthony Memorial UnRest Home Womyn's Land Trust in Athens County Ohio.

A Personal Retrospective On My Campus Ministry Years
By Rev. Paul C. Walley

"36 years as a campus minister in one place? You've got to be kidding!"

No, I'm *not* kidding. It's true – and I loved the whole ride. I guess you could say longevity has its value, especially if you are comfortable with the niche you are in. I was. One of my board members said that it was a natural fit: this ecumenical campus ministry and me. I agree. It was at **State University of New York in New Paltz, New York**. I also am continuing on with the small church I pastor part-time in West Camp, New York.

What I'd not like to do here is bore you with an endless history of "I did this – then I developed that – and then ..." and on and on and on. I'd rather hit the high notes, lift up the things I most remember or that stand out for me as I reflect back on my many years in campus ministry.

Let me kick it right into high gear with this: I decided early on that I would try some things that I enjoyed or got me excited. My hope was that students and faculty/staff might join in because they liked them too. For the most part, this thesis worked well. Occasionally something would flop. So then we would let it go and attempt something else. I tended to keep the programs or ventures that worked well (as they say, "if it ain't broke, don't fix it") over the years.

So, you *newbies* out there in campusland, do an inscape search. If it turns you on, try it. (Now I am assuming that you have some moral scruples and are not doing anything illegal or foolhardy.) But there *has* to be room to experiment. I once had a communion worship using hot rolls with butter on them, leading one student to term this unorthodox service "hot buttered God." If you are going to explore, develop a somewhat tough skin to ward off your critics. But keep your warm heart and creative mind. They are invaluable gifts of God in this unpredictable ministry.

My first love was our retreats. It is my contention that these weekends/weeks are the most lasting experiences you can give to your students and colleagues. So we had a rafting retreat to start the fall semesters discussing our river challenges (five in each rubber raft) as a paradigm of the Christian life. The Presbyterian ministry team of the church we stayed in overnight (sleeping bags on the floor) were a talented musical team and fired us up with new songs. We also had a theatre retreat in the NYC church of an Episcopal priest I knew, seeing "The Elephant Man" and discussing it with the actors. A fall retreat at Weston Priory was a favorite of mine, rousing the students for a 5 a.m. Vigil in candlelight and sharing with these Benedictine Brothers. My wife and I took our canoe and let students use it on a nearby lake. Our Fall Retreat in Vermont was the most traditional: three worship services (each different) closing with joyful communion.

In addition, I got the Habitat for Humanity bug and initiated a campus chapter with our student activities director and a student in a fraternity (he became our first president). Each spring we went on HFH's *Collegiate*

Challenge, 15-20 students building houses in snowy West Virginia to the sunny beaches of South Carolina. In 2008 after I retired the chapter went to *New Orleans* and asked me to go with them. Habitat attracted students who *didn't* go to church but just wanted "to help people." We tried many *other* things along the way but these were my staples.

An on-campus activity we ran each year was called Skip-A-Dinner. It netted over 1,000 sign-ups with students giving up the cost of a meal (the College took it off their meal card). The success was when I invited the sororities and fraternities to sit at our sign-up tables on campus. With such a cross-cut of campus, they got their friends into it and put us over the top most years. I also ran around taking *photos* and offering *prizes* for top volunteers. Money raised was given to the United Nations World Food Program, CROP, and Trinity Church Soup Kitchen in NYC.

Oh, yes, we did the traditional stuff like weekly Bible studies, Word and Worship on campus in our office, and monthly visits to our supporting churches. The trick in all this was our talented Peer Ministry Team (3-6 students each semester) who got student stipends (small) and worked their tails off for our ministry. One semester they did a liturgical dance to a conga drum they had learned at an ecumenical student retreat. Another semester they performed "Puppets Go to Church" for the children's sermon (while lightly roasting the local pastors!) in churches.

Faculty & staff showed up for an early morning monthly discussion series with video segments on authors writing short stories with Christian connections. We moved it to the lunch hour for better attendance and it became a brown bag b.y.o. thing. The Food Service supplied homemade cookies and beverage. We had Christian guests mostly, but some other faiths too.

Speaking of other faiths, I am pleased to learn my successor is continuing the interfaith Thanksgiving dinner on campus. I went to one my first year after retiring. It was great to see the huge circle of prayer by various student reps from our spiritual multifaith mix on campus. (Yes, Wiccan and the Pagan Student Society were welcomed as well).

We did tons of *other* interesting things over the years. Not all were initiated by me or the SCC. I did occasional guest lectures. Students invited West Point cadets for joint activities for a time. For a while I showed short movies in the residence halls at 10 p.m. We had a covenant house student community the first four years until family came along and we re-shaped our ministry more as an outreach mission. Carole, my devoted wife and partner, led and taught sewing at a detention facility nearby with students assisting her. We ventured into a state prison for worship and discussion with adult inmates (ours was the first co-ed group to be granted regular entrance), enjoying the correctional facility gospel choir each Sunday. I heard attendance increased when we came ~ partly because of our lively and attractive students, I am sure! (as well as the Spirit of Christ in our midst). This ministry was enabled by the Episcopal prison chaplain and colleague.

Sure, I had some down times. One pastor talked his governing body into de-funding us. But a lay member of this church brought it to the congregation and they reversed their own council! I wondered if I should seek another calling and did take a gifts assessment test, very intense – but it only confirmed that I was in just the right position for/with my gifts and personal style. I had my disagreements with students at times (one slammed down her keys and stormed out, vowing never to return to our campus office!). Another student over-extended his SCC time to the neglect of his studies; I had to throw him out of the office "until you get your grades up!" (He has since become a pastor of a Lutheran church in the Midwest and is still a close friend).

My dear wife had serious mental issues and cancer which caused much stress our last ten years. But through it all, God kept us together as we struggled and served. My *swing dancing* gives energy and new life to me socially. Our *children* encourage me as they forge their own lives and careers in their social work, teaching and administrative worlds. My *first grandchild* arrives in August! My *wife* is looking down on all of this with pride and gratitude, like me. What a wild and wonderful ride this amazing thing called campus ministry has been for me. *Alleluia!*

Backing Into a Calling and the Ripple Effect!
Susan Yarrow Morris

It was a vibrant time in the pioneering ecumenical effort known as Campus Christian Ministry at the *University of Washington* in Seattle, Washington in the early 1970's, much as it was on other U.S. campuses of both private and state colleges and universities. On one hand, many UW students, faculty and staff were questioning "the way it's always been done" in their particular academic and administrative settings, challenging cultural norms related to civic and community life, and taking actions responding to peace and justice issues in local communities and in the world. On the other hand, sizeable numbers of the UW community clung to traditions (sororities, fraternities, athletic teams, etc., for example) common to campus life. In this context, the ecumenical (eight Protestant denominations and Roman Catholic) staff was pulled together, supported by various denominational and ecumenical sources and UMHE (United Ministries in Higher Education) and charged with "doing ministry" at the UW in the late 60's, early 70's.

In 1972, I was invited (i.e., "called") to join the CCM staff to design and direct a Marriage Preparation program which would reflect the ecumenical spirit of the ministry and yet honor denominational premarital particularities, an idea which had been identified as appropriate for campus ministry, by its staff and Board. I was to be a (very!) part time staff person funded with a small stipend. My prior experience, post B.A. in Social Work and Religion, had been in various church, agency, and health care settings. This invitation to envision and develop such a program/ministry lit a vocational and spiritual spark for me. I knew and respected a few of the staff members already, and was eager to be a part of this unique venture. And so I began backing into ministry!

After consulting with CCM staff and area clergy, I designed and directed an ecumenical Marriage Prep program which became one of CCM's many core ministries, building bridges between local parishes, communities, and CCM. Serving over 125 couples a year in weekend or weeknight workshops, these were the primary components of the Marriage Preparation program during my 16 years on the staff (1972-1988):

- an articulated and relevant covenant theology at the heart of the process and content of the workshops, leaving specific denominational doctrines to be conveyed by the officiating pastors to couples. Our task was to help couples sense a connection between God's covenant with humankind and all creation and our response to live in embodied covenant love with one another.
- an MP faculty of 40-50 persons from many denominations and faith traditions – couples and singles, clergy and lay – who became in many ways a covenant community, volunteering to lead workshops as authentic (not perfect!) human beings, to participate in ongoing continuing education

events, to contribute to workshop design and content, and to explore in their personal and professional lives what it means to live in healthy, life-giving covenantal relationship with another.

• financial, organizational and spiritual support from all participating Protestant denominations and the Roman Catholic churches in the area.

• a Participant Couple's Workbook of over 125 pages of exercises, resources and handouts designed for use with couples in the workshop process; these were gathered (and refined for use in the MP program) from experts in marriage and family life, theological studies, and other social and behavioral sciences, as well as my own and MP faculty members' ongoing ideas.

• development, in the mid 80's, of a Committed Relationship Preparation program for same gender couples, in which I invited several lgbt couples from different denominations to help rewrite all the MP materials to make them appropriate for use in such workshops, as well as adding topics unique to lgbt couples. These couples were then trained to lead the CR workshops. We held about two such weekend workshops a year in those years before I left CCM. Sadly, there was little staff energy to continue that piece of the program after 1988, even though the MP program continued under new and creative leadership. Once again, CCM was a pioneer, enabling and supporting this unique CRPrep program. (Note: Through the years, all the language used in exercises and resources for all the workshops became inclusive, so the same materials could be used.) (Note: With the blessing of the UCC, I was honored to officiate in 1985 for a same gender couple's Covenant Service, and have been privileged to witness many more in the years since. With the passage of the Marriage Equality law in Washington state last year, many of those couples have returned to celebrate their covenants anew, as well as to marvel at the working of the Holy Spirit in the unexpected, justice making context of an election process!)

Several participant couple follow-up support programs were offered over the years, providing topical marriage enrichment gatherings, using various formats. As well, pages of local resources and bibliographies and referral lists were provided participant couples during the workshops.

Over the years, this model for an ecumenical Marriage Preparation program was used in several other campus ministry settings in Washington; local leaders were trained and materials shared. As word of the program's integrity and popularity spread, it became a resource not only for the UW community but for churches and pastors throughout our state and some colleagues were glad to use the MP/CR model in their parish and campus settings in other states. I was asked to present the model, process and materials in several national and local marriage and family life conferences and agencies. Our written materials were about to be published when Pilgrim Press went through some major bureaucratic changes, and the whole project was suspended and never revisited.

Characteristics which were most appealing and unique for this particular Marriage Preparation and Committed Relationship program model were:
- covenant theology basis for all topics (communications, roles and expectations, family of origin, intimacy, etc.),
- participatory workshop style,
- leadership community,
- workshop process (using a variety of approaches to topics),
- high value on creating a safe and trusting ecumenical setting for couples to reflect, discuss and learn;
- inclusion of domestic violence (awareness and prevention and strategies for responding) in the topics addressed,
- its viability as a truly ecumenical ministry.

As this program and its "ripples" became the primary focus of my work at CCM and I interfaced more and more with staff colleagues and area clergy, I was invited to take on other responsibilities....preaching and speaking at the CCM's worship services and local churches, joining colleagues to teach or lead classes, workshops or retreats in Feminist Theology, Alternative Living Arrangements (my family and two other families were living in a covenantal community on an island farm and many were intrigued with this topic – it was the 70's, after all!), weekly Bible text study, theology of human sexuality (based on James B. Nelson's EMBODIMENT and his consultation with us for many years) and, with David Royer, my UCC colleague at CCM, teaching courses in LIFEwork Planning with training from Dick Bolles (former campus pastor himself!) The Vocations Working Group of the UCC, under Verlyn Barker's guidance, was spawned from this effort and similar programs offered by colleagues around the country.

I began taking courses and seminars whenever possible in theological studies, as I "backed into" my calling. Vancouver School of Theology in Vancouver, BC and Pacific School of Religion in Berkeley, CA were the closest seminaries for my academic needs at the time. It was clear that my commitment to my family and living community on Whidbey Island mitigated against leaving the area for three years to complete a B.D. or M.Div. To augment my local studies (at Seattle University's Jesuit seminary, and independent work with theologians in the Seattle area), I attended summer sessions for several years at PSR and VST and the Institute for Campus Ministry at Valparaiso University. I was given standing in the UCC as a Licensed Minister to serve at CCM in 1982, and was blessed for this call in a special worship service at CCM, surrounded by my colleagues of many traditions, a humbling and joyful time.

My own journey to ordained ministry continued when I chose to leave CCM in 1988 to return to local parish ministry, serving two Seattle UCC churches until my retirement. Continued studies and a uniquely designed process led to my ordination in 1994 at Plymouth Congregational Church, UCC, in Seattle, where I was serving. I retired in 2004 after serving as Marriage Minister and Associate Pastor at Fauntleroy Church, UCC, in Seattle for eight years. In both those churches, I continued to lead Marriage Prep, Marriage Enrichment and family life workshops and classes as part of my ministry....a great joy! I surely believe that my incredibly rich CCM experience serving within a staff of ecumenical colleagues committed to mutual support, shared vision, and theological integrity was a seminal factor in my choice to serve in churches with multiple staff configurations for the rest of my ministry.

The moment I retired, I was asked by the FaithTrust Institute (Rev. Dr. Marie M. Fortune, Founder and Director), to write a book to help pastors feel skilled and confident addressing domestic violence in their premarital counseling. This was called *OPENING THE DOOR: A Pastor's Guide to Addressing Domestic Violence in Premarital Counseling* and was published by the FaithTrust Institute in 2006. It includes theological underpinnings as well as specific approaches to the topic of domestic violence within workshop or individual premarital counseling sessions, several copy-ready handouts, and an appendix of related articles and resources. It is being used, I understand, in a variety of pastoral settings, including campus ministry and chaplaincy, local parishes and seminaries. Amazing ripples from a small program begun in 1973 in the context of campus ministry! (www.faithtrustinstitute.org)

Residing with my husband in a lively retirement community near Olympia, Washington since 2009, I'm occasionally invited to provide a pastoral presence for persons and couples in this community and in our local UCC/Presbyterian church. As I use some of the same premarital resources we designed in 1975 with engaged couples in their 80's and 90's, I smile with deep gratitude to God and former colleagues who nudged/called me into campus ministry long ago!

Susan Yarrow Morris and husband Dave live in Panorama Retirement community in our own home on Chambers Lake, a part of the 140 acre campus, in Lacey, WA. Our active lives include an extended family, professional engagements, sharing table and hearth with many, musical adventures, Seattle Mariners and The Church of Baseball (of which I seem to be Bishop!), gardening, travel, and church/volunteer commitments.

It's Us or Them: Campus Ministry at Texas Tech
Roger Loyd

In his excellent history of the Northwest Texas Conference (*And are we yet alive?*), historian David J. Murrah devotes a section to what he calls "the camping war." He explains that, beginning in 1970, the conference began to offer alternative camps for senior high youth, one that came to be called "One Way" for more evangelical youth, the other was offered as the "traditional" camp, with its staff being known as the conference's liberals, including me. As Murrah narrates it,

> This issue, more than any others, became a dividing point that forced churches and individuals to make a distinct choice between "evangelical" and "liberal." That issue was the conference's summer camping program. (Murrah, 186-187)

During my three years of pastoral ministry in Northwest Texas (1971-74), I had been an active staff member of the traditional camps for high school youth. The bishop and cabinet, in June 1974, appointed me as the United Methodist campus minister for **Texas Tech University**, carrying with it the title, Director of the Wesley Foundation, as well as responsibilities for teaching in the religion department of Texas Tech, made up of its campus ministers. I gladly accepted the appointment and moved my family from Levelland to Lubbock.

As I described to Murrah, the conference's polarization affected the Wesley Foundation greatly. Though we made every effort to include students of all persuasions, recruiting them from United Methodist churches in the conference and beyond, the students who came to the Wesley Foundation were typically not those from more conservative congregations. About the work that my predecessor Gene Sorley and I did, Murrah quotes another distinguished historian, McMurry's Robert Monk, who said,

> Both Gene and Roger were trained in the newer theologies and were certainly better attuned to the changes in student perspective. ... But their theologies tended to represent the 'liberal' positions in the conference theology. (Murrah, 251)

Murrah proceeds to document the disagreement by discussing the ministries to college students offered through St. Luke's United Methodist Church, whose pastor was Ed Robb (a founder of the Good News movement). Murrah explains,

> The Texas Tech Wesley Foundation found itself competing with Robb's church for students. "[Robb] was very clear that he was pulling in a whole other direction than I was pulling," [Loyd] said, "and neither of us would change what we were doing." (Murrah, 251)

With this sort of push-and-pull going on, I neither had time nor interest to look to the wider world of campus ministry outside of Texas, so being asked to

257

prepare this document on my relationship with the National Campus Ministry Association is frankly a bit unusual, but sooner or later I often do what my friend Betsy Alden asks of me. I certainly know and respect many of my campus ministry colleagues around the country.

What did campus ministry at Texas Tech involve? First and foremost, it was an effort to connect with the students at the university, both those who identified as Methodist and others as well. We offered a varied program, including a weekly meal and discussion, worship opportunities, off-campus retreats to Sacramento and Ceta Canyon Methodist camps, summer hikes with students in the New Mexico and Colorado mountains, special events such as film festivals and late-Saturday-night viewing parties for "Saturday Night Live" ... as well as instruction in courses in New Testament and Old Testament, which students could take for credit through Texas Tech. Moreover, we prepared the musical "Celebrate Life!" for public presentation (in the basement of our Wesley Foundation, where we had a large room with a stage), and involved about fifty people as actors, musicians, director, stagehands, and the like. As best I recall now, we offered the musical three times, to good crowds. I also remember quite well the storeroom downstairs, in which was a full run of *Motive Magazine,* a vanguard Methodist periodical which went out of business in 1972 after publishing an issue written and edited by lesbians and feminists.

Looking back through the reports I submitted to the Northwest Texas conference, as found in the conference minutes of my years at Tech (1974-80), I also see that building maintenance and repair was a frequent topic. After all, the Wesley Foundation building had been built in 1950, through a generous gift from Dr. and Mrs. M. C. Overton of First Methodist Church, but needed continuing attention to such matters as a new roof, new linoleum in the basement (for which the students and I removed the old, asbestos-laden tile by hand, with straight-edged hoes, carrying it out to the alley and dumping it into the city's garbage bins by the barrelful), and updating and repairing the Wesley Lodge (a retreat center at nearby Buffalo Springs Lake owned by the Wesley Foundation), for which I was manager and schedule coordinator.

The 1978 report mentioned an event, World Hunger Emphasis Day, at Tech, sponsored by all of Tech's campus ministry groups, during which students fasted for 30 hours, donating the proceeds to an offering for CROP. It notes that State Senator Kent Hance spoke to the students during the event. (Conference Minutes, 1978, 141)

An excerpt from the 1979 report further illustrates the kind of campus ministry we offered:

But even more, the Wesley Foundation is people. Campus minister Roger Loyd, his staff, the people of the Wesley Foundation board, the students, the international groups, community groups, and many others... people who matter, being served by the Wesley Foundation. For instance, the Sunday night supper and worship time has more than doubled in attendance, because of the warmth of relationships existing among the people involved. Every activity is co-led, with one student leader aiding the campus minister in planning and carrying out the program. (*Conference Minutes*, 1979, 15)

The 1980 report lists various features of my campus ministry: "as teacher, as counselor, as United Methodist Student Loan officer, as group leader, as guest preacher, as one who is available to students and other Tech people." (*Conference Minutes*, 1980, 166) The same report notes that John Rakestraw, Jr., was on the staff of the Wesley Foundation in an unusual combination of duties, as campus ministry associate and part-time secretary!

During the years 1979-80, I was also called upon to be the part-time executive for the **Texas Commission on Campus Ministry**. My predecessors had been Wallace Chappell and George Yates, who passed along the records of that organization to me. When I became a member of the library staff of Bridwell Library at Southern Methodist University, I donated that collection to the library. Anyone wishing further information about the TCCM can consult their online guide (a statewide resource on higher education assembled by the library of the University of Texas). Robert Monk, himself a former campus minister, provided a helpful historical note to the records.

One may look back at the whole history of the Wesley Foundation at Texas Tech from its founding in 1935 by going to its website. As they celebrated their 75th year of service in 2010, they gathered historical information and presented it at the following location: http://ttuwesley.org/who-we-are/our-history.

From 1980 forward, the Wesley Foundation has clearly been identified with the more conservative theological parts of the conference. Its leaders have all graduated from Asbury Theological Seminary, where it has sent many of its graduates to prepare for ministry in Northwest Texas and beyond. Though I have characterized this group as "them" in my comments, I believe that they are doing their ministry to honor God and to serve Jesus Christ and his Church as best they can, as of course I did also.

As I reflect on those years of my life, the one regret I have is the requirement by SMU that I keep my appointment to Bridwell Library secret until June 1, 1980 (because the Board of Trustees had not yet voted its approval). The result was that I was unable to bid farewell to my students, my staff, or my board, but had to rely on letters to them instead. We were able to say good-bye to St. John's United Methodist Church, our across-the-street neighbor and strongest supporting congregation, and its excellent pastor, Ted Dotts; our families' friendship continues to this day.

Fortunately, the technology available now makes re-connecting with many of those students and others quite simple, through electronic mail and social media.

Roger Loyd retired as Director of the Divinity School Library at Duke in June 2012. He and his wife Leta continue to live in Durham, NC, where he devotes his energies to the church and various nonprofit agencies. But he reserves some of his time to support the Duke women's basketball team!

Speaking Truth to Power
By Rev. Bernadine Grant McRipley

My first exposure to campus ministry came as a member of the Trenton Campus Ministry (TCM) board. I was active with Christian education and ecumenical activities in my presbytery. At that time I was an ordained elder who had taken continuing education courses at Princeton Theological Seminary. When Mercer County opened a new community college the TCM board decided to start a campus ministry there. The supporting denomination churches were American Baptist, Presbyterian Church(USA), Evangelical Lutheran Church in America,, United Church of Christ and United Methodist Churches.. There was also some support from the denominations. Their other two ministries were traditional ones at a state college and private college. The community college was a new brand at that time with only commuting students. Moreover they did not come direct from high school (as many do now) so the age of most was in the late twenties. Evidently the TCM board had enough confidence in me to appoint me their chaplain (the college's terminology) *to Mercer County Community College* (MCCC).

MCCC 1973-1980
With a board open to experimentation and learning the nature of this new kind of campus and students, we were able to initiate a chaplaincy program as an integral part of student services. The most memorable ministry that we did was for an abused wife. A counselor informed me of the situation and asked for help. I was currently working with a female county executive working to start a shelter for abused women but at that time there was a long way to go. My board rallied to the circumstance, even informing me to take all the time I needed and helped with resources for the woman and her son. Contact with some local churches resulted in finding a safe place to live, free legal help and a place in a church daycare center for her son. When the woman asked why we were helping a stranger, I told her it was because we are Christians.

The ministry serving there called for establishing a presence with staff and their programs which resulted in being able to reach students. This included the Black Student Union, one of the few student groups on a commuting campus. I worked with the financial aid director and chaired a community outreach program to students on financial aid. Finances were a problem for many students. Our churches were sometimes called to provide a helping hand. The college gave me an office and support. In turn I was expected to participate as staff including serving on college staff search committees, including chairing the call of the dean of its urban campus. In MCCC's' beginning, our ministry was able to do more with our part-time ministry because the college was experimenting with reaching out to the community.. They sponsored a non-credit course which I taught on conserving the environment using denominational materials. It was open to the public which was part of the mission of the college.

TCM was able to cooperate with the college where the mission of the two overlapped. Before leaving Mercer to go to Trenton State, I received a UCC grant that was used to start a mentor program. It was continued by the next TCM chaplain, the Rev. Nancy Schluter who recently retired as chaplain at Rider University. ("Chaplain" is the title designated by the institutions.)

New Jersey United Ministries in Higher Education (NJUMHE), 1974-1980

When NJUMHE came into being, I was one of the campus ministers who attended loosely coordinated meetings. I became coordinator for NJUMHE. I divided my time between MCCC and UMHE, both were part-time. This was when I was also enrolled in the Master of Divinity program at Princeton Theological Seminary. NJUMHE was financially supported by American Baptist, Presbyterians, Reformed Church in America and the United Church of Christ. Although the United Methodists were not an official UMHE member, they also played an important role in the ministries to students and staff.

The ministries were located as far north as Newark and Hoboken and south as Camden, including the campuses I served part-time while being part-time UMHE administrator. There was only one full-time ministry at Rutgers, the State University. The ministries I served at MCCC and later at Trenton State College while also serving UMHE were greatly enhanced by the institutions and staff. The presidents at both institutions included our ministry because we provided much needed services to their students. I *was treated as adjunct staff and given office space and services. For UMHE I worked from home with no support staff. Some support came from the New Jersey American Baptist office and later from Reform Church staff. Much of my New Jersey UMHE travel was made possible by Clyde Robinson of the Presbyterian Church.*

Doing campus ministry while serving UMHE gave me a better sense of actual ministry at that time. At Trenton State College (now College of New Jersey), there were traditional aged students who lived in dorms on campus. However it was called a "suit-case" setting because many students went home for the weekend which meant ministry focused on Monday-Friday. This was also true at some other UMHE campuses. For me. this resulted in establishing a presence with faculty and staff whenever possible as well as with student groups. We were on their turf and learned to use that to our advantage. This allowed me to work with the student run Women's Center and its advisors from the Women's Study program. Since many of the students were education majors, I was able to get the local female superintendent of education to address the group. It was also my first opportunity to work with a female rabbi. It was illuminating for this group of heavily Roman Catholic women to engage with a female rabbi and an African American protestant minister (I was ordained as minister of Word and Sacrament by that time).

The ministry there somewhat mirrored life. I also worked with the Black Student Union members who were seeking their place on campus and into the world, including two African students who shared their dream of returning home and becoming a leader.

There was joy in weddings, especially in the memorial chapel in June, but the campus was not exempt from death. Four students were killed in a car crash and it affected the whole campus. The administration asked the Council of Campus Ministries to participate in a memorial service. In a mostly secular environment, it was clear the students responded to the spiritual care given to them. We clearly had a place on their turf.

At a National Campus Ministry Association meeting, I was able to get administration approval for two student services staffers to do training on avoiding or combating racist acts. I had participated in such a training event with staff and student leaders. There was a bonus to having TSC staff on our turf. Interacting with campus ministers gave them a deeper understanding that campus ministry is more than Bible study for a small number of students. This helped to interpret our ministry.

I eventually left a ministry I loved because I could no longer afford to serve in it. It served me well in a parish and gave me a solid foundation when I later worked in the PCUSA Washington D.C. office. Under the guidance of church policies I pursued justice issues as when serving in campus ministry. My colleagues in NCMA showed the value of higher education is not for prestige or economic advancement. The principles of those ministries always included justice. "Speaking truth to power" in Washington with Catholics, Protestants and Jews is harder than it sounds, but campus ministry never was a pushover.

After I retired from the Presbyterian office in Washington I began having health problems, so moved closer to my two sons and granddaughters, now all in PA. I have gotten involved in biblical theology, especially the biblical concept of justice and women in the Old and New Testaments. I am Parish Associate Emerita at Slackwood Presbyterian Church and am also involved with Planned Parenthood, using "Rev." in a highly Catholic area where that church is very visible and vocal. It is a pleasure to reconnect with campus ministry friends and colleagues. God bless!

Places I've Loved…And Never Really Meant to Go
By Helen R. Neinast

By any measure, it was a strange way to begin a career in campus ministry. I had just finished my M.Div. at Duke and was awaiting word of my first appointment.

My district superintendent finally contacted me (as a recent seminary grad and a female and part of a clergy couple, I was fairly far down the hierarchy of appointments). There were two appointments available—one a small church high in the New Mexico mountains, the other an ecumenical campus ministry at a state university near the Mexican border.

As it happened, their decision had been made: they "didn't want a woman to have to drive in the mountains in winter," so I was appointed to the campus ministry near the Mexican border. **Western New Mexico State University** is in Silver City—a beautiful town in the Gila Wilderness where copper mines were struggling and the university president would later be indicted for using state funds to add to his gun collection.

A strange beginning, and one with plenty of challenges: the student population was largely commuter, majority Hispanic, mostly Catholic and often worked two jobs to support their families. It was also very isolated—far from Santa Fe and Albuquerque, two hours to the nearest movie theatre.
And I loved it.

I learned how to reach students through the only stable population on campus—faculty and staff. I benefited from the very best in ecumenism—support from three denominations and a committed board. I made my first post-graduate foray into local and national politics: it was the 1970's and the Equal Rights Amendment was being debated. (I still can't believe it's never passed.) Our campus group dealt with the red herrings (unisex toilets) and the true realities (equal pay for equal work) and we sponsored educational events for town and gown. The local newspaper covered one of these events. The headline for the story was "Campus pastor says things were better when God was a woman."

That got my board's attention.

But they stood by me, and I was privileged to work with students, faculty, and staff on issues of spiritual formation, ethics, community and worship. My tenure in the Gila Wilderness was a time of great growth. I came to understand things about both myself and about ministry in higher education that might not have come to me any other way. (Though, just for the record, I can drive in the mountains during winter, and do so to this day.)

From southern New Mexico's sparse landscape I moved to Nashville, Tennessee's lush hills and immediately felt claustrophobic. Both the physical environment and the demands of working in an under-staffed national higher education agency were enormous. At a time when the church was (and still is) in dire need of ordained clergy, the agency that supported work with colleges and college students had seen severe staff cuts, and the local churches that supported local campus ministries were cutting budgets and closing ministries.

Once again, it was colleagues and mentors whose support and unabashed cheerleading helped me find my way through to campus ministers, chaplains, colleges and universities where the church's work was sometimes rag tag and tattered, sometimes thriving, sometimes desperate, sometimes wildly creative—but always on the front lines of ministry in higher education.

One of the first things that became apparent to me when I took the job of director in the *United Methodist Board of Higher Education and Ministry* is that ministry professionals in the field have a love-hate relationship with their judicatories. There's love for the support and resources judicatories can bring to bear, and there's hate for some of the ways those judicatories sometimes bring those support and resources to bear. Standing before my second or third such love-hate crowd, I redacted the old attorneys joke: "What do you call ten church bureaucrats dead in the bottom of a river? You call it a good start." Some laughter, some loosening of tension. I also told them I suspected most of them spelled Nashville with a silent "g"—gNashville—and from there we were on our way together.

The ten years in Nashville were extremely rewarding and extremely frustrating. Listening to those who had been called to ministry in higher education, with all their enthusiasm and energy was a privilege. Getting them the resources and support they needed was often an exercise in frustration. It is hard to impact something as big and unwieldy as a church agency trying to respond to the ever-changing landscape and mission of campus ministry.

But we tried. And it seems that what mattered could sometimes be as simple as a one-on-one phone conversation with a campus minister having a bad day (or semester) or as tedious as the efforts to publish a national directory for higher education that connected people for support and resources.

There were some important and concrete projects that came from GBHEM during those ten years. The United Methodist Student Movement was revived (within the context of renewed support for the ecumenical student movement) and became an important player on the national stage. Support for Campus Ministry Women increased, as did ministry with women on campus. Resources for ethnic-racial ministry were strengthened. The idea of campus ministry as "student work plus" became a bridge for conversation and understanding between campus ministries, annual conferences, and national work. And we produced a great number of resources from the national office geared toward students, campus ministers, chaplains, annual conference boards, and ecumenical agencies.

For the record, Dr. Julius Scott, chief administrator of the entire Division of Higher Education, was a pivotal mentor to me. He was energetic, kind and challenging. He treated me with a sense of respect and a sense of humor; he brought out the best in me...even in my rookie years. He challenged me to think, and taught me how to make hard decisions. I am in his debt; I carry great affection for him.

After ten years' of constant travel, the novelty of airports wore off and left me worn down. I took a break from ministry in higher education. I gave myself to writing (and supported myself with a paper route, an entirely different form of travel). I worked as chaplain at a psychiatric hospital in Florida. It was during this time I co-authored two of my favorite books for college students: *What About God? Now That You're Off to College* and *With Heart and Mind and Soul: A Guide to Prayer for College Students and Young Adults*. These were wonderful collaborations with Tom Ettinger, my husband of four years. I did small pieces of consulting work. I rested.

Then my husband, also a United Methodist minister, came across an opening for a United Methodist campus minister at **Emory University**. Tom was serving a local church at the time, but he had several years of campus ministry experience at two state universities in Florida. "Wouldn't it be great," he said to me, "if we applied for the position together?" I was happily ensconced as a hospital chaplain, and I'm never keen on moving, but I figured no campus ministry board would go out on a limb to consider hiring co-campus pastors. I could afford to be generous with Tom on this one.

So, I said, "Sure. Go ahead and apply for us." I settled back into hospital chaplaincy, certain that this was the end of it.

Six months later, we moved to Atlanta and spent ten years working together at Emory. From the beginning, our time there was extraordinary. And the end? The end, too, was extraordinary—so extraordinary that I reckon it's sufficient to say, "The rest is history."

Helen R. Neinast currently consults for the General Board of Higher Education and Ministry. She lives with her husband Tom Ettinger in the northeast Georgia mountains, where she continues her work as a writer.

For Such a Time as This
By Betsy Alden

Since we decided to solicit and collect the Pages of the Sages for NCMA's 50th Anniversary, I sat down in the fall of 2013 to write my own memoir. I now see that what follows reflects the gender/age differences between coming into campus ministry in the mid-1970's as a young wife and mother, receiving a very specialized "call" to work with community college ministry, and receiving the benefit of many memorable mentoring relationships with "older and wiser" campus ministers whose stories we are documenting in this collection.

*As I served on the North Texas UMC Board of Ordained Ministry from 1980-88, I came to realize that my call was similar to that of other **women** of that time, who had experienced the same recognition that their gifts and graces were needed in a particular context, and that ordained ministry was the best way to fulfill their particular calling. Since this was not the norm in the appointment system of the UMC, I wanted to describe how and why I responded to this unanticipated vocation to campus ministry, and what life was like, both personally and professionally, during the decade that I began my ministry, 1974-84. As my later feminist studies taught me, "the personal is political," so I see my career, in retrospect, as a series of serendipities and synchronicities, leading to my sense that, like many of my colleagues, like Esther, perhaps we were called "for such a time as this."*

Serendipities and Synchronicities, As They Happened

The Coming of Community Colleges to Dallas. In August of 1970 my neighbor suggested that she and I (both mothers of 3 pre-school children) drive out to the new campus-under-construction of the Dallas County Community College District—Eastfield College. She thought we each might find some part-time teaching with our hard-earned Masters degrees (hers in math, mine in English) from before babies. We traded hours with our baby-sitting club and headed out to Mesquite, TX, a blue-collar suburb 20 minutes from us on I-635, and came home to announce to our husbands that they would need to do some babysitting on a couple of weeknights that semester. I plunged into teaching 2 sections of Freshman Comp and Lit, startled to find my students ill-prepared for college-level work. Most were women who had never had a chance to attend college, Vietnam veterans on the GI Bill, balancing school with jobs and families, and aspiring young adults whose chance at a "career" depended on acquiring an Associate degree.

As I continued to teach at Eastfield, also picking up Saturday classes, I discovered that using a Journaling process greatly improved my students' abilities to write and reflect on their reading more coherently. I required that they each keep a journal, to be handed in three times in the semester-- not graded, but I told them I would read through them and make constructive comments. And did they write! This was the first time, many told me, that anyone had encouraged them to articulate their ideas and attitudes, and they had a lot to say! As I read and commented, I was more and more conscious that I did not have the professional training to respond to some of their existential crises and their outpouring of questions of faith and meaning in their lives, as they tried to connect with the probing and provocative literature they were being exposed to.

I had always been active in the Presbyterian Church, currently teaching our high school class, so I naturally wondered how the Church, at large, was ministering to the thousands of students who were now attending classes on the seven campuses of the flagship Dallas Community College District. I found out that most of the churches (often Southern Baptist or Catholic) were ignoring this aspect of their members' lives, even making the women feel they should be attending their Circle meetings or preparing for the church's Christmas Bazaar instead of studying for finals.

A Life-changing Meeting. In August of 1972, as our station wagon headed for our usual vacation with my family in the NC mountains, we stopped off at my husband's 15th high school reunion at a park in Nashville, TN. He was delighted to see his old friend Richard Beauchamp, now a UMC minister, who happened to ask me what I was doing these days. I told him that I was teaching and considering whether I should go back and get an MSW so I could respond more helpfully to my students' needs. And Richard said, "Well, my Yale PhD roommate is a Dean at Perkins School of Theology in Dallas, so when you get home, just give him a call and ask if you can sit in on some of their pastoral care classes."

The day after we returned from NC, I called LeRoy Howe, gave him Richard's greetings, and relayed the suggestion, to which LeRoy said, "Can you come in today so I can meet you? Classes start tomorrow." I hastily arranged for child care, made the drive to Perkins for the first time, and left LeRoy's office 2 hours later with a course schedule, an enrollment form ("You should just take the courses for credit in case you might want to transfer sometime"), a promise of a full scholarship, and the assurance that Perkins welcomed all, even though I had no intention of becoming a "minister."

"The Providential Call." Once on the Perkins campus, attending a few classes, I realized I was not much different from the other students (though I was a little older, with a family) and that my interests and inquiries were congruent with seminary students. By the next year, I went to see LeRoy again, wondering if, perhaps, I "should" enroll full-time (now that my children were 4, 6, and 8 and in school part of the day), but concerned that I did not know if I had a "call." Again LeRoy was very helpful; he referred me to Reinhold Niebuhr's description of "the providential call"—being in the right place at the right time to perform a particular ministry. He liked my idea of perhaps developing a new ministry with the community colleges and affirmed my call to this. So I filled out my official application to Perkins, using Dag Hammarskjold's quote from a bright yellow 1970's Abbey Press poster I already had on my kitchen wall. Later, I would realize how this became a self-fulfilling prophecy for my career. *"I don't know Who, or what, put the question, I don't know when it was put. I don't even remember answering. But at some moment I did answer Yes to Someone, or Something, and from that hour I was certain that existence is meaningful and that, therefore, my life, in self-surrender, had a goal."*

A Bit of Advice on the Run. In the summer of 1973, I went to see the Presbyterian minister who was in charge of the Committee on Care to apply for candidacy for ministry and was told that the idea of trying to become a minister with three small children was not wise, and that I should come back later "when your kids are older." Shortly after, I was headed downstairs to class at Perkins and a woman I had known in our Presbyterian church was walking upstairs, so I called out and told her of my experience, and she yelled back, "Forget the Presbyterians—they just make it all too hard for women. I've become a Methodist!" That fall our family decided to join Spring Valley United Methodist Church, one-half block from our house. I had attended a couple of classes with Don Benton, the pastor (who was working on his D.Min. degree), and we occasionally car-pooled to Perkins since his wife was my daughter's Brownie Scout leader. Don welcomed us enthusiastically, and that winter he told me that he wanted to sponsor me, along with four young men he had mentored, as candidates for the Order of Deacon, the first step to full ordination in the UMC.

Obviously I had not fulfilled the requirement of being active in a local UMC for the requisite period of time, so, as we were in his office one afternoon, he called Zan Holmes, then the District Superintendent, and told Zan that he would like to have that rule waived since I was "a mature woman with a family" who had always been active in her local Presbyterian Church, had completed the necessary hours of seminary, and the church would be "lucky" to have me. I was probably the only deacon candidate who did not know what a UMC "Administrative Board" was, but the Board of Ministry told me to study up on that, and I got through the first hoop. (The next summer I took Methodist Polity and learned it well enough to be elected Bishop at our mock-Jurisdictional Conference, an honor also probably bestowed because I brought a cake to class for John Wesley's birthday on June 17.) So I was duly ordained with the sixteen male deacons and one other married woman. My parents came for the ordination and were supportive, though they really could not imagine what I was getting myself into. And neither, of course, did I.

A Coincidental Introduction. In September of 1974, standing in line for the weekly Perkins Community Lunch, a seminary friend commented, "Oh,

Betsy, aren't you interested in doing some kind of ministry with the community colleges? The man behind you is Wally Chappell, Director of the Texas Campus Ministry Commission, and you should meet each other." I greeted Wally, who was very interested in my ideas, and he completely surprised me by saying, "I just got a notice of a workshop in Iowa next month on the very subject of community college ministry, sponsored by United Ministries in Higher Education. If you'd like to go, I'd be happy to send you to it."

Yes! I called my mom in Indiana, who agreed to come and take care of the kids so I could go to Des Moines, and from that moment on, my course was set. At that conference I met most of the national leaders in ecumenical campus ministry who would continue to influence and affect my work for the next 25 years. They all realized the church needed new strategies for ministry with commuter and community colleges, and had come together to brainstorm and create new models for campus ministry without a residential "center." As we shared our interests, Wayne Bryan, who had grown up in Dallas, suggested I be in touch with the Dallas Council of Churches to create a Task Force for Community College Ministry, which I promptly did. I had continued to teach part-time at Eastfield throughout seminary, so I had some ideas about how to work with faculty and local churches.

Since the community colleges used "mission" language in their own publicity, Dwight Judy, one of the pastors near the campus, helped me formulate the phrase "churches and colleges together in mission to their community." When I called the first meeting of this Dallas Council of Churches task force, *every* major judicatory sent a representative, realizing they needed to relate to the burgeoning numbers of their members who were attending, teaching, or working on the six campuses that surrounded Dallas and one right in the center of the city. (Statistics at the time showed that one of every four adults in Dallas County had some relationship to the community colleges.)

Learning to "Network." In 1976, I was given my "field education" placement as an intern at First UMC, Dallas, under Ben Oliphant and Jim Ozier. FUMC was open to experimental ministries and agreed to support my convening all of the big downtown churches for a Conference on Community College Ministry, which generated many ideas for innovative ways to connect churches and campuses. Then, with some success in spreading the word, I applied to the Texas Campus Christian Life Committee for a $5000 grant to "create" the **Dallas Community College Ministry (DCCM).** My seminary friend Martha Gilmore's husband Jerry happened to be on the Dallas Community College District Board, and he assisted in getting permission from the District for this new non-sectarian ministry to "be" on their campuses.

In 1977, several pastors and community leaders agreed to serve on a new DCCM Board, and I wrote and received a grant from the local Fikes

Foundation for $20,000 so that we might expand the ministry with part-time campus ministers on several of the campuses. We hired a Disciple minister, an AME seminarian, a Roman Catholic seminarian, and a part-time secretary and set up the office on the back porch of our home (with a propane space heater and two big desks salvaged from FUMC—one for me, and one for Norma, one of those "returning women students" I recruited as our new secretary.) Other judicatories and some churches "contributed" program money or staff, and pledged to include the DCCM in their campus ministry budgets.

Becoming a Campus Minister—for Real. I had been too busy creating the DCCM to finish my seminary coursework, but managed to test out of two leftover Church History courses so that I could finally graduate (summa cum laude and valedictorian—another score for women in ministry!) and be eligible for an appointment from the North Texas Annual Conference in May of 1978. Some of my Board members had managed to convince the UMC North Texas Conference Powers That Be to create a new appointment for the Dallas Community College Ministry—and to appoint me to it. But I was unprepared for the backlash on the floor of Annual Conference when this was announced. Some of my own *fellow* seminarians objected to appropriating the funds for a new campus ministry, and much discussion ensued about "how can one person offer ministry at seven campuses" (ignoring the fact that this would be an ecumenical ministry, also supported by other judicatories). Finally the matter was settled, as a respected elder stood and said he thought we should give it a chance: "Seems to me John Wesley did pretty well covering his parishes all over England!" The vote was called, the DCCM was officially sanctioned, and I had a new job.

I had continued to teach English throughout seminary, so my transition into the role of campus minister (and Director of the DCCM, under the Greater Dallas Conference of Churches) was not difficult. I asked faculty colleagues to let me come to their classes and speak on whatever subject might be relevant, so that I could become identified *as* a campus minister. In Sociology, I was given a textbook called *Organizations, Institutions, and Behavior* which made the point that, "Over the years, the Church has dealt with their *deviant* clergy in a number of ways—burning at the stake, excommunication, and more recently, giving them a pastoral role on college campuses." Remember the 70's?? That anecdote itself launched me into many fascinating conversations with students (and faculty) over the changing nature of the church in society.

On our initial five campuses, we tried anything people asked us to do. Jerry Miller worked with Eastfield's Continuing Ed program to offer courses for "Elders" (usually through local churches), using oral interviews to help them tell and record their life-stories (a new idea, pre-computers and the memoir-writing age!); Tom Slater at Mountain View created new courses on African-American studies; Father Christian helped music students develop and perform an Oratorio for local churches. I helped create the Everywoman

Center at Richland for returning women students. We held Religious Awareness Days at our campuses, working with Religion faculty to bring speakers to discuss everything from "Creationism and Evolution" to Harvey Cox on *The Secular City* and Margaret Mead on *Rethinking the Future* to a workshop on "Sex and the Single Girl." Obviously, many of these programs were of interest to the surrounding community, and brought new people to these amazing campuses. It was all win-win, with DCCM serving as a link, providing extra people-power through our networks of church connections, and garnering publicity for campus programming.

Seizing the Moment. A particularly fruitful connection occurred in 1978 when I saw a billboard on the North Dallas Tollway one fall afternoon which read "Oh Come, Ye Successful" (advertising Johnny Walker whiskey), and almost went off the road. I went right home, pulled out my *Alternative Christmas Catalogue*, written and published by Bob Kochtitzky in Jackson, MS, called him up, and said, "Can you come to Dallas so we can mount a campaign against the crazy commercialism of the holidays here?" He jumped on this chance to start an *Alternatives* crusade in Dallas; I rallied the campuses and area churches to host workshops; we had talk radio shows and much newspaper publicity; and hundreds of Dallas folk attended the workshops and developed strategies for reducing their Christmas consumerism. *"Whose Birthday Is It Anyway?"* was the Alternatives slogan, and it hit home in consciousness-raising. *CBS Evening News with Walter Cronkite* featured one of our workshops on TV, the DCCM produced an Alternative Holiday card to inform recipients that a gift had been given to a charitable organization in their name, and we filled orders for these for weeks-- at that time the Heifer Project and other non-profits had not yet caught on to this "marketing" idea.

Through UME, I met Neil Merritt, President of Ealing College of Further Education in London, and we brainstormed the idea of offering community college students a chance to "study abroad" at his college. A generous member of our DCCM Board (Jeanette Early) offered to fund scholarships for 2-4 students a semester, and the DCCD recognized her philanthropy as making a significant contribution to their students—and expanded the program.

The Dallas County Community College District, coupled with this investment by the Dallas Conference of Churches in the DCCM, gave us access on a broad scale to make a significant impact with our programming, and all of our staff worked at a constantly stimulating (and exhausting) pace because the rewards were so evident, and we were thrilled to be part of such a lively and satisfying ministry.

Joining the National Campus Ministry Scene. In the summer of 1978, I thought I should connect with the larger world of professional campus ministry and, after arranging for coinciding summer camps for my children, I ventured off to the National Institute for Campus Ministry (NICM) week-long conference in Denver with Jim Forbes, Bernard Lafayette, Bob Johnson, and Brother David Steindl-Rast. Shortly thereafter, I was invited to be one of NICM's seven new interfaith "Program Directors" across the US, to support and develop programs in our regions. At one of our meetings in New Orleans, as a Hillel Director led us (and the crowded roomful of tourists waiting in Preservation Hall for the next jazz set) in singing "Kum BaYa," I realized how happy and lucky I was to have escaped suburbia and bridge clubs for this.

By spring of 1979, when Bill Hallman and Clyde Robinson asked me to join UME's Community College Task Force (the group that had sponsored that first community college ministry conference I had attended in 1974), they suggested that we produce a "how to" slide show. They commissioned Wayne Bryan, who had become a professional photographer and script-writer, to come to Dallas and film the DCCM in action. (Ironically, it was Wayne who had first suggested I go to the Dallas Council of Churches to get started. And he had just produced another UME slideshow "Islands and Bridges" featuring the community college ministry of Robert Thomason in Jacksonville, FL.) The resulting production, "DCCM: The Church and the Community College in Mission," launched me into "Show and Tell" venues all over the country, and, happily, quite a number of new community college ministries resulted from sharing these models.

The UMC Board of Higher Education was interested in our work and asked me to be a consultant for community college ministry with UMC Wesley Foundations; they also sent me to the Ministries to Blacks in Higher Education (MBHE) annual meeting in Atlanta, and I was appointed to that board, as well as being elected to the UMC National Committee on Campus Ministry (1979-83). So I had the chance to employ all my networking skills between the various campus ministry organizations, connecting efforts initiated by one of them to each of the others and sharing insights. Clearly, it was the "right place, right time" for an energetic young clergywoman to bring the (mostly) men-in-charge together.

Praxis: Inventing a Model for Service-Learning. Meanwhile, in Dallas, I invited some Richland students to participate in Faith Development interviews—based on a research project my friend Jim Fowler had done at Harvard, showing "stages" of faith development analogous to Piaget's and Kohlberg (and later Gilligan)'s models for cognitive and moral development. In this intensive series of interviews, I became aware that these mostly "adult" community college students felt their lives were much too scattered—with school, jobs, family, only "18 minutes of discretionary time" on campus (to get from the parking lots to their classes!)—and that they felt they were missing a "meaningful" connection to the "real world" of social and community issues.

I had known, through national campus ministry connections, of Thad Holcombe's Praxis Project which he operated as part of the Free University in Tulsa, OK. I had read liberation theologians in seminary and knew the revival of Aristotle's term for "experiential education" by Gustavo Guttierez in base communities in Latin America, based on the pedagogy of Paulo Friere, advocating "action/reflection/action/reflection" for "making meaning" of one's experience in deeper and more satisfying ways. So I proposed that DCCM work with a few faculty to offer students an alternative to the required freshman English "research paper" by providing opportunities for service in the community throughout a semester, including concurrent "reflection sessions" with other students, and a final oral or written presentation (with appropriate footnotes and documentation) on their new understandings. We called it "Praxis" and within a few semesters we had over 900 students enrolled—in a wide variety of courses.

UME arranged for our community college task force to attend the national meetings of the Association of Community and Junior Colleges (AACJC) to give presentations on this successful partnership between the churches, the community, and the campuses, and I discovered that other campuses (mostly universities) were beginning to engage students similarly in what was soon designated "service-learning." Soon I was asked to serve on the Board of the new International Partnership for Service-Learning and was exposed to some of the best practices in this emerging pedagogy. The PRAXIS Project we developed also became a model for engaging students in community college ministry, and we developed a packet of materials to assist others in creating their own programs. Sybil Shuck, my stalwart secretary (and former Board member), managed a filing system for all these paper records, which was eventually put onto a computer data base in 1990.

Keeping It All Together. In May of 1982, I received my Doctor of Ministry degree from Perkins/SMU-- my dissertation title was *Vocational Discernment: Reclaiming "Calling" for Laypeople in the Church*). I was finally free from "owing" some professor a term paper (I had to request several "extensions" over these years!)—after ten continuous years of seminary/post-graduate work, teaching, and creating the DCCM. My only response to "How can/did you do it all?" was that I was blessed with abundant energy, a quick mind, and a lot of help from my friends—and that God must have "wanted" me to do it because I was sustained and enlivened by almost each venture. When I began Perkins at age 30, my children were 3, 5, and 7; when I finished at 40, they were 13, 15, and 17. Somehow I had managed to keep up with being a Cub Scout den mother (motto: "Keep it simple; make it fun!"); "Witchie-Poo" Hallowe'en visitations at their elementary schools (and at Perkins, where the Dean saw me racing to class still in costume and yelled, "I knew we could count on you, Betsy!"); fostering a pregnant teenager and helping her finish high school; piano and ballet carpooling; doctor and orthodontia appointments; soccer games and Eaglette performances; help with homework ("Why don't you do your speech on the E.R.A.?"); teaching the Confirmation classes for Becky and Joey at Spring Valley UMC; arranging for family vacations and summer camps, birthday parties, and holiday occasions, usually with several extra folk around our ping-pong table for Thanksgiving dinners. Family and ministry constantly overlapped, with the DCCM office in our house, enlisting the kids to collate and fold brochures; UME and NCCM colleagues staying with us; DCCM Board parties; and much juggling of schedules, travel, and help with school projects. Katy, Becky, and Joey had become teenagers who took it all in stride. Unfortunately, my husband felt that he had not "signed up" for this lifestyle, but we agreed to stay married till the children were out of high school, and he was a steady presence for them as I continued to pursue my career.

Two defining moments stand out as confirmation of my calling to ministry in higher education. In 1979, several male clergy encouraged me to "run" for a place on the General/Jurisdictional Conference slate the next year (as soon as I was eligible), so that a clergywoman might be elected to the delegation. (They also let me know that if I wanted to "move up" in the clergy hierarchy I "should" be in parish ministry.) So that summer I spent several days on Retreat and worked my way through Dick Bolles' *The Four Boxes of Life and How to Get out of Them,* using his personal values clarification exercises to discern what mattered most to me. This time apart for reflection made it very clear that I did NOT want to pursue ministry in the local church, with its attendant jockeying for power. I loved being able to teach and work with students and faculty and to connect the churches with the campuses. I wanted to be with people who shared my interests in education, to prioritize my children above a parish's demands, and I had no desire to climb the ladder of church bureaucracy. So that settled that—and I have never been tempted to forsake my allegiance to ministry in higher education.

A while later, around 1982, I was attending a UMC National Committee on Campus Ministry meeting in NYC, and had brought my teenaged daughter Becky with me. As she joined us to wander the city streets and interact with my colleagues over dinner, she turned to me and said, "Mom, these are your kind of people." I had intuitively known this, but I was delighted that she recognized this, as well!

When the seminary wanted to offer a course on campus ministry, my UME colleague Mark Rutledge and I developed a syllabus for a two-week summer course, which we offered at Perkins and at St. Paul, and shared with others. I attended my first NCMA Conference in Georgetown the summer of 1982, and was thrilled to be with so many ecumenical colleagues who shared a vision for the church's ministry in higher education, as we listened to concerts by Sweet Honey in the Rock, spoke with our Senators, and studied "Politics, Peacemaking, and Poetry" with Will Campbell. Phil Berrigan was in jail, but his activist wife Elizabeth McAlister came and inspired our new Campus Ministry Women's group.

Thereafter, I attended every NCMA Conference until 1997, and when Mark Rutledge and I were married in 1987, many of our NCMA colleagues

274

came to our Balloon Fiesta wedding in Albuquerque, officiated by dear friends Helen Neinast and Clyde Robinson.

A New Job Prospect. PRAXIS/Service-Learning was booming and becoming well-known throughout Dallas, we now had paid staff on all seven campuses of the DCCD, and I, as Director, found that I was spending more of my time being an administrator and personnel director than a campus minister. I decided to apply for a one-semester sabbatical, with my salary going to my able assistant Jerry Miller, while I took time to assess "Where to, from Here?" My proposal was approved and I looked forward to my first real "rest period" ever. And then United Ministries in Education advertised for a national *UME Communications Coordinator*, and I heard from many (and also felt myself) that "this job has your name on it," so I applied and was hired by Bill Hallman in the fall of 1983, just before I was to begin my sabbatical. Fortunately, everything was in place for Jerry to "take over" the daily operations of DCCM, but my leaving meant that we had to find new office space (i.e., not in our house), a new Director would need to be appointed by the UMC, and all the history and info that was in my head and paper files had to be transferred to my successor. And I would need a new secretary and have to set up my UME office (which could still be in my home), and be ready to start in May!

So—no time for personal projects! Just a little more leisure from the day-to-day, as I personally "recruited" the clergywoman (Georjean Blanton) I thought would be best to take over as Director, lobbied with the UMC for her appointment, was given a new DCCM office in the Presbyterian church near Brookhaven, cleaned and cleared boxes of files and records, sadly said farewells to my amazing DCCM Board, found a terrific new UME secretary in the neighborhood, and we purchased our first computer.

The first decade of my ministry was coming to an end, and I was about to embark on the next adventure. One child had left for college at the University of Texas, and two others were close behind as NCMA met in Fort Worth in 1984 to discuss Time-Management with Ann McGee-Cooper and Spirituality with Paul Jones, and I was initiated into the UME national staff of seven "bureaucrats" who carried their denomination's portfolios for campus ministry—Bill Belli for the American Baptists, Larry Steinmetz for the Disciples, Mark Harris for the Episcopalians, Gary Harke for the Moravians, George Conn and Clyde Robinson for the Presbyterians, Verlyn Barker for the UCC, Bill Hallman as our Chair, and, thank goodness, Shirley Heckman for the Church of the Brethren, so I had another terrific mentor—and a roommate for all those meetings for the next five years.

We worked cooperatively with the United Methodist Board of Higher Education and Ministry (especially with Helen Neinast, who became my dear friend and traveling companion) to create and publish resources like the *Directory of Campus Ministers* (with 1700 entries and all the judicatory and ecumenical organizational contacts), *Church and Campus Calling*, and UME's quarterly *Connexion* newspaper--all involving *printed* copies, in the days before digital computers, email, Fed-Ex, and cell phones! We spent lots of time on airplanes and at our Selectric typewriters, and long-distance phone charges were built into our budgets!

Verlyn Barker has nicely documented UME's work in his memoir, and it was my job to publicize all of that with the sponsoring denominations until 1989, when national ministry support staff had to be reduced. But I was happy to be offered a full-time position teaching English at Central New Mexico Community College in Albuquerque, where my new husband Mark Rutledge was campus minister at the University of New Mexico. We worked together to develop an extensive service-learning program on both campuses for seven years, while I also served as Program Coordinator for NCMA and Director of Clergy Continuing Education for the New Mexico Council of Churches. We spent our summers enjoying the free travel perks of my daughter's new job with American Airlines, doing house-swaps in the British Isles, conferences at Ghost Ranch, and caring for aging parents in Indiana and California.

The Grand Finale of Serendipities. In 1995, Oli Jenkins, the UMC campus minister at Duke University, which was my alma mater, was visiting us in Albuquerque and suggested that we should "swap" jobs and homes for a year. We loved the idea, and, after a year of negotiations with our Boards, Mark and I set out for Duke in August 1996. As we crossed into North Carolina, having missed the "green" for 30 years while living in the Southwest, I remember saying, "I don't think we are going back!"

During our "year" at Duke, chaplain Will Willimon mentioned to the newly-appointed Director of the brand-new Kenan Institute for Ethics that she might want to talk to me about service-learning as a pedagogy for its goal of "infusing the curriculum with ethical discourse." Elizabeth Kiss and I had lunch, and I had a new job, creating and directing Duke's wonderful Service-Learning Program for the next ten years, teaching a Public Policy course on Women as Leaders, and settling in to our new life with Duke/Durham, just three hours' drive from the family retreat my parents had built in 1969 in the Blue Ridge mountains. My mother's desire had always been to get her family back to North Carolina, and now I had truly come "home."

Then imagine my delight when, coincidentally with my 2008 Retirement party, Duke's new President Richard Brodhead titled his Mission Statement "Knowledge in the Service of Society." This is what campus ministry has always been about, and I hope it is what I have always been about—I could not have landed in a better place.

"And the end of all our exploring will be to arrive where we started and to know the place for the first time." (T.S. Eliot)

"Officially" retired, Betsy Alden continues to teach Duke's Intergenerational Ethics class, mentor younger women, and keep up with her three children, five grandchildren, and campus ministry friends around the country. She has been part of a Women's Spirituality group in Durham for fifteen years, and she and Mark love to read and listen to good literature on audiobooks on their walks and Road Trips. They welcome friends in both their Durham and mountain homes, and cherish these relaxing times with family and friends, including many Sages of NCMA and nine of Betsy's Duke '64 dormmates, who gather each year. An unexpected gig has been traveling together to perform destination weddings all over the country for many of Betsy's former Duke students!

Every Morning is Easter Morning
By Alice Riemer-McKee

My love for campus ministry started as a college student at Carroll University (then Carroll College) from 1957-1961. As college students, we met at First Methodist Church in Waukesha, Wisconsin with a member of the church as our leader. He introduced us to the Methodist Student Movement in Wisconsin, and for me the rest is history. I soon received a state leadership position and for the next three years, participated in jurisdictional events and national happenings. I met Jamison Jones from Nashville and the Board of Higher Education and Campus ministry and traveled with him to events around the country. My senior year in college I served as president of the state MSM for Wisconsin.

After graduating from Carroll, I took a teaching position in Neenah, Wisconsin. Because I was lonely as a single woman in town, and with the blessings of two of the area pastors, I started an Ecumenical Adult group for singles like me. The group grew quickly and at the end of the year, one of the pastors called me in to talk about going to seminary. I was flabbergasted! I didn't know that women went to seminary, and I didn't even know where the nearest one might be. He walked me through the process, the conference gave me a scholarship named Ideas Unlimited, and I broke my teaching contract for the next year. Soon I boarded the train for Evanston, Illinois and then Garrett Biblical Institute (now Garrett Theological Seminary). Thirteen women were enrolled at that time, and not one in the BD degree program (now Master of Divinity degree). It was my dream to return to Wisconsin to work with students on one of the major university campuses as a Christian Educator.

Soon a young man named Doug McKee arrived at seminary from Meadville, Pennsylvania, having graduated from Penn State and serving as president of Inter Varsity. We met and were married several months later. Doug finished Garrett and I was told by my bishop here in Wisconsin that they would give Doug an appointment as a pastor, but there was no place for me. It was something about couples not working in the same conference! I never asked what that meant, and I am sure he was glad I didn't push it further. So, instead of finishing Garrett, I taught second grade in the inner city of Chicago. Doug was later ordained in the East Wisconsin Conference where he served local churches for almost ten years and then was called by a senior pastor in Colorado Springs in 1975 to join his staff. We moved west and lived there for over thirty years. Doug joined the Rocky Mountain Conference.

In 1978, we moved to Laramie, Wyoming, where Doug was appointed to serve as Interim Senior Pastor, and I was asked if I was interested in exploring the idea of rebuilding the Wesley Foundation at the *University of Wyoming*, Laramie. It had been inactive for many years, and I was to get back to the conference in a year to tell them if it might be feasible. However, in less than two months, I had a group of students meeting with me at the church who wanted more than just talking about the future. They made it clear that they were ready to move forward now. Our funding at that time came from an oil well near Cody, Wyoming and five cents for every gallon of gas pumped at a local gas station in Laramie. The Foundation owned the land on which the gas station stood. The rest is history as there has been a campus minister appointed to the Wesley Foundation ever since.

In 1979, Bishop Melvin Wheatley called Doug and me, and asked if we would be interested in moving to Boulder, CO to serve as campus ministers at the Wesley Foundation there. We were thrilled to be asked and we spent eleven years serving the *University of Colorado* campus. Doug was appointed and I was hired by the local board. We defined the ministry as being a denominational ministry that worked ecumenically. We were proud of our roots as a strong and historic Wesley Foundation, but we were also just as proud of our work with the ecumenical community on campus and in the wider Boulder community.

Since my love of campus ministry was birthed in the Methodist Student Movement and Doug's was nurtured through Inter Varsity, it became obvious very quickly that we appealed to two very different groups of students. I always said that if a student walked in the door and was wearing Docker pants, an Izod shirt with the collar up, and was a B School or Econ major, they were coming to see Doug. If the student was an Arts and Science major or Civil Engineering student, and glad to be dressed—they were coming to see me. I think this is one of the examples of why we were a good team. Doug talked an evangelical "language" that was new to me. I shared my love of a church beyond our walls with him, and it became a strong piece in how we did campus ministry. Bishop Wheatley said that if we did not offer Sunday worship to the students, he would reappoint Doug somewhere else. For the Bishop this piece was crucial. In those days, this model worked, and worship meant fifty to sixty students on a Sunday morning and communion every Wednesday night at 10:00 p.m. Maybe this is why during our time at Wesley, eight students entered full time ministry in the United Methodist Church, the Seventh Day Adventist Church and the United Church of Christ -- one is now a professor at Phillips Seminary in Oklahoma. The United Methodist students are now serving churches in Minnesota, Wisconsin, Colorado, Montana and Georgia. Today we also have students actively working in their local churches of many denominations here in the states and abroad.

Participating in local and national mission projects was part of our yearly schedules. As I write this, I am remembering sending students to Haiti, to projects within Boulder and throughout Colorado and beyond. We taught our students the fine points of protesting such things as the manufacturing of triggers for neutron bombs at Rocky Flats—located between Boulder and Golden, Colorado. Sunday nights at 4:00 p.m. you could find us as a group sitting along the road across from the plant and having worship. That plant finally closed.

A lot of energy and time went into monitoring the many cults and sects that found the Boulder/Denver area attractive. At one point, it was estimated that there were close to a hundred groups in the area. We documented such things as how large the group was, where they were located, who the leader was, the average length of stay for a person who joined, what they were eating and wearing as well as the daily routine. Some were very small, others were known nationwide. Names that come to me now include The Unification Church at 777 Broadway—a former sorority house on campus; the Church of Scientology which had a large office building right down town in Boulder; the Boston Church of Christ and their infamous chocolate chip cookies that they passed out during exam time in the dorms; and my favorite because of their very brightly painted bus—Jesus Christ Lighting Amen, who spent summers in Boulder and winters in Florida.

I would be remiss if I didn't mention fund-raising which was a major part of my position as director. In those days, I found it easy to raise money for campus ministry from the conference, the local churches, parents and alums. I am sure I could not do it again today. Doug and I also held very visible conference positions—I chaired COSROW and he chaired Board of Pensions and Health Benefits. This put us in front of the conference in ways beyond campus ministry which I think was a plus.

The local ecumenical campus ministers were very active as an organization and we always presented a united front when approaching the university and other organizations for recognition or information.

Many of the students still write about the power of the retreats we held each semester as well as the classes taught, like Disciple 1 and 2. They also remember Easter Eve services that sometimes included a baptism of a student, Easter Sunrise Services up on Flagstaff Mountain and singing "Every Morning is Easter Morning" by Avery and Marsh as their theme song at many worship events throughout the year.

It was not all work and no play. Social activities were popular depending on the year.

Thanks to the UMC Board of Education and Don Shockley, we were able to secure grant money for an Ethnic Ministry Center. For at least five years we had three ethnic pastors doing part time work on campus working with students.

In the midst of serving the campus, Doug and I raised two sons in Boulder. They were as comfortable on campus as were the students. They could dumpster dive at the end of the semester like pros, have summer jobs on campus, enjoy some special friendships with the students, live in a home located right across the street from campus that was open to students day and night, experience rock concerts in the football stadium which was almost in our front yard, watch Frank Shorter train for the Olympics as he ran by our home, get paid for being in a live segment of "Mork and Mindy", and benefit from the excellent Boulder schools.

In 1990, I decided to complete my seminary education and work towards ordination. We both asked for local church appointments in the conference, and we were sent to western Colorado where we served separate local congregations. Obviously, it was no longer a problem for couples to work within a conference so I enrolled at Wesley Seminary in Washington, D.C., and through a special summer program I finished and was ordained in the Rocky Mountain Conference. We were asked in 1998 to serve together at Hilltop UMC in Salt Lake, and we retired from there. Doug had been diagnosed with prostate cancer in 1994 and his cancer returned while we were in Utah. It was his wish to die in Colorado so we moved back again to Grand Junction, Colorado where he passed away in 2002.

I moved to Wisconsin in 2004 as I have a son and family here. And as life often goes full circle, I am now on an area committee looking at the possibility of bringing campus ministry back to the University of Wisconsin, Oshkosh. As I share some of my long ago experiences with campus ministry with the group, I wonder how I would serve the campus today. This is what I am trying to discern as a committee member.

Doug and I made a strong commitment to participate in jurisdictional and NCMA organizations, where many of you reading this became our friends. As I am enjoying your writings and stories, I am recalling some special times shared with many of you. Thank you for all that you taught us and for your friendships.

Thanks be to God who called all of us to serve the campus then and now.

"Every morning is Easter morning, from now on. Every day is resurrection day, the past is over and gone!" Amen.

The McKees returned to the local parish until 1999, when Doug's prostate cancer returned. Their final service on Christmas Eve in Salt Lake City ended with the two of them walking down the aisle at midnight singing "Joy to the World." It was a glorious ending. After Doug died in 2002 in Grand Junction, CO, Alice moved to Neenah, Wisconsin in 2004 where she is near a son and family including two of her four grandchildren. She is now volunteering in a program for people with stage one/stage two dementia and their caregivers.

Sage Report
by Ruth Dunn

Am I really a sage? Maybe so, if that means I've learned something in 80 years! One of the things I've learned is that my life has been full of surprises, which most of the time worked out better than what I had planned.

In terms of history, I had planned to become a conservationist with a state or national park, and went to Miami University in Ohio to learn how to do that. But as I anticipated graduation in 1956, I discovered that at that time, women couldn't do it - so I was almost back to square one.

Fortunately, I had also taken a minor in religion, with a dynamite professor from the University of Chicago Divinity School named Stan Lusby. I immediately responded to his process theology orientation, and took every class he taught. At the same time I was involved all four years in the Presbyterian Westminster Foundation, and had a very good experience there. The campus minister was Dale Robb, who actually lived at the Westminster House with his wife and two small children. (I wonder now how they survived that!) Among other valuable experiences, Dale sensitized me to a number of social justice issues, especially ones related to racism. We got involved in a number of local situations, like barber shops and the NAACP, and campus issues like restrictive clauses in Greek organizations, and I was hooked for life.

By 1956 denominational campus ministries were burgeoning, and many were hiring women as second staff persons, many without training. With Dale's encouragement, I decided to go for a campus ministry career, with training, and Stan Lusby got me a full scholarship to the Divinity School. He warned me it would be tough - said, "You'll really suffer up there!" and I did, because I was stretched far beyond what I could have imagined, but it was the best education I could have gotten. Professors included people like Court Rylersdam, Walter Harrelson, Marcus Barth (son of Karl), Joe Sittler, Bernard Meland, Bernard Loomer, Jaroslav Pelikan,and Seward Hiltner. They did make me suffer, but I made a lot of friends who suffered with me, and I couldn't have asked for better.

By the time I had finished, Presbyterians were ordaining women, but the campus ministry thing fell apart. The denominational programs were collapsing and partnering ecumenically with each other, and many ministers were losing their jobs. The one interview I got was for Religion Coordinator at Cornell, and was told I would have intimate relationships with 2000 students. I didn't get that job!

But I had met a student from Indianapolis named Paul Crafton, who with his wife Sue was Director at the Westside Christian Parish in an African American ghetto area in Chicago. They were in charge of a house in which lived several young conscientious objectors (Vietnam era) sponsored by the Brethren Volunteer Service, who worked with youth in the area. When Paul graduated, they started a similar program in Indianapolis, and I went with them.

After helping set up that program, I moved to New York City, where I worked in a couple of community centers sponsored by the YWCA in housing projects in the Bronx, and I got a lot of first-hand experience working in the inner city. I got involved in the Judson Memorial Church in Greenwich Village, pastored by Howard Moody, and through them attended the March on Washington.

When the YW left those programs (weren't good at co-ed work) I went back to Indy, lived at Fellowship House and worked at a Presbyterian inner city center, where eventually Headstart got started. I became a Headstart teacher there, and later in a Catholic School. That's where I made friends with a liberal thinking nun, and together we started an interfaith study group, and also became involved in a new Christian Inner City Association. Through that experiencee I was present when Bobby Kennedy announced to an ethnically mixed group of folks that Martin Luther King had been killed that morning in 1968.

I was invited to teach at the preschool in the lab school at **Indiana State University in Terre Haute**, and while doing that volunteered with a UCCF program there. When that campus minister left, I replaced him -- I was a campus minister at last!

The first year was wonderful - I loved it! I also loved my collegial relationships with campus ministers at seven other state campuses through the Indiana Commission of United Ministries in Higher Education. Unfortunately, there was also a Wesley Foundation just down the street and ICUMHE decided they would no longer fund either of us unless the boards merged into one. That was accomplished at the middle of my second year, and I was established as co-director with the Wesley pastor. However, he was not about to work on that basis with a woman. I remember vividly the day he slammed his fist on his desk and said, "You will NEVER be my equal!" He got the board to bust me to his personal assistant, and was allowed to control everything I did. He embarrassed me in public every way he could, and made life miserable for me. I didn't know then how to put it into the words, but I was being professionally abused in much the same manner as if it were spousal abuse.

I had to hang in for the rest of the semester, and certainly learned a lot about what it feels like to be an abuse victim. Even the three men who had come to the new board from my old board told me not to complain - they wouldn't support me because they didn't want to appear un-ecumenical. I left at the end of the semester.

It wasn't until, after a series of odd jobs, that I became a campus minister at **Vincennes University**, and finally came to terms with the anger and humiliation of that previous experience. In those days we had Campus Ministry Women, NCMA, and Presbyterian Ministers in Higher Education meetings all at the same place. At my first CMW meeting (at Lewis and Clark in Oregon) I was encouraged to tell the whole story. They listened, without judgment, and. cried with me, and the healing started. I became a different kind of person after that. (I almost left this part of the story out, but decided it was too strong a part of what had happened to me as a woman campus minister not to tell.)

Those three organizations were very important to me, and I attended for about ten years. I value the colleagues I met there, and am happy I will see some of them this summer. One of the most important was Clyde Robinson.

I had 19 good years at Vincennes. Vincennes University Junior College was a state owned two year school, with dormitories, so it was both residential and commuter. UCCF was ecumenical, with a good number of local churches involved. I learned a lot about board development, and fund raising! When I started there, ICUMHE forbid us to raise money; by the time I left we didn't get anything from them if we didn't raise half of our funds. That's part of the history of campus ministry!

At first many of my students were from mainline denominations; by the end most were from evangelical churches or no church at all. Discussions were often lively - I remember a Bible study where a Missouri Synod Lutheran guy was complaining because they weren't even supposed to smile in his church, and a Pentecostal girl said "Wow! Last Sunday I ran all around the sanctuary three times before I collapsed." We certainly learned a lot from each other.

In addition to doing things like Bible study, worship, weekly fellowship meals, retreats and other typical things, I was the unofficial chaplain to the university. I had many faculty and staff contacts, did some programming with them, participated in many memorial services for students and faculty/staff, and in graduations. The university president and I respected one another, and on that small campus a lot was possible. It was interesting to be invited to participate in programs we had started which the university took over, like a Christmas tree- lighting service for the community and the school, and a coffee house for students. I guess they were our gift to the university.

Some important things I initiated: cooperation with an art professor and some Chinese students in the construction of their own Lady Liberty statue which became a prayer center during the Tiananmen Square situation, prayer services for the community before and after the first Middle East war, being ready to stand up to the KKK when they threatened to disrupt a homecoming parade (they never did it) and several multicultural retreats in cooperation with the international student advisor (from Afghanistan) and the Black student advisor. A colleague, Bob Epps, led one of those retreats. We were part of a watch group when trains carried nuclear waste from Trident submarines through Vincennes. A highlight was getting to know a South African student who was a member of the ANC, and came to the US when death threats were made on him. He got Naomi Tutu to speak at VU when I took him to see her in Terre Haute. I was fortunate to go on trips to the Yucatan peninsula of Mexico with Jack Diel, and to China with some other campus ministers from Chicago (whose names my brain is blocking.)

About eight years after I started we invited the Catholic Diocese to share our facility - a former Methodist parsonage - and have Newman Center there. I had a creative partnership with several young Catholic campus ministers. I also had a good relationship with the university counseling center, and a number of the faculty in various departments, like the nursing school.

I managed to get a D.Min in Pastoral Care and Counseling at Christian Theological Seminary in Indianapolis by commuting for several years on my day off, and did a lot of special counseling with women in the community who had been abused.

In about my 17th year, I had to get some students to haul me to my feet after sitting with them on the floor, and I said, "Just call me Grandma!" Well, they did. From then on that was my title. I realized it was a term of endearment and respect, but I knew it was time to think about retiring, which I did 18 months later in 1998.

I have moved to Ohio, where my brother and his wife gave me an acre of ground on a farm they still own but don't live on anymore, and I put up a nice double-wide house. It is peaceful and quiet here, and surrounded by fields and woods. I love it! I have many members of a large extended family not far away - in and around Cincinnati and Oxford -- and many friends, but I can have solitude when I need it.

I did stated supply and interim stints at a couple of small churches. and because I can't get campus ministry out of my blood I became president of the Ohio Campus Ministry Board, (one of the last such in the US, and going out in December, but will stay as a volunteer organization for campus ministers), moderator of the Higher Ed Committee of the Synod of the Covenant (Ohio and Michigan), and recently a member of Campus Ministry Advancement. The Synod had been exciting because it is very diverse racially and ethnically, and very committed to social justice and peacemaking involvement. I will go off membership of all three organizations at the end of this year, and maybe then I will learn how to retire.

I have already slowed down – with more time to read, relax and have fun. I am doing some painting – oils, watercolor, and pastels, and someday might be able to call myself an artist. I have a small involvement in Presbytery, and am in touch with the Presbyterian Peace Fellowship and Rick Ufford-Chase.

I have had the opportunity to meet Walter Brueggemann, who lives near Cincinnati, and attend several series of his lectures and discussions. I am a big fan, and he helps me to work on my present concern – how can I, as a retired clergywoman, make a contribution to the healing of this terribly broken world? I don't have any answers yet, but at least I'm not as discouraged as I used to be before I met Walter.

As for reflections on all of this - my career as a campus minister, after all the preliminary jobs and education that helped prepare me for it, has definitely helped define the woman I have become. I have learned that God works in mysterious and surprising ways, offering many of those opportunities for growth that process people call eternal objects. The ones I have chosen to take advantage of have transformed me in many ways.

I have slowed down, now that I am 80, and have some neuropathy and arthritis problems, but I'm not ready to throw in the towel and stop being involved as best I can – but at a much more relaxed pace!

Portals of Love and Openers of Doors
An Invocation for NCMA's 50th
By Odette Lockwood-Stewart

Friend and colleague Rabbi Patricia Karlin-Neumann quoted a student who, in a workshop with poet and playwright Merle Feld, wrote these words when she was asked, "If you were to write your own Mezuzah..."

God, you know I have no space to call my own. I am a wandering ship, my anchor still stowed safely in its hold. My doorways are always changing, my homes always temporary, I have no constancy save myself and you. Let this token remind me that whether I am entering into my quiet domain or entering the world beyond my room, you are with me, part of me, part of my shifting life. Help me to be a portal for love, and Torah, and an opener of doors.

May this student's reality and prayer guide NCMA's 50th story telling. My particular story of ever changing doorways in campus ministry includes varied calls; strategic conversations; changing generations; ministry in the Western U.S.; NCMA experiences; change making and being changed. May we each, may we all be portals for love, Torah, Gospel, and openers of doors.

My Calls to Campus
My call to campus ministry began in 1970 as a student worker at what was then San Fernando Valley State College in Los Angeles (now *California State University, Northridge*). I worked with campus ministers Al Axelton and Daniel Statello at "the Dialogue Center." Through campus ministry I opened to new worlds and my questions were taken seriously. I met and learned from Caesar Chavez and Paulo Freire before I knew who they were. The walls between personal faith and social justice crumbled as I followed Jesus.

As the first in my working class immigrant family to graduate from college, I found a lifeline in campus ministry in every sense of that word.
While in seminary at Boston University School of Theology, I was part of a small group that founded the Anna Howard Shaw Center, and I served as the first Student Director of the Center. My first full time campus ministry position was as founding Director of the Landberg Center for Health and Ministry at *University of California, San Francisco*, an ecumenical campus ministry with medical and nursing students launched by a patient's bequest received by the only ecumenical campus ministry in the city at that time, Ecumenical House at San Francisco State University. I then served as Wesley Foundation Director at *San Diego State University*, and later for eight years at *UCLA*. In 1993 I became the first full time Director hired to re-start a Wesley Foundation at *UC Berkeley*.

I also served three pastorates, most recently 9 years as pastor of Epworth United Methodist Church in Berkeley.

From 2000-2004 I was the first Program Director of Contextual Education at Pacific School of Religion, and in 2012 I returned as faculty member and Director of Field Education and Contextual Learning.

Because of a life changing mission study trip to Chile in the early 1970s, I am called to initiate and facilitate what Robert McAfee Brown called, "Creative Dislocation," immersive learning experiences that change world views and open new worlds every year and in every setting.

Strategic Conversations and Actions

Strategic and contextual conversations for mission and ministries in higher education have also been part of my call: through the General Board of Higher Education and Ministry and the National Committee on Campus Ministry of the UMC, through NCMA, regional denominational and ecumenical commissions, forming partnerships to launch new ministries and movements (e.g. Ecumenical Black Campus Ministry, 2000 California and Nevada Campus Ministry Mission Strategy). Board development, contextual analysis, and model development have been my primary consulting areas.

Current trends in student demographics, economic and educational disparities, divisions between delivery of services and learning outcomes, student indebtedness, graduate employment rates, and for-profit initiatives in "untapped" higher education markets that leverage and "unlock" assets of campus ministries and colleges and universities all require strategic thinking and campus ministries are uniquely placed conversation partners in discerning discipleship, justice and meaning in the ways ahead for church and campus. May each doorway be a portal to love, Torah, and Gospel, and may we be openers of doors.

Changing Generations in Campus Ministry

Women entering campus ministry in the third wave of the 1970s and 1980s responded to the "in but still out" realities of a field challenged by changing contexts, diminished support, and long tenured staff. Hospitality to new generations of colleagues was not a core practice in a time of seeming scarcity.

I recently found correspondence from campus ministry colleagues and regional leaders explaining to me why the compensation package for the campus ministry I was just hired to direct would leave with the former campus minister to a new site and therefore I would have to live in the campus ministry building.

While lay and clergy women had founded and served campus ministries for many years, top denominational and para-church leaders were overwhelming white males, and local Directors as well (though with an increasing number of women program associates). Women found and founded new ministries and new models of leadership bridging campus and community.

Campus Ministry Women was a network where women mentored and supported one another and acted together. In CMW it was never only about women in campus ministry. I remember a Campus Ministry Conference in Illinois where we gathered at the home of the Illinois governor to protest that Illinois was one of fifteen states to refuse to ratify the Equal Rights Amendment (which failed in 1982 due to those fifteen states). Access to education, wage equity, sexual violence, and international solidarity with women struggling against injustice were foci of our gatherings and action.

One vivid memory I have from an NCMA Conference held at Temple University was when Womanist theologian Dolores Williams was asked during Q and A (in a long, energetic and highly descriptive question) what she thought about a complex and controversial denominational reorganization in one denomination. She was silent for a moment and then responded, "I think it is simply another realignment of the white male power structure."

The West

The expansion, changing realities and leadership of public higher education in the western U.S. has not always been reflected in the focus, funding, studies, conferences, histories or strategies of denominational or ecumenical ministries in higher education.

A few anecdotes worth sharing from my experience that hopefully prompt interest in scope and particularity of stories from all regions:

Herman Beimfohr was Campus Minister and Director of the Wesley Foundation serving UCLA from 1936 to 1975. His tenure included pre-WWII, WWII, Korean War, and Vietnam student eras.

By 1936 there were student centers or campus ministries at junior colleges, teachers colleges, public and private universities throughout the Western U.S. serving thousands of students.

Until it closed in 1999, the Landberg Center at UC San Francisco initiated Anatomy Lab burial rites, a CPE program for medical students in Haight-Ashbury, community clinics with Glide Memorial Church, advocacy for a health science women's center, and immersive courses on Cross-Cultural Perspectives on Health Care and Healing.

In 1972 Mary Alice Geier wrote *There's a Community College in My Town* and in 1987 she co-wrote *We Got Here From There: a Reflective History of the Southern California and Southwest Conference of the United Church of Christ: on the Occasion of Its 100th Anniversary, 1887-1987.*

In 1996 Stanford, UC Berkeley, UC Davis campus ministries created *Tet Ansamn*, a multi-year ecumenical student network of teams and solidarity with the ti eglise movement and the people of Haiti.

NCMA

NCMA provided me primary professional affiliation, development, theological study and strategic working papers, collegiality, and an ecumenical community of accountability during the necessary season of rebuilding denominational bases for campus ministry.

NCMA also connected me to lifelong friends and adventures. Through conference planning committees, international delegations and exchanges, learning and teaching at institutes and academies, writing devotionals and serving on editorial boards, student conferences, and lay theological institutes, through serving on the NCMA executive committee and then as president, I have been changed and challenged by dear friends, wise teachers, brilliant students, colleagues, comrades, sisters and brothers. You know who you are! I am so grateful.

Happy anniversary, NCMA.

This anniversary and the interest of seminarians has prompted me to develop a course proposal titled "Changing Ministries in Higher Education."

Odette Lockwood-Stewart serves as Director of Field Education and Contextual Learning at Pacific School of Religion in Berkeley, serves as a delegate to UMC General Conferences, and, with her husband Jim, keeps up with their four children and extended family.

Campus Ministry: A Space and Time for Holy Hospitality
By Jan Rivero

The year was 1994. The General Conference of the United Methodist Church had just convened. And word came out immediately about a letter signed by eleven bishops of the church stating that as a Church we were not of one voice on the issue of homosexuality. The debate had begun. As I read the news report, one clear thought came to me: "You'd better know where you stand on this because you are going to need to know." My journey to a deeper understanding of the human family, my call, and myself had begun.

In the summer of 1996 I was reappointed for a third year by Bishop Pennel to serve as campus minister to the Wesley Foundation at *The University of Virginia*. As is true for most campus ministers, I was preparing for a summer focused largely on clean up from the previous year, recuperation, including time for family, rest and renewal, and preparing for the year to come.

Shortly after graduation in May, I began to undertake that task of cleaning up. On this particular day, I was culling through old minutes from the meetings of the Wesley Foundation Board of Directors. Reading through a particular set of minutes from the earliest years of the Foundation, I came upon an action taken by the board to allow the then Gay Student Organization to meet weekly in the Wesley Foundation building. "Interesting," I thought. It seemed to me in the moment to be a courageous decision, but one that seemed in the moment to have no impact on the current state of our ministry. Nearly thirty years later, in 1996, the group, now the LGBT Student Association, still met weekly in the Wesley building, providing a safe space for students who were deserving of just that, safe space and time to be in a supportive community. Little did I realize how important the discovery of those minutes would be, to the campus ministry and even to my own ministry.

In October that year, I was summoned by the District Superintendent to his office without warning or explanation. As soon as I arrived he quickly ushered me into his office and showed me a seat. Some conversations you remember close to verbatim for a lifetime. This is one of those.

"I understand that the gay student group meets in your building. Is that true?" he queried.

"Yes it is," I replied.

"Well, you need to kick them out."

"Oh. I'm sorry. I can't do that."

Face turning red and appearing angry, he replied, "You have to. Their meeting in the Wesley building violates the Book of Discipline."

"Well that may be true, but the Board of Directors made the decision years ago to allow the group meeting space in the Wesley building, and I am not authorized to overturn that decision."

He was stunned. Evidently in his mind he imagined that I would roll over and obey without question. It was as though he thought this was a decision made on a whim by a group of "youth" who didn't know better, and it was my job, as their leader to show them the error of their ways.

At this point I am relatively certain that this was one of those God moments: that I had been given that information from the Board minutes for "a time such as this." And I relaxed into the moment, trusting that God would give me the words, even though I was scared out of my wits!

The next words came quickly and easily, "You are on the Board of Directors and I invite you to have this concern placed on the agenda for the next meeting." I'm fairly certain he was even more stunned, but I had no intention of backing down and doing his dirty work. Rumors around the conference were of his aspirations to become a bishop. I wasn't interested in contributing to his campaign.

The conversation devolved from there, but I did offer to call the Board Chair and have his concern placed on the meeting agenda. Then I went and found a quiet place to look on the mountains, restore my emotional balance, and consider my next steps.

Newly composed, I called the Board Chair, we met for lunch and mapped out a strategy which would result in the Board taking steps to both educate and examine its building use policy. My next step was to arrange to meet with the Bishop. I needed to know where he was going to be on this. If he would be supportive, great; but if not, I needed to know. Surprisingly, I was able to get on his agenda fairly quickly.

I've had some pretty difficult conversations with bishops over the years, so I approached this one with a certain level of dread. Of course by the time I sat in his office in Richmond, he was well aware why I was there. Nevertheless, he asked questions as though he was hearing this for the first time. The questions were insightful and helpful to my thought process. But the take home for me that day was two statements he made that I will never forget. First he said, "Your job is to give the Board the information they need to make a good decision. I trust boards to make good decisions." I took a deep breath of relief. Then he said, "And we want to make sure this isn't about you." My interpretation: "I have no intention of moving you over this." Deeper sigh of relief.

With that affirmation, I returned to Charlottesville and began the tasks of equipping students, board members, local laity. Our Board moved to offer a six weeks series of conversations on the church and homosexuality, using the UMC curriculum readily available at the time. The sessions were led by others: former campus ministers, ordained clergy faculty, local church clergy. We extended invitations to the local churches in the Charlottesville area, but attendance was low and the audience was by and large "the choir." There were one or two lay members of the church next door who attended because they were genuinely looking for insights on the issue, but by and large most in attendance were students who were already supportive of the stand the Board had taken years prior. For some, these were their very friends who were "under attack."

The second action the Board took at that meeting was to name a task force that would examine the building use policy, seek like documents from other ministries, and come to the Board with recommendations for potential revisions. They went to work, and at their last meeting of the academic year in April of 1997 they presented their report: recommended revisions to the building use policy that was more welcoming and affirming than the one that had been in place for many years. The Board approved the policy by a vote of 17-2.

Fast forward one year. In June of 1998 I was appointed, "on loan," to be the Director of the Wesley Foundation at *UNC Chapel Hill*, following the twenty two year tenure of Manuel Wortman. The Wesley building, like the one in Charlottesville and many others across the country, had been built in the 1960's and its use was always being redefined. Shortly after my arrival I was welcomed by the Sunday morning "tenants" of our chapel, the Revs. Rick and Jill Edens, pastors of United Church of Chapel Hill. A year or two prior, their sanctuary had been "condemned" and so the congregation was worshipping in the Wesley chapel while they conducted a building campaign and program for a new campus north of town.

Two or three weeks after arriving, Rick and Jill came back to visit me, this time to inform me that Jimmy Creech was scheduled to preach in their worship services in September. Rick and Jill, having had roots in the Western North Carolina Conference, were well aware of the potential repercussions of this for me. They offered to worship elsewhere on that Sunday. I declined their thoughtful offer. At the time, Jimmy was still ordained in the UMC, though he had charges against him and was awaiting another church trial. Jimmy was a guest of this UCC congregation. Wesley was not endorsing or sponsoring; we were landlords. In my mind there was not a single thing wrong with having him preach for these guests in "our house." So I let it go, though I was personally disappointed because I had made a commitment to preach in a congregation in Virginia that weekend, so I could not be there.

In the meantime, I made an appointment to meet my new District Superintendent, for no other reason than for him to know who I was, a pastor on loan from Virginia, appointed to ministry on a campus in his district. We met for an hour or so, exchanged call stories, and I went on my way. When I got to my car to return to Chapel Hill, I had my hand on the door handle when I thought "You forgot to tell him about Jimmy Creech." For about thirty seconds I stood there, "Do I go back? Do I let it go? Do I go back? Do I let it go?" My intuition prevailed: "You didn't think of it while you were in there. Let it go." And let it go I did.

Late August brought students back to campus. It was an exciting time, an exhilarating time. New faces. A new to me campus. Lots of energy, joy and opportunity for ministry. In early September, however, I walked into the office one morning and listened to a voicemail from my Board chair. "Call me as soon as you get this."

"I had a call from the District Superintendent. He says that Jimmy Creech is going to be preaching at Wesley and he wants to know what you are going to do about it."

If that call came today I would say, "Seriously?" But it was 1998 and things were different then. Things were different. I was not!

"I'm not going to do anything about it."

"You're not?"

"No, I'm not."

"But the DS said you have to."

I proceeded to explain to him all that I had said to Rick and Jill that day: we are not sponsoring, Jimmy is still clergy in good standing, there is no ground on which to take action.

"OK. I will deliver the message."

Apparently a letter had been sent from United Church to all the local churches in the Chapel Hill area inviting them to come worship at Wesley to hear Jimmy. And apparently there was (at least) one clergy recipient of that letter who took offense and wanted it stopped. To my resistance the DS said to my Board chair, "Well the Cabinet is meeting right now. and we will decide what you are going to do."

That was the last I heard of it. The DS never spoke with me about it directly. And apparently he never got back in contact with the Board Chair.

Jimmy came and preached. I went to Virginia and preached. And when I got home that night and turned on the local news, there was Jimmy, standing and talking to a reporter right in front of the Wesley building. But I never heard another word.

Fast forward several more years. A beloved colleague who once held a campus ministry position in Virginia was now a District Superintendent. He had been invited to come spend some time with our Wesley residential community as part of a grant we had received for developing a culture of call through intentional residency. Come to find out from him that my story had become legend in District Superintendent training school because he had heard it from both of my previous DS's. He said he had heard stories about me. When I pressed him about it, he said, "Jan is just being Jan."

Well those of you who know me know how that made me bristle. This colleague came to talk with my students about his "ministry of reconciliation." So I wasn't going quietly into the night on this one. I looked at my colleague and stated with conviction that I had clearly been called to a ministry of holy hospitality that was no less valid or significant than his ministry of reconciliation. I think he "got it."

Within just a few weeks of that I sat in a meeting of North Carolina campus ministers with Bishop Kammerer. We spent the afternoon with her.

She shared her vision for campus ministry. She asked how she could support our work. Well you know me. Jan, being Jan, just had to ask "Please tell us what you see to be the role of campus ministers with regard to the issue of homosexuality."

I don't remember her response with the same clarity that I remember the rest of this story, but I do remember her clearly saying these words, "As campus ministers, you have a ministry of hospitality. And in that regard your ministry should be open to all." She said something else about her role as enforcer of the Book of Discpline, but as you can tell, I didn't pay much attention to that part!

In the spring semester following, someone in the office of Student Affairs extended me the invitation to participate in a panel Q&A along with other campus ministry colleagues at UNC. The subject: how different faith perspectives view homosexuality. About twenty students attended, a few of whom were participants in ministries of Wesley, and one of whom was carrying what my husband would describe as "a Bible big enough to choke a mule." The conversation was well controlled by the moderator, who had students write questions on pieces of paper that were placed in and retrieved from a fish bowl. The moderator tempered the language in a few instances. As the panel progressed it was clear to me that the students had an angry, biased agenda. They were not there to learn as much as they were there to inform. Perhaps they were using this as an opportunity to find out where they would most feel comfortable.

By the time the questions passed to me, I had determined that never again would I have this conversation with anyone who could not acknowledge that they had a friend or family member who was gay or lesbian. But there I was, so I had to speak. My message was simple and clear and came straight from I John. "Let us love one another, because love is from God; everyone who loves is born of God and knows God." Students pushed back, but I would not budge. I would not argue. I would not even state my position beyond that. I was finished with the conversation.

That portion of the story came full circle last year however, when one of those students in attendance was front and center at a wedding I performed for two young women who first met at Wesley.

Now, some twenty years after the debate began and, I pray, the UMC approaches the end of its debate on this subject, I give thanks for the presence of God who walked with me through the dark night on this issue. I know that my words and my actions offended some, but for many more they were words and deeds that brought healing and hope. That was not a journey I ever would have chosen, but I am confident that I walked it faithfully.

Since leaving campus ministry in 2010, Jan Rivero has served as University Relations Director for Stop Hunger Now, a Raleigh, NC based, international hunger relief organization. She lives in Chapel Hill with her husband, Jeffrey Pugh. They enjoy traveling together and are looking towards retirement in 2018 when they will move back to Virginia to be closer to family.

Using the Church's Empty Spaces for Theater and the Arts
By Jerry Miller

This is the personal Foreword to a forthcoming book about how to combine ministry, theater, and the arts by a former campus minister who did just that. His story is so engaging and inspiring that I wanted to include it in our Sages collection. It illustrates how our ministries on campus also nurture US and prepare us for further callings in other stages of our lives!

I have started theaters in four churches in the Chicago area from the ground up over the last 14 years with the help of others both within the church and in the community. Let me tell you a little bit about my journey and how I came to this place of passion.

When I was 13 years old I was the narrator for the Putnam Junior High School Christmas Pageant in Oklahoma City. The only role available for me in the pageant, other than the narrator, was the role of a shepherd. I didn't want to be just a shepherd in the pageant and besides most of the shepherds were playing poker backstage while the rest of the pageant was going on. It didn't seem that they were really into the story of Mary and Joseph and the babe in swaddling clothes in the manger.

I loved having the chance to narrate the play. I loved the spotlight shining on me and my ability to move the audience emotionally as I read the words of Scripture and contemporary narrative. It was magic. I was home. Everybody told me how wonderful I was. My mom said, "When people tell you how wonderful you are just tell them that it is a gift that God gave you." And I thought to myself, "I worked really hard on this; why should I tell them that?" Even then my ego was a little inflated. But my mom was right. It was a gift.

My dad didn't like the idea of my being an actor. He wanted me to become a minister because acting was "sissy" stuff but my mom liked the idea of me being in theater, and she chauffeured me to all my acting events.

In deference to my dad, I chose the ministry although that was not the only reason. The church had nurtured me and loved me as a young person. I was involved with regional youth events and camps. I was elected to youth leadership positions in the Disciples of Christ Church in Oklahoma and was encouraged and mentored to enter the ministry. And the church also nurtured me to use my gift of acting Dr. Ralph Stone and Reverend Royce Makin of the Disciples of Christ denomination created opportunities for me to perform in the plays that they had written for Crown Heights Christian Church in Oklahoma City, as well as at regional events for Disciples of Christ Churches both within and without the state. So it was the church that enabled me to use my gifts of ministry and acting. And it was also a minister in the church who literally saved my life.

I grew up as a young gay man in the '60s in Oklahoma City, Oklahoma – a difficult experience. At school I was told by peers who were not in my church

296

group or theater group, that to be gay was a sin, that it was wrong, and that God didn't make "queers." I was beaten up. I was yelled at. I was rejected by the majority of my peers at school. This was a painful journey and I contemplated suicide at the age of 15. But I found solace in the church and on the stage. From the church, I learned in Vacation Bible School that "Jesus loved me and all the little children of the world." It was a youth minister who encouraged me to continue my journey even when I wanted to end it all. I am eternally grateful for the unconditional love of Reverend Ken Compton. In theater I found an inclusive community. I felt safe with these adventurous and talented people. They enjoyed acting as much as I did. I set a goal to win the Drama Award in both junior high and high school, and I did!

I received my undergraduate degree from Phillips University in Enid, Oklahoma, a small private religious university funded by the Disciples of Christ. I loved Phillips, where I was included and had great fun being a member of the Varsity Fraternity, serving as Vice-President of the Phillips Student Senate and parliamentarian for the Oklahoma State Student Senate and as a dorm counselor. I was exposed to a larger world by later living in a large city as compared to the small town of Enid, but I will always be grateful to Phillips because it offered me many opportunities for leadership; I was also able to take a study trip to Europe and visit nine countries on a trip led by Dr. Robert Simpson, my philosophy professor who made me fall in love with philosophy.

After graduating in 1967, I attended Perkins School of Theology at Southern Methodist University in Dallas, Texas. My friend Lance Roberds encouraged me to attend Perkins rather than continue my graduate education in Theology at Phillips because he felt that Dallas would be a larger arena for coming into contact with people at the forefront of social justice.

My roommate at Perkins served as the Student Body President. The Dean of Perkins at the time asked my roommate to let him know if there were any "gay" students as he would "like to weed them out." So I was very closeted during my time in Theology School, but I am happy to say that my roommate friend is now a Bishop in the United Methodist Church and very supportive of my journey!

Perkins School of Theology, despite the homophobia of the Dean, was great in instructing me about injustice and oppression. The Vietnam War was going on at the time and we were taught that it was not a "Just War." I participated in rallies against the war, and I remember seeing members of the CIA taking photos of people in the crowd.

I learned about racial injustice when I picketed a "Whites Only" washateria across from the S.M.U. campus. I was asked by an undergraduate student who had initiated and led the picket for several months to continue as the leader because he had grown weary, and his studies were suffering due to the time required of him. Several Perkins professors and theology students joined me in the picket, and eventually there was a resolution with the owner of the washateria and the sign was taken down. But I saw first hand the hate directed at people of color. The Dallas police would arrest us unless we kept moving and had $5.00 in our pocket; the American Nazi party came out in their uniforms and threatened us; many Southern Methodist undergraduates would drive by and yell "N.......Lover;" and the owner placed a sprinkler hose outside so our shoes and pants would get wet during the winter. But because we picketed and persisted in dialogue with the owner, the sign finally came down.

I went to my first gay bar on a field trip at Perkins designed to desensitize me to the gay population in Dallas and how to minister to them. There, I talked to our "tour" guide who had a friend who was 16 and suicidal and asked me to visit with him. I was sent into a poorer, all black section of Dallas to survey people about their medical needs. The experience of being the only "white" person in the neighborhood was eye opening. My time in Dallas expanded my experience with different cultures, political issues, and the arts.

After Perkins I served as Director of The Corner at Highland Park United Methodist Church in Dallas. The Corner was a community arts and recreation center that had an afterschool program for "latch key" youth, a summer day camp program, and a variety of activities for all ages. The program also hosted Emeritus Educational and Arts courses for Older Adults. Unfortunately, all the creative emerging ministries at Highland Park UMC were disbanded because the church was suffering budget deficit, but I will always be grateful to Reverend Bill Dickinson, the pastor who was so supportive of creative ministries prior to his death.

After my service at Highland Park United Methodist Church, I served as Minister of Education at First Christian Church in Denton, Texas, where I produced my first play with the youth group. We grew a youth choir that started with four people and, with the help of our Youth Choir Director, expanded to 50 youth.

Back in Dallas, I worked as a campus minister for the **Greater Dallas Community of Churches Community College Ministry**, where I had the opportunity to meet such people as Robert Short, the author of the *Gospel According Peanuts*, and Maggie Kuhn who started the *Gray Panthers* to fight against ageism in all its forms. Maggie Kuhn taught me that there are no limits due to age. Kuhn was an outstanding advocate for older adults, and I was later inspired by her to produce a play on successful aging called *Don't Wait Up for Me* at Lincoln Square Arts Center in Chicago.

Maggie also inspired me to write a course with twenty of my older adult friends at the Mesquite Senior Center in Denton, Texas entitled "Successful Aging." It was the only course in the 1970's written and taught by older adults. This course was recognized by the National Science Foundation, and I was invited to attend a conference on "Society and the Senior Citizen" with other persons on the forefront of addressing the needs of seniors in Higher Education.

Under the leadership of our Director Betsy Alden at GDCCC, I was able to create a workshop and course book on *Successful Aging*, an Emeritus Chorus and Senior Citizen Camp, and, inspired by the model created by Noel Buell in California, I started an Emeritus Institute for seniors on three of the campuses of the Dallas Community Colleges. This was an innovative concept at the time—an "idea whose time had come," and I was at the forefront of this movement to develop Lifelong Learning opportunities. Seniors could take community college courses from the community service division for only $5.00, so I hired the teachers and created a variety of courses, including Computers, How to Create Your Own Cable TV Show, Book Studies, and Basic Acting. We also published a book containing the "oral histories" of some of these students to give to their families.

Through the *Praxis Project* that was part of our ministry on campus, we placed undergraduate students as volunteers in over 50 social service agencies in Dallas, and many of them had a chance to work with the older population in senior citizen centers and nursing homes This service-learning model, in which student service was part of their academic coursework, was replicated on many other campuses across the country.

After serving eight years for the Greater Dallas Community of Churches Community College Ministry, I moved to Santa Fe, New Mexico to work in an Antique Shop and Art Gallery that my mother had opened. We carried the works of a variety of artists including my older brother Willis and my sister Sallie. We also sold Indian jewelry made by our friends from the Pueblos, and I worked for five dollars an hour in my mother's shop. I lived with my mom, and when I wasn't working in the shop I pursued my acting career, performing in several productions of Santa Fe's *Shakespeare in the Park*. I took acting classes from Nicholas Ballas, secured a talent agent, and earned my Screen Actor's Guild Card. I acted in a lot of plays in Santa Fe but I had done about all I could do with my acting career there.

At the age of 50, I made a big move--I decided to go back to school to obtain my MFA in acting. To be considered for a professional acting school at the time you had to audition for the University Regional Theatre Audition Committee before two judges. My regional audition was at the University of Arizona, and the two judges had to agree that you had talent in order for you to be passed on to the national auditions. At the regional audition, I performed two monologues and sang a song. The audition site had a tape recorder for us to use, but there was something wrong with the volume control on the tape recorder, and I could not hear the music as I sang. The two judges passed me on to the national audition but told me, "Please do not sing at the next audition." Luckily, I can now sing in musicals after taking voice classes. And I am very thankful for my current vocal coach, Marc Embree at DePaul University in Chicago.

The national audition was in Long Beach, California. I remember students some 30 years younger than I was asking me if I was a judge or professor. I informed them that I was auditioning to attend graduate school as a student. I felt quite comfortable auditioning for graduate school as an older adult. As I learned from Maggie Kuhn "There are no limits. Use It or Lose It." Here, there were about twenty judges from various professional schools of acting in the United States. I was nervous, to say the least. I did my best and I did not sing. The auditions were in the morning, and in the afternoon, each person who had auditioned was handed an envelope with a list of the schools that wanted to interview you as possible MFA candidates. I was thrilled to be invited for interviews by five schools.

It is very hard to get into a professional school of acting for a graduate degree. Most schools take five to ten students per year. Some graduate schools take a lot more than ten and tell the students that they will get scholarships in their second year but then cut many from the program after the first year. It seems unfair but this is the way it is. After the interviews in Long Beach, I was extended an invitation by the University of South Carolina to be a graduate MFA (Master of Fine Arts in Acting) candidate. Attending a professional acting school was something I had always wanted to do. I was honoring a lifelong love.

The MFA program at the University of South Carolina is a three-year program-- two years taking classes, teaching classes to undergraduates in acting and public speaking, and performing in main stage productions; then the third year is an internship. My internship was at the Milwaukee Repertory Theater in Milwaukee, Wisconsin, where I was the first MFA acting candidate from the University of South Carolina to intern (most students interned at the Shakespeare Theatre Company in Washington, D.C.), and being there was a tremendous experience. It is a "state of the art theater" with incredible productions and a large subscribership. The theatre can seat up to 4,086 people. I understudied most of the major male roles of the season and performed small roles in the productions. . I had the opportunity to meet and work with Actors Equity Union actors from all over United States and even a director from Russia who directed his adaptation of The Gambler, a short novel by Fyodor Dostoevsky reflecting on his own addiction to Roulette. Included in the roles I understudied, were the father in *Six Characters in Search of an Author* by Luigi Pirandello and the role of the father, the tenant farmer Phil Hogan, in *Moon for the Misbegotten* by Eugene O'Neill.

After my internship in Milwaukee, I moved to Chicago. I had acquired my union cards in both the Actors' Equity Association (AEA) and the Screen Actors Guild (SAG), and I worked as an Equity actor quite a bit the first two years in Chicago, but acting does not pay well so I decided to enter the corporate world, working as a trainer for Arthur Anderson. (But I continued to perform in local Chicago Theaters in the Evening). I worked at Arthur Andersen for almost five years when the firm was indicted in June of 2002 for obstruction of justice for shredding documents pertaining to its audit of Enron. The indictment put 28,000 people out of work in the United States and 85,000 people living outside of the US. The Supreme Court removed the indictment in May of 2005 on the basis of the jury not being given clear instructions on what it was to decide.

It has been said that God does not shut one door without opening another one. Someone also said that the journey in the hallways leading to the next door can be difficult. But as a result of Arthur Anderson closing its doors, I I made some interesting detours along my journey! I generated income by cleaning houses, being a personal assistant to a doctor friend, and serving as a part-time executive assistant. I was very poor.

I started attending Berry Memorial United Methodist Church in Chicago-- just a couple of blocks away from where I lived. I served on several committees at the church and suggested to the pastor, Reverend Sherry Lowly, who was quite receptive, that we do a play. The play was *Mass Appeal* by Bill C. Davis. The play has two characters, Mark, a bisexual seminarian, and Father Farley, an alcoholic Catholic Priest. It is a story of a friendship that occurs even though Mark and Father Farley are at the opposite ends of the theological spectrum and demonstrates how religious institutions can be oppressive to an individual's life and journey. I have initiated this play at three theaters that I have started.

After the play in 2001 a Fine Arts Committee was formed to create a season of plays at Berry Memorial UMC, and Dr. Marti Scott, who was the District Superintendent of the Northwestern District of the United Methodist Church at that time, appointed me as a part-time Minister of Fine Arts with Bishop Joe Sprague's endorsement. A group of talented artists within and without the church formed a Fine Arts Committee at Berry and we established the Lincoln Square Arts Center, including *Beast on the Moon, Godspell, The Gin Game, The Normal Heart, David and Lisa, Angels in America,* and *Bang Bang You're Dead.* The Lincoln Square Arts Center continues to this day and, since 2001, has produced nearly 30 plays.

Since that first theater was established, I have created three other theaters in United Methodist Churches in cooperation with others from both within and outside the church. I served as Artistic Director/Minister of Fine Arts at the James Downing Theatre at Edison Park United Methodist Church in Chicago, Passion Theatre at Euclid Avenue United Methodist Church in Oak Park and am currently working with Edge Theatre at Epworth United Methodist Church in Chicago. I owe a great deal of gratitude to. Reverend Dr. Marti Scott, who placed me in three of these positions of ministry. Had it not been for her there would be no story to tell.

As a result of all these experiences, I believe that overcoming oppression and rejection to arrive at a place of self -love has made me more sensitive to issues of social justice. And I believe that theater, in conjunction with the church, can address social justice issues in an extremely significant way-- not just for LGBTQ people but for oppression wherever it occurs.

Today I am an active actor, director, writer, grant writer, producer and consultant to churches on doing theater in their empty spaces. I retired from full-time ministry in October of 2012 but continue to perform, write and produce arts events for churches. The church has encouraged me to fight for justice for those living on the margins--to be the Body of Christ for the world.

The theatre has demonstrated inclusiveness, creativity, and communicating through the art form. Addressing social justice issues through theatre in the church has been and continues to be my passion, and my hope is that this book inspires and encourages you to do theater in your church's "empty spaces" for social justice.

Empty Space: Creating a Theater in Your Church, Step by Step by Jerry Miller was published by Amazon in October, 2014. The website is www.creatingatheaterinyourchurch.com

A Calling for a Season
By Debra Brazzel

My diverse experiences in campus ministry span a period of over 25 years, from Texas to North Carolina. I enjoyed almost everything about working in ministry in higher education, and found it to be a very welcome place for a feminist clergywoman to explore new dimensions of ministry—and of herself. But I chose to "give up" this vocation to "take on" full-time motherhood for almost fifteen years before designing a new career—as a "minister for all occasions"!

In the summer of 1984, beginning my 3rd year of seminary at Perkins School of Theology, SMU, I took a campus ministry course with Betsy Alden and Mark Rutledge. I loved the class and was intrigued by the idea of meeting people where they were by bringing the church to the campus. The campus ministry programs we explored were creative, relevant and meaningful. With serendipity (another word for grace), there was an opening for a part-time campus minister at **Mountain View Community College,** and I was hired for this position at one of the seven campuses of the Dallas Community College District. The Dallas Community College Ministry was sponsored by the North Texas Conference of the United Methodist Church and the Greater Dallas Community of Churches, with more than 200 Christian and Jewish member congregations. This was the ministry that Betsy created before taking a position as National Communications Coordinator for United Ministries in Higher Education. I worked with her successor, Georjean Blanton, and six other wonderful campus ministers.

Providing campus ministry on a community college campus was challenging because all of the students were commuters. Most of them had one or two jobs, in addition to their college work, so they were busy! How do you connect in meaningful ways with people who are literally coming or going? The Praxis program was a creative way to meet these students where they were – in the classroom! Each semester, I worked with 25 classes and presented the opportunity for service learning to hundreds of students. I was able to meet with 30-50 students a semester to meaningfully reflect upon their experiences with the people they served, to engage each other in significant conversation and to deepen their exploration of the courses they were taking. It was a brilliant model, especially for the community college context.

I was there for five years. Very quickly, I realized that I needed to build an ongoing community, and the obvious starting place was with faculty and staff, the people who stayed through the constantly changing student population. I formed wonderful relationships with the faculty who offered Praxis through their classes, with the counseling and programming staff and with the administrators. They were kindred spirits, and I found many enduring friends and discovered many collaborators for ministry outreach to students and staff. (Ann Fletcher, a counselor, hosted a post-wedding brunch for me at her home).

I formed a spirituality group for faculty and staff that met once a week for years for meditation and spiritual practice. With Ann Fletcher, I founded the Buddy Program that paired American students with new immigrant students (mostly from Laos, Vietnam and Cambodia), in which students met for casual conversation, and out of this growing community, we formed an International Club that met weekly. We made literally thousands of homemade eggrolls to raise money for the group to plan activities that helped strangers become friends. On eggroll days, you could smell them wafting through the campus the moment you entered the doors! We went bowling, camping, to people's homes and even a spring break trip to Florida. We had one young African-American man with severe cerebral palsy who found loving support and community in this group. I loved being part of it.

As I engaged more meaningfully with the community at Mountain View, I was offered a part-time job as a grant writer/administrator of a program we called Life Transitions. This allowed me to stay on at Mountain View after graduating from seminary and, with the campus ministry position, gave me full-time work and a full-time ministry appointment. The grant allowed us to set up an on-site day and evening child care program for adult women returning to school, where we offered counseling, financial aid and programming since most of the women were single mothers struggling to provide for their families. I had already established a women's spirituality group for students that met weekly, which fit very well with this focus on women in transition. I did collaborative programming with the counseling center and with Guy Gooding, who coordinated student programming. I was also asked to teach a World Religions course for a couple of semesters and an Ethics course. I was the staff "pray-er" for community gatherings -- opening days, graduations, holidays. I learned to be comfortable with people of many religious traditions and those of no tradition. We even held the first Interfaith Worship Service at the college. I will always be grateful for my time at Mountain View and know that my openness to people of many different cultural and religious backgrounds was nurtured in this community.

My next campus ministry position was Assistant Dean of *Duke University* Chapel from 1991-1994, Associate Dean from 1994-1996, Acting Dean from 1996-1997, and Associate Dean from 1997-1998. I was also Director of Religious Life for Duke University from 1991-1998-- challenging and varied work that I loved!

Having worked as a campus minister for five years, I was naturally supportive of the campus ministers at Duke. In my tenure, we grew from a staff of 14 to 20 campus ministers. Unlike many campuses, where denominational and para-church staff were antagonistic toward one another, we had a collaborative approach that welcomed and provided funding and space for many Christian groups. With a commitment to interfaith presence, we invited a Muslim imam to the staff, welcomed a Buddhist monk and supported the rabbi's work to raise funds for a Jewish Life Center. We also added a Black

Campus Ministries staff position. Each campus minister was hired by the university and given a nominal annual salary and a staff identity card. This gave them status as university staff with access to university buildings and resources. My position as a university administrator afforded me the opportunity to make connections that helped boost the visibility and credibility of the campus ministry staff as a whole and helped us advocate for the needs of the various religious communities at Duke.

Most of the denominational campus ministries at Duke did not have individual houses, but instead had small offices in the basement of Duke Chapel. All the campus ministries, those with and those without offices, shared a secretary, a conference room, a lounge, a kitchen, a computer room, and a copy machine. A lot of coordination was required but this became one of our strengths. Because the staff knew each other well, they were better able to negotiate conflicts when they arose. It also created an atmosphere of trust that allowed people to speak the truth to one another without destroying friendships.

We worked hard to foster these relationships. The campus ministry staff had two retreats a year (a two-day retreat before school started and a day-long retreat after it ended). We met bi-weekly for business meetings where we addressed everything from "who left the kitchen a mess" to strategies to ease racial tension and work for justice (the Rodney King beatings and the ending of apartheid were in this era). We also met bi-weekly for staff development. We invited people from the university that our staff needed to know (i.e., the Vice President for Student Affairs, the Director of the Counseling Center, the Dean of Students and many others). Sometimes staff shared their knowledge or interests with the group. Sometimes we dealt with problems, like the presence of religious cults on campus (we developed a student brochure on "How to Discern Healthy From Destructive Religious Groups"). We worked on annual service projects including Gleaning Day, CROP Walk, and the OXFAM fast. We invited religious speakers such as Tony Campolo, the Brothers of Taize, John Shelby Spong, Thomas Moore, Thomas Berry, Matthew Fox and Huston Smith (one of our colleagues said he wouldn't attend but would pray for us, and that was okay!). We hosted a two-day regional Renovare Conference with Richard Foster for more than 500 people. We held several ecumenical and interfaith worship services annually including Blessing of the Animals, Holocaust Remembrance, an Advent Service of Lessons and Carols and Ash Wednesday. We sponsored religious art exhibits and plays such as Mark's Gospel by Max McLean and the Gospel of Luke by Bruce Kuhn. The possibilities were limited only by time and imagination.

Duke Chapel provided extra funding to campus ministry groups for programming, especially international and domestic mission trips. Fall break, spring break, and summer mission experiences gave students the chance to work in places of great need. I co-led a student group to Washington D.C. over spring break with the Catholic campus minister, Sister Peg, and again the next year with the Episcopal campus minister, Ann Hodges-Copple. Twice, I was a member of a medical mission team to Honduras with Duke physicians, nurses and medical students. As anyone who has ever done mission work knows, the impact you make on the places and people you visit is small; the impact these relationships and experiences make upon you is inestimable. Through the Chapel we were able to sponsor hundreds of students for mission. Many others were sponsored for spiritual renewal through youth conferences and pilgrimages to places like Mepkin Abbey and the Monastery of Christ in the Desert.

As a worship leader at Duke Chapel, I got to know students, faculty members, choir members, and people from the community who participated in one of the most vibrant university chapels in the country with weekly worship attendance from 1000-1700. Planning and participating in more than 60 worship services a year at Duke Chapel, I was blessed to hear some of the best preaching in the world (including Peter Gomes, Barbara Brown Taylor, Thomas Long, Samuel Proctor, Walter Bruggemann, Elizabeth Achtemeier, Fred Craddock, James Earl Massey and of course, William H. Willimon, my boss). Being a part of such exceptional weekly worship gave me the opportunity to hone my worship and preaching skills.

There were also many university services. Opening Convocation for freshmen featured Maya Angelou (she encouraged and challenged Duke students for 24 consecutive years, beginning in 1989). The annual Founder's Day was full of pomp and circumstance and distinguished guests. Baccalaureate services were so well attended that even with limited tickets, it required three services. I was part of the historic inauguration service for Nannerl Keohane, the first woman president of Duke. Other memorable services included the funeral of Terry Sanford and memorial services for Doris Duke and Princess Diana. Weekly Choral Vespers and Taize prayer services deepened the life of the spirit and provided consecrated moments for prayer in the beautiful Chapel worship spaces. In addition to these "university functions," I was often called upon to exercise the roles of ministry by officiating at weddings, funerals and baptisms, and counseling students and adults.

Outside of worship, there were numerous opportunities to connect with students and the extended Duke Chapel community. In the summer of 1996, I led a group of students and community members on a 10-day spiritual pilgrimage to Taize in France. I was blessed to go on three international Duke Chapel Choir tours - to Poland and the Czech Republic in 1993, to England in 1995 (where the choir sang the Messiah at St. Martin in the Fields) and a ground-breaking trip to China with 200 members of the Chapel Choir in 1997.

One of my passions since seminary has been women's spirituality. At Duke, I found a kindred spirit in Martha Simmons, the founding director of the Duke Women's Center. Beginning in 1993, Martha and I led women's spirituality classes called "Exploring Women's Spirituality Through

306

Literature" for graduate and undergraduate women. We led these classes/groups for five consecutive semesters and utilized many resources to tap into women's experiences of the sacred. Some of the women continued to participate over several years and we added new women each semester. In 1994-95, we offered the same course for twelve women through Duke's continuing education program. The women who attended the community classes ranged in age from 30 to 60+, and in these women, we found a hunger for depth and connection to God and each other. The 1994 class formed an ongoing women's spirituality group that has met monthly for twenty years! Martha and I are a part of the group, and in the way of women's spirituality, the leadership is shared. My life has been immeasurably enriched through these experiences of the sacred in and through women.

In 1997, I was invited to serve on a steering committee which was charged with identifying thirty women to commit to meet for 10 months in the Women's Spirituality Project to develop a women's spirituality curriculum. Dennis Campbell, the Dean of the Divinity School, provided funding for the project. The women were from many denominations, clergy and lay people, with one Jewish participant. There was a two day opening retreat, followed by monthly gatherings and a closing two day retreat. Many different readings and spiritual practices were explored and each section was evaluated. Unfortunately, there was a change of leadership at the Divinity School and the curriculum was never repeated. However, a group called Spirited Women formed at the end of this project and continues to meet twice a month for shared spiritual practice with rotating leadership. I participate in both these ongoing women's spirituality groups, and the groups meet once a year for a weekend retreat.

Subsequently, some of us participated in a year-long women's spirituality course at Duke Divinity School with Teresa Berger, who taught an undergraduate class titled "Women's Vocations: Leadership, Power, and Constraint in the Christian Tradition." This rich experience provided some of the inspiration for Dr. Berger's 2005 book, *Fragments of Real Presence: Liturgical Traditions in the Hands of Women.*

In 1995, I was part of a delegation of 10 clergy and laity from Durham, North Carolina for a trip to our sister city, Kostroma, Russia. We were joined there by clergy and laity from our sister city, Durham, England. The purpose of the visit was to strengthen the ties between our cities and churches. We explored ways that the western church responds to the needs of our communities through mission outreach. As the Russian Orthodox Church emerged from decades of being "forbidden," their priests were faced with the tremendous task of rebuilding churches and meeting the dire needs of their congregations. Many continuing relationships between the three sister cities were established. Some of those Russian church leaders later made visits to Durham, North Carolina and our churches have helped support their work.

I have had other wonderful experiences in ministry at Duke beyond these years on staff at Duke Chapel. I worked at the Kenan Ethics Institute, taught classes through Duke Divinity School's Course of Study program, and worked with the Lilly Endowment for Vocational Discernment and the PathWays program at Duke Chapel. Through all my work in college and university settings, I have found that campus ministry is primarily relational. Just as Christ ate with people and drank with them and touched them and sat down with them around campfires, so do campus ministers. We share countless meals and stories; we build trust, often through our vulnerability to one another; and we are transformed, even as we seek to transform. The best worship experiences arise out of our connectedness to each other and to God. I could not have found better work in ministry.

The needs of my family led me to leave full-time ministry. Being a working mother with one child was manageable, but after I had twins in my early forties, I felt I could not do justice to my family and my job and stay whole. Many women in ministry face this dilemma, and I was fortunate that we could live on my husband's salary, augmented with my part-time ministry work.

The intense physical caregiving required for infant twins and a three-year old made it clear that I had to find a way to nurture myself. When I discovered yoga, it felt like a drink of cool water in the desert. From the first class, I wanted more! In addition to several classes a week, I did a six-month Anusara immersion program in my first year of practice. Then, as soon as I was eligible, I signed up for an EmbodiYoga teacher training for a year, then the advanced training for a year, then two years assisting. (All of this training meant one weekend a month away from relentless caregiving demands and gave my husband a chance to be closer to our children). I also did a yearlong Mindfulness Based Stress Reduction program at the Duke Center for Integrative Medicine. It was never my intent to teach yoga and mindfulness, only to get more of it for myself, but it was so life-giving that I had to share it! I have now been teaching restorative yoga and mindfulness for seven years. The contemplative practices of yoga, mindfulness and meditation have deepened my spirituality and influenced how I do ministry.

Now that my children are older, I am returning to full-time ministry with a new venture called "Minister for All Occasions." (DebraBrazzel.com) I offer a variety of ministry services, including designing rituals for special events especially targeted to those outside the local church. I teach yoga and mindfulness to groups and individuals, lead retreats and workshops, and reflect with others on their journeys. Despite the challenge of re-entering the professional world, I do not regret my choices. I have new skills and understandings I would not have gotten otherwise, and my own children are as stimulating and provocative as college students—and I will get to see how they turn out!

A Peculiar and Extraordinary Journey:
From Virginia Western Community College to the
Mekong Delta of Vietnam and the Townships of South Africa
By Steve Darr

In the visionary days of Community College Ministries in 1984, I was fortunate to work with Charles Downs, president of *Virginia Western Community College*. His vision for higher education, community, and culture was truly global, and he constantly worked to bring global interests to bear in the vocational and technical world of the community college. Charles and I had talked about ways to involve community college students in global experiences, when along came John Killian, a brilliant Biology professor. I suggested that we try a project with the Peace Corps in the Dominican Republic by sending VWCC students with John Killian to work on a rural project developed in the Haitian bateyes near La Romana. Charles agreed. John jumped on board and learned Spanish in three months and was off to La Romana with a host of students by the spring of 1985.

Later on, I wondered if this could not be a bigger opportunity. Could our ministry's program to take students to the Dominican Republic appeal to other colleges? In fact, there is no other educational institution whose resources match the needs of the developing world and our own local communities better than the community college.

A Peacework school garden in the Zamane Township of South Africa
At the same time, the Contra war was raging in Central America. I joined a peacemaking trip to Nicaragua and Guatemala sponsored by the Presbytery and wondered if the same student volunteers who worked in the Dominican Republic could not also serve as agents of peacemaking and change in a place like Nicaragua where homes and schools were being destroyed in the war. Could volunteerism be that powerful? Could we, in fact, bring together, volunteers from two sides of a global conflict to demonstrate the compelling need for peace? It seemed like a simple idea. It took two years to find the right partners. The model of engaging local citizens in the bateyes of the Dominican Republic served as the model for bridging the Cold War in Nicaragua. I had to come up with a name and chose *Peacework*.

The phone rang at 7:30 am ET on April 21, 1989. I'm glad I was home and not in the shower! Yuri Alexandrin was calling from the Soviet Peace Fund in Moscow. They were ready to accept my invitation to support a joint peacemaking volunteer effort in Nicaragua. CEPAD accepted the challenge of hosting this tri-lateral effort. In August 1989, 8 volunteers from the US and 8 volunteers from the Soviet Union rebuilt 5 houses for war-displaced families in Esteli. Word spread. Before the first project ended, we were planning a similar event in Mexico and a second in Nicaragua.

A global volunteer program was about as far from the imagination of the board of directors of Community College Ministries as any concept could get. However, it made sense to the board of directors to support a new program called Peacework that would promote the involvement of college students in global service regardless of the college or church or other connections they have or where they are enrolled. Peacework was thus launched as a completely independent, non-aligned 501(c)3 non-profit organization so that the new volunteer program could work with anyone, anywhere, at any time without any predisposition whatsoever to religious or national affiliation, ethnicity, political persuasion, or culture. In fact, this element would be fundamental to the new idea. Peacework was a product of the people and interests of Community College Ministries, including the college president Charles Downs, and launched from those ideals that make the community college an open-door institution.

The idea has grown steadily since its inception in 1989, working on projects such as housing in Nicaragua and Mexico, health care in Malawi and Peru and Guatemala and Haiti, education in Belize and Trinidad and India and the Dominican Republic, engineering and construction in Vietnam and Cameroon and Russia, working with children in Russia and South Africa and India and the Czech Republic and Ghana, and a host of other projects and sites. Peacework has developed projects with academic departments, programs, campus ministries, chaplaincies, student organizations, or professional schools with Gettysburg College, Milton Academy, Northeastern University, American University, George Washington University, University of Virginia, Virginia Commonwealth University, the University of Mary Washington, Virginia Tech School of Construction and Architecture & Urban Studies and Agriculture and the Pamplin College of Business, Patrick Henry Community College, Virginia Western Community College, Lynchburg College, Roanoke College, Southern West Virginia Community College, Virginia Highlands Community College, Penn State, Morehouse College, Spelman College, Duke University's Global Health Program and Duke Engage, North Carolina State University, Meredith College, Rhodes College, the University of Arkansas Colleges of Engineering and Education and Business and Agriculture and Medical Sciences, the Clinton School of Public Service, Hendrix College, Oklahoma State University, Northeastern Oklahoma State University, North Central College, Gateway Technical College, the University of Wisconsin in Madison, Boise State University, Arizona School of Health Sciences, Rochester National Technical Institute for the Deaf, Wake Forest University, St. Lawrence University in Toronto, the University of Toronto, Waynesburg University, DePauw University, Siena College, and others.

Several campus ministers were instrumental in launching Peacework and its projects. Rod Sinclair brought a Soviet delegation to his campus in 1987 to speak about peacemaking. It was a member of that delegation from Moscow who said his organization, the Soviet Peace Committee, could not sponsor the project but that he would find an organization that would. Woody Leach started the Global Issues Advocate program at Virginia Tech that sent students to Haiti. Clyde Robinson made the initial overtures to a Vietnamese group that would launch our post-war efforts in the Mekong Delta, Nha Trang, Dalat, and Hanoi. Kathryn Adams at Youngstown State is one of dozens of campus ministers who have taken delegations to the former Soviet Union with Peacework and is still doing so today.

I also learned a valuable lesson from the community Hunger Hikes at Virginia Tech, the power of multiplication. One walker can get a contribution for one dollar for one mile. But ten dollars per mile for ten miles walked by 300 volunteers generates $30,000 in donations. It works for individuals, too. Nearly 20,000 volunteers have participated in Peacework projects with hundreds of community partners in over 25 countries. I would estimate that those 20,000 students and others have touched the lives of a million children and their communities around the world and those children have changed the students' lives in profound ways. It all started with an idea and a phone call.

Peacework operates today under seven key principles. (1) The bottom line is improving the lives of people who live on the margins of society and who often lack basic resources and where modest investment of sweat and funding will launch a new project or bring an important community project to completion. (2) When students live in a community and work alongside local citizens, their own lives and careers are profoundly changed. Every one of us enters these experiences knowing very little about the conditions in which people live and work around the world and our worlds are forever changed by this experience. (3) Peacework's foundational principle is not "helping people" but rather "working alongside" local community or village partners in the process of their own development and with a full appreciation of indigenous self-determination. This is not our concept. It belongs to Jerry Aaker who worked with Heifer International. Read his book, "Partners with the Poor" especially page 137. (4) Our organization wants to match the human and material resources of those who have them with those who don't. (5) We take care of you. Security and safety is the highest priority. (6) No one's culture or customs are better than another's. Everything is planned with respect for the culture and customs of the participants on all sides. (7) Good things can come in both large and small doses. I like short-term projects that are manageable and effective, but I love to see long-term partnerships in development come from these relationships. Long-term relationships best utilize resources and offer the most effective outcomes.

I hope those outcomes will have specific, measurable benefits and lead to positive, lasting social change and foster new opportunities for young people where there were no or very limited opportunities before. I also hope that these experiences will inspire those who participate to be change agents throughout their lives.

God's Earthen Vessel
By Laura Lee Wilson (Morgan)

Campus Ministry is a vital mission ministry of the church. Why would I make such a bold statement? I was privileged to serve 18 years on campuses ministering to students, faculty, staff and administrators. God called me to be the earthen vessel assisting students to become the next generation of Christian leaders. I served four years part-time at **Western Maryland College (now McDaniel College)** as the Coordinator of Religious Life then was appointed full-time to the Wesley Foundation Campus Ministry at the **University of Delaware** for the next 14 years. Sharing some stories may help you understand why Campus Ministry is essential on our campuses.

But he's already made it plain how to live,
what to do, what God is looking for in men
and women. It's quite simple:
Do what is fair and just to your neighbor,
be compassionate and loyal in your love,
and don't take yourself too seriously –
take God seriously. (Micah 6:8, *The Message*)

While many students spent their spring break partying, students connected with campus ministry spent their spring break on mission trips. For the Wesley Foundation at U of D, our spring break trip was to Lumberton, NC, to serve the Lumbee Nation and others in the community. Before our week of service began, we had a day of play at Myrtle Beach. One particular year, Holy Week was spring break week. On Palm Sunday we gathered on the beach to have worship. The service included a baptismal renewal liturgy. One student spoke up and said, "Wait! I have never been baptized." I was surprised because of her faithfulness and her willingness to serve God in many ways. We had had many talks about God and God's son. Before I could complete whatever I was saying, she enthusiastically asked, "Will you baptize me now?" "Of course I will with much joy!" Into the Atlantic Ocean we went. As I looked at her and she at me, the rest of the students followed into the water forming a circle around us. She was baptized in the name of the Father, the Son and the Holy Spirit surrounded with the circle of love from her peers. Today, she is a leader in her local church.

A knock came on the office door. The door opened before I could acknowledge the knock. Before he sat down, he announced, "I have had it! God is pulling at me so strongly! What do I do to go into ordained ministry?" This student is currently serving in the Susquehanna Annual Conference as an elder in full connection.

...for I was hungry and you gave me food,
I was thirsty and you gave me something to drink,
I was a stranger and you welcomed me, I was naked and you gave me clothing,
I was sick and you took care of me,
I was in prison and you visited me... (Matthew 25:35, NRSV)

She sat in my office and told me of her stepfather's verbal abuse. She started to cry, "I can't go home and face that again. I only get peace when he is gone. I need help to find a place to live here for the summer. I have a summer job. Help me, please!" She and her husband are youth leaders in their local church.

The phone rang at 8:30 am. The assistant to the President of the University said, "The President wants a service at 1:00 pm today. Can you do it?" This was after the most horrific event our country had experienced, 9-11-2001. He had been present that September evening when over 4,000 students came quietly to the Vigil that I had organized along with my colleagues. More than 8, 000 on campus attended or watched on their computers or the TV screens in the student centers. That year the President's Christmas card showed several pictures of the Vigil, including the campus spiritual leaders.

"...God plays no favorites! It makes no difference who you are or where you're from –
if you want God and are ready to do as he says, the door is open..." (Acts 10:34-35, The Message)

"Would you be willing to lead a Bible study for the opposing football team?" was the question. I said, "yes." I went to where the visiting team was staying. I had a short Bible study, shared a few thoughts, and we held hands and prayed. That afternoon as I watched the game, I could not cheer against the visiting team. I could not cheer for U of D. I saw the visiting team as my brothers in the faith instead of the opponents.

"I can do all things through him who strengthens me" (Philippians 4:13, NRSV)

Over my tenure I was privileged to participate in local, national and international campus ministry/chaplain organizations. The connectedness of colleagues supported my faith and commitment. We would share leadership ideas and affirm one another. I was so humbled when I was asked to attend the European Students' Chaplains' Conference in 1995 in Modling, Austria. The United States delegation was invited to an after conference meeting with Johan Kijne, where I was asked to be the Chaplain to the Chaplains at the First International Conference for College and University Chaplains and Campus Ministers. The Conference would be held in Durham, England, in 1996. The year was filled with joy as I met so many international colleagues while we worked on providing worship experiences. Each morning service was provided in the tradition from which the leader was a member. The larger services were ecumenical. Sharing on the Prep-Co was incredible. Leading the departing worship service was awesome. Having friends/colleagues remember the worship services unto this day is priceless.

Reflections/memories cannot be completed without a few words about Campus Ministry Women. Yes, there was a separate national organization for women serving in campus ministry/higher education. We planned a conference each year that would be held either before or after NCMA. The organization had to cease because of the all too often expression, "…not enough money in our budget." Unfortunately many campus ministry units have ceased because of that reality. However, for the time of Campus Ministry Women, we would sing, dance, share liturgy, cry, laugh, and just be us for a few hours. It was what fed many women in their ministries. Food for the journey!

God's earthen vessel

My experience of ministry in higher education was rooted in the teachings of Jesus the Christ, where all were invited and welcomed to be a part of the community of faith– and accepted unconditionally.

Campus ministry is the church in the midst of a secular community, and its spiritual leaders provide biblical hospitality through sharing the grace, love and forgiveness that God has freely given.

I humbly acknowledge now that I was the catalyst empowering and enabling the campus community to search for God's initiative in their lives. I was a teacher, mentor, a counselor and preacher. I was called to be a faithful learner while nurturing faithful minds for faithful service. I was called to set the example by leading and enabling others to bring their faith to life through serving our community, the community-at-large, and the global community by offering my gifts, my skills, my talents and my love for all God's people.

I was called and I said "yes!" I served God, the church and the campus making disciples for Jesus the Christ as we shared in transforming the world in his Holy name.

And that, my dear grandchildren, is a snapshot into my calling. If God calls you, answer quickly. The journey may not be smooth, but it is priceless. With all my love to Dereck, Mikayla, Alycia, Bryce, Carter, and Caleb; Nicholas, Michael, Heather, Brandon, Cole, and Claire.

The Scripture texts quoted above fed me throughout my campus ministry days and beyond.

Laura Lee C Wilson (Morgan) is living at Stoner's Farm in Littlestown, PA. She is care giver for her husband, Ralph, who has a rare autoimmune disorder. Morgan enjoys her family of 4 children, 12 grandchildren and 3 great grandchildren. She says, "Life is busy and good."

DREAM Catching
By John Feagins

After serving local church appointments in La Feria, Laredo, and San Antonio, Texas, I was privileged to serve as director of **San Antonio United Methodist Campus Ministry** from 2008 until 2013.

I had big shoes to fill. The venerable David Semrad had provided exceptional leadership for two and a half decades, consistently raising the consciousness of students and helping them Christian values, witness, and action for social justice. David's ministry deployed both teaching and example, ranging from the "Hot Potato" lecture series, where faculty, experts, and students could interact, to the "Urban Plunge" that placed students on the city's transit system, to ecumenical action and international mission projects. My transition into campus ministry would not have been possible without his friendship and support.

In November of 2010, was on campus at the University of Texas, San Antonio leading an open air discussion called "Seek & Speak." When we finished, I noticed another group of students organizing nearby to demonstrate for the DREAM (Development Relief and Education for Alien Minors) Act. Curious, I approached, and received a quick education about the DREAM Act.

Dreamers are undocumented students who have been raised within the United States. Having been brought here by their legal guardians, they broke no laws when they entered the U.S. They are intelligent, adaptive, successful, helpful young adults, educated in the public education system, many of whom also desire to serve in the military. Dreamers are American in every way except their place of birth and legal status.

Having served in Hispanic ministry along the Mexican border and in San Antonio, and personally knowing several students who would benefit from this legislation, I realized how important it was, and that there were clear moral implications for Christians in its adoption.

The students were using a bull-horn to call out to people to come sign their petition, yet with limited response. After sitting with them for a while, I explained that I was a campus minister with extensive public speaking experience. I said, "If you would like, I could help you on that." They were quite tired of yelling and let me have a try.

I began by calling out with questions like "How many of you know the golden rule? How many believe we should live and let live? How many cherish your freedom? How many would want to live under the fear that a police state would come to your home, arrest you, and ship you off to a third-world country? How many of you can tell the undocumented person from the citizen? The student sitting next to you in class could disappear tonight!"

In short order, a long line formed to sign the petition. The students also secured signatures of University leaders, including the president. At the end of the afternoon, we exchanged information, and they graciously invited me to other events they were holding.

Students on several campuses had been demonstrating as well, and Senator Majority leader Harry Reid, D-Nev, had promised to move a vote on the legislation before the end of the year. The UTSA students were concerned with securing the vote of Senator Kay Bailey Hutchison, who had once supported the measure, only to later conform to the bias of her party.

The demonstrators explained to me that they were launching a hunger strike (actually a careful fast monitored by doctors) to pressure Senator Hutchison to support the DREAM Act before the mid-term elections changed the political character of Congress.

I was blessed to join them on various occasions, for prayer vigils and to be invited by them to speak in public and to the media concerning the DREAM Act. On a number of occasions, I delivered public sermons, on campus and in front of the San Fernando Cathedral, laying out the inconsistencies in the ideology of those who oppose the DREAM Act, yet support family values, lower taxes, more national security, integrity in the stewardship of public funds, and such. The last sermon challenged those who claim a literal interpretation of scripture to apply the Parable of the Sheep and the Goats to the plight of the dreamers:

Matthew 25:41 *"Then he will say to those on his left, 'Depart from me, you who are cursed, into the eternal fire prepared for the devil and his angels.* *42 For I was hungry and you gave me nothing to eat, I was thirsty and you gave me nothing to drink, 43 I was a stranger and you did not invite me in, I needed clothes and you did not clothe me, I was sick and in prison and you did not look after me.'*
44 "They also will answer, 'Lord, when did we see you hungry or thirsty or a stranger or needing clothes or sick or in prison, and did not help you?'
45 "He will reply, 'Truly I tell you, whatever you did not do for one of the least of these, you did not do for me.'
46 "Then they will go away to eternal punishment, but the righteous to eternal life."

I explained that the word for "stranger" is *xenon*, from which the word xenophobia is derived. It means foreigner or alien. According to the teaching of Jesus, those who seek the unjust, uncharitable, irresponsible and immoral deportation of dreamers are liable to divine judgment.

During the month long course of the demonstration, I invited Rev. Lorenza Smith, a ministry colleague and immigration activist serving a church in San Antonio, to join their efforts. Rev. Smith joined their fast and chose to be arrested with the students when, after failing to get a response from Senator Hutchison, they remained in her office past closing hours. This demonstration gathered national attention to this cause.

The students and I had many conversations prior to the sit-in, including a conversation about the distinction between civil disobedience, the intentional disobedience of an unjust law, and radical disobedience, breaking the law in the process of political demonstration. The sit-in was an instance of the latter, done to express solidarity with those who are unwelcome within the United States and considered trespassers.

For the Dreamer, remaining, working, living, loving, sharing, making good grades, buying, selling, and paying taxes, are all *civil disobedience*. They live in a world where a mere traffic stop could result in deportation and separation from family. For everyone else, any act of friendship, hospitality, support, or love toward the Dreamer is an act of civil disobedience. So xenophobic and misanthropic is our law!

UMCM supported the students' efforts in a number of ways. We helped students travel to Washington where they met with the UM Board of Church and Society. We accompanied them with prayer and pastoral support. We marched with them and gathered other church leaders to their cause. We opened the Methodist Student Center to their meetings and teach-ins, and we brought them to a prayer service at La Trinidad UMC where I now serve as pastor. We hosted film screenings of undocumented filmmaker Pablo Veliz's "Cardboard Dreams." (Benita Veliz, Pablo's sister, spoke at the Democratic National Convention.)

Ultimately, while the DREAM Act failed in Congress, it succeeded within the UMC, with a resolution approved at the 2012 General Conference.

The DREAM Act hunger strike ended with a community-wide pot-luck supper held at Jefferson United Methodist Church, where my spouse, Rev. Raquel Cajiri Feagins, herself an immigrant from Bolivia who graduated first in her class from a U.S. High School, welcomed Mayor Julián Castro and leaders from many civic organizations to express appreciation for the courage and integrity of the student demonstrators.

This solidarity and work did not take place without some controversy. Our own UTSA student group was indifferent, and some were uncomfortable with these efforts. A few of our board members were offended, and suggested I should not become involved unless our student group wanted to be involved. I explained that I was a campus minister, not a young adults pastor serving a private social group. My duty was to the entire campus, students, faculty, and staff, even to God, as pastor and as witness. While it may have offended some, our efforts opened many doors and relationships for ministry that have continued to this day.

In the Spring of 2013, I received word that I would be appointed to La Trinidad UMC, an historic downtown congregation built in part by the efforts of refugees and immigrants from Mexico. Several of the students I met during that demonstration continue serving the cause of social justice to this day, and some of them work in the same ministry area as La Trinidad UMC. Those friendships, partnerships, and alliances forged in campus ministry now extend to the world parish, as the passion and hope for justice continues to extend the mercy and grace of Christ to those he came to save.

Obituaries of Recently Deceased Colleagues

Because these friends were well-known to so many of us over the years, we wanted to include them among the NCMA Sages in this volume. Sadly, we do not have their memoirs, but we do have many joyful memories of their times with us.

Charles Doak, October 10, 1931-February 7, 2011

Charles W. Doak, a founding NCMA member and President, 1973-74, was a campus minister at the University of Idaho and University of Southern California before coming to UCLA in 1968. He joined the civil rights marches in Montgomery and Washington DC, and later he and his wife Jan participated in mission trips to the Middle East and to Northern Ireland. He was committed to interfaith dialogue, brought the Academy of Judaic, Christian and Islamic Studies to UCLA and later served as Executive Director of the University Religious Conference. He was instrumental in establishing the Chancellor's Committee on Religion and Ethics that resulted in the UCLA Center for the Study of Religion. He served on the Institutional Review Board at UCLA Medical Center.

Chuck wrote and published a *History of the Presbyterian Church's Ministry in Higher Education*, which is in the Yale United Ministries in Higher Education archives.

Charles served in leadership roles in many local, regional and national organizations of the Presbyterian Church. He was President of Meals on Wheels, several parent-teacher groups and the UCLA Campus Choir. He was a voracious reader of theology, current affairs and history, and an avid tennis player. He enjoyed his friends, tennis partners and community life in Santa Monica, and also for the last ten years part-time from his home in Taos, New Mexico.

Harold James Wells, 1936-2013

Harold James Wells, activist, political junkie and friend of many died on Thursday, December 12, 2013 in Des Moines, IA. Harold was born in 1936 in Russell, Arkansas, smack dab in the middle of the great depression, which explains both his lifelong inordinate love of pot luck dinners and his inability to ever throw anything away. Ever.

Harold loved the opera, symphony, ballet, and all manner of plays. More often than not he would wake both of his young boys to the sounds of WOI public radio FM, blaring the likes of Puccini, Carmen and Bach. A true dream come true for grade school aged boys. He was not all highbrow and college-educated however, and had a wonderfully eclectic record collection, where the likes of Isaac Hays, Simon and Garfunkel, and Elmore James all waited patiently for the curious and prying fingers of his young boys.

Who knows what drives people to become themselves. Perhaps it was Harold's intimate familiarity with the cruelty of others. Cruelty fostered in the dark recesses of intolerance and insecurity. Perhaps, it was his kind soul. Whatever it was, it led to a lifetime of helping others. It led to a lifetime of protests, demonstrations, marches, and counseling. He was tireless. He marched for civil rights in Arkansas in the 1960s; he marched on Washington in the 1970s for the ERA. In the 1980s, he fought for peace with STAR*PAC and finally he fought for equality for all, regardless of sexual orientation.

In 1976, Harold opened the Thoreau center, a community center where like-minded people could congregate, people from across the aisle could debate, and everyone could let down their hair and have a good time. For four decades there have been weddings, birthday parties, political functions, French Club meetings, poetry readings, gypsy jazz shows, and old fashion house parties too numerous to count.

Over the last 77 years Harold has been a campus minister, teacher, politico, sexologist, rape counselor, rabble-rouser, raconteur, and dreadful cook. He rarely paid a bill on time and punctuality remained an absolute stranger to him until the very end.

He is survived by his two sons Malcolm (Janel) and Gregory Wells, to whom he has given the love of music, the arts, sports, and most of all the gift of an open mind and the ability and desire to question the man, though at times he has regretted that last gift. Harold also has four wonderful, riotously spirited grandchildren who are as talented as they are diverse.

A Lifetime of Advocacy for Campus Ministry:
a Tribute to Barry F. Cavaghan
Sent by Barry's family, shortly after his death on May 20, 2014

Barry Frank Cavaghan, Sacramento, California, completed his work at Union Theological Seminary and felt called to be of service at small community churches. He spent one year at 29 Palms near Joshua Tree National Park in a temporary pastoral visiting position. He was called to a Presbyterian church in Corning in 1957.

His work with the youth of that church over several years caught the attention of Sacramento Presbytery who urged him to accept an assignment as regional campus minister in 1961. He served Sacramento State, Sacramento City, American River and Sierra Consumnes Colleges until the late sixties when funding declined dramatically and he was given a sabbatical to prepare for another profession.

He attended the Counselor Education program at California State University, Sacramento, earned a second master's degree and qualified as a licensed marriage and family therapist in 1971. He remained active in campus ministry, however, becoming president of the UMHE (United Ministries in Higher Education) which became the CCCM (California Campus Christian Ministry), a support group for campus ministers. In this role, he visited campus minsters, raised support money and organized conferences for exchange of ideas and resources between campuses and from guest speakers and educators.

He enjoyed serving as a guest preacher at many churches throughout Northern California for more than 50 years. Barry loved all things that soared: he was an avid recreational pilot; he was awed by the beauty of the natural world; he climbed challenging mountains; and he found inspiration in great music, great ideas, and the triumph of the human spirit. He was devoted to his family and gave of himself fully until his sudden and brief illness.

In April 2014 Barry was diagnosed with inoperable liver cancer. His first and most poignant regret was that he would miss the July NCMA meeting in St. Louis.

.

Bill Ng
1934-July 22, 2014

Born at the Chinese Hospital in San Francisco, CA to the late Lily and Edward Ng, Bill was the adoring father of Jeremy and Grace Dolezal-Ng; caring partner/friend of Carol Dolezal.

A strong person of faith and a dedicated Presbyterian pastor, Bill was actively committed to a lifetime of social justice and working for the disenfranchised. He lived out Martin Luther King's vision of the Beloved Community and worked to inspire others to do the same. His first call as pastor was to serve Faith Presbyterian in South Central LA when demographics were changing and racial tensions high. Bill was nurtured by the San Francisco Chinatown communities at the Presbyterian Church and Cameron House. His career also included service with Mental Health Services at Manzanita House and Director of the Indian Welcome House in LA in the 1960's which provided social services to Native Americans who had been forced off their land to urban areas.

For many years, he was Campus Pastor for Unitas, an ecumenical ministry at UC Berkeley.

He served as Resident Director of Berkeley Presbyterian Mission Homes, from 2001 to present. Prior to that he was Executive Director of the Indo Chinese Housing Development Corporation in SF Tenderloin. Concurrently, he volunteered as President of the Cameron House board and was a major force in bringing to light the pastoral abuse there. As a survivor, he worked tirelessly to help heal that community's wounds.

Bill graduated San Francisco State University, followed by a M.Div from San Francisco Theological Seminary and MSW from UC Berkeley. Bill was a lifelong student and loved sports. He was an avid fan of the Giants and 49ers,

320

but it all started with the SF Seals . When Bill met Carol, he said with all his accomplishments, he missed out on having children. In 1998 twins Jeremy and Grace were born and remain Bill's greatest accomplishment and legacy.

Apartheid: Campus Ministry with the University Community
By Bill Ng
(Written in 1997 for an earlier NCMA publication)

It was spring 1985 when the anti-apartheid movement for South Africa was heating up at UC Berkeley. This was the second year of demonstrations for the university to divest. Radical students and other concerned individuals were gathered together on campus ground sleeping overnight until the University system divested its investment in South Africa.

They challenged the police on one particular morning as they vented their emotions. I recall getting up early that morning to watch as the campus police broke up the demonstrators who were sleeping overnight in their make-shift wooden houses. Trash cans and other articles were tossed on the grounds as demonstrators scattered in many directions chased by police. Violence began to escalate.

At that point I felt the spirit of Christ calling on the faith community to act. It was time for the religious community to be present. I got on the telephone and called a number of my clergy friends to be present the next day as a symbol of non-violence. They came in the afternoon and we stood at strategic places. The mood changed and that particular demonstration by clergy was a significant witness. There were no more violent acts by either side after that day.

Clergy presence made a big difference during the rest of the anti-apartheid movement. A member of the University staff forwarded to me a letter of commendation from Chancellor Ira Heyman's office for our clergy' s non-violent action. Several months later the University system divested. Clergy presence can and did make a difference. It was one of the most spiritual moments in my years as a campus minister. I thank God for that special "kairos" moment.

George M. Conn, Jr.
1935-October 4, 2014

George Conn accepted his first call to the Shenandoah Church in Johnson City, TN. Over the next 37 years, George would serve as the Presbyterian Campus Minister at East Tennessee State University, Johnson City, TN; College Pastor, St. Andrew's Presbyterian College, Laurinburg, NC; Chaplain, United States Navy and Marine Corps Education and Development Command, Quantico, VA; Pastor, University Church, Tuscaloosa, AL; Director, Office of Higher and Public Education, General Assembly Mission Board, PCUS, and staff to UMHE; Associate for Racial Ethnic Schools and Colleges, General Assembly Council, PC(USA); Pastor, Massanutten Church, Penn Laird, VA. Following his retirement in 2001, he continued to serve churches as interim pastor. George served the larger church in numerous capacities, including as a member of the Advisory Committee on International Evangelism PC(USA); the General Assembly Council (Worldwide Ministries Division); and the Council of the Synod of the Mid-Atlantic.

George was born in Bristol, VA. He was an avid fly fisher, loved great music, a good drink, and a bad joke. He was a loving father and devoted husband. He and his wife lived many places and traveled to more than 49 countries, but he called himself a son of the mountains and yearned to return home.

George devoted his life to his faith, and was especially dedicated to civil rights, social justice, and higher education. His contributions were recognized with honorary doctorates from numerous schools and colleges across the country.

George honorably served 27½ years as a Navy Chaplain, 24 of which were with the Marine Corps. He retired as a Captain in 1990. He was the National Chaplain, Marine Corps Reserve Officers Association (2002-2004).

Prayers for Hard Times
by Walter Fishbaugh

Walter I. Fishbaugh was God's beautiful child whose gifts of perception, articulation, and love remain with us although his physical presence has been gone more than twenty years. His eyes saw realities in his fellow humans that escaped their own and those of their sojourners. His heart felt more deeply than almost anyone I knew. His commitment to his Creator infused every part of his life and work. And, to the wondering amazement of those of us who listened, his words, even in what might otherwise pass for daily conversation, flowed like poetry whose right hand was love and whose left was grace.

Before his death he left a large collection of prayers to the care of his friend, William Belli. Bill in turn has put Walt's 100 Prayers for Hard Times and Hard Hearts and a bonus of benedictions into a simple notebook and distributed it to some of us. (by Wayne C. Bryan)

Walt wrote in his introduction:
I hope that many of these prayers will be heartily and thoughtfully prayed by many other congregations. I hope that they will be freely adapted to the personality and situation of other clusters of the faithful.... Let us keep in mind that prayer doesn't really come from us. It is His Spirit thrusting and probing within us Who breaks out in our praying, giving evidence of God's continuing enticement of our spirits out toward Him. Let us pray!

i.

O Lord God, out of a dense inertness
You have spoken
the universe into
lively motion.

And in the midst of the whirling spheres you have given us a world – a place to be – a speck of blue and green on which to live and for which to care.

And you have caused to be upon this earth nations and races and all sorts and conditions of people, that we might find you and love you – and find one another and love one another.

Finding you, O God, and finding one another
have proven to be
<u>one</u> thing –
<u>one</u> search –
<u>one</u> indivisible enterprise of the spirit.

We are ashamed, O God, that after countless generations there is still so much of it left to be done. We and our earth are in peril because we have not fully found you, nor loved you deeply enough. We know this because, as persons and nations and peoples, we are still estranged from one another.

In Jesus Christ, your son our Lord, help us so to find you and so to love you that we shall link our lives with all those who share His and our humanity. Save us in him, O God, until we shall be bound up together in the bundle of life and love that we call your kingdom.

Come and reign over us, Ancient of Days. Amen.

ii.

O good and blessed God,
Father and Friend, Creator, Sustainer,
Center and Circumference,
Source and Destination
– be all and in all to us, we pray.

Help us to know that no matter how occupied or pre-occupied we are, we deal with you. Behind every appearance and every circumstance there is the Divine Presence.

Remind us that we cannot distance ourselves too far away as to be beyond your care or outside your eager concern.

And when we feel alone, or adrift,
or estranged, or forgotten,
remind us that these feelings are not reality,
but reflections of our own dimness of faith.

If we have come to this holy time and place in depression of spirit or coldness of heart, restore a right spirit within us and rekindle such an affection for one another and for you that we shall be reborn – renewed in body, mind and inner-ness, so that the week we now begin may carry through each day some of the energy and glory of this encounter.

For it is in the name and Spirit of Jesus, our Lord, we pray. Amen.

iii.

Thrust us out, O God, into the lively stream
of your concern for this world!

Let the beat of your Father-heart give a singing and marching cadence to us as your people. May we hear its rhythm within our worship, drawing us into step with each other and into harmony with you.

For too long, O Lord, we have had to occupy ourselves with our own affairs. We are weary of expending energies tinkering with our documents and our real estate. Our uneasiness makes us irritable and petulant. These are important things, deserving of our best thought. But they channel our concerns narrowly. They shrink our horizons. They so magnify secondary things that we are in peril of losing our calling in the distortion.

There are so many things to decide that we stagger under the burden.

Refresh us and renew us, O God, for our mission. Rouse us from our weariness. Call us to greatness of spirit. Help us to find ourselves as a people, O Lord. Stamp us by Your Spirit, as a church whose program and purpose intersect in the passion of Jesus, our Lord, for this lost and undone world.

In His name. Amen.

NCMA Newsletter

NCMA: The First Thirty Years
(1964-1994)

There was a beginning. It was 1964 and what we now call the National Campus Ministry Association took form in a windowless meeting room of the old Pick Mark Twain Hotel in St. Louis.

Present there were representatives of seven major denominations, all Protestant ministers, all male, and all sharing a vision for the church and ministry in higher education. It was a cross section of campus ministry professionals in the 1960's, both in age and gender. Each had a history of involvement in the denominational gatherings of campus ministers in regional and national settings.

According to Chuck Doak, some had been in gatherings earlier that year where the agreements were hammered out for "a single association." Four denominations had taken this initiative: Disciples of Christ, United Church of Christ, Evangelical United Brethren, and United Presbyterian. They would be joined in the St. Louis meeting by representatives of three additional communions: American Baptist, Lutheran (NLC), and Presbyterian US. (Southern). Methodist participation came later.

In the post World War II years, the character of campus ministry had changed. With the majority of students now in state and public colleges and universities and a new ecumenical spirit abroad, the old and almost universal pattern of denominational foundations or houses at major campuses was shifting. Most campus ministers found themselves relating to other campus ministers in either merged or visibly cooperative ministry. New ministries were almost always established with an ecumenical base.

The need for an association of campus ministry professionals at a national level was clear. Denominational gatherings still had a place, and may still, for purposes unique to each and vital to the internal politics, credibility, and accountability within a given denomination, but professional development and communication needs called for a new structure.

What was envisioned was a national expression of a reality common to many campuses, namely, a strong sense of common ministry by the various Protestant Christian churches. A variety of terms were in use to describe these ministries, among them "joint," "united," "cooperative," and "ecumenical." It was the desire of that group of founders in St. Louis in 1964 that their new structure or association embody the spirit of unity that marked the local scene.

The initial funding and staffing of this association came, in part, from participating denominations and from the emerging United Ministries in Higher Education (U.M.H.E.). Membership dues were only a part of the financial base and budget. The churches and their representatives saw the new association as an extension of their time-honored concern for the equipping of clergy and lay leadership for the work of ministry in higher education.

There was considerable discussion of the name for this new association. Some present felt strongly that the words "higher education" should be included, or the word "university," to indicate the setting and the status of those engaged in this ministry. It needed to be seen as a professional association and more than a "fellowship." The term "campus ministry" was not used as universally as it is now, thirty years later. Campus ministers were still being called "student workers," "university pastors," or "foundation directors."

The ultimate choice of "National Campus Ministry Association" reflected the concern for a name that was inclusive, with which both women and men, lay and clergy could identify. At the same time, N.C.M.A. was seen as an ecumenical body, representative of the Christian denominations in covenant in its formation, and not, therefore, intentionally an interfaith organization. Membership would be open to all engaged in ministry in higher education and who supported NC.M.A.'s goals and objectives. As constituted, there was no attempt to accommodate to a broad spectrum of theological viewpoints. If a denomination certified that one was engaged in ministry in higher education, that made one eligible for membership.

In 1964, fewer than 10% of the membership were women and nationally probably a like percentage were active in full-time positions. The first women added to the Executive Committee came in 1970. One woman was asked to serve, but, to her credit, she declined to be a token woman and stated she would serve only if a second woman were asked. They both came and were instrumental in sensitizing a male dominated association. The first woman to serve as a N.C.M.A. president was Ann Marie Coleman (1981-83).

In the early years, U.M.H.E.-deployed staff persons attended Executive Committee meetings in an ex-officio role. These included, at different times, David Rich, Ron McNeur, Dick Bolles, Verlyn Barker, and Myrv Delapp. David Rich served as Executive Secretary on behalf of U.M.H.E. and for a number of years handled N.C.M.A. membership and communication services out of his office in Valley Forge.

Executive Committee meetings were twice a year, the winter meeting during the 1960s being almost always in Chicago, the exceptions being meetings in Louisville (1966) and Little Rock (1970). In the 1970s, a pattern evolved of a February meeting in a central U.S. city and a summer meeting during the annual conference, or in the fall when there was no conference.

The summer conferences began with the organizational meeting at Michigan State in East Lansing in June 1965. In 1966, a conference was held at the University of Georgia campus in Athens, and a 1967 convocation at Michigan State drew 475 participants around the theme "Issues in Higher Education." In 1969 there was a gathering of N.C.M.A. during the American Association for Higher Education (A.A.H.E.) annual meeting in Chicago. Meeting concurrently with A.A.H.E. became a pattern for the next few years. Sending representatives of N.C.M.A. to various other professional association meetings was an early strategy of involvement in the academic world.

Denominational caucuses often were held during N.C.M.A. conferences and in the 70's, Campus Ministry Women organized and, subsequently, Campus Ministry Men formed to meet the special needs of N.C.M.A. members. Representation on the Executive Committee, now called the Coordinating Committee, was primarily by geographic region. Initially, there were two representatives from each of six regions, later reduced to one, plus at- large members to represent underrepresented constituencies. Initially the President was elected for a three-year term and Dick Yoe (U.C.C.) served from 1964 to 67. The second elected President, Wally Toevs (U.P.U.S.A.), served a two-year term and that has been the prevailing pattern since.

The changing constituency and agenda of N.C.M.A. has been a mirror of the changing patterns of higher education ministry. N.C.M.A. began in 1964, the same year that four denominations came together to form United Ministries in Higher Education (U.M.H.E.). An ecumenical spirit and imperative reshaped national and local structures. The churches were rethinking and reaffirming a traditional emphasis on higher education, recognizing that the vast majority of its students were now in state colleges and universities rather than in church-related colleges. The non-traditional students, women, and ethnic minorities became the focus of specialized ministries. The student activism of the 60s and 70s was shaped and led by campus ministries committed to "prophetic inquiry" as a valid mode of ministry. Civil rights, peace-making, draft counseling, problem pregnancy counseling, ecology, and gay and lesbian rights were issues and activities that commanded the attention of denominational and ecumenical ministries. An early N.C.M.A. conference in the 1960s focused on the cybernetic revolution. All of these issues were addressed in both annual conferences, and regional gatherings and in the N.C.M.A. Newsletter and Occasional Papers.

In the first years, the Executive Committee sought to plan and help fund, annually, a series of continuing education events for the membership. In 1969 there were six of these and in 1970, twelve! Responsibility for such events shifted to the regions during the 1970s and the annual conference became the major focus of national strategy. Print media became the primary medium of communication among the membership with the beginning of the Newsletter and the publication of Occasional Papers. Editors have included Dave Steffinson, Dan Earnhardt, Bob Turner and Sally and George Gunn. Betsy Alden and, now, Ken Mcintosh have served as Editors of the Occasional Papers in recent years. In 1994 we recognize those who have been in campus ministry over thirty years and those who have provided leadership over the years. There is always a new generation coming on the scene, but that which changes least of all is the commitment of a company of men and women who find their calling and the meaning of ministry in the world of higher education.

As professionals, let us make that profession a profession of faith in the One who calls and who goes before us in all the challenges of each new day. Chuck Doak concludes his 1989 "Brief History of the N.C.M.A." with these words: "N.C.M.A. has struggled with the themes of Exodus, Wilderness, and the Promised Land. The future will be no less an opportunity to live with these themes. Even more important will be Death and Resurrection experiences in the Faith that will enable N.C.M.A. to continue its pilgrimages of hope."

So be it.

NCMA Conferences 1964-2014

Year   Location   Theme

1964 - Mark Twain Hotel, St. Louis, MO, Founding of NCMA

1965 - Michigan State University, East Lansing, First Plenary Meeting of NCMA

1966 - University of Georgia, Athens, "The Search for Wholeness"

1967 - Michigan State University, East Lansing, "Issues in Higher Education"

1969-1974 - Chicago, IL

1973 - Washington, DC, created the Council for Professional Religious Ass. In Higher Ed

1975 - Colorado Women's College, Denver, "The Future of Ministry in Higher Education" with
    Robert Bellah, Matthew Fox, Beverly Harrison, Paul Harris

1976 - Regional Conferences

1977 - Berea College, "Doing Theology, "Living the Questions" with Ann and Harry Smith

1978 - Regional Conferences

1979 - Macalester College, St. Paul MN, "The Future: We Can't Get There from Here" with
    Hazel Henderson, Rosemary Reuther, Sharon and Tom Neufer-Emswiler

1980 - Colorado Women's College, Denver, "Social Interaction" with Robert Rankin

1981 - University of CA, Berkeley, "Beyond Chicken Little: Locating in Dislocation" with
    Robert Bellah, SF Mime Troupe, Robert Parsonage, Donna Schaper, Carol Christ

1982 - Georgetown University, Washington, DC, "Politics, Peacemaking, and Poetry" with Will
    Campbell, Sweet Honey in the Rock, Joe Brown and Ruth Love

1983 - Mexican-American Cultural Center, San Antonio, "Faith-Fiesta-Liberation" with Virgil
    Elizondo, Sanford Gottlieb, Brady Tyson, Ricardo Ramirez

1984 - Texas Christian University, "Stayin' Alive with the Right Stuff for the Big Chill"

1985 - Lewis and Clark College, Portland, OR, "The Painful Wisdom of Survivors: Images of
    Hope and Renewal" with Douglas Huneke

1986 - Duke University, Durham, NC, "On Jordan's Stormy Banks: The South as Paradigm for
    Values in Conflict" with John Westerhoff, Doris Betts, and Doug Marlette

1987 - University of Pennsylvania, Philadelphia, with Vincent and Rosemary Harding, Delores
    Williams, Bob Edgar

1988 - University of San Diego

1989 - Baldwin-Wallace College, Cleveland, OH

1990 - Episcopal Divinity School, Cambridge, MA

1991 – Dillard University, New Orleans, LA, "Jambalaya, Crawfish Pie, File Gumbo:
    Overcoming Homogeneity" with Cain Hope Felder

1992 - Four Regional Conferences: Fairbanks, AK; Fayetteville, AR; Minneapolis; El Paso

1993 - Howard University, Washington, DC, "The Future is Upon Us: Images of Things to
    Come" with Bruce Birch, Mary Cosby, and Diana Chambers

1994 - Michigan State University, East Lansing, MI, "Stepping Out on the Word of God:
    Campus Ministry in A Changing World" with Tex Sample and Edwina Gateley

1995 - University of Tulsa, OK, "Rounding Out Communities: Stories of Living Circles"

1996 - Collingwood College, University of Durham, England, "Truth in Exile: A Challenge to
    Church and University" with Catherine Keller and David Jenkins

1997 - University of San Francisco, CA, "Soul Matters: The Arts, The University, and Campus
    Ministry" with Daniel Berrigan, Janice Mirikatani, and JoAnne Henry

1998 - Yale University, New Haven, CT, "Holy Wilderness: Professional Religious Work on
    Campus"

1999 - Estes Park, CO, "Unto the Hills…Onto the Campus: Passion and Practice for Ministry in
    the Twenty-first Century" with Marcus Borg

2000 - University of British Columbia, Vancouver, BC, Canada, "Phoenix Rising: Wisdom,
    Spirituality, and Community in the University"

2001 - Hampton University, VA, "Come to the Waters: Living Out Our Baptism Through
    Campus Ministry" with Sharon Parks

2002 - Radisson Hotel O'Hare, Chicago, IL, "Something's Brewing: The Changing Face of Campus Ministry"

2003 - St. Mary's University, San Antonio, TX, "Borders/Frontiers" with Jim Wallis of *Sojourners*

2004 - Griffith University, Nathan Campus, Brisbane, Australia, "Dreaming Landscapes: Spiritualities and Justice in Learning Communities"

2005 - Columbia University, "Campus Ministry and All That Jazz" with Douglas Adams and James Forbes

2006 - Lewis and Clark University, Portland, OR, "None-Zone" with Marcia McFee

2007 - Vanderbilt University, Nashville, TN, "The Blues and Rhythm of Campus Ministry" with James Lawson

2008 - University of St. Mary, Leavenworth, KS, "Convergence: Bridging Ministry-Visioning Congregation & Community"

2009 - Case Western Reserve University, Cleveland, OH

2010 - American University, Washington, DC, "Finding Holy Ground: Converging Streams of and Justice"

2011 – University of CA, Berkeley, "Neither Jew Nor Greek: Creating Multicultural Communities of Faith on Campus"

2012 - Yale University, New Haven, CT, International

2013 - Agnes Scott College, Decatur, GA, "Interfaith is the New Ecumenical" with Eboo Patel

2014 - Washington University, St. Louis, MO, "Generation to Generation"

NCMA Presidents 1964-2014

1964-67	Dick Yoe
1967-69	Wally Toevs
1969-71	George Gunn
1971-72	Glenn Martin
1972-73	Robert Johnson
1973-74	Chuck Doak
1974-75	Sam Slie
1975-76	Allan Burry
1976-77	Donald Collins
1977-79	Harold Wells
1979-81	Allyn Axelton
1981-83	Ann Marie Coleman
1983-85	Bob Breihan
1985-87	Delton Pickering
1987-89	William Ng
1989-91	Odette Lockwood Stewart
1991-93	Thad Holcombe, Jr.
1993-94	Mary Sloan Baugh
1994-96	Phil Harder
1996-98	Ken McIntosh
1998-2000	David Moore
2000-2002	Brian Young
2002-2004	Kristin Stoneking
2004-2006	Karen Bush
2006-2008	Jan Rivero
2008-2010	David Jones
2010-2012	Paul Walley
2012-2014	Cody Nielsen

List of Contributors with Campuses and Dates of Service

Betsy Alden, Dallas Community College Ministry, 1976-84; UMHE Communications Coordinator 1984-89; NCMA Program Coordinator, 1989-1992; Central NM Community College/UNM 1989-96; Duke University, 1996-2010 (34)

Verlyn Barker, University of Nebraska, 1956-1959; National Staff for Ministry in Higher Education, United Church of Christ, 1961-1996; President of United Ministries in Higher Education, 1970-1980; President,World Student Christian Federation Trustees USA,1991-96 (38)

Chad Boliek, University of Idaho, 1960-1971 (11)

Dick Bowyer, Fairmont State University, West Virginia, 1963-2006 (43)

Debra Brazzel, Mountain View (Dallas) Community College,1984-89; Duke University,1991-98 (12)

Bob Breihan, University of Texas, 1951-55; Director, Texas UMC Campus Ministry Foundation, 1955-61; University of Texas, 1961-1980. (29)

Wayne Bryan, Stephen F. Austin College (TX), 1962-66; Drake University, 1966-75; University of Florida, Gainesville 1975-1978 ; University of Texas, Austin, 1981-89 (24)

David Burnight, University of California, Davis 1951-1966; San Diego State University, 1966-1994 (43)

Barry Cavaghan, Sacramento State University; CA UMHE/ Campus Christian Ministry, 1965-2005 (40)

Robert Cooper, Denton (TX) Wesley Foundation, 1952-56; West Texas State 1956-5; Texas A&M 1957-6; Texas A&I 1961-65; Southern Methodist University, 1965-92 (40)

Steve Darr, Virginia Tech, Blacksburg, VA Community College Ministries; Peacework, 1984-2014 (30)

Howard Daughenbaugh, Tulane University, 1958-69; University of Illinois, 1969-73 (15)

K. James (Jim) Davis, University of Minnesota, Duluth, 1968-77; University of Puget Sound, 1977-2006 (38)

Ruth Dunn, Vincennes University, 1979-98; Synod Higher Ed Committees, 1998-2014; Campus Ministry Advancement Board, 2010-14 (35)

Robert Epps, Washington University, St. Louis, 1964-73; Indiana University, Bloomington, 1973-90; Campus Ministry Advancement Board; 1990-2014 (40)

John Feagins, San Antonio United Methodist Campus Ministry, TX, 2008-2013 (5)

Don Gibson, University of Oklahoma, 1961-83 (22)

Jan Griesinger, World Student Christian Federation, 1971-75; University of Ohio,1976-2004 (32)

George Gunn, University of Georgia, 1950-54; University of Arkansas, 1960-73; Office of Higher Education, Presbyterian Church, U.S,. 1973–76; NCMA Co-Founder, 1964; President, 1969-71; Newsletter Editor (with Sally), 1991-96 (25)

Philip Harder, Willamette University, 1968-71; Southern Oregon State College, 1971-76; Portland State University 1976-1998; NCMA President, 1995-6 (30)

Emmett Herndon, Stetson University; Emory University; Georgia Tech 1955-90 (35)

Thad Holcombe, University of Tulsa, 1967-84; University of Oklahoma, 1984-91; University of Kansas, 1991-2013; NCMA President, 1991-93 (46)

Diane Kenney, Stanford University, 1969-74; Danforth Foundation, 1974-5; Mills College,1975-6; Youngstown State University, OH 1977 -82; University of Southern California, 1982-2012 (43)

Odette Lockwood-Stewart, University of California at San Francisco,1979-81; San Diego State University1981-85 ; UCLA,1985-93 ; UC Berkeley 1993-97; NCMA President 1989-91 (21)

Roger Loyd, Texas Tech University, 1974-1979; Director, UMC TX Commission on Campus Ministry, 1979-80 (6)

Thomas Mainor, William and Mary College, VA, 1967-71; Campus Urban Ministry, Presbytery of Norfolk 1971-79; Virginia Campus Ministry Forum, 1980-82; Medical Center, Norfolk, 1982-85; University of Illinois Med Center, Chicago, 1990-95 (20)

Tom McCormick, University of Washington, 1966-1985 (19)

Marna McKenzie, University of California, Berkeley, 1969-76 ; UMHE, N. California, 1972-89; San Francisco State University, 1979-85; UMHE national staff,1987-91. (24)

Bernadine McRipley, UMHE, Trenton, NJ , 1974-80 (6)

E. Thomas Miller, Presbyterian Campus Pastor at UNC, Chapel Hill, (1963-66); University Pastor, West Virginia University, Morgantown, West Virginia University,(1967-1976); Minister to the Campus and Assistant Professor of Humanities, Austin College, Sherman, TX (1976-1982) (19)

Jerry Miller, Eastfield Community College, Dallas, 1978-87 (9)

Susan Yarrow Morris, University of Washington, 1972-88 (16)

Helen R. Neinast, Western New Mexico University, 1975-78; Director of Campus Ministry, UMC Board of Higher Education and Ministry, 1980-89; Emory University, 1992-2002 (20)

Hugh Nevin, United Campus Ministries of Suffolk County, 1963-1972; Long Island United Campus Ministries, 1972-1978; three interim roles related to the New York State Council of Churches, 1979-1982; Union College, 1982-1994; University at Albany-SUNY, 1994-1996 (33)

Thomas Niccols, Ohio University, 1958-70; Hiram University 1970-91 (33)

Tom Philipp, State University of New York (SUNY), Oswego, 1965-72; Long Island United Campus Ministry, 1972-2005 (40)

Delton Pickering, Louisiana State University, 1961-71; Memphis State University, 1971-76; Director, Ecumenical Campus Ministry, Baltimore, MD, 1976-88; NCMA President, 1985-87, Secretary-Treasurer, 1987-93 (33)

James Pruyne, Illinois State University, 1955-1995 (40)

Ted Purcell, Western Carolina University, 1970-74; North Carolina State University, 1974-89; Duke University, 1989-2010 (50)

Jim Ray, University of Illinois,1963-69; University of Pittsburg, 1969-83; Youngstown State University, 1983- 95 (32)

Alice Riemer-McKee, University of Wyoming, Laramie 1978-79; University of Colorado, Boulder (with husband Doug McKee), 1979-90 (12)

David Rich, University of Maine, 1961-63; Northeastern Regional Secretary, UMHE, Valley Forge, PA 1968 - 1975; Executive Director for the PA Commission for United Ministries in Higher Education,1975-1990 (24)

Jan Rivero, United College Ministries in Northern Virginia, 1981-1984, University of Virginia, 1993-98; University of North Carolina Chapel Hill,1998-2010; NCMA President, 2007-08; Stop Hunger Now, 2011-2014 (19)

Clyde Robinson, Duke University, 1966-68; National Staff (PCUSA) to UMHE, 1969-1997(33)

David Royer, University of Washington, 1965-91 (26)

Mark Rutledge, University of CA, Berkeley,1956-7; San Jose State1961-67; IA State 67-71; Monterey Peninsula College, 1971-73;Northern Illinois University,73-80; University of NM 80-96; Duke University, 1996-2013 (52)

Don Shockley, Birmingham Southern College, 1964-72; University of Redlands, CA, 1972-79; Emory University, 1979-90; UMC Board of Higher Education, 1990-99 (35)

Harry Smith, University of North Carolina 1952-69 (17)

Robert Thomason, Milledgeville, GA Wesley Foundation, 1966-69; Emory University 1969-74, Jacksonville, FL Campus Ministry 1974-84, United College Ministries in No. VA, 1984-97; NCMA Admin Officer/Editor 1998-2006 (40)

Paul Walley, State University of NY (SUNY), New Paltz 1971-2007 (36)

Harold Wells, Drake University, IA, 1968-80

Jim Wilson, Eastern Kentucky University, 1963-69; Northeast Louisiana University, Monroe, 1969-97 (34)

Laura Lee Wilson (Morgan), University of Delaware, 1991-2005 (14)

Manuel Wortman, UNC, Greensboro, 1969-70; Appalachian State University, 1970-75; UNC, Chapel Hill, 1975-1998; UMC Western NC Executive for Campus Ministry, 1998-2003 (34)

Darrell Yeaney, Emporia (KS) State University, 1962-69; University of California, Santa Cruz, 72-86; University of Iowa, 1986-98 (33)

Email Addresses of Contributors

Betsy Alden	alden@duke.edu
Verlyn Barker	barkerv@me.com
Chad Boliek	cb4@desertgate.com
Dick Bowyer	rorbow@aol.com
Debra Brazzel	debra.brazzel@gmail.com
Bob Breihan	bobbreihan@gmail.com
Wayne Bryan	lwbryan@bellsouth.net
David Burnight	burnightD@cox.net
Barry Cavaghan	peggygtc@gmail.com
Steve Darr	steve@peacework.org
Howard Daughenbaugh	hdaughenb@aol.com
K. James Davis	kjadavis42@gmail.com
Ruth Dunn	ruthdunn77@gmail.com
Robert Epps	eppsro@gmail.com
John Feagins	jpfeagins@yahoo.com
Don Gibson	dsgib33@att.net
Jan Griesinger	ucmjan@frognet.net
George Gunn	greatgunns50@gmail.com
Philip Harder	ahacamwa@aol.com
Emmett Herndon	hernatl@comcast.net
Thad Holcombe	tjholcombe@gmail.com
Diane Kenney	pdk0751@gmail.com
Odette Lockwood-Stewart	olockwood@psr.edu
Roger Loyd	roger.loyd@duke.edu
Thomas Mainor	tommainor@hotmail.com
Tom McCormick	mccormicktr@msn.com
Alice Riemer-McKee	acriemermc@aol.com
Marna McKenzie	mjmckenzie@cybermesa.com
Bernadine McRipley	mcripley2000@yahoo.com
Jerry Miller	gaev5@yahoo.com
Susan Yarrow Morris	sym@comcast.net
Helen R. Neinast	hneinast@windstream.net
Hugh Nevin	hnevin@nycap.rr.com
Tom Philipp	tjphilipp@aol.com
Delton Pickering	deltonpickering@aol.com
James Pruyne	jwpruyne@gmail.com
Ted Purcell	forjuls@aol.com
Jim Ray	jimray@zoominternet.net
David Rich	davidcrich@cox.net
Clyde Robinson	clyderobi@gmail.com
David Royer	royerdb1911@gmail.com
Mark Rutledge	betmark@msn.com
Don Shockley	donshock@mac.com
Robert Thomason	thomasonrobt@gmail.com
Paul Walley	walleyp@newpaltz.edu
Jim Wilson	jwilson228@cox.net
Laura Lee (Wilson) Morgan	revlauralee@comcast.net
Manuel Wortman	wortman21@gmail.com
Darrell Yeaney	suedy2@comcast.net

41922766R00189

Made in the USA
Lexington, KY
02 June 2015